CERES™
Celestial Legend
Volume 14: Hagoromo

STORY & ART BY YUU WATASE

Editor's Note: At the author's request, the spelling of Ms. Watase's first name has been changed from "Yû," as it has appeared on previous VIZ publications, to "Yuu."

English Adaptation/Gary Leach

Translation/Lillian Olsen
Touch-Up Art & Lettering/Susan Daigle-Leach
Cover & Graphic Design/Hidemi Sahara
Editor/Gary Leach

Managing Editor/Annette Roman
Director of Production/Noboru Watanabe
Vice President of Publishing/Alvin Lu
Sr. Director of Acquisitions/Rika Inouye
Vice President of Sales & Marketing/Liza Coppola
Publisher/Hyoe Narita

Printed in Canada

Published by VIZ Media, LLC
P.O. Box 77010 • San Francisco CA 94107

Shôjo Edition

10 9 8 7 6 5 4 3 2 1

First printing, February 2006

www.viz.com
store.viz.com

VIZ GRAPHIC NOVEL

Ceres

Celestial Legend

Vol. 14: Hagoromo

Story and Art by
Yuu Watase

TÔYA: His former memories regained (with his new ones still intact), Tôya has always felt that his existence required something he couldn't name. Since the moment he first drew breath he has been seeking something...and, once he found it, he knew its name—*her* name—was Aya. Even death seems unable to impede Tôya's quest, or stay the forces drawing him and Aya together.

AYA MIKAGE: A direct descendant of Ceres, Aya is the human vessel of the celestial maiden, able to communicate with Ceres and call her forth...but unable, it seems, to use her celestial powers to protect those she loves. Pregnant and consumed with grief over the loss of Tôya and Chidori, Aya has decided to stop the slaughter and cruelty of the Mikages in the only way she knows: by surrendering and joining the mysterious C-Project.

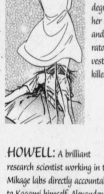

CHIDORI KURUMA:
A childlike teenager with a hopeless crush on Yûhi, Chidori possessed celestial DNA, which gave her some degree of celestial power...and made her a target of the Mikages. Kidnapped and imprisoned in the C-Project laboratories, Chidori was surgically harvested for her genetic material...then killed while trying to escape.

AKI MIKAGE: Aya's twin brother and host to (or hostage of, more like) the angry, Ceres-obsessed "Progenitor." Although Aya still believes that, somewhere deep inside, her brother still exists, the longer he is exposed to the insane love of the Progenitor for Ceres (who of course inhabits Aya), the less the real Aki remains.

HOWELL: A brilliant research scientist working in the Mikage labs directly accountable to Kagami himself, Alexander Howell ("Alec") spends what little time he doesn't spend in the lab watching anime, playing video games, collecting action figures...a real *otaku*, in other words.

MRS. Q (ODA-KYÛ): Eccentric yet loyal-to-a-fault servant (?) to the Aogiri household...and not without a few secret powers of her own.

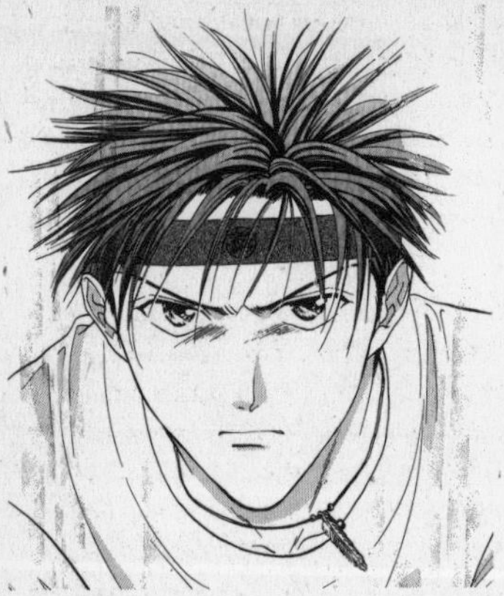

CERES: A *ten'nyo* or "celestial being" prevented from returning to the heavens after her *hagoromo* or "celestial robes" were stolen, Ceres bears little love for the descendants born of her union with a mortal male—the being known as "the Progenitor."

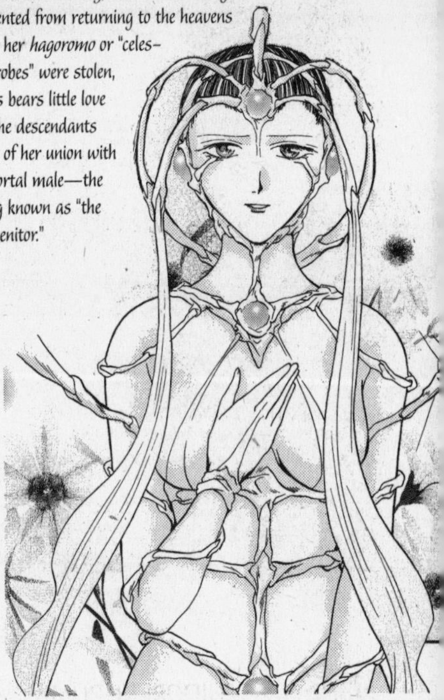

YÛHI AOGIRI: Once it hurt just to look at her, but gradually Yûhi is learning to accept (if not understand) the love Aya bears for his rival, Tôya. Another benefit? The knowledge that he can still care for and love—without necessarily being *in* love with—someone.

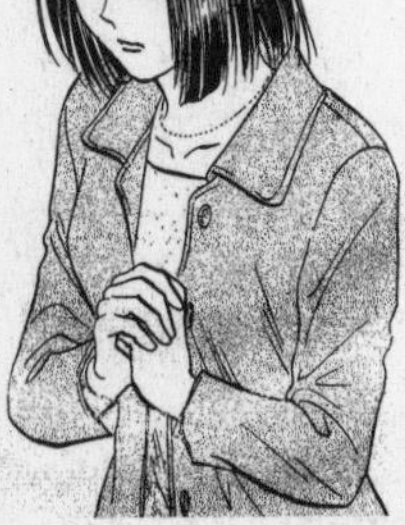

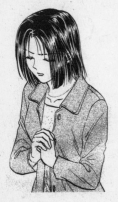

SUZUMI AOGIRI: Current head of the Aogiri household (after her husband, Yûhi's half-brother, passed away) and possessor of some *ten'nyo* or "celestial" blood herself. A "big sister" figure to both Yûhi and to Aya, from the start Suzumi's protection and support has meant a great deal...maybe even the difference between Aya's life and death.

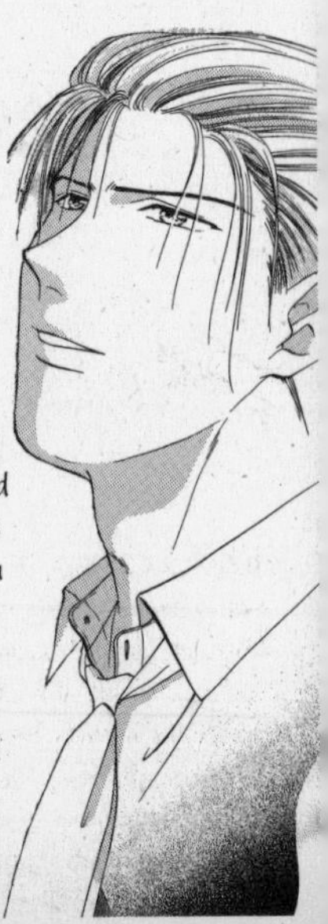

KAGAMI MIKAGE: Scion of the family empire and founder of the nefarious "C-Project." His passion mistaken by Aki/The Progenitor as lust for Ceres, the true purpose behind Kagami's search for Ceres' *hagoromo* is slowly being revealed.

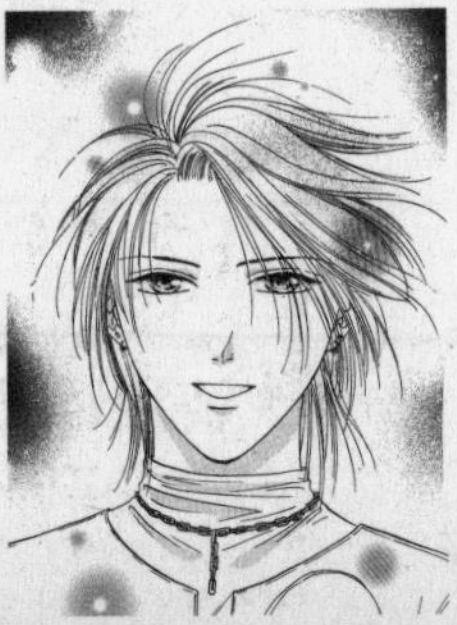

SHURO: Another celestial, who once passed herself off as a man (as part of the wildly popular Japanese pop duo GeSANG). Grappling with her own fate, Shuro used her last, glorious burst of power to breach the defenses of the C-Project.

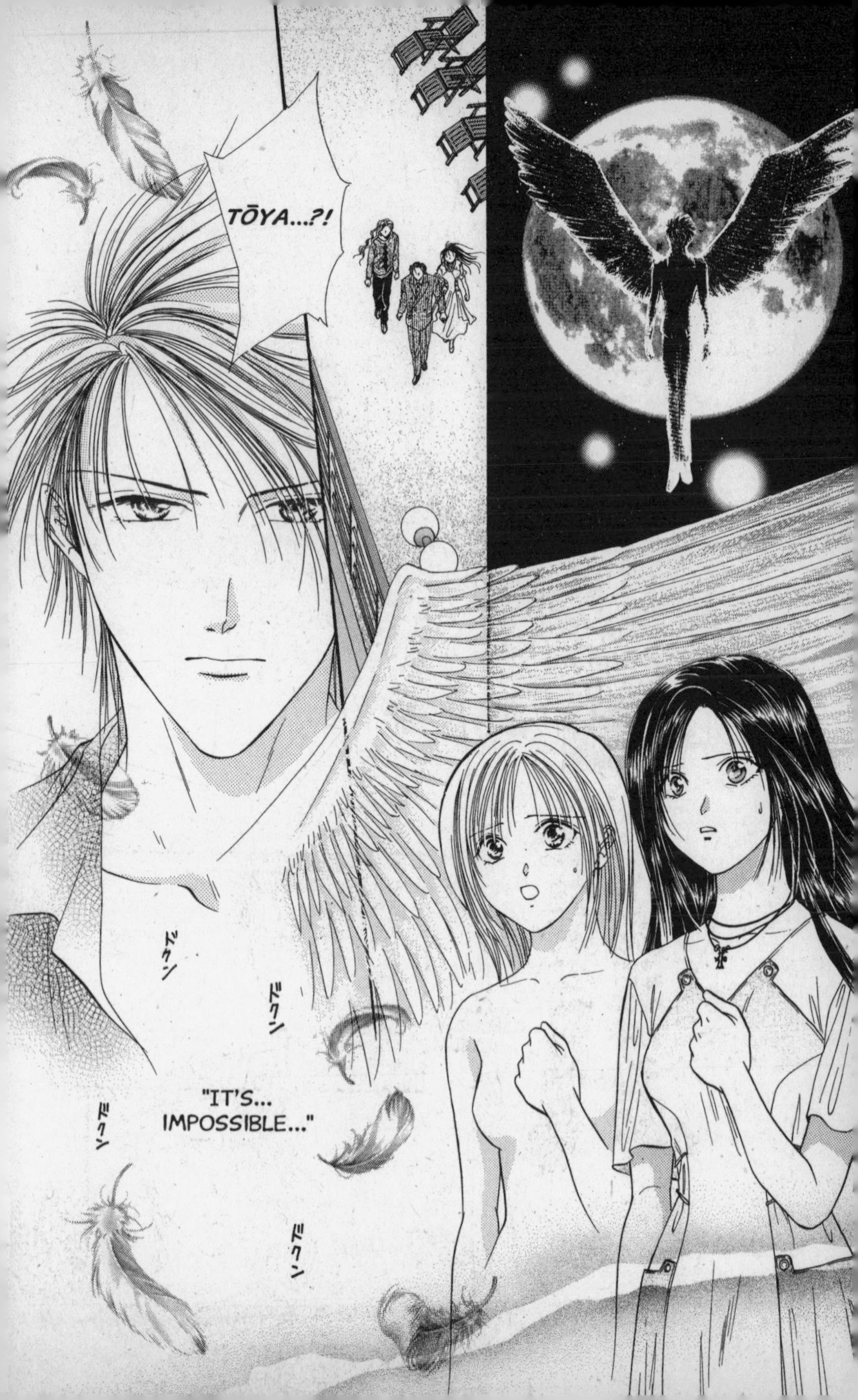
TŌYA...?!
ドクン
ドクン
"IT'S... IMPOSSIBLE..."
ドクン
ドクン

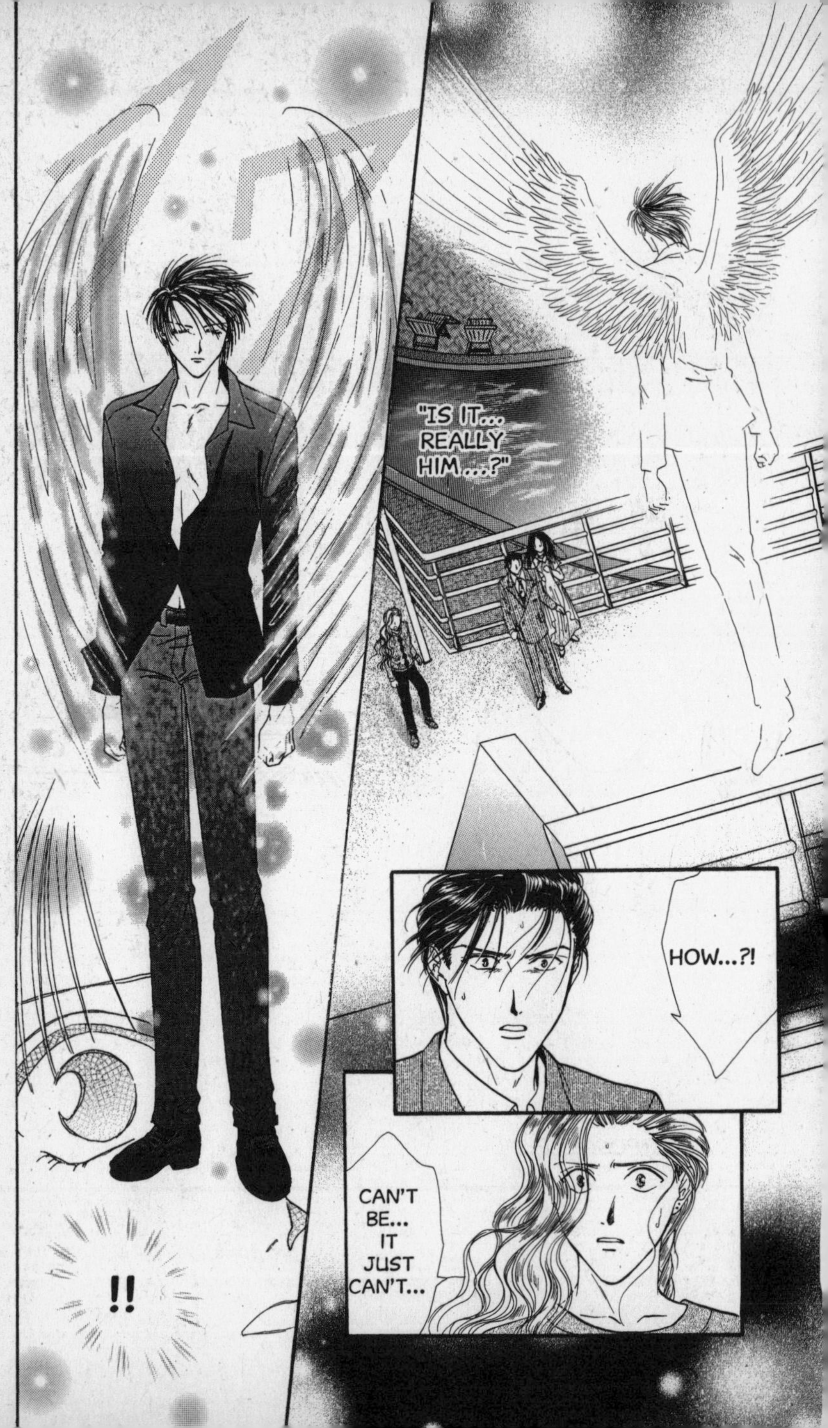
"IS IT... REALLY HIM...?"
HOW...?!
CAN'T BE... IT JUST CAN'T...
!!

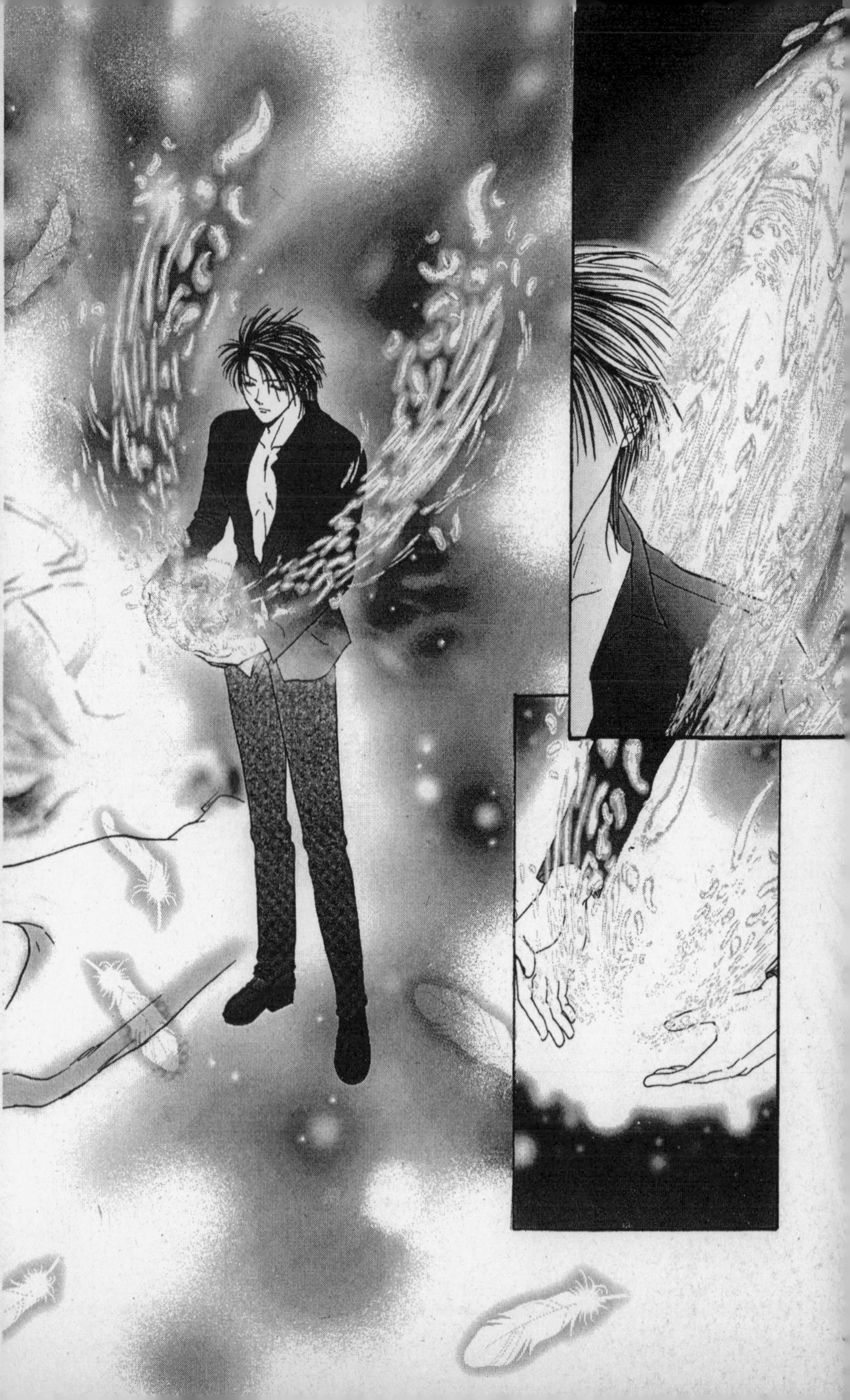

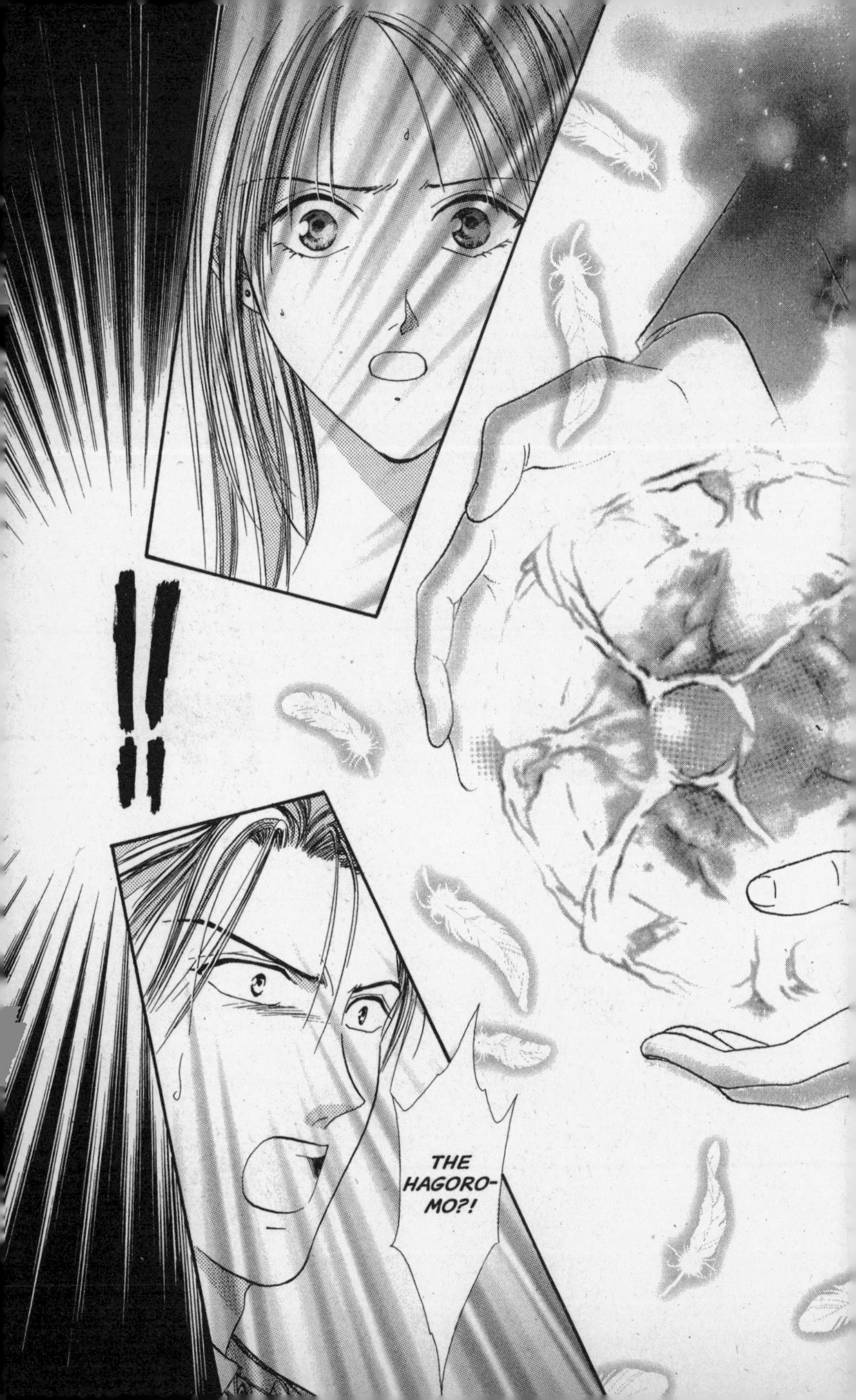
!!
THE HAGORO-MO?!

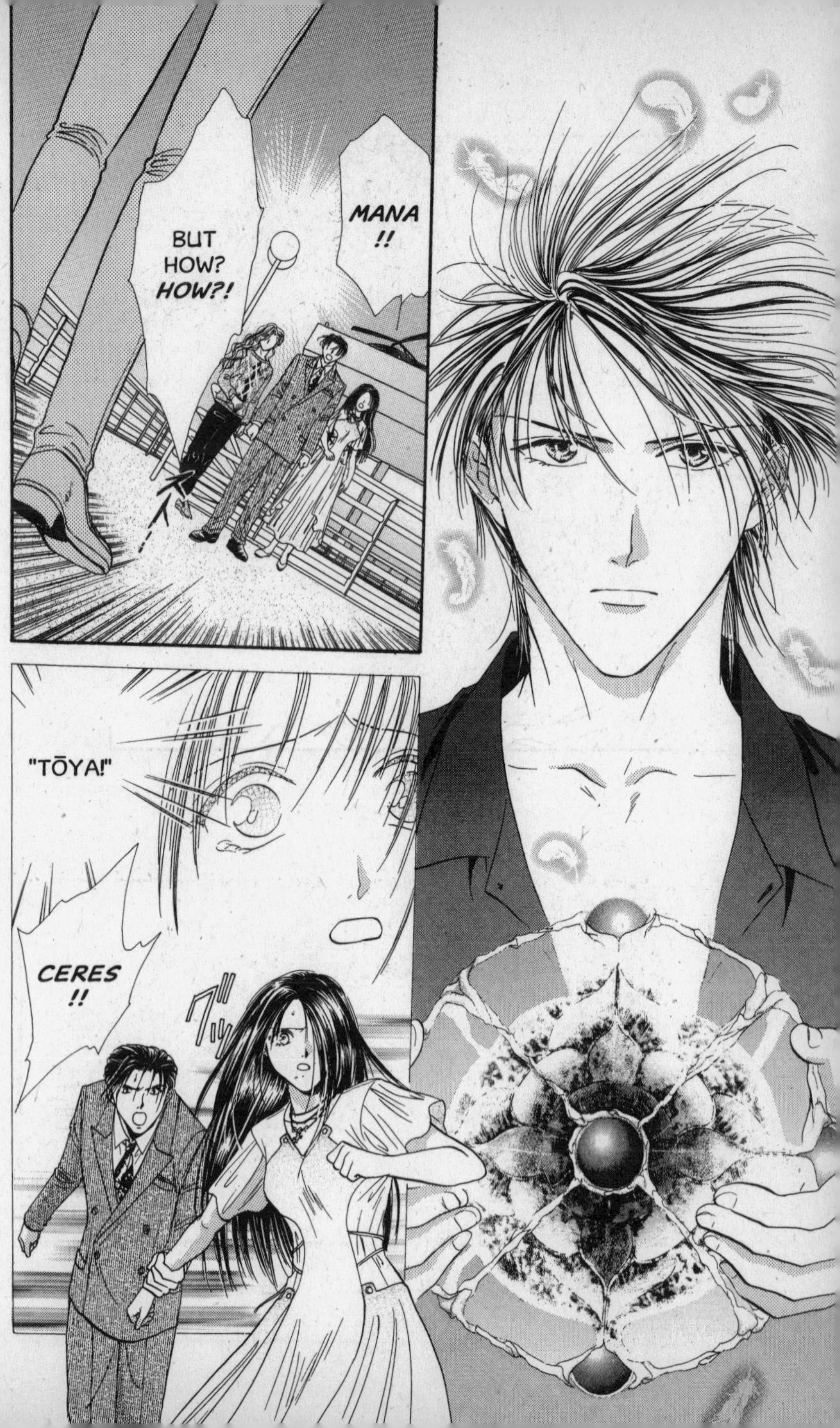
MANA !!
BUT HOW? HOW?!
"TŌYA!"
CERES !!

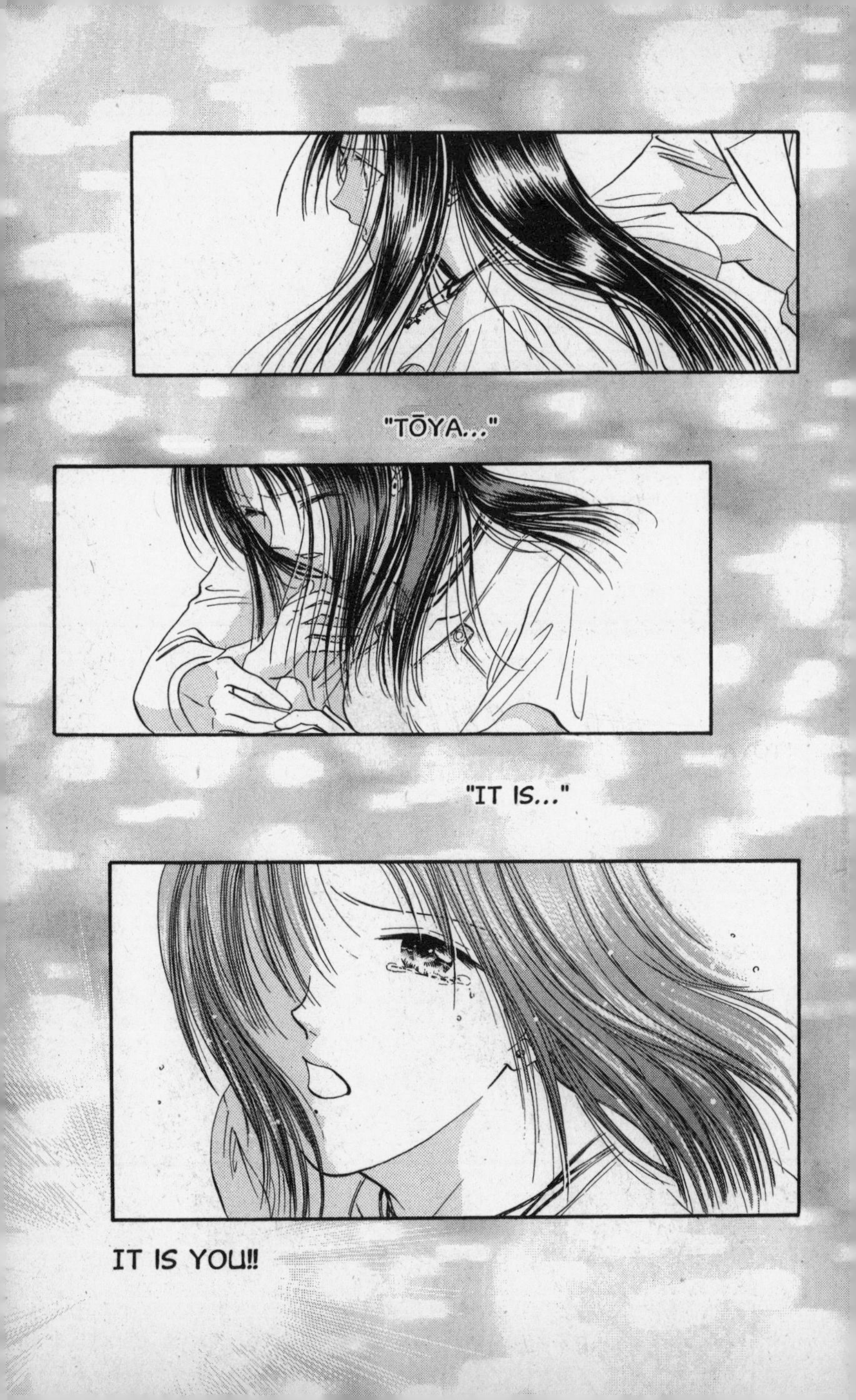
"TŌYA..."
"IT IS..."
IT IS YOU!!

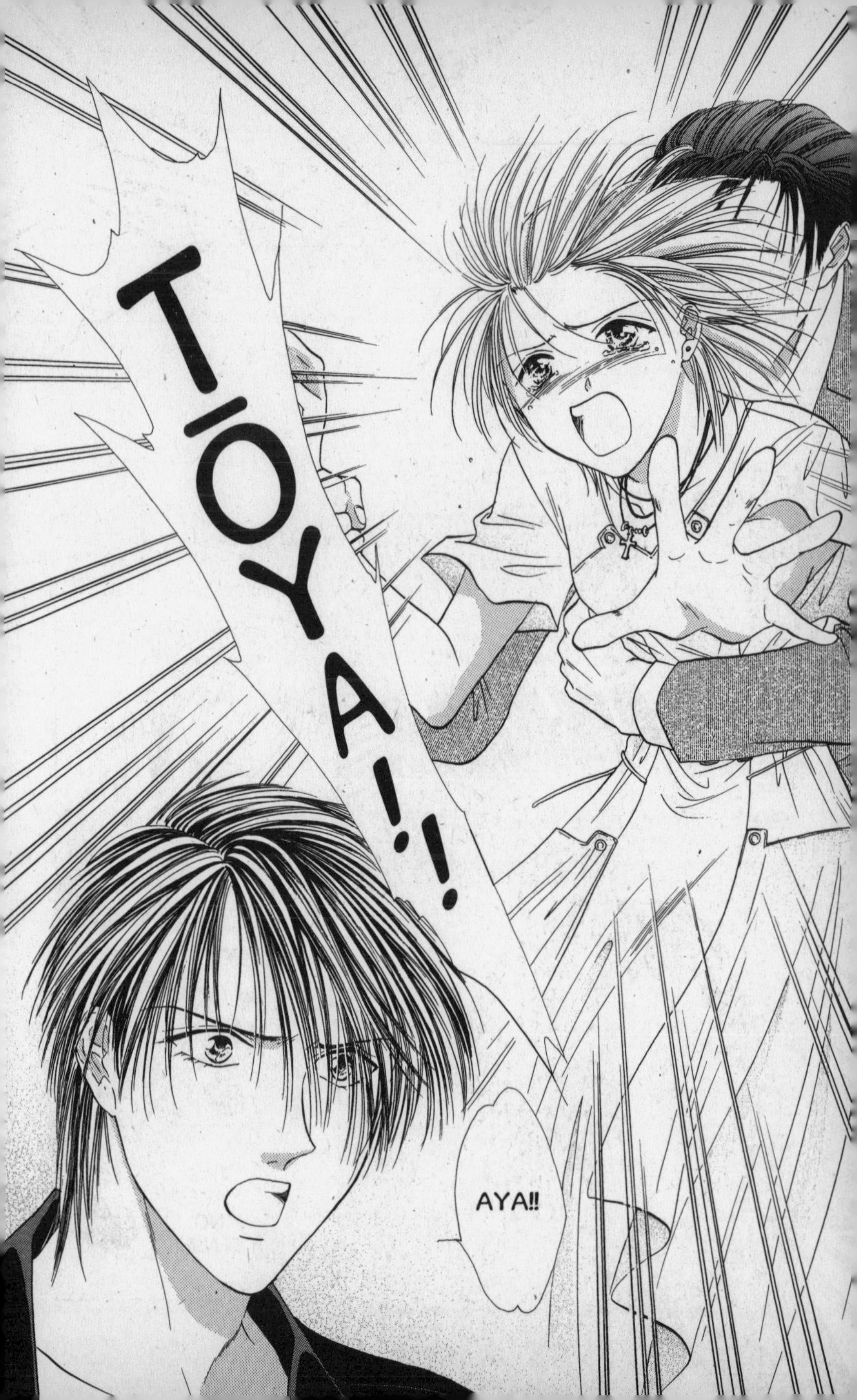
TŌYA!!!
AYA!!

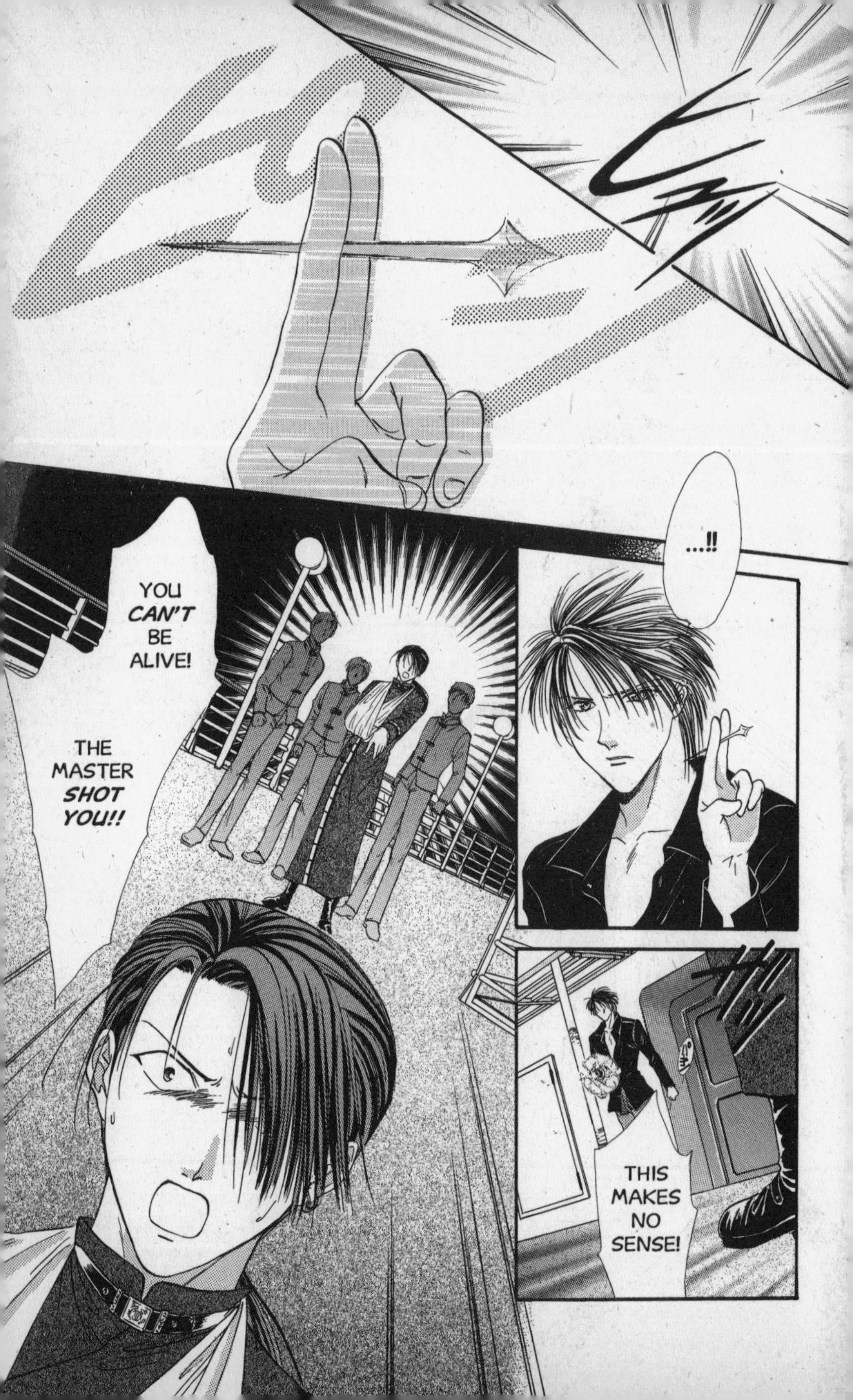
...!!
THIS MAKES NO SENSE!
YOU *CAN'T* BE ALIVE!
THE MASTER *SHOT YOU!!*

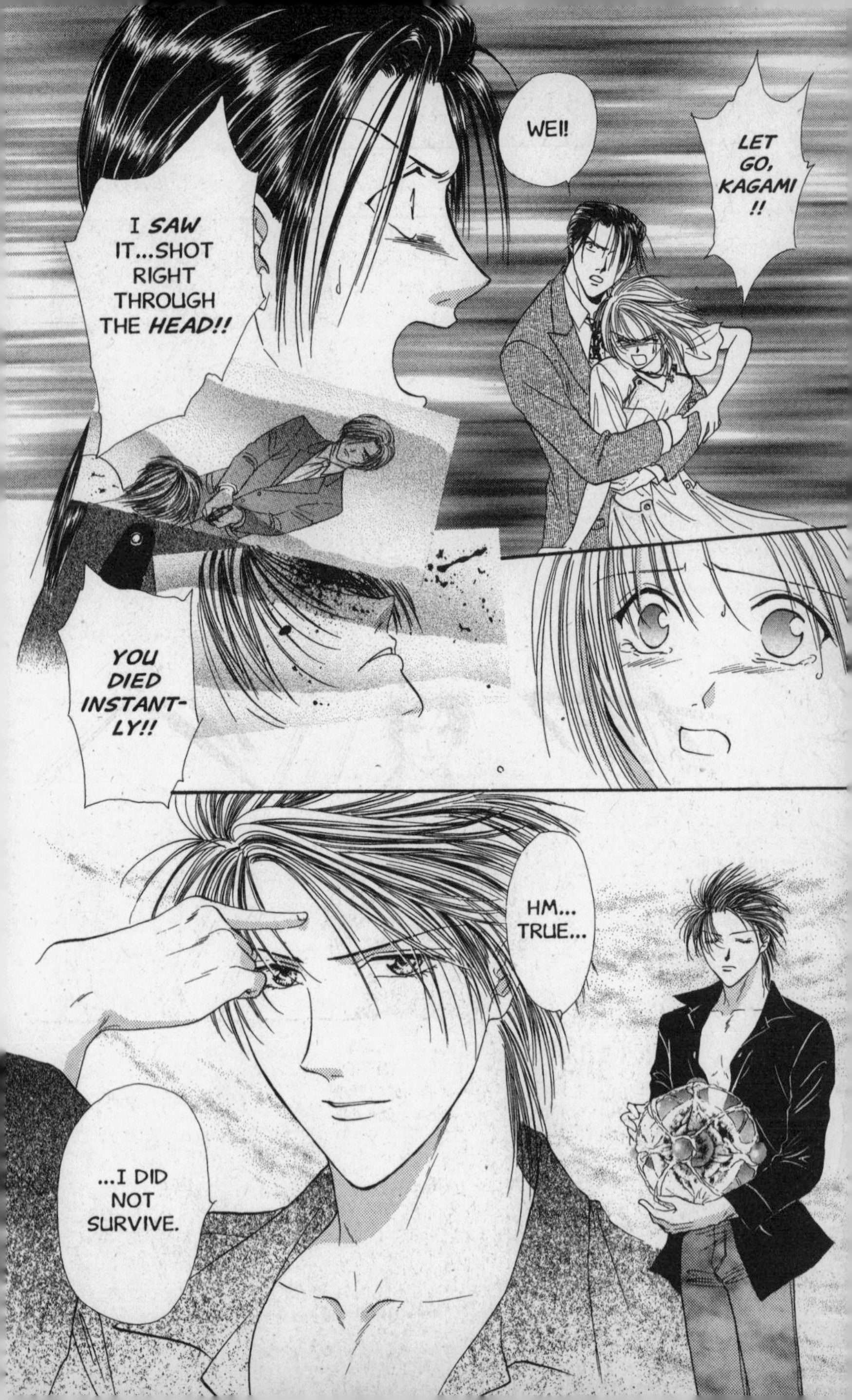
LET GO, KAGAMI!!
WEI!
I SAW IT...SHOT RIGHT THROUGH THE HEAD!!
YOU DIED INSTANTLY!!
HM... TRUE...
...I DID NOT SURVIVE.

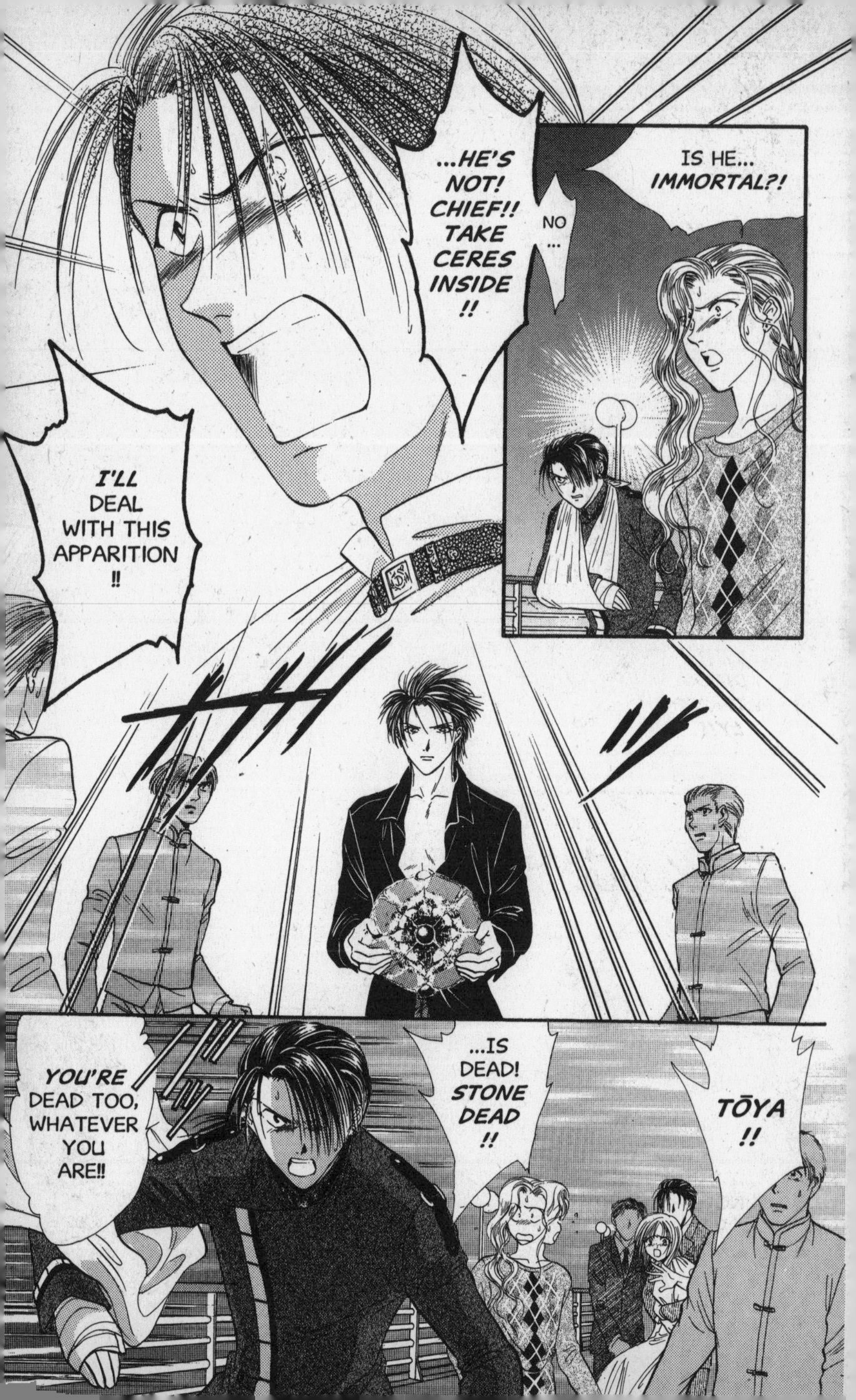
IS HE... IMMORTAL?!
NO ...
...HE'S NOT! CHIEF!! TAKE CERES INSIDE !!
I'LL DEAL WITH THIS APPARITION !!
TŌYA !!
...IS DEAD! STONE DEAD !!
YOU'RE DEAD TOO, WHATEVER YOU ARE!!

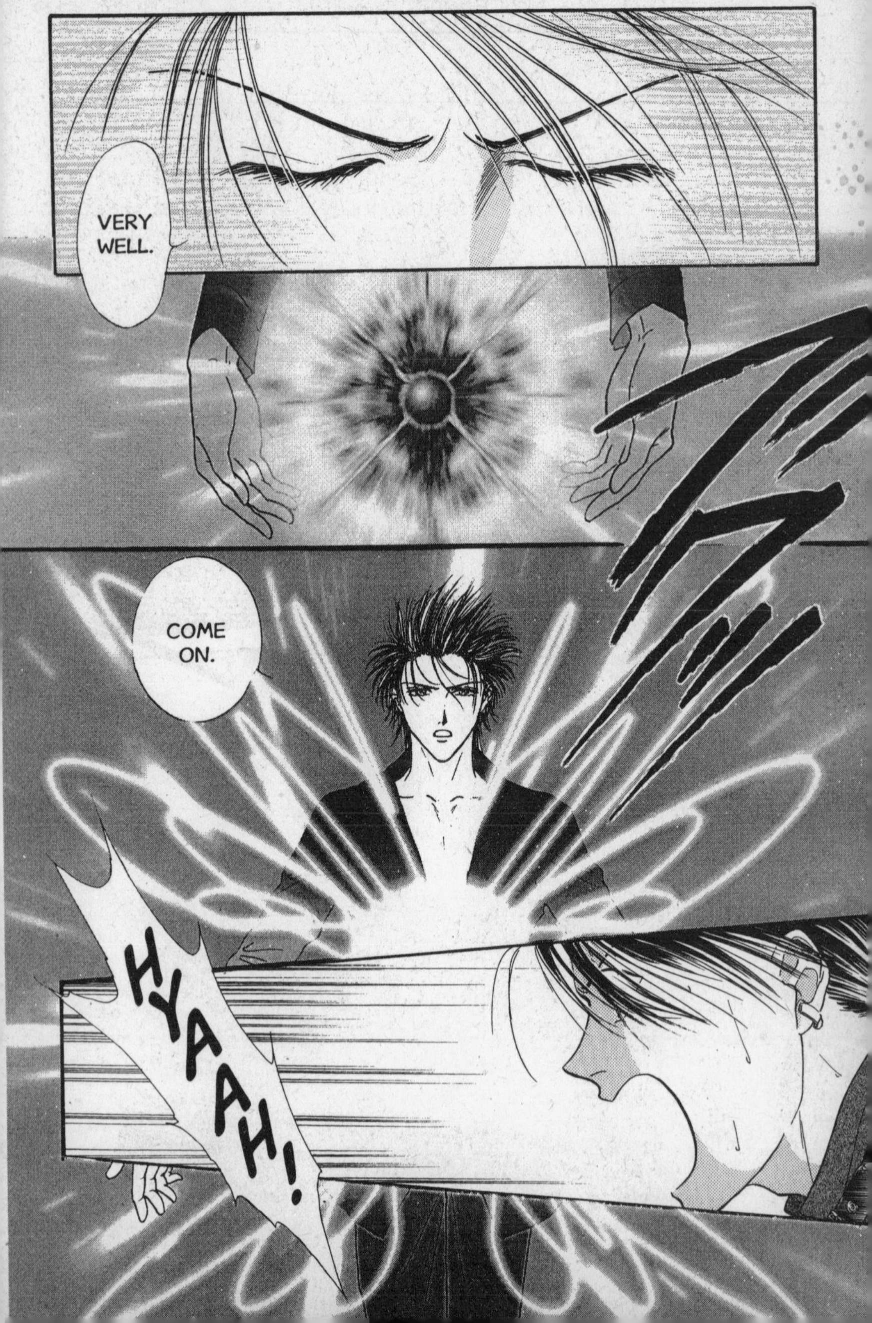
VERY WELL.
COME ON.
HYAAH!

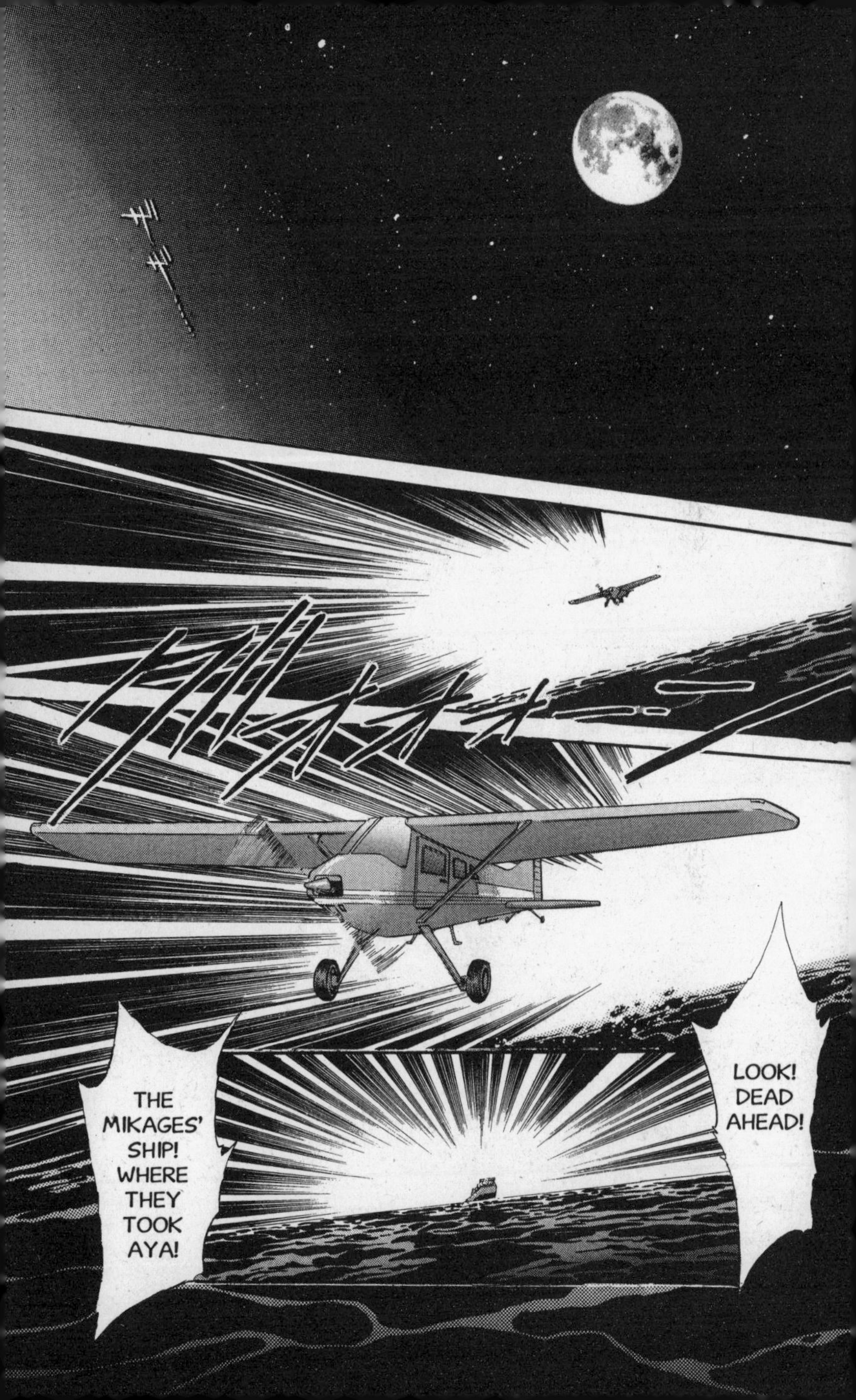
LOOK! DEAD AHEAD!
THE MIKAGES' SHIP! WHERE THEY TOOK AYA!

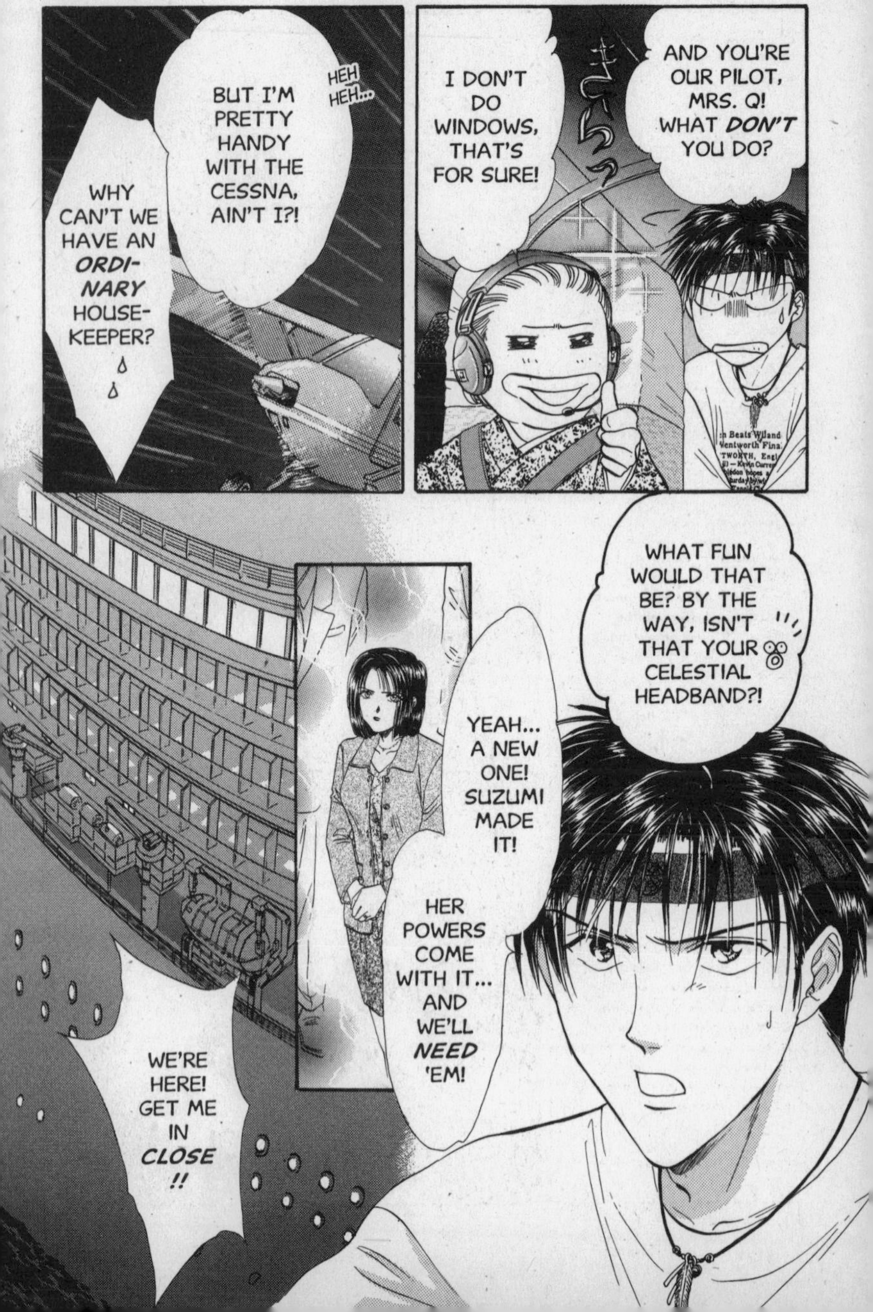
AND YOU'RE OUR PILOT, MRS. Q! WHAT *DON'T* YOU DO?
I DON'T DO WINDOWS, THAT'S FOR SURE!
BUT I'M PRETTY HANDY WITH THE CESSNA, AIN'T I?!
HEH HEH...
WHY CAN'T WE HAVE AN *ORDINARY* HOUSEKEEPER?
WHAT FUN WOULD THAT BE? BY THE WAY, ISN'T THAT YOUR CELESTIAL HEADBAND?!
YEAH... A NEW ONE! SUZUMI MADE IT!
HER POWERS COME WITH IT... AND WE'LL *NEED* 'EM!
WE'RE HERE! GET ME IN *CLOSE*!!

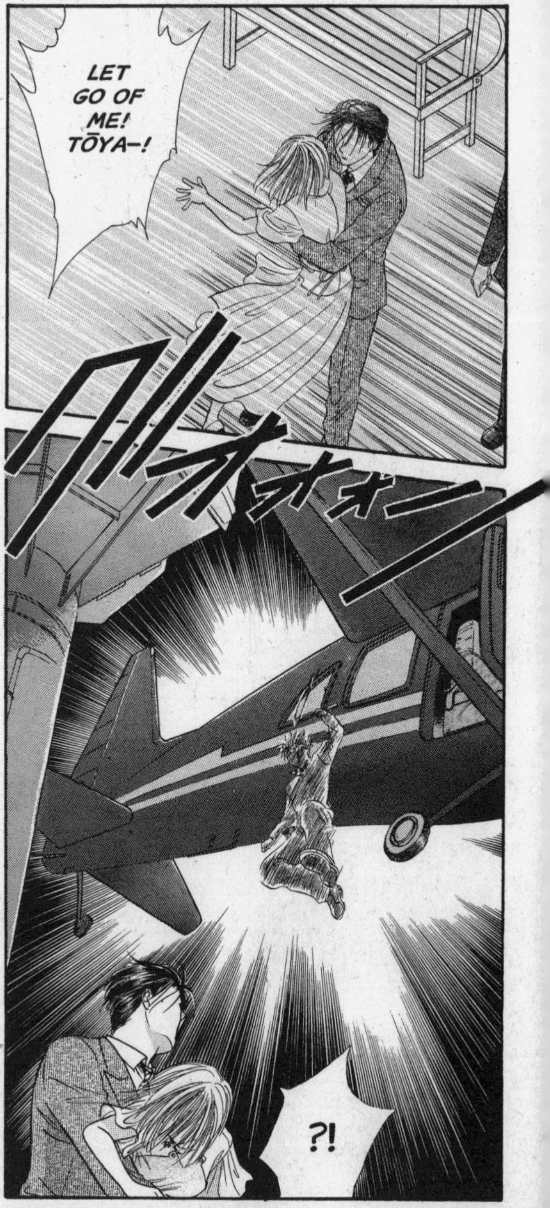
LET GO OF ME! TŌYA–!
?!

Hi!! This is, finally, the final volume of **Ceres**!! Thanks a lot for sticking with me for so long!! Okay, bye now.

...Just kidding. Don't worry, I'm still writing the rest of these columns. And now, **Ceres** is going to be an ANIME! Starting Thursday, April 30, [2000] at 6:30 on WOWOW. Since the broadcast isn't scrambled, you don't even have to be a subscriber. You only need a BS digital antenna and a tuner, and the picture should clear up only for that time.

Actually, the subject of animating **Ceres** came up two or three years ago, and it's only now become a reality. Readers have been asking me when it would get animated. Well, I was keeping quiet until it was official.

It's tough keeping such secrets.

They had sent me a copy of the character model sheets a loooong time ago. But I gather rumors spread quickly through the internet. ◡ Some details didn't correspond to what I knew, though.

People without an antenna and the tuner might be upset, but broadcasting **Ceres**, as is, on heavily regulated commercial broadcast would be hugely problematic! (Ha ha!) All of it's against code!! (Oh boy...) Broadcast regulations are so strict! (It's my own damn fault the manga is so risqué!) They considered changing some content...but the anime production staff objected, saying "it wouldn't be **Ceres**!!" I didn't even have to interject... ◡ So thanks to them, **Ceres** is intact with all its hardcore, adult (???) themes. Go buy the videos!! (I'm so blatant!) I'll be doing new art for the covers! (More work to do...) But the packaging for the rental copies will have anime art on their covers...I think?!

My art will only be on the copies for sale?

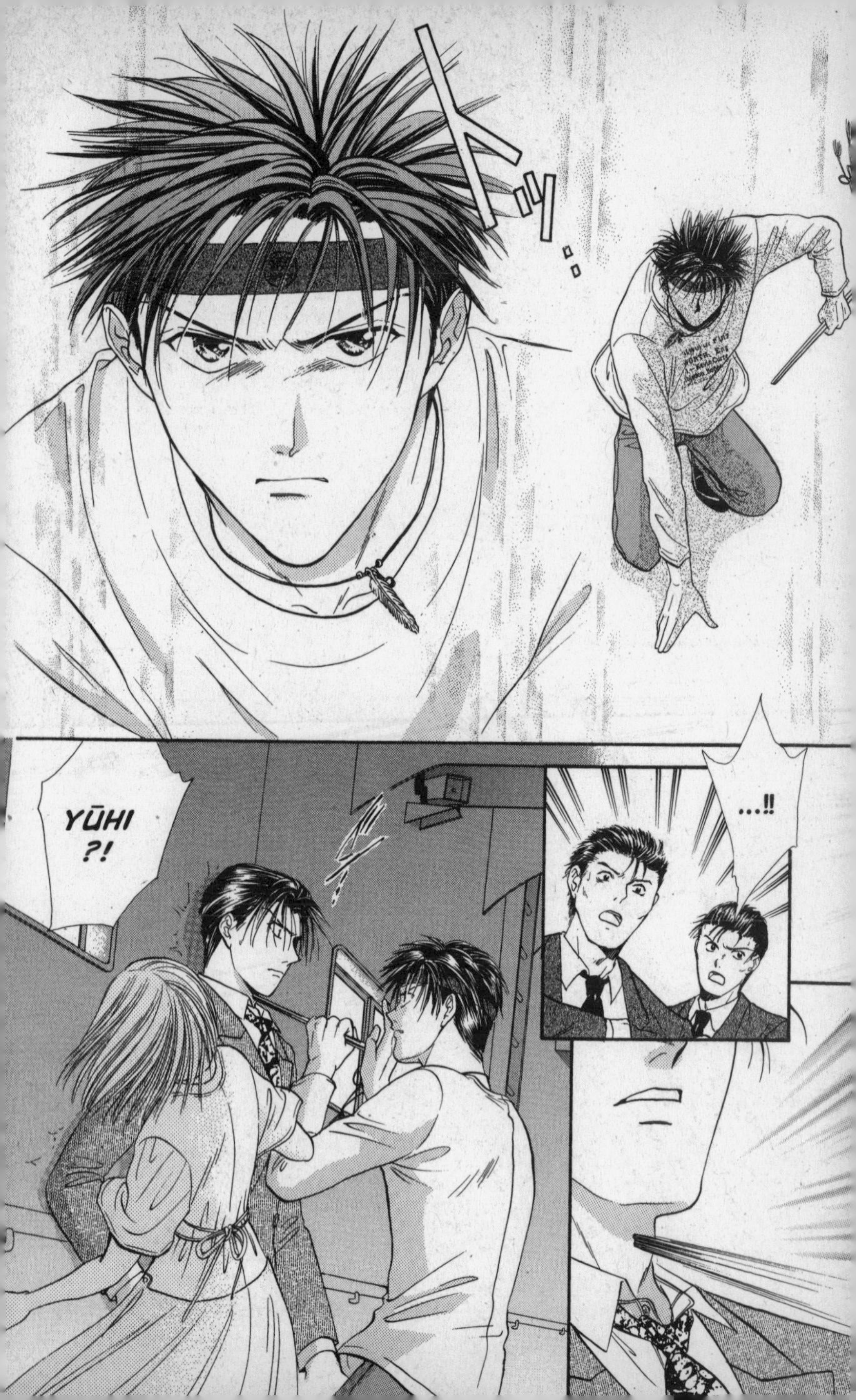
...!!
YŪHI ?!

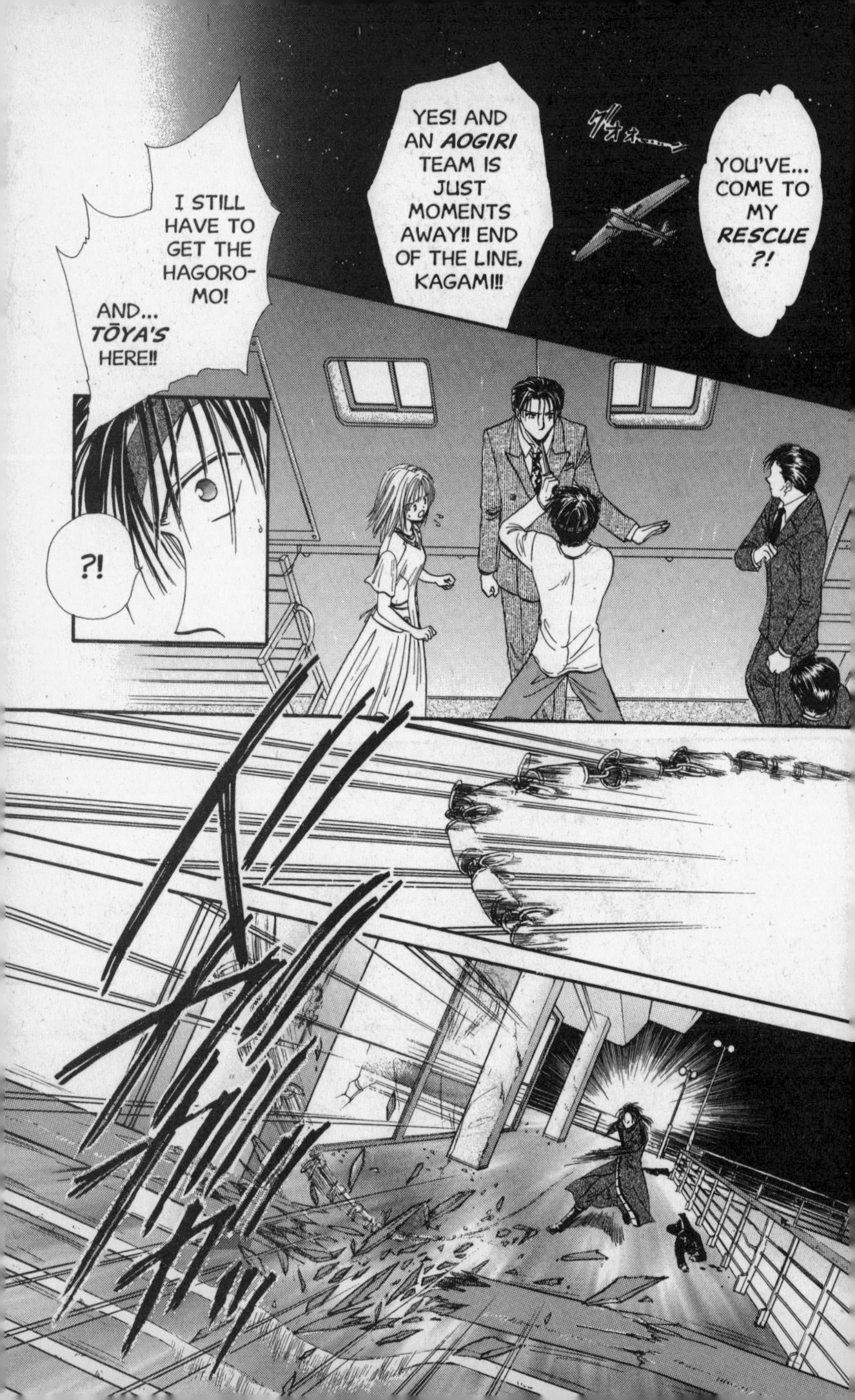
YOU'VE... COME TO MY *RESCUE* ?!
YES! AND AN *AOGIRI* TEAM IS JUST MOMENTS AWAY!! END OF THE LINE, KAGAMI!!
I STILL HAVE TO GET THE HAGORO-MO!
AND... *TŌYA'S* HERE!!
?!

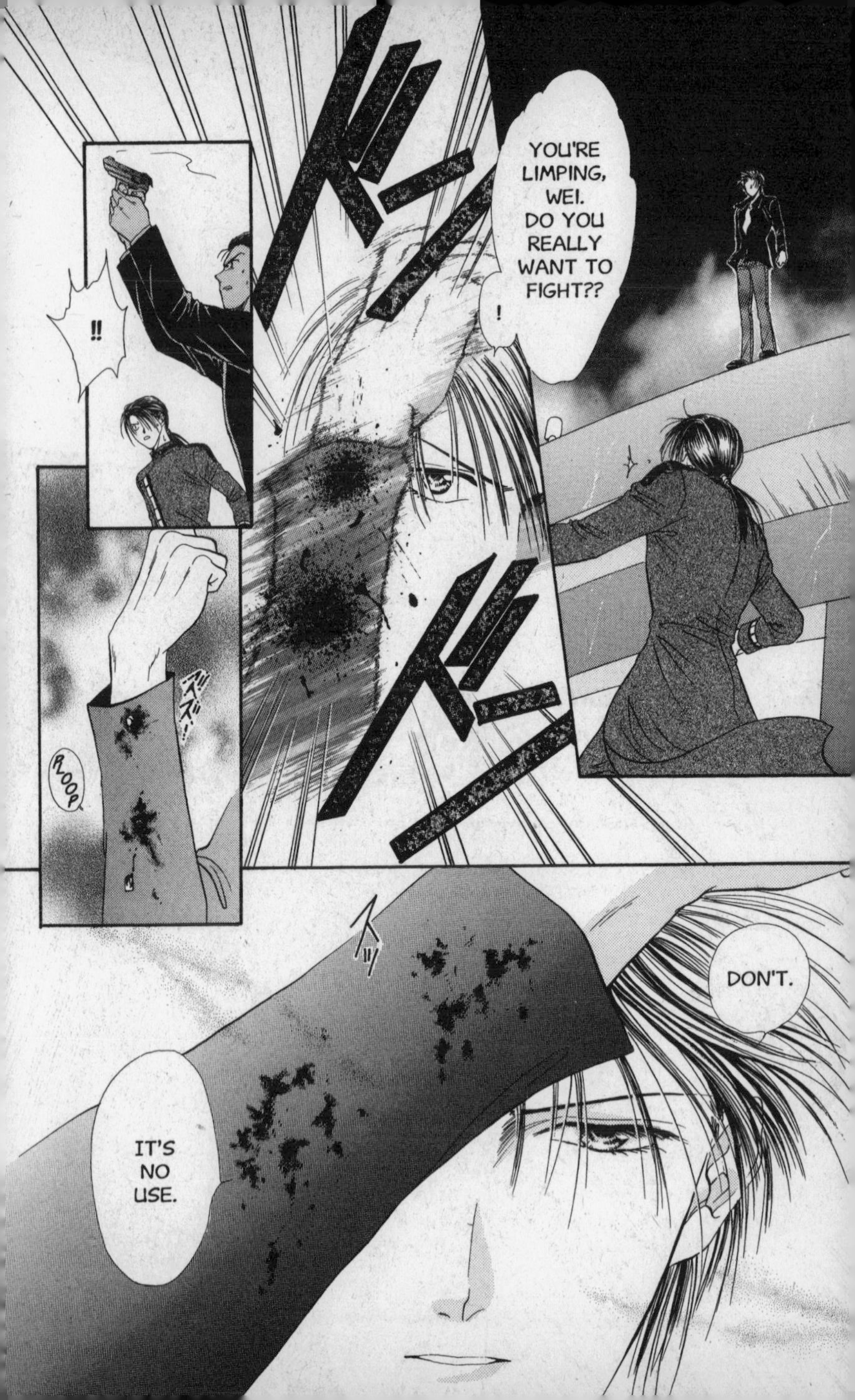
YOU'RE LIMPING, WEI. DO YOU REALLY WANT TO FIGHT??
!
!!
BLOOP
DON'T.
IT'S NO USE.

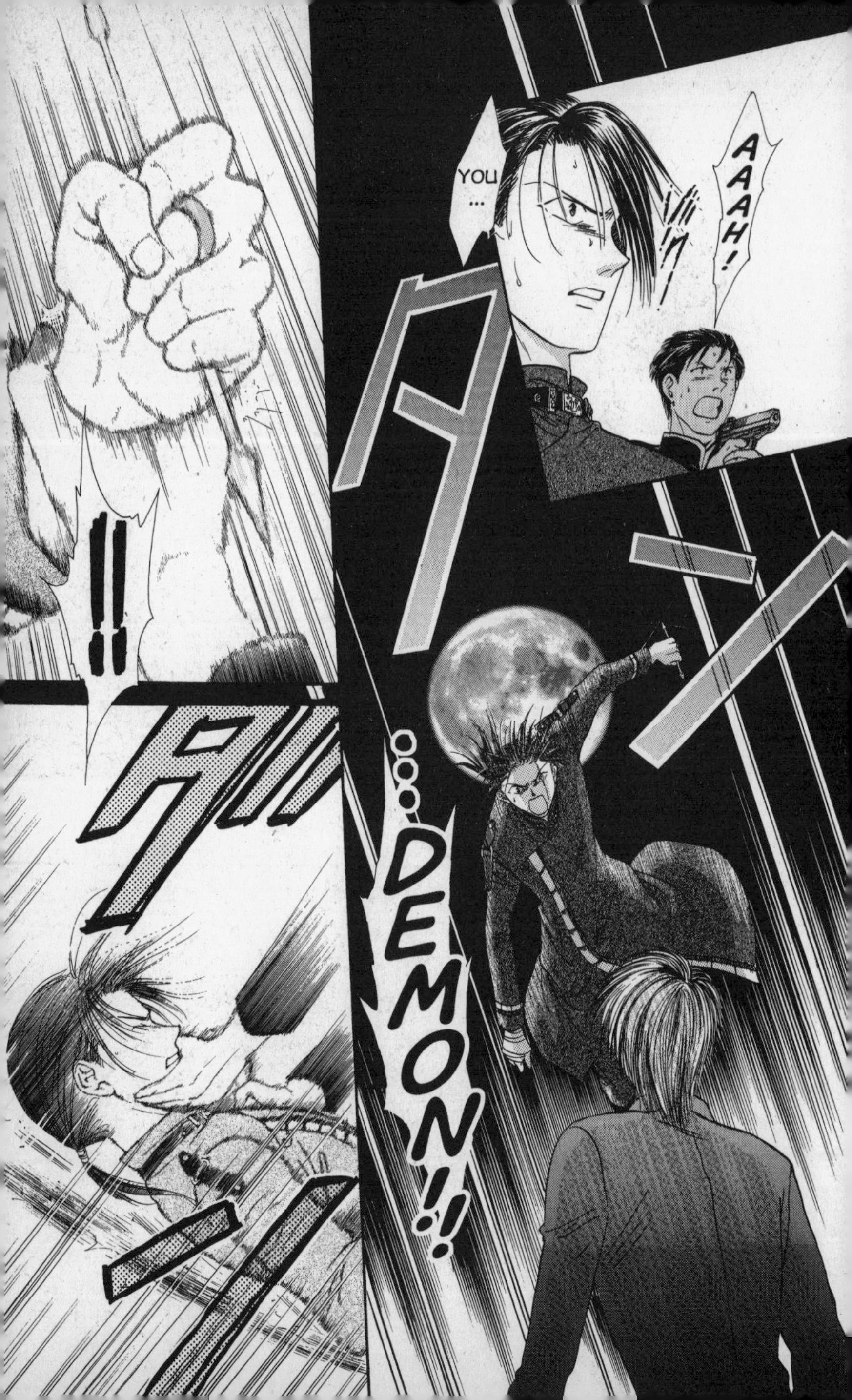
AAAH!
YOU ...
...DEMON!!
!!

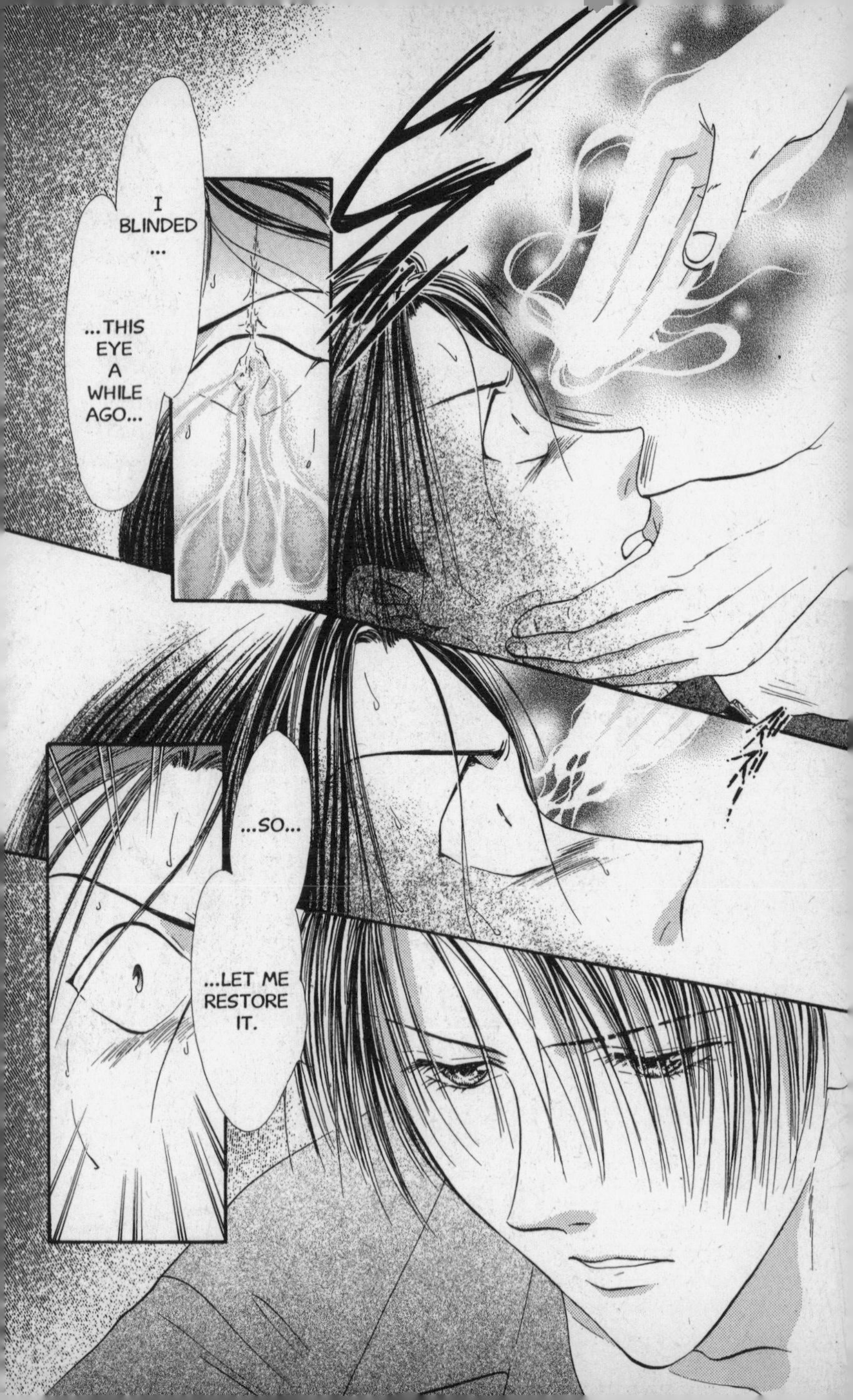
I BLINDED ...
...THIS EYE A WHILE AGO...
...SO...
...LET ME RESTORE IT.

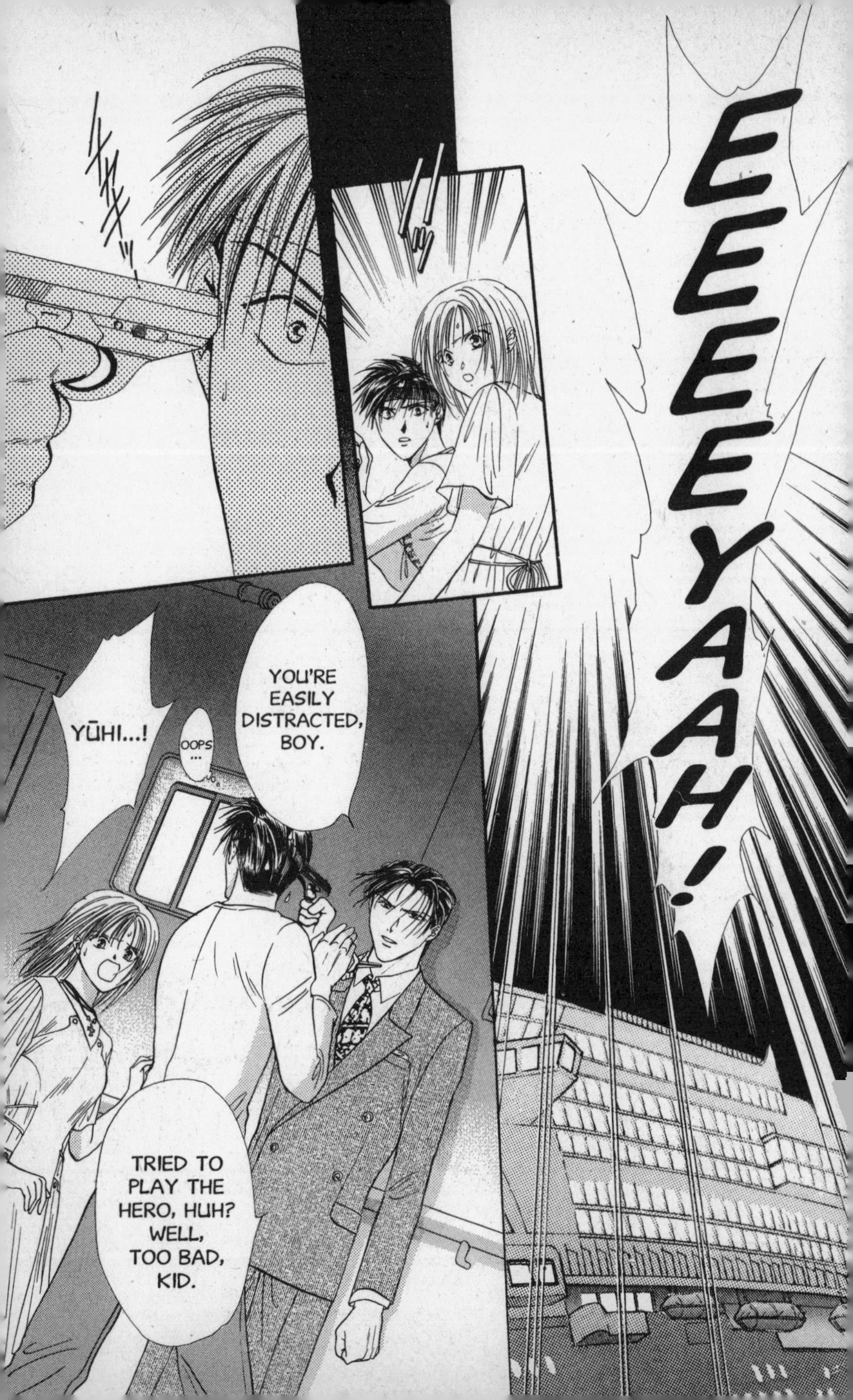
EEEEEYAAH!
YOU'RE EASILY DISTRACTED, BOY.
OOPS...
YŪHI...!
TRIED TO PLAY THE HERO, HUH? WELL, TOO BAD, KID.

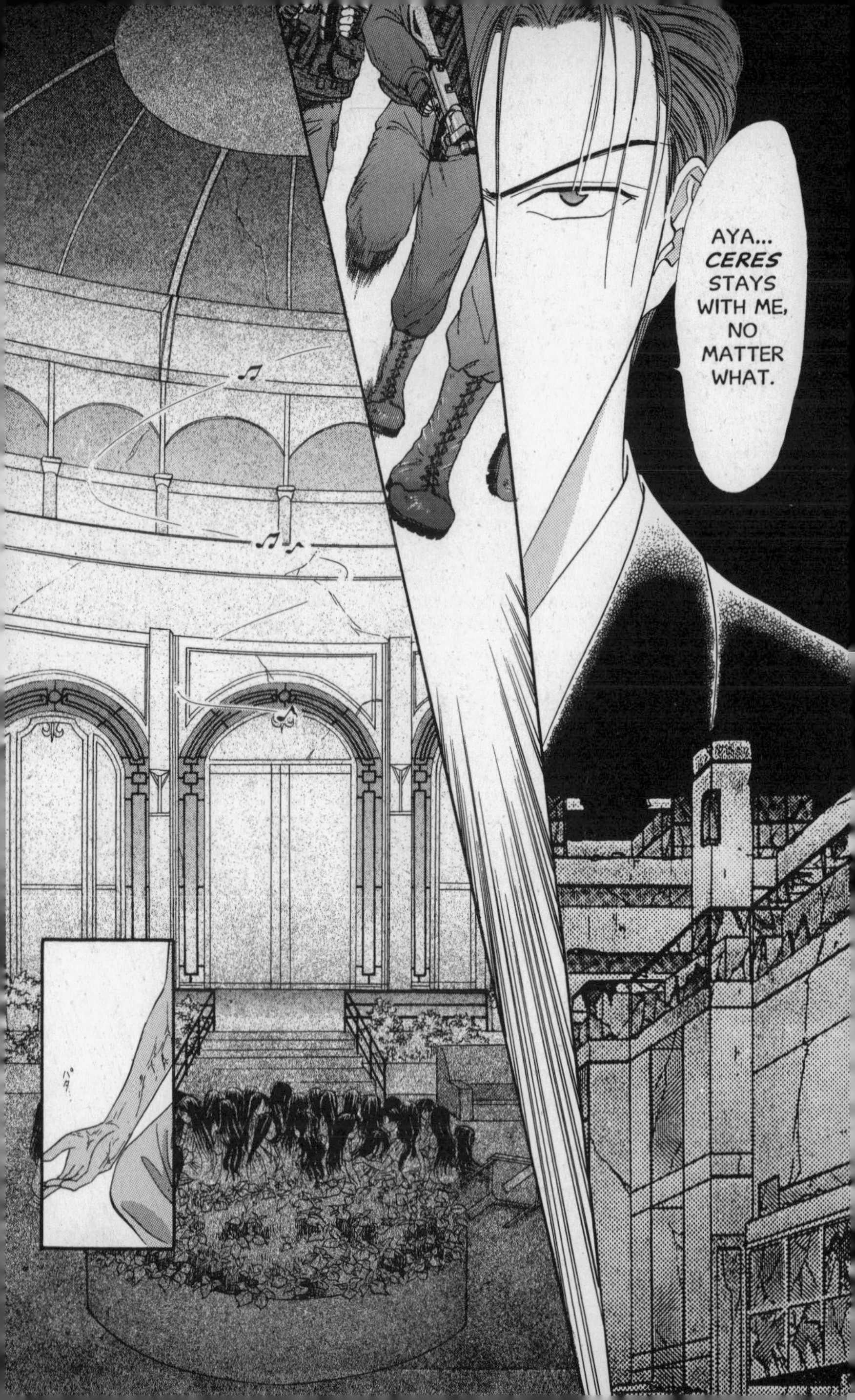
AYA... *CERES* STAYS WITH ME, NO MATTER WHAT.
パタ

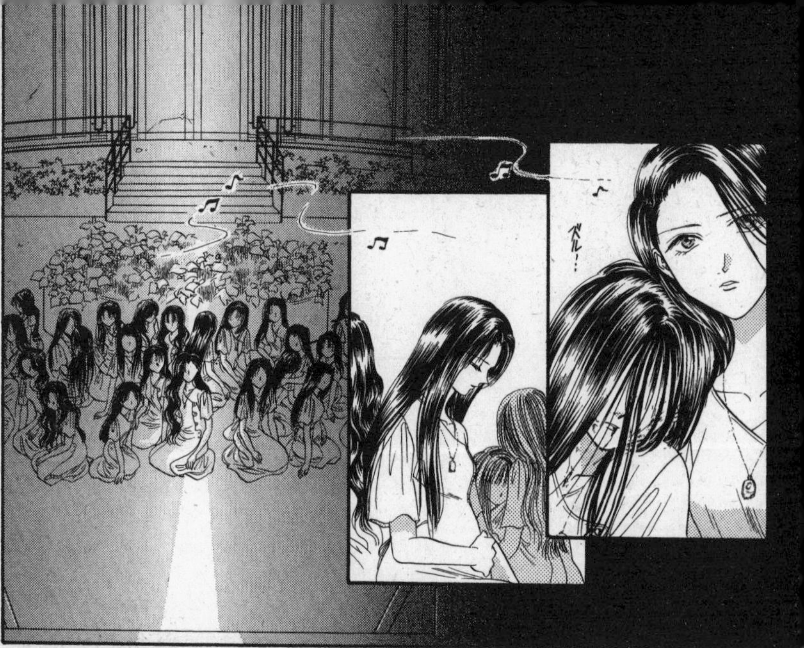
ズル…!
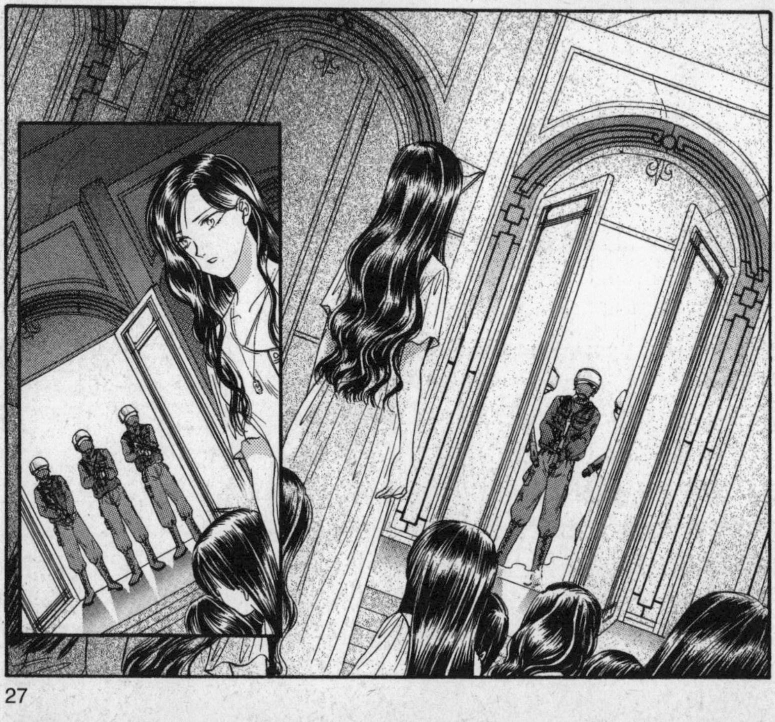

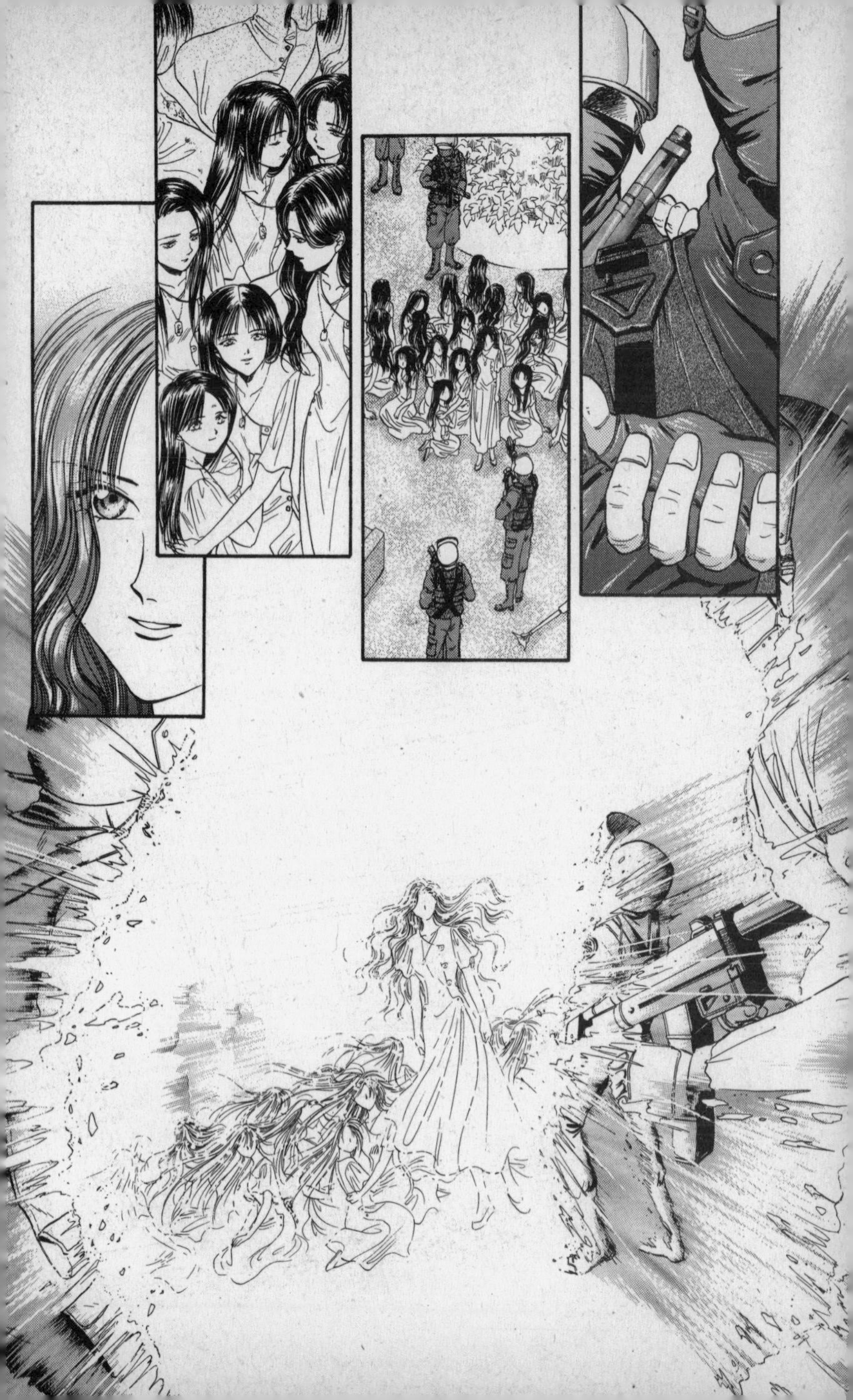

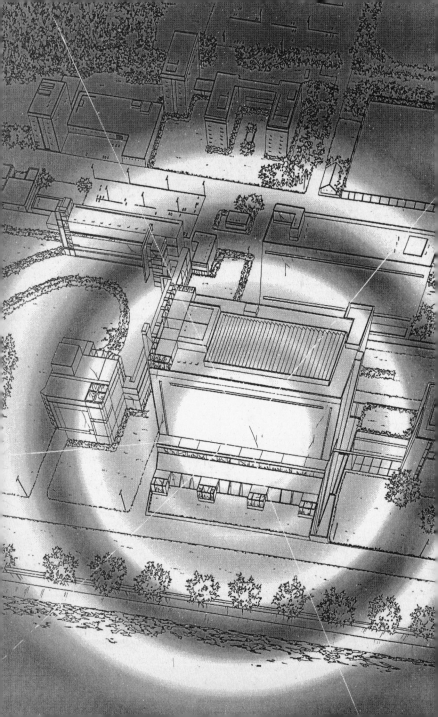

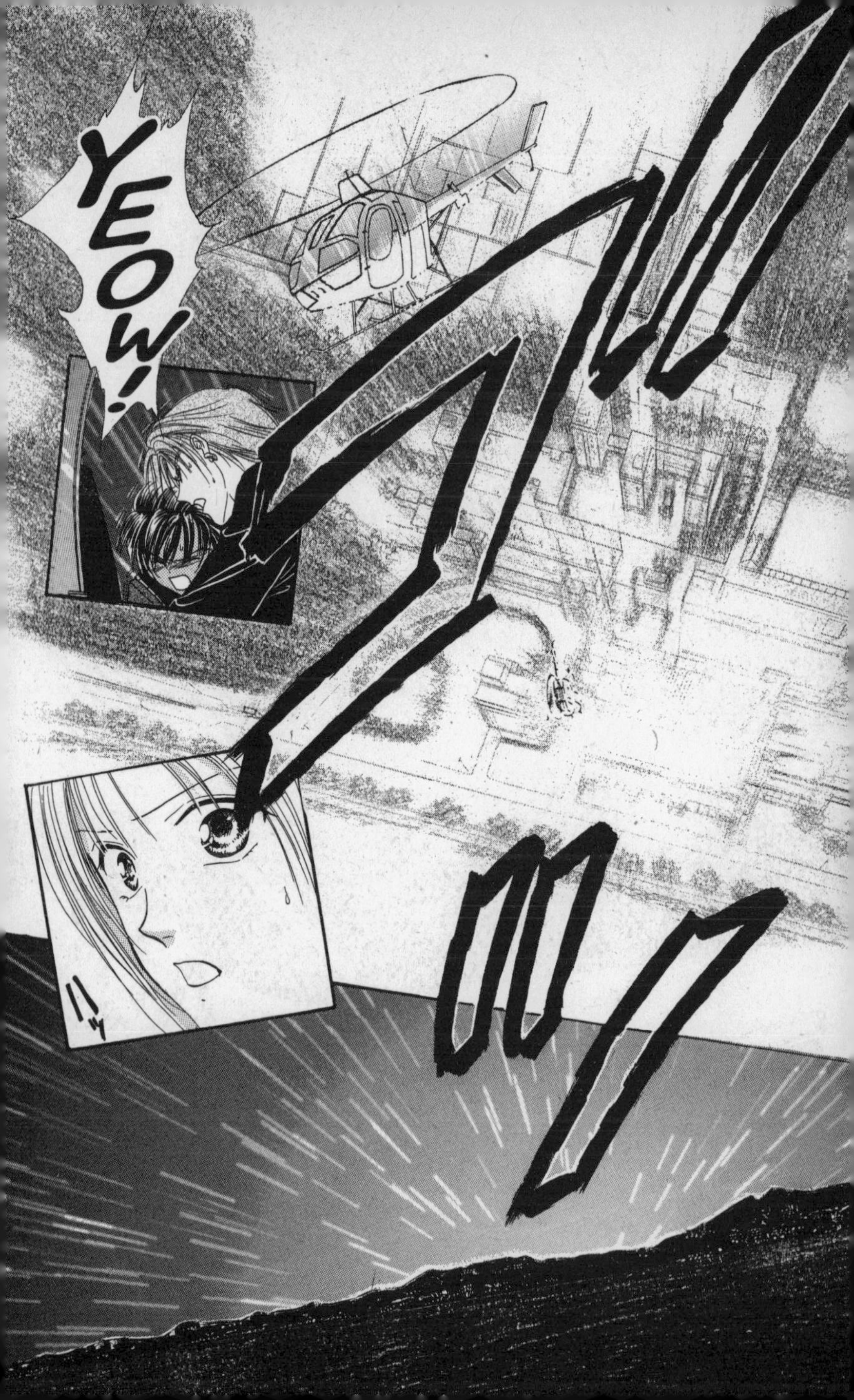
YEOW!
ハッ

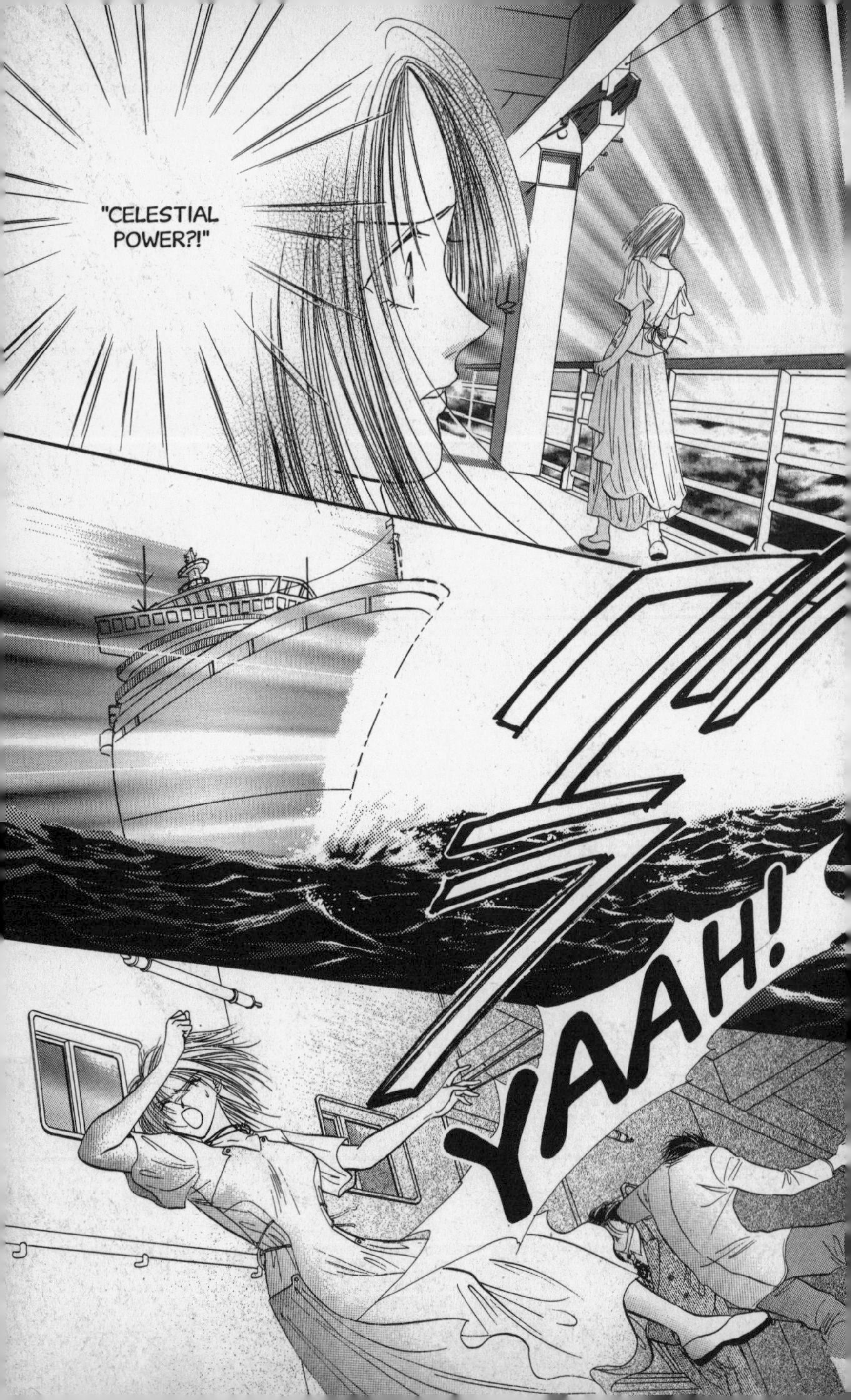
"CELESTIAL POWER?!"
YAAAH!

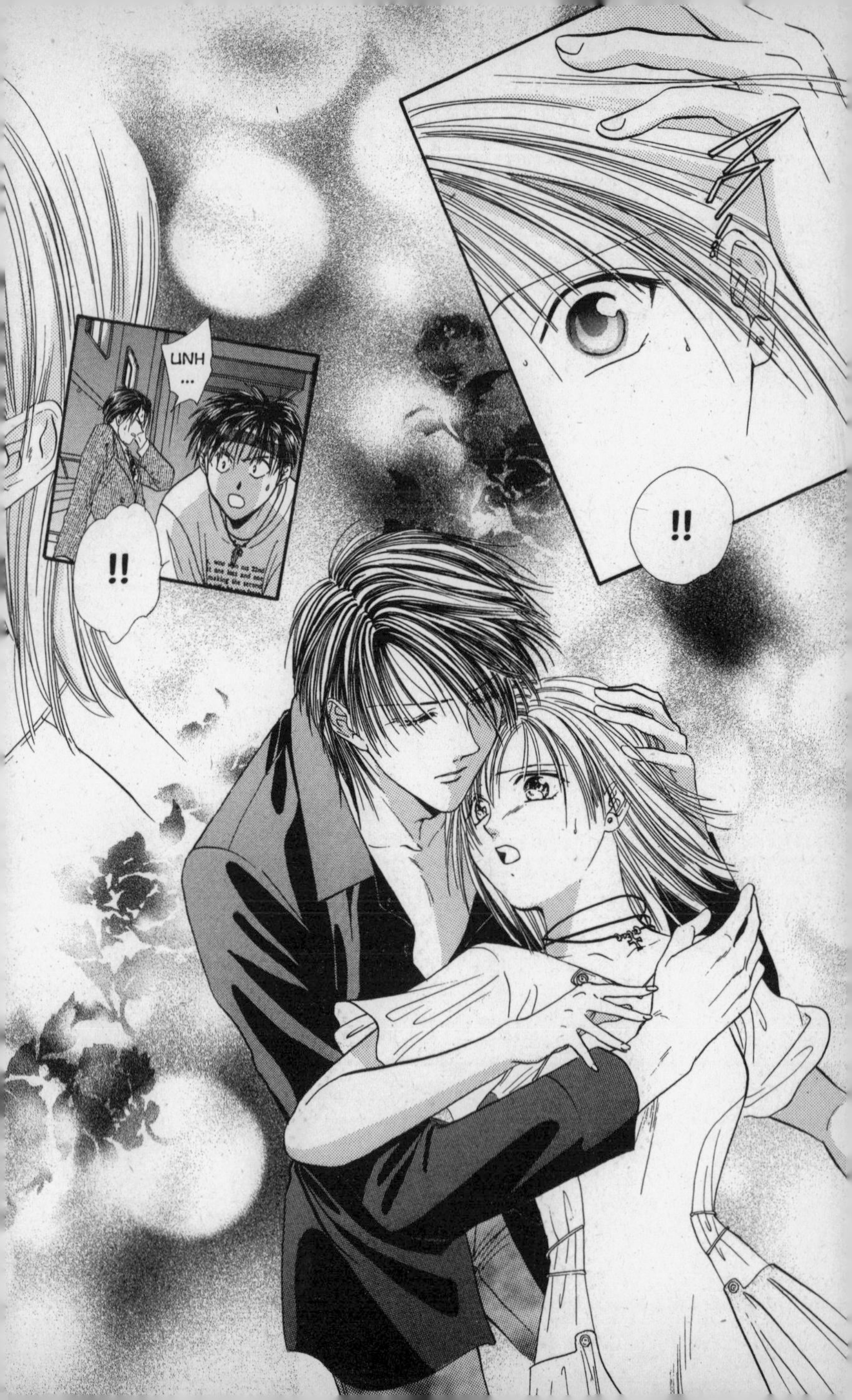
!!
UNH ...
!!

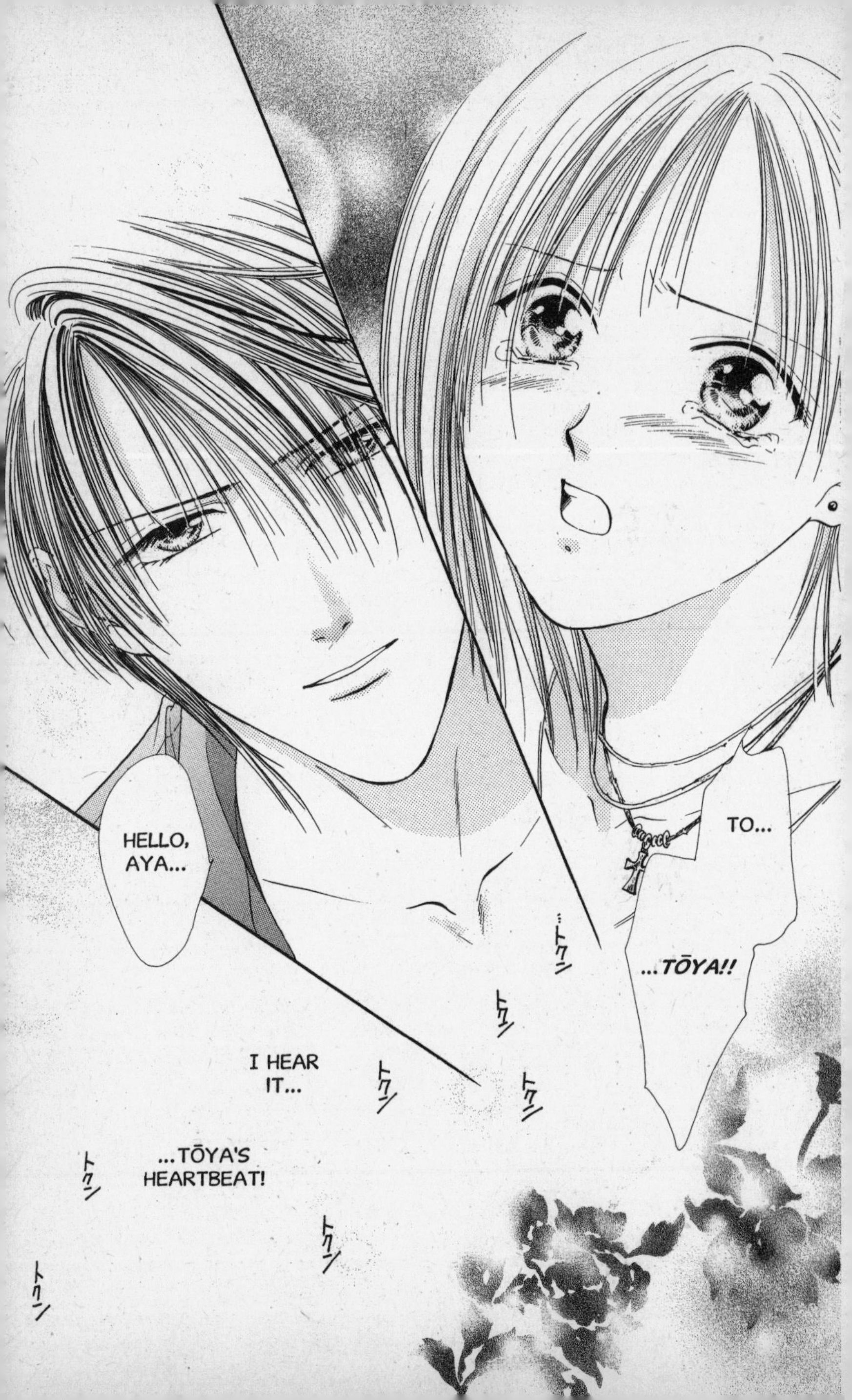
TO...
...TŌYA!!
HELLO, AYA...
トクン
トクン
トクン
I HEAR IT...
トクン
...TŌYA'S HEARTBEAT!
トクン
トクン
トクン

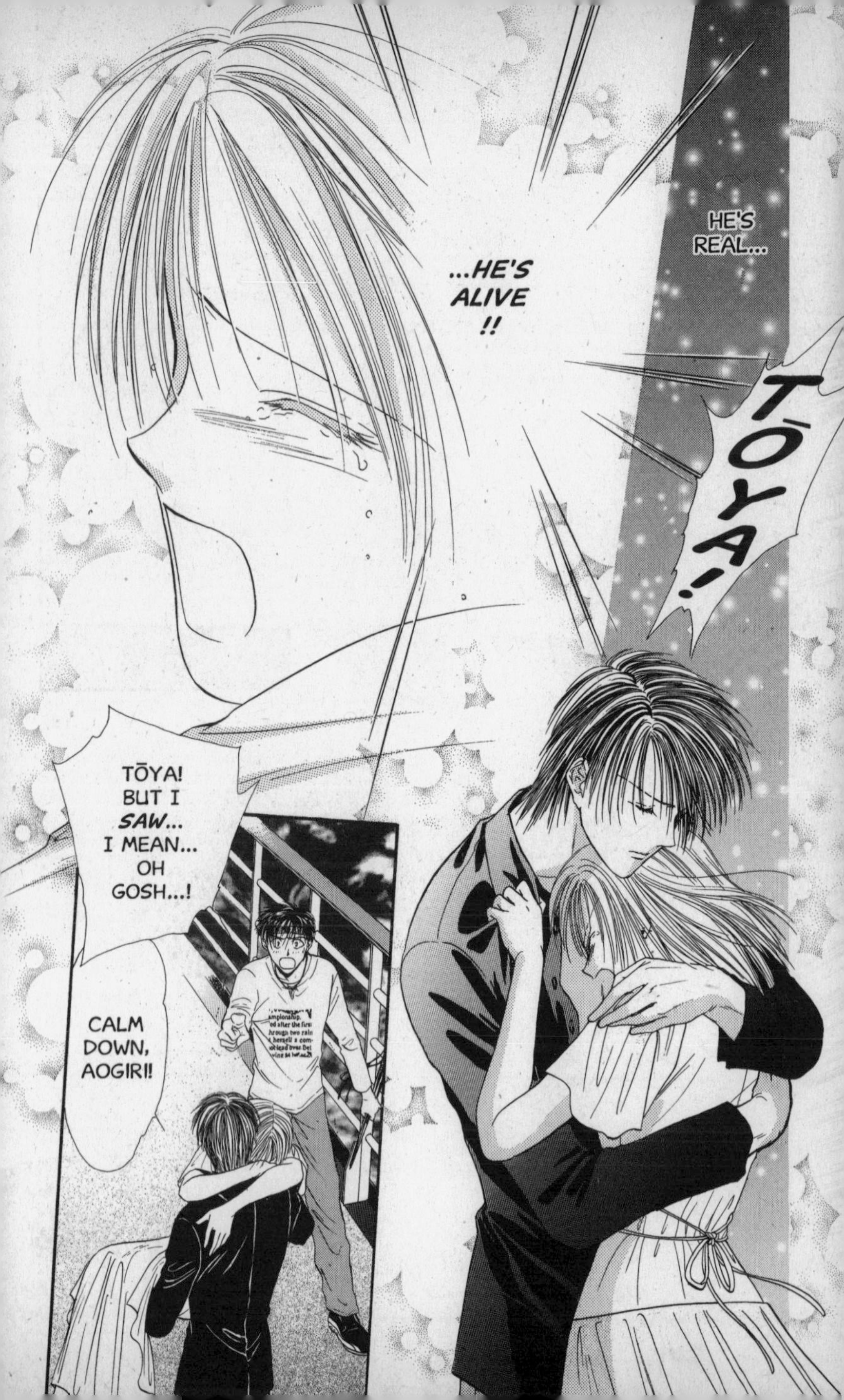
HE'S REAL...
TŌYA!!
...HE'S ALIVE !!
TŌYA! BUT I SAW... I MEAN... OH GOSH...!
CALM DOWN, AOGIRI!

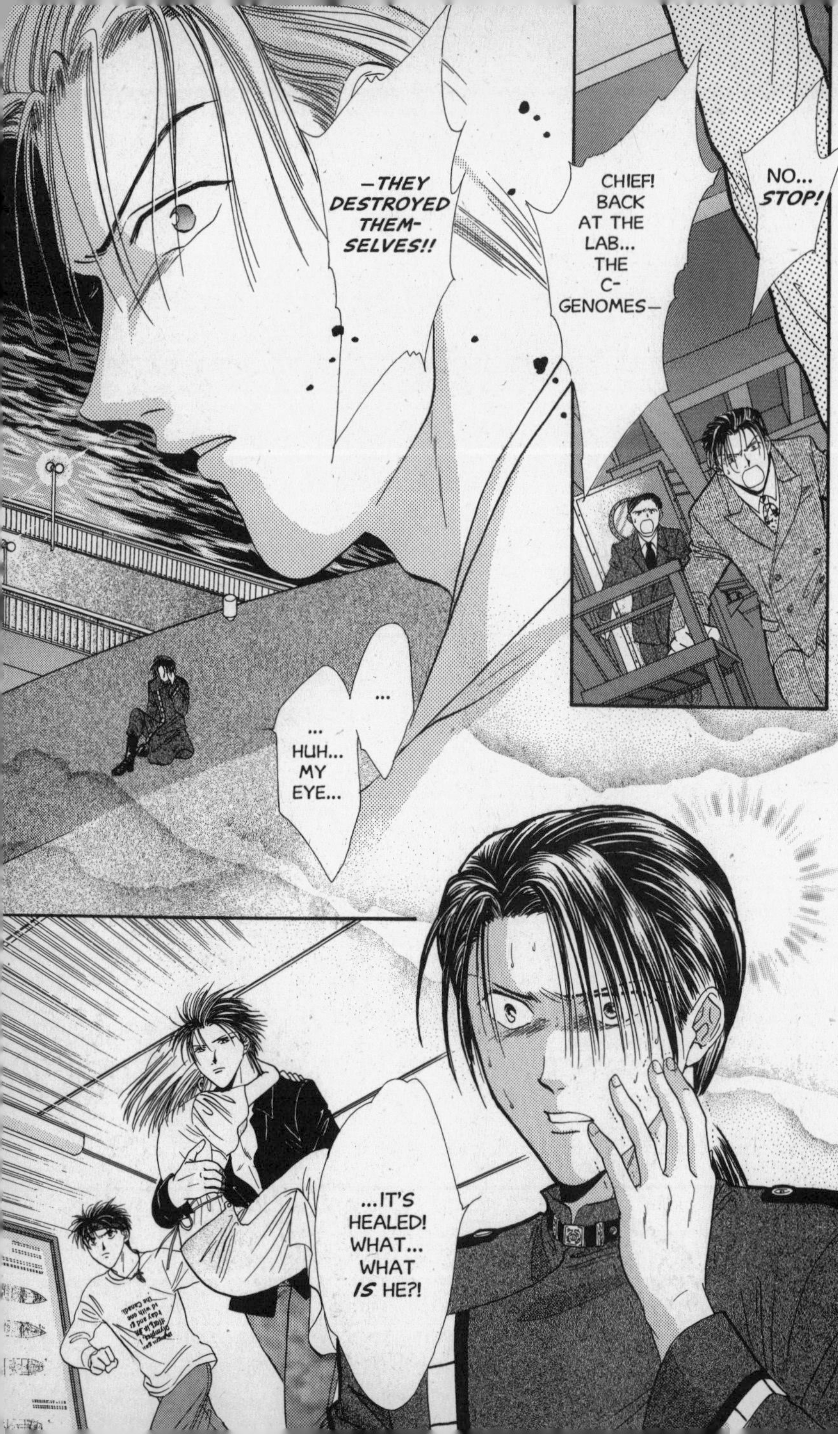
NO... *STOP!*
CHIEF! BACK AT THE LAB... THE C-GENOMES—
—THEY DESTROYED THEMSELVES!!
...
... HUH... MY EYE...
...IT'S HEALED! WHAT... WHAT *IS* HE?!

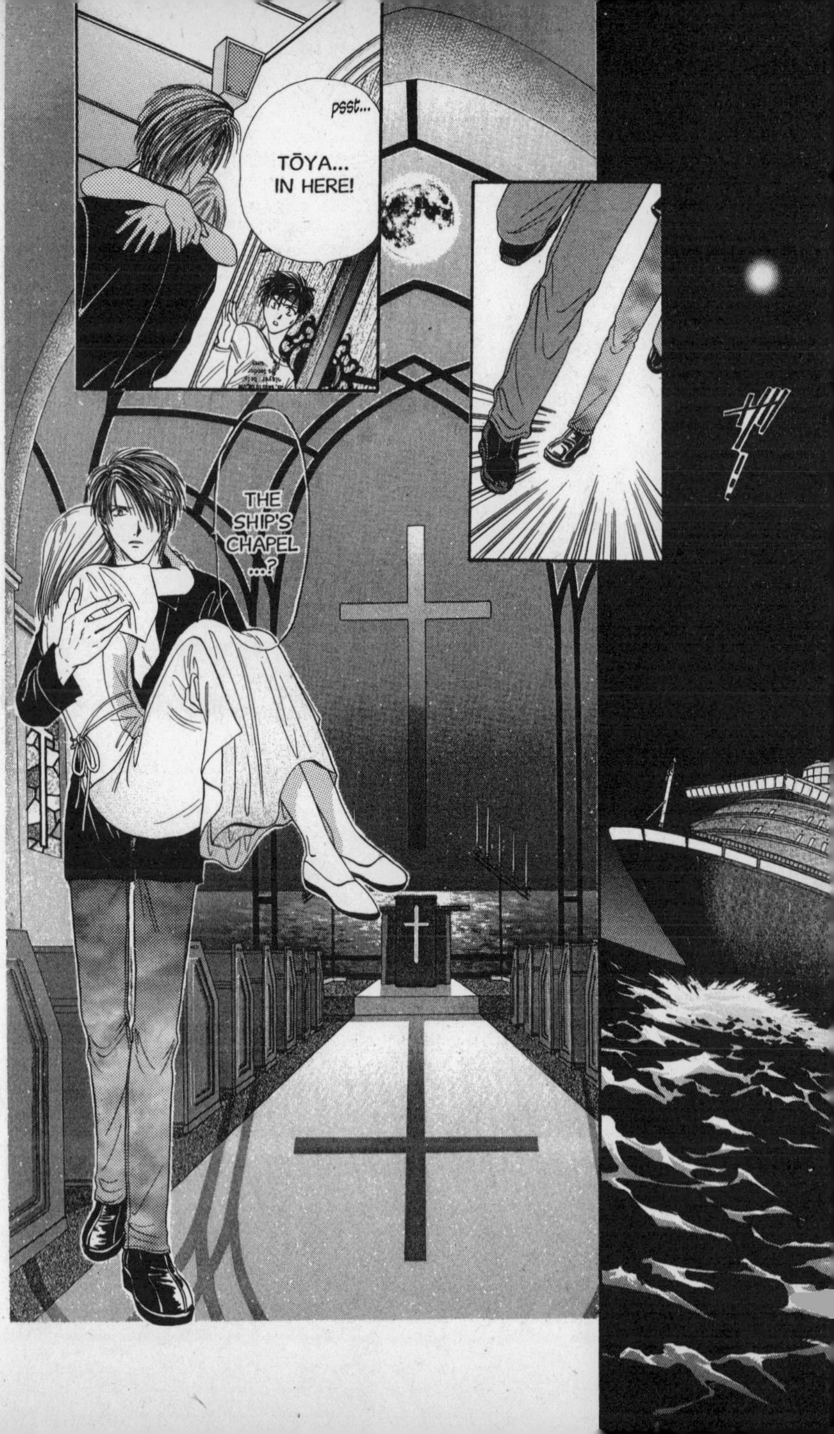
psst...
TŌYA... IN HERE!
THE SHIP'S CHAPEL ...?

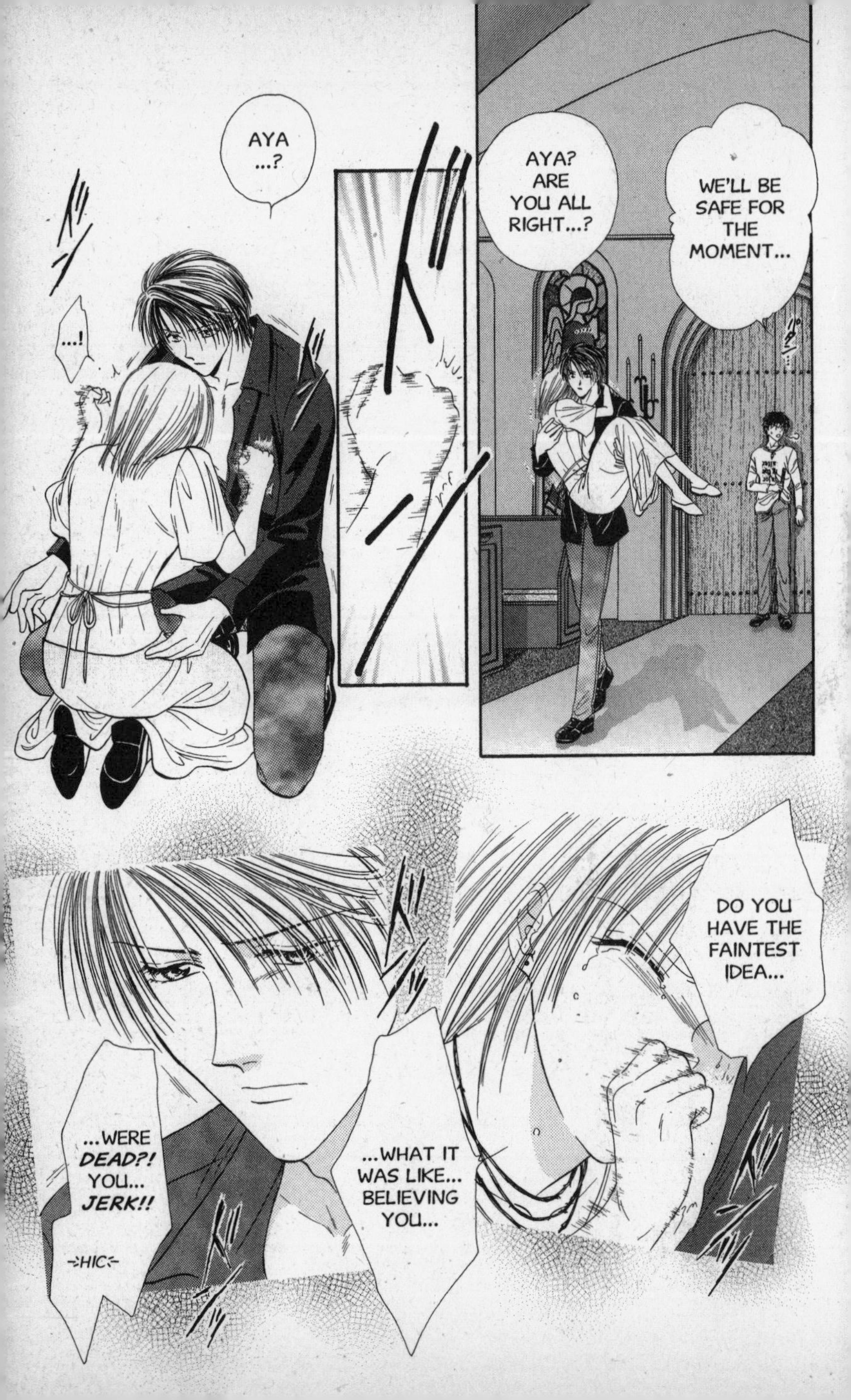
WE'LL BE SAFE FOR THE MOMENT...
AYA? ARE YOU ALL RIGHT...?
AYA ...?
...!
DO YOU HAVE THE FAINTEST IDEA...
...WHAT IT WAS LIKE... BELIEVING YOU...
...WERE *DEAD?!* YOU... ***JERK!!***
HIC

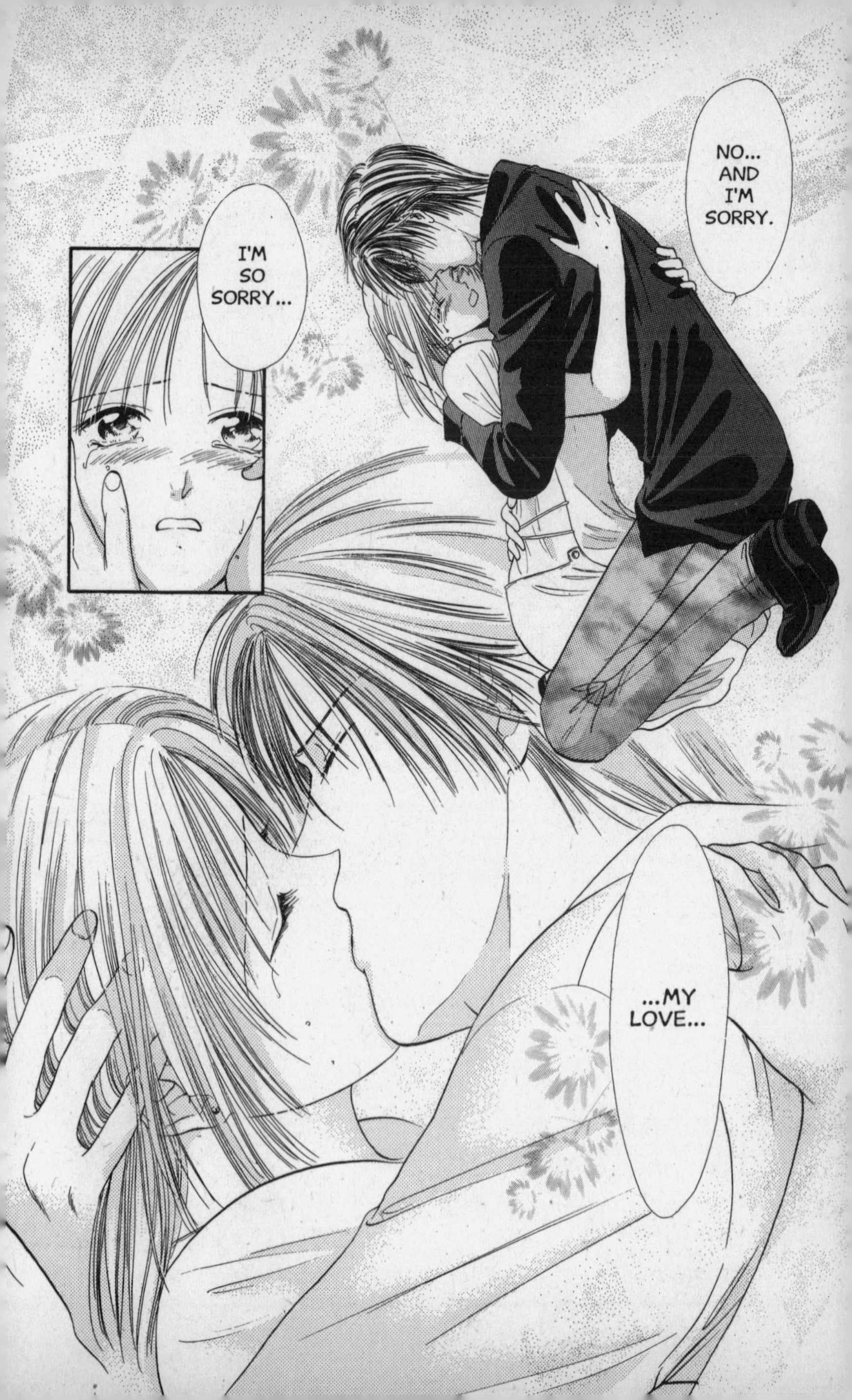
NO... AND I'M SORRY.
I'M SO SORRY...
...MY LOVE...

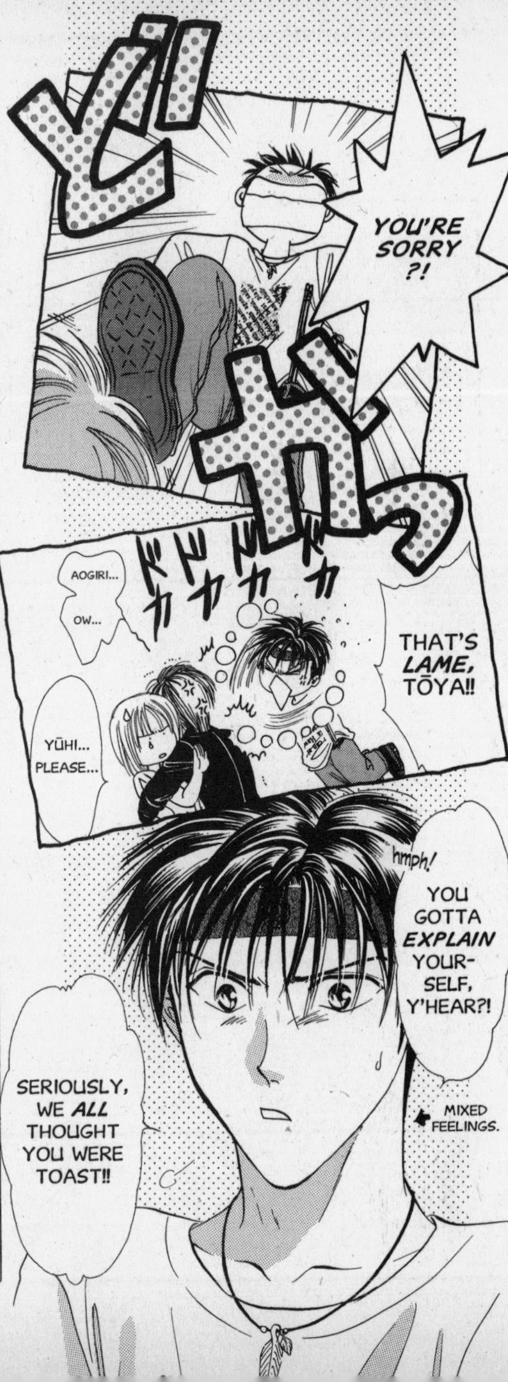
YOU'RE SORRY ?!
THAT'S *LAME*, TŌYA!!
AOGIRI...
OW...
YŪHI... PLEASE...
hmph!
YOU GOTTA *EXPLAIN* YOURSELF, Y'HEAR?!
SERIOUSLY, WE *ALL* THOUGHT YOU WERE TOAST!!
MIXED FEELINGS.

I don't know all the details at this point (late January) so I can't say much, but by the time you read this, you'll have access to plenty of accurate news.

Anyway, I could understand wanting to animate **FY**... but **Ceres**? Studio Pierrot's sure got some guts (I don't mean to be rude – I'm glad, very glad)!! The color scheme and mood are very different from **FY**, and overall it feels much more mature. It's so exciting.

However...the story might change a lot. You might become confused when certain events and characters are missing...but please enjoy the anime as something independent and different.

...That's all I can say for now.

The art for all the episodes is going to be overseen by Mr. Hideyuki Motohashi (who worked on **FY**). And it's all drawn on cels, which (I hear) is rare these days. Digital anime seems rather jagged on close-ups. Cels are prettier, so that's good...but it's harder on the staff! As for the voice actors, many of them are new talent (?)...(or is it just I haven't heard of 'em?!) Personally, I wouldn't want them to use seasoned celebrities anyway...I hate it when people go, "It's so-and-so's voice!" before they listen to it as the character's voice. I was a bit worried, but Studio Pierrot sent me tapes, and I double-checked them and gave them my blessing! I don't want to hear any complaints! ◡̈ I approved them myself!! That's how the characters sound in my mind, so that's how they're supposed to sound!! ◡̈

× × ×

...So the manga's concluded, but please watch the anime. Uh-oh, the novels...!! ◡̈ The first one will come out around April 25. The first had to be about Tōya, of course. Personally, I think the stories about Kagami and the Guardinals will be good, too...(I couldn't fit them in the manga!)

This is shōjo manga after all.

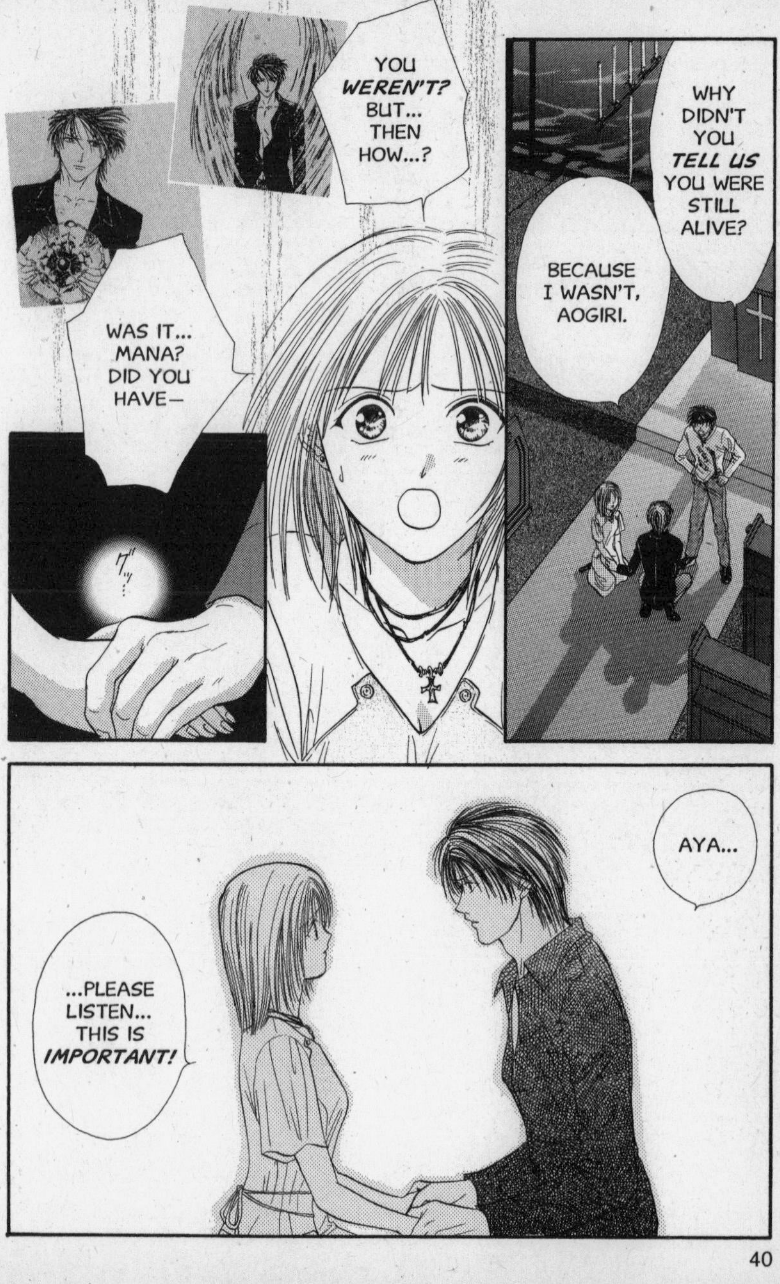

WHY DIDN'T YOU *TELL US* YOU WERE STILL ALIVE?
BECAUSE I WASN'T, AOGIRI.
YOU *WEREN'T?* BUT... THEN HOW...?
WAS IT... MANA? DID YOU HAVE—
AYA...
...PLEASE LISTEN... THIS IS *IMPORTANT!*

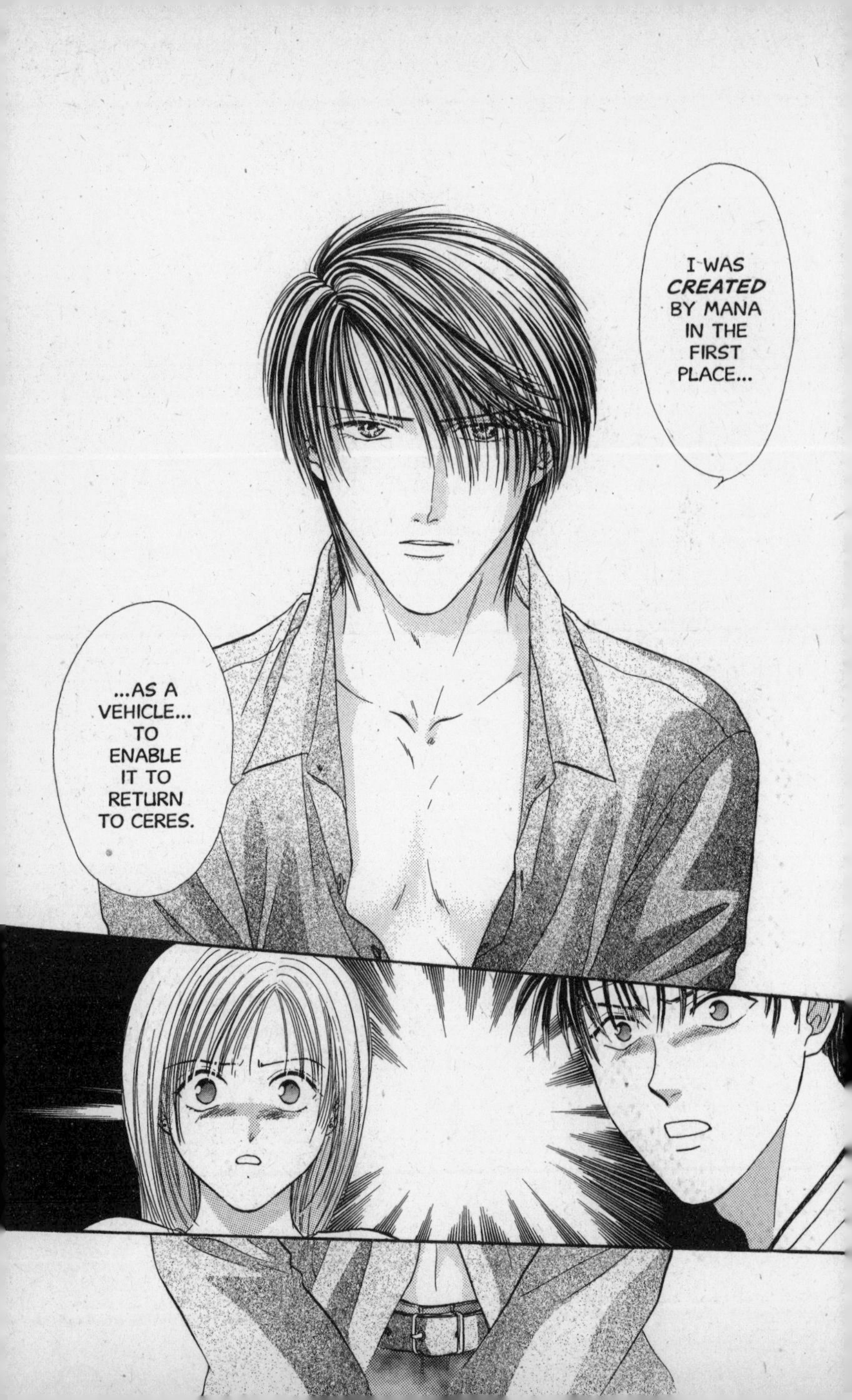
I WAS *CREATED* BY MANA IN THE FIRST PLACE...
...AS A VEHICLE... TO ENABLE IT TO RETURN TO CERES.

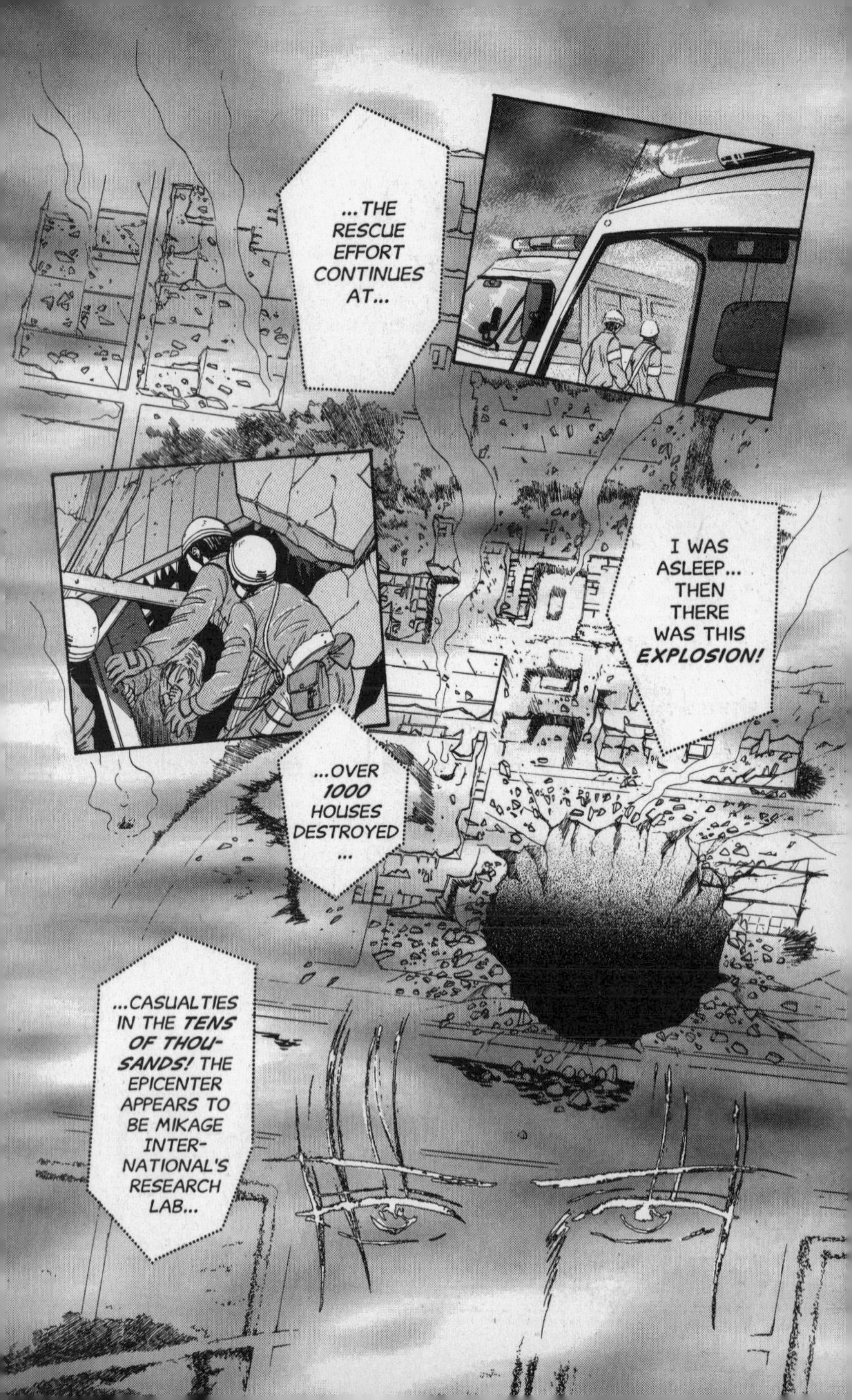
...THE RESCUE EFFORT CONTINUES AT...
I WAS ASLEEP... THEN THERE WAS THIS EXPLOSION!
...OVER 1000 HOUSES DESTROYED ...
...CASUALTIES IN THE TENS OF THOU-SANDS! THE EPICENTER APPEARS TO BE MIKAGE INTER-NATIONAL'S RESEARCH LAB...

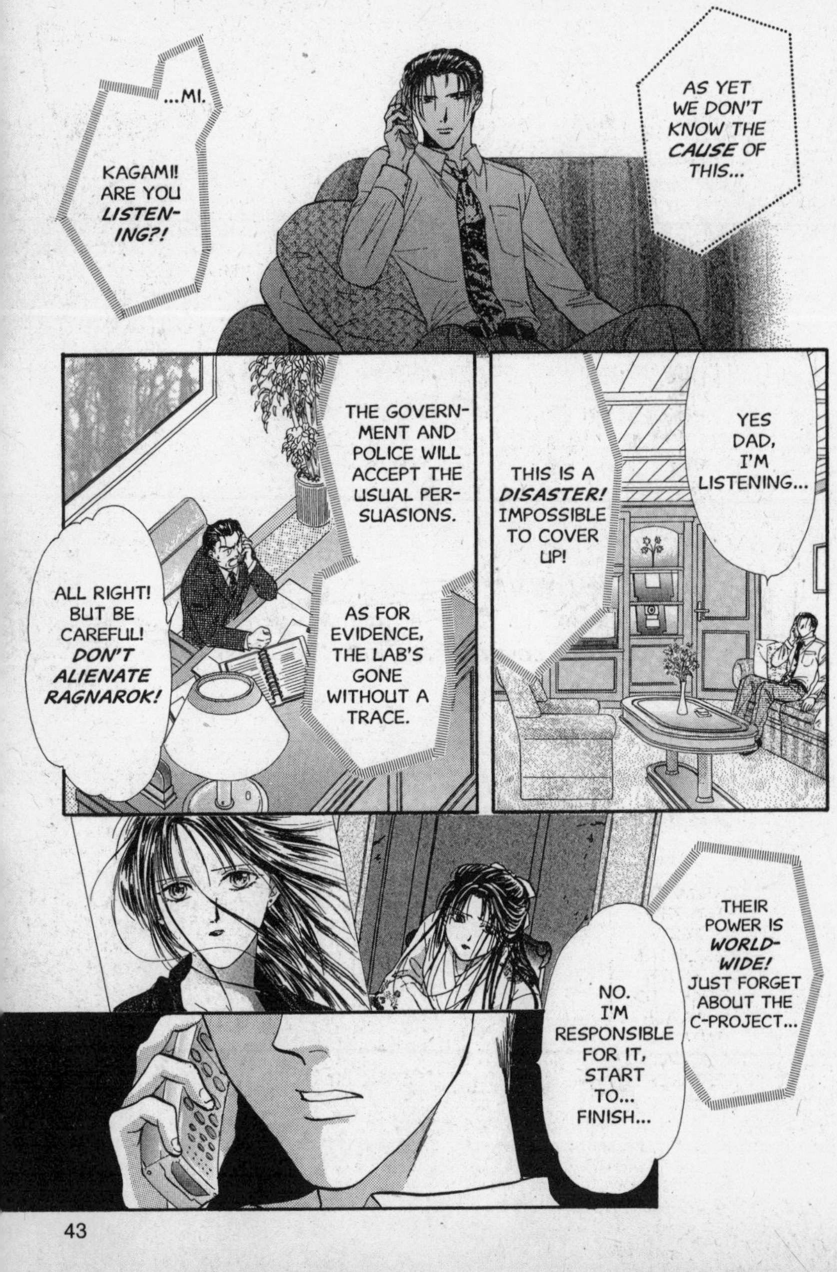
AS YET WE DON'T KNOW THE CAUSE OF THIS...
...MI.
KAGAMI! ARE YOU LISTEN-ING?!
YES DAD, I'M LISTENING...
THIS IS A DISASTER! IMPOSSIBLE TO COVER UP!
THE GOVERN-MENT AND POLICE WILL ACCEPT THE USUAL PER-SUASIONS.
AS FOR EVIDENCE, THE LAB'S GONE WITHOUT A TRACE.
ALL RIGHT! BUT BE CAREFUL! DON'T ALIENATE RAGNAROK!
THEIR POWER IS WORLD-WIDE! JUST FORGET ABOUT THE C-PROJECT...
NO. I'M RESPONSIBLE FOR IT, START TO... FINISH...

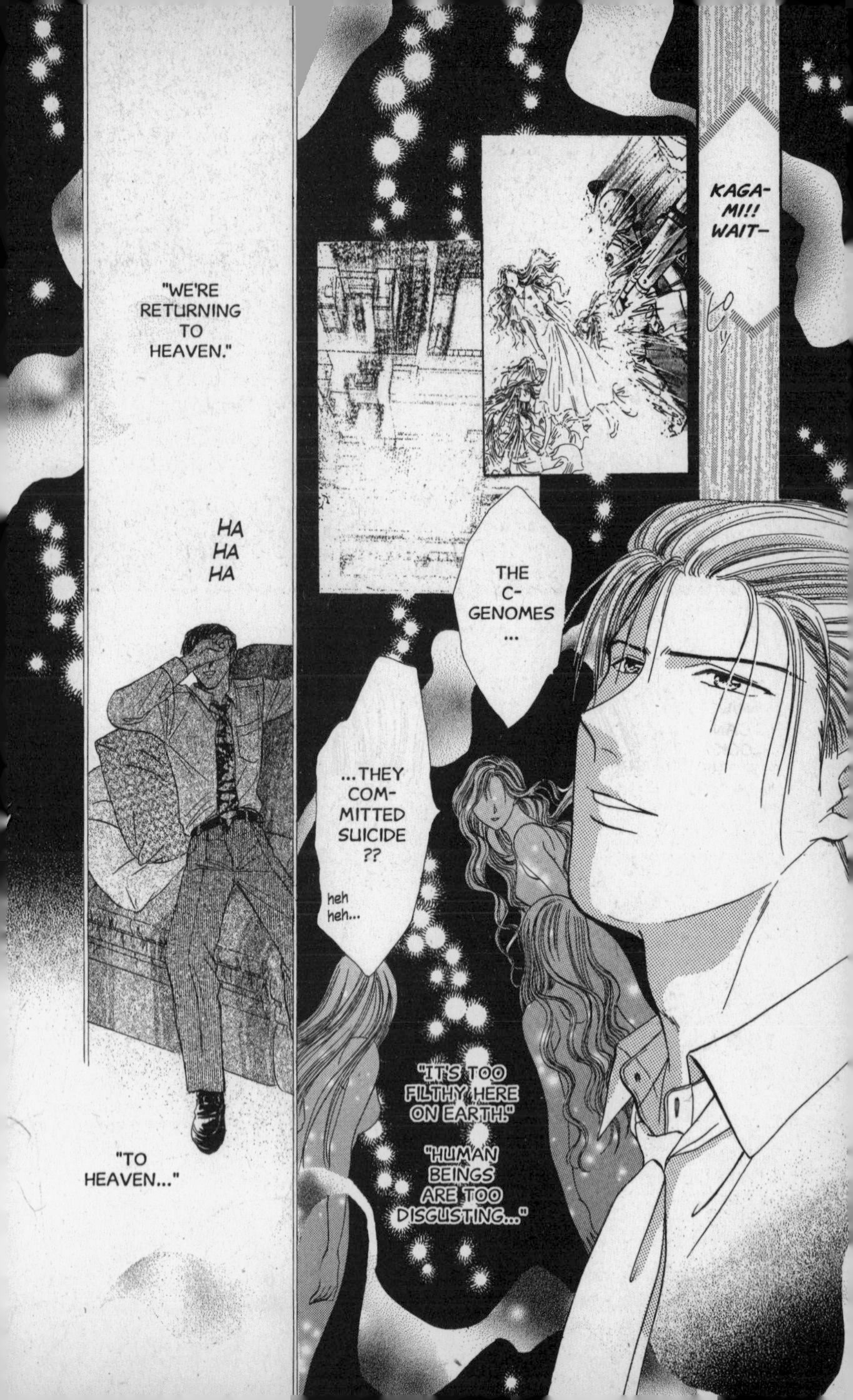
KAGA-MI!! WAIT—
THE C-GENOMES...
...THEY COM-MITTED SUICIDE??
heh heh...
"IT'S TOO FILTHY HERE ON EARTH."
"HUMAN BEINGS ARE TOO DISGUSTING..."
"WE'RE RETURNING TO HEAVEN."
HA HA HA
"TO HEAVEN..."

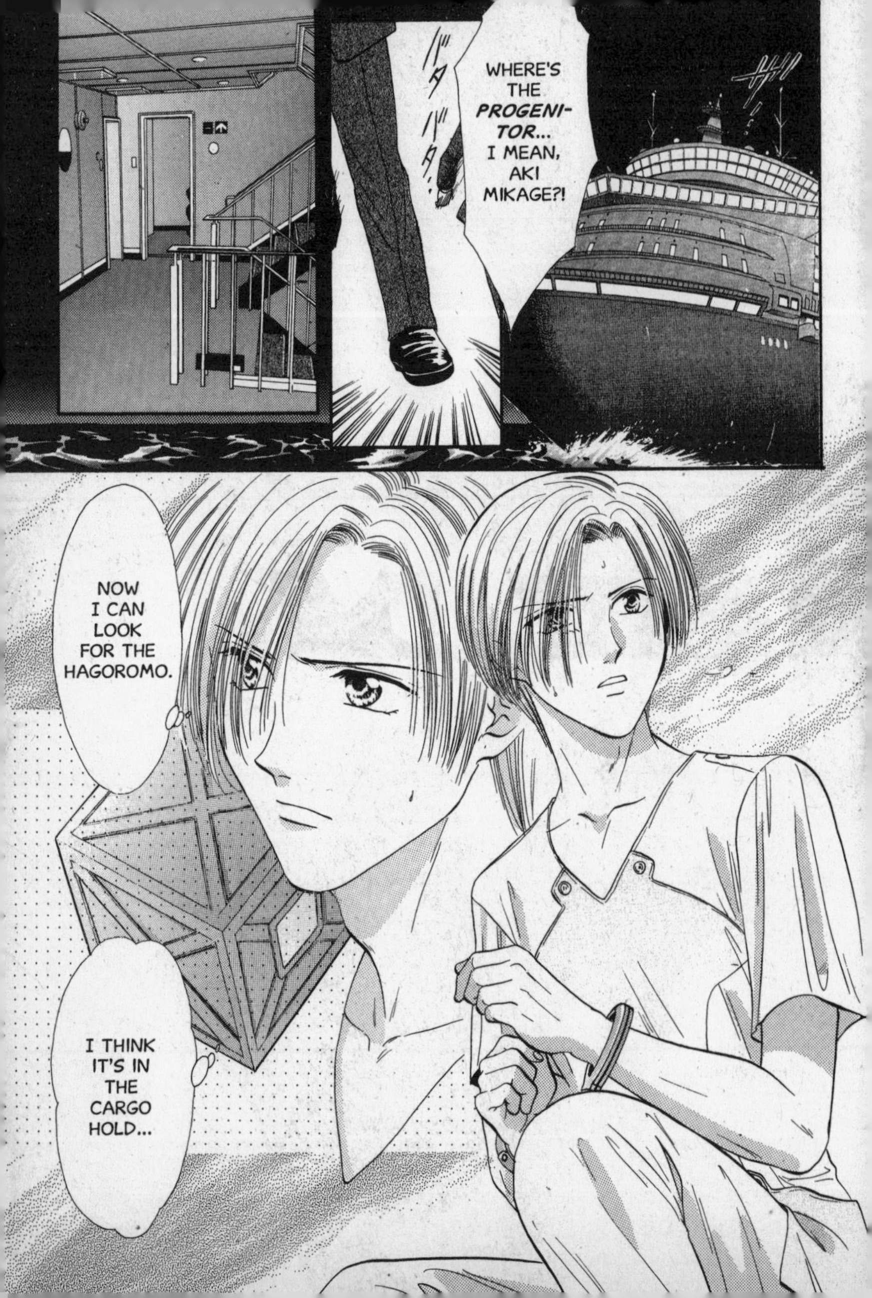
WHERE'S THE *PROGENITOR*... I MEAN, AKI MIKAGE?!
NOW I CAN LOOK FOR THE HAGOROMO.
I THINK IT'S IN THE CARGO HOLD...

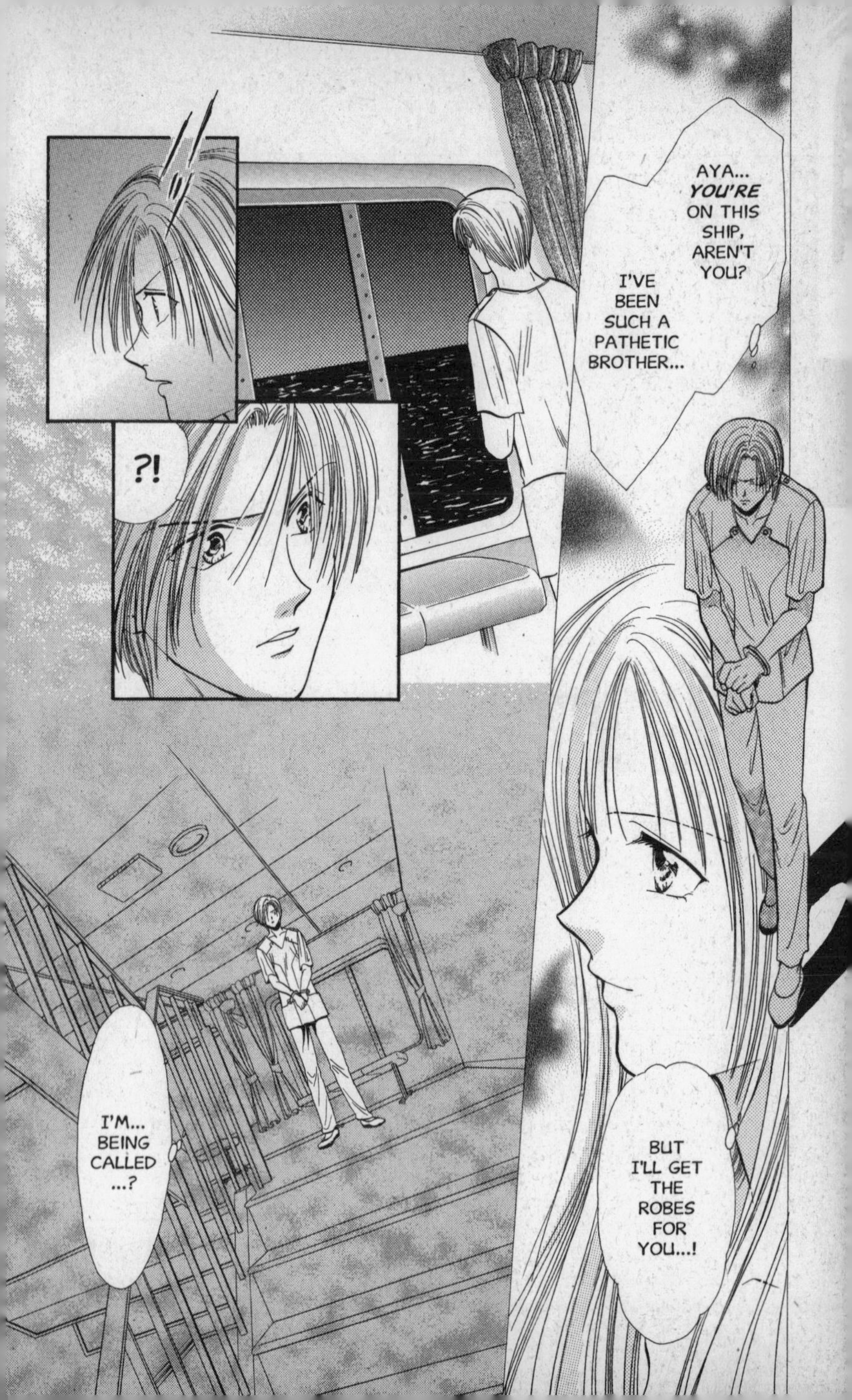
AYA... *YOU'RE* ON THIS SHIP, AREN'T YOU?
I'VE BEEN SUCH A PATHETIC BROTHER...
BUT I'LL GET THE ROBES FOR YOU...!
?!
I'M... BEING CALLED ...?

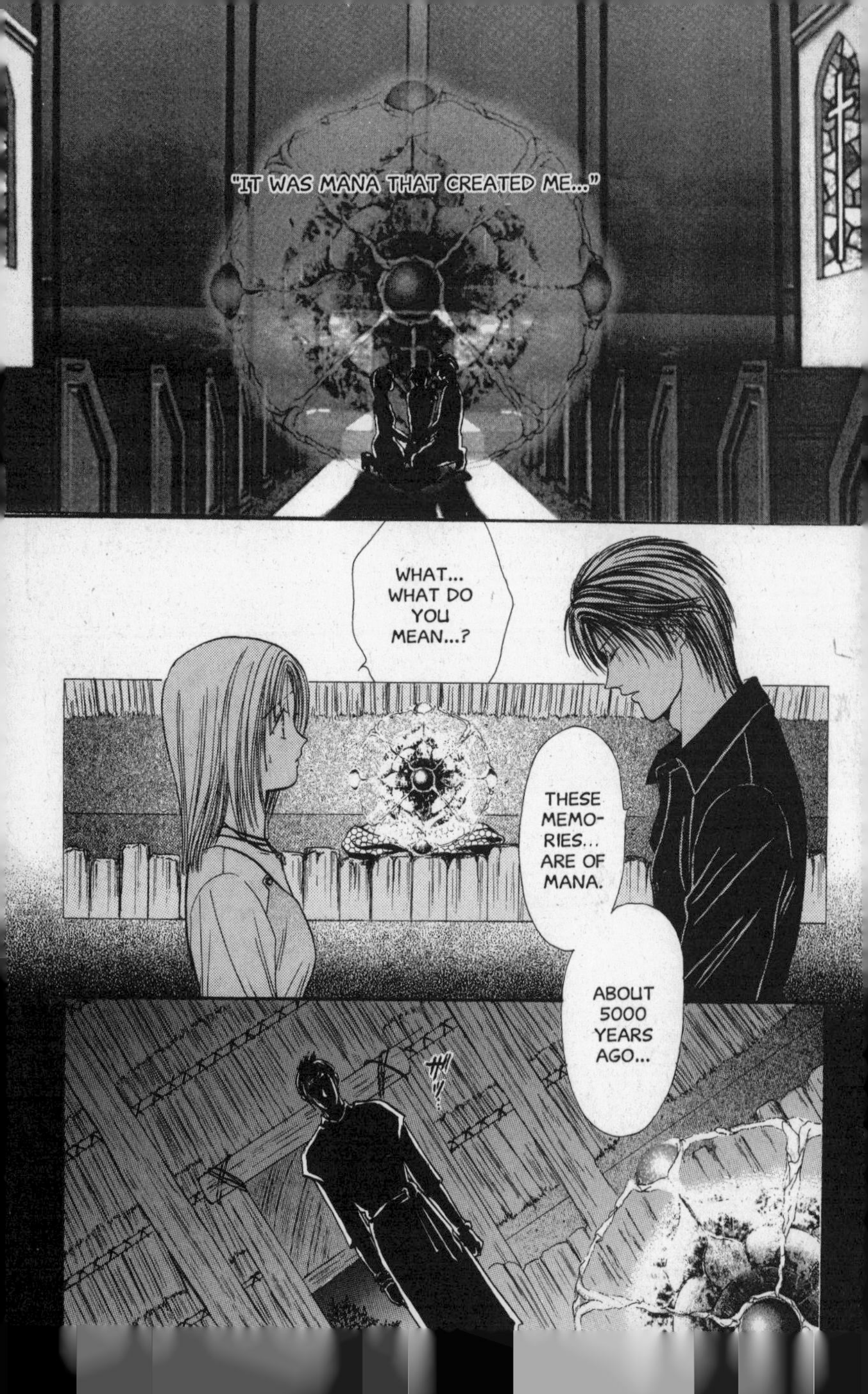
"IT WAS MANA THAT CREATED ME..."
WHAT... WHAT DO YOU MEAN...?
THESE MEMORIES... ARE OF MANA.
ABOUT 5000 YEARS AGO...

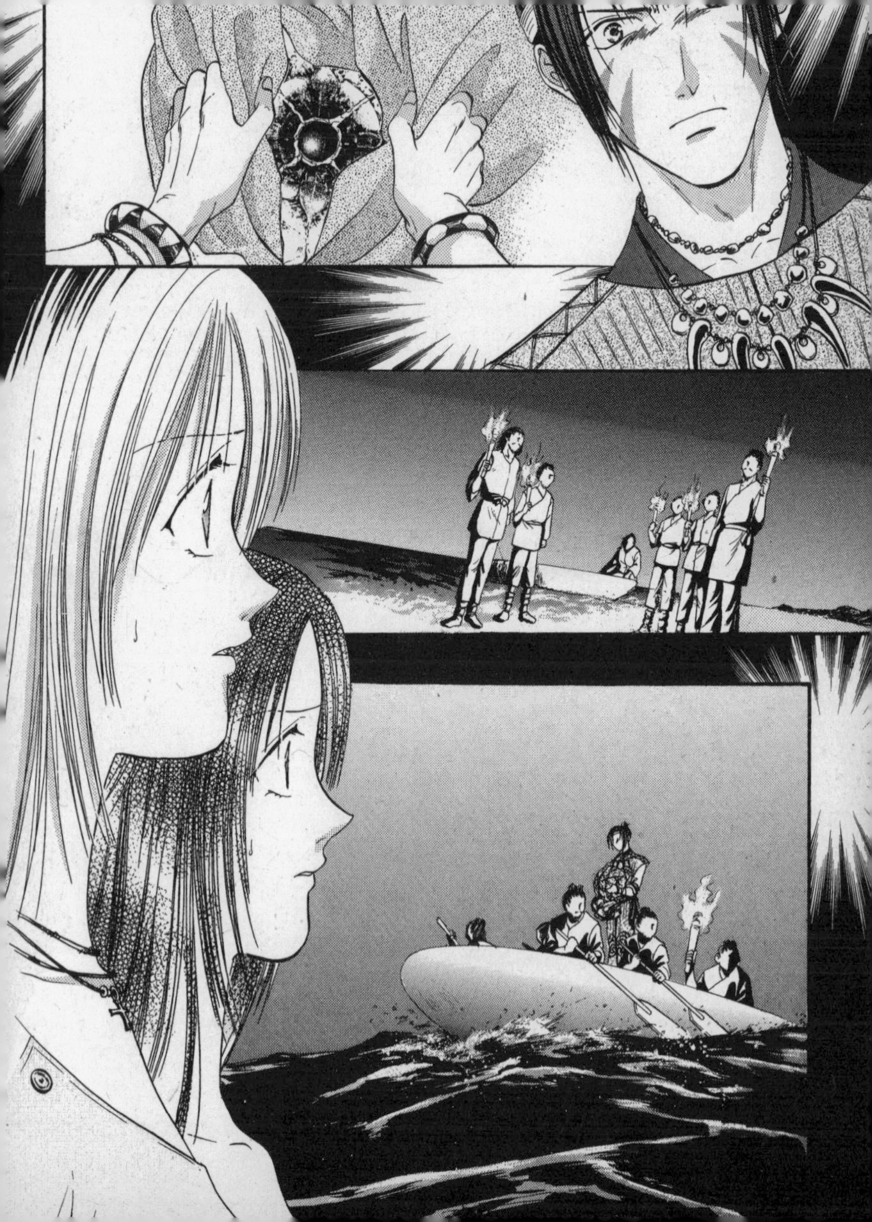

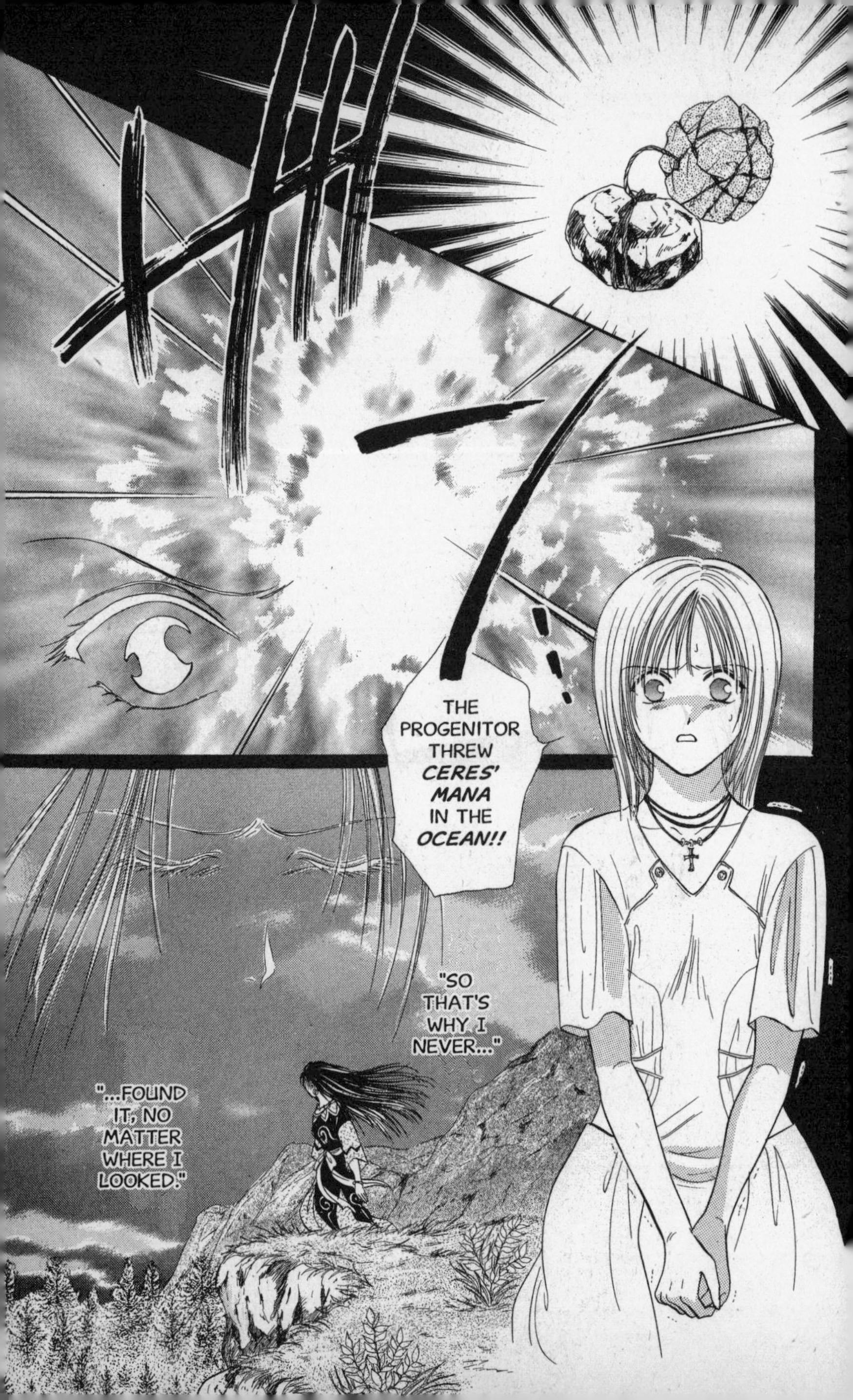
THE PROGENITOR THREW CERES' MANA IN THE OCEAN!!
"SO THAT'S WHY I NEVER..."
"...FOUND IT, NO MATTER WHERE I LOOKED."

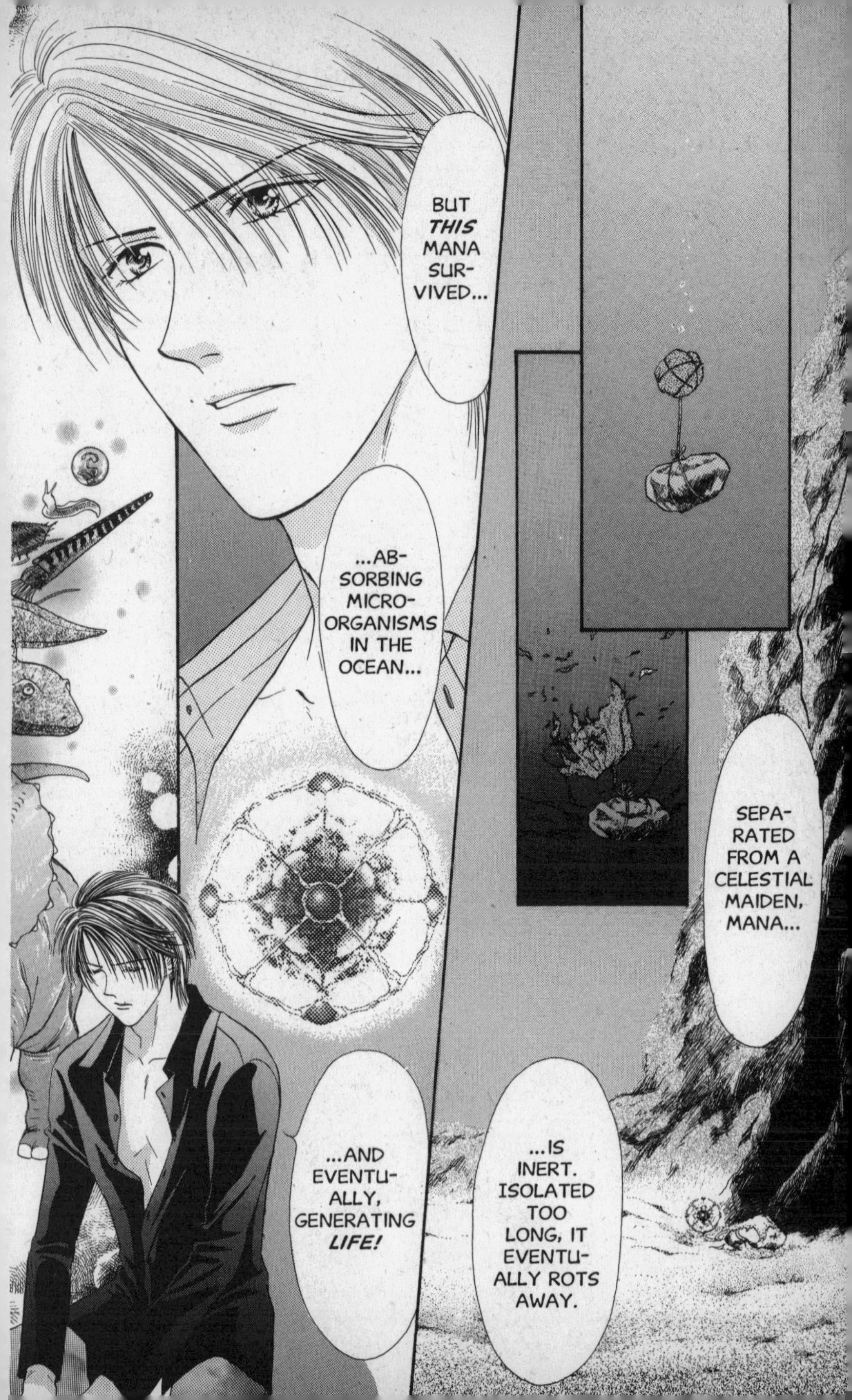
SEPARATED FROM A CELESTIAL MAIDEN, MANA...
...IS INERT. ISOLATED TOO LONG, IT EVENTUALLY ROTS AWAY.
BUT *THIS* MANA SURVIVED...
...ABSORBING MICRO-ORGANISMS IN THE OCEAN...
...AND EVENTUALLY, GENERATING *LIFE!*

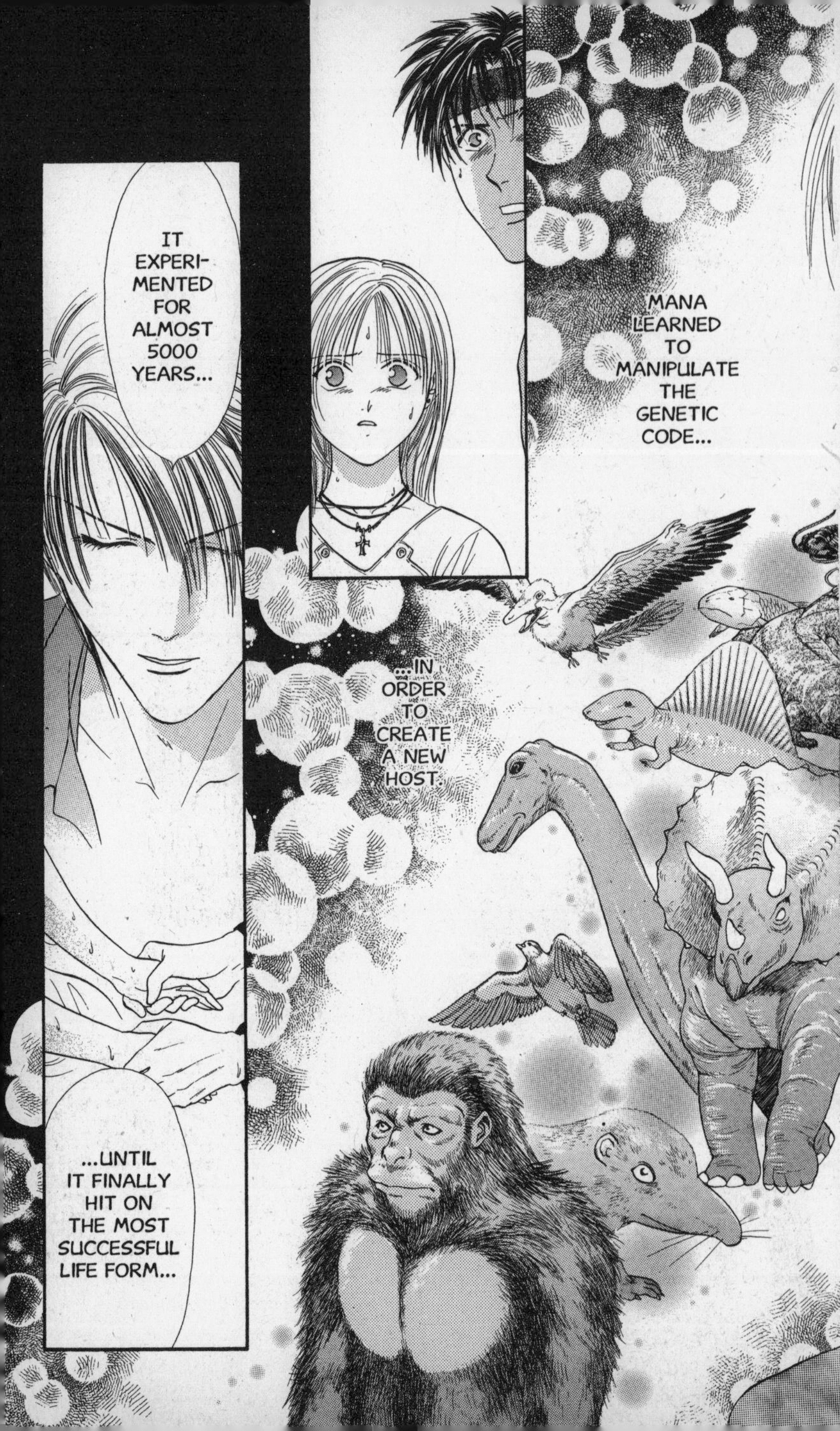
MANA LEARNED TO MANIPULATE THE GENETIC CODE...
...IN ORDER TO CREATE A NEW HOST.
IT EXPERIMENTED FOR ALMOST 5000 YEARS...
...UNTIL IT FINALLY HIT ON THE MOST SUCCESSFUL LIFE FORM...

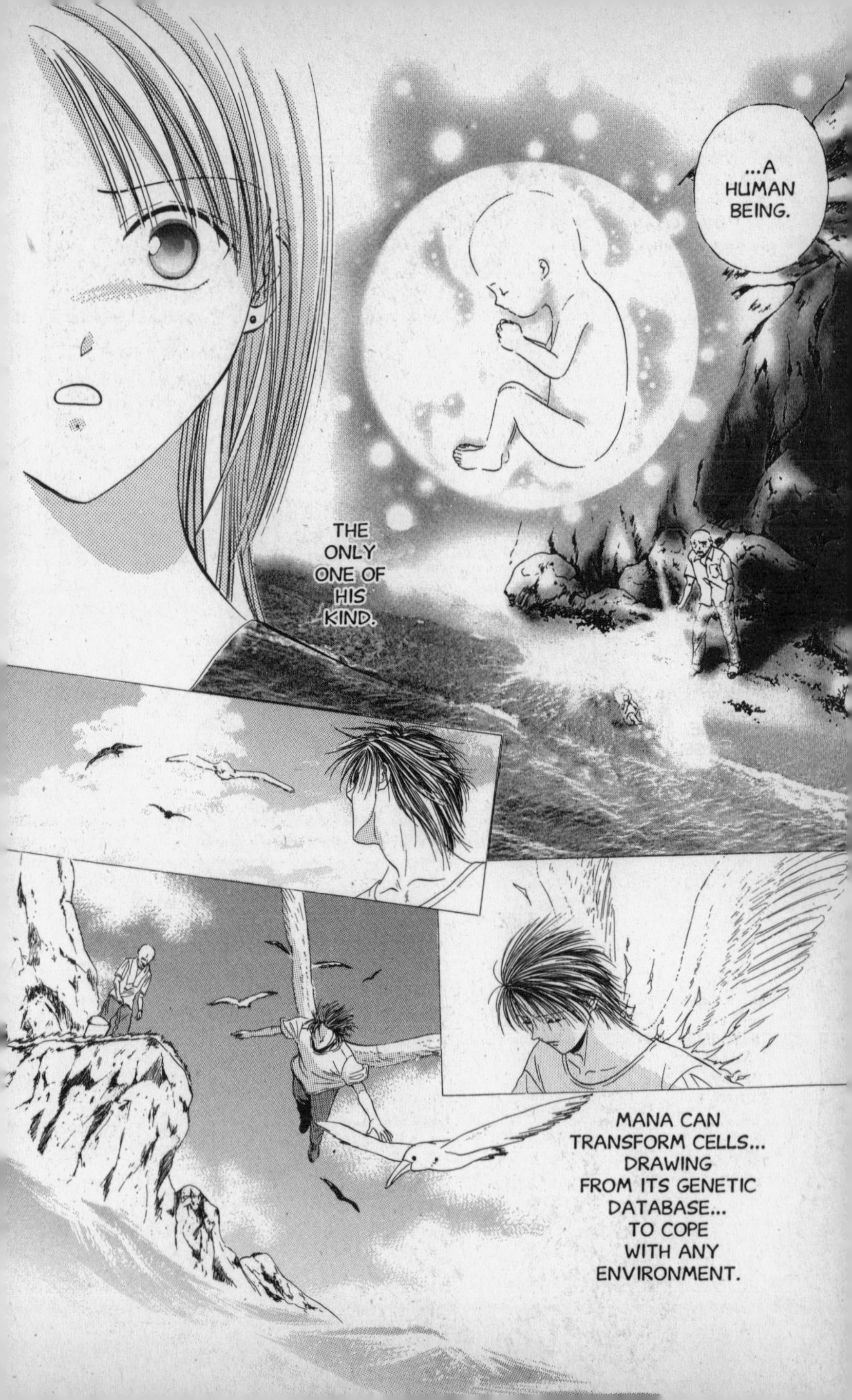
...A HUMAN BEING.
THE ONLY ONE OF HIS KIND.
MANA CAN TRANSFORM CELLS... DRAWING FROM ITS GENETIC DATABASE... TO COPE WITH ANY ENVIRONMENT.

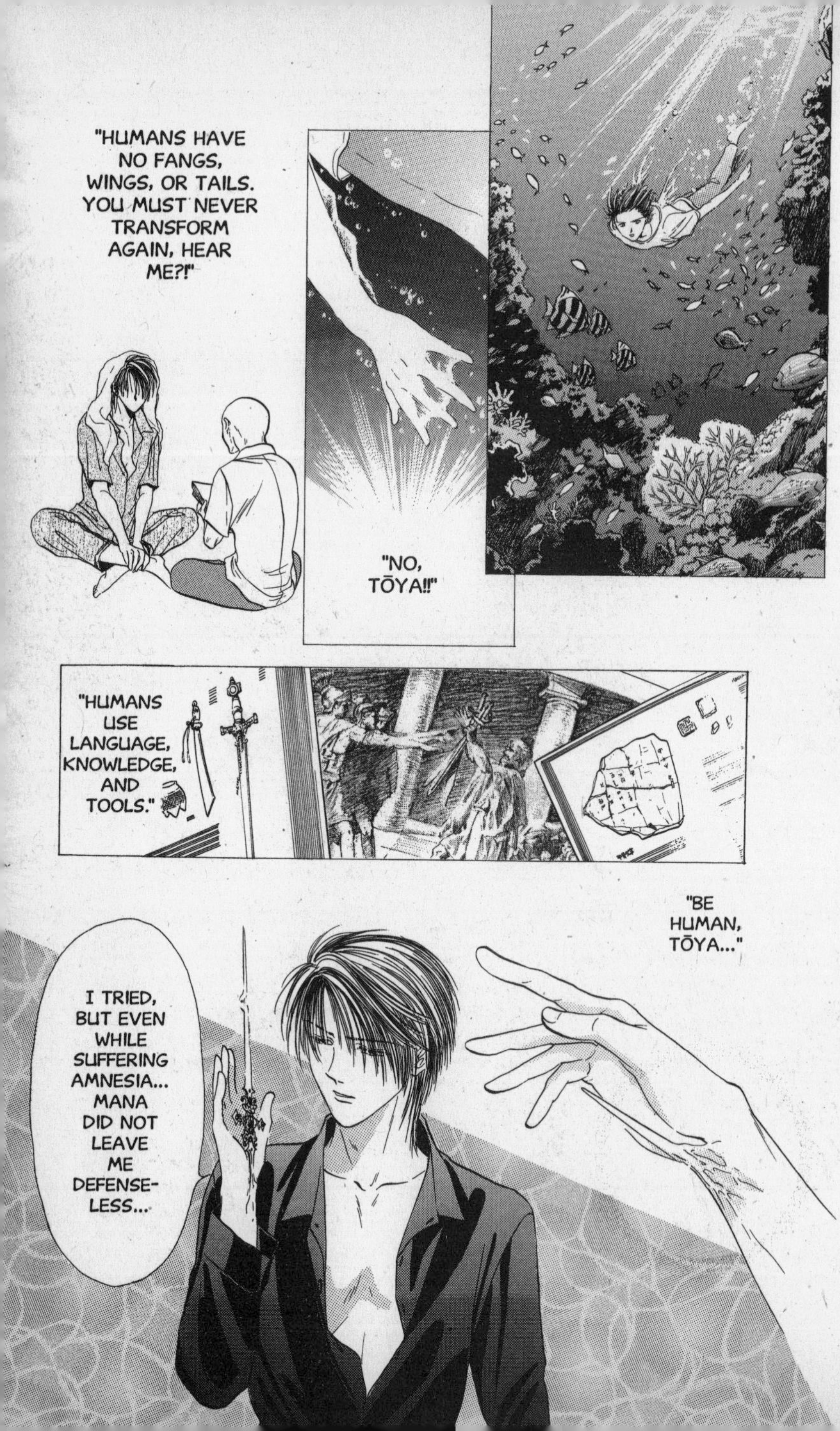
"NO, TŌYA!!"
"HUMANS HAVE NO FANGS, WINGS, OR TAILS. YOU MUST NEVER TRANSFORM AGAIN, HEAR ME?!"
"HUMANS USE LANGUAGE, KNOWLEDGE, AND TOOLS."
"BE HUMAN, TŌYA..."
I TRIED, BUT EVEN WHILE SUFFERING AMNESIA... MANA DID NOT LEAVE ME DEFENSELESS...

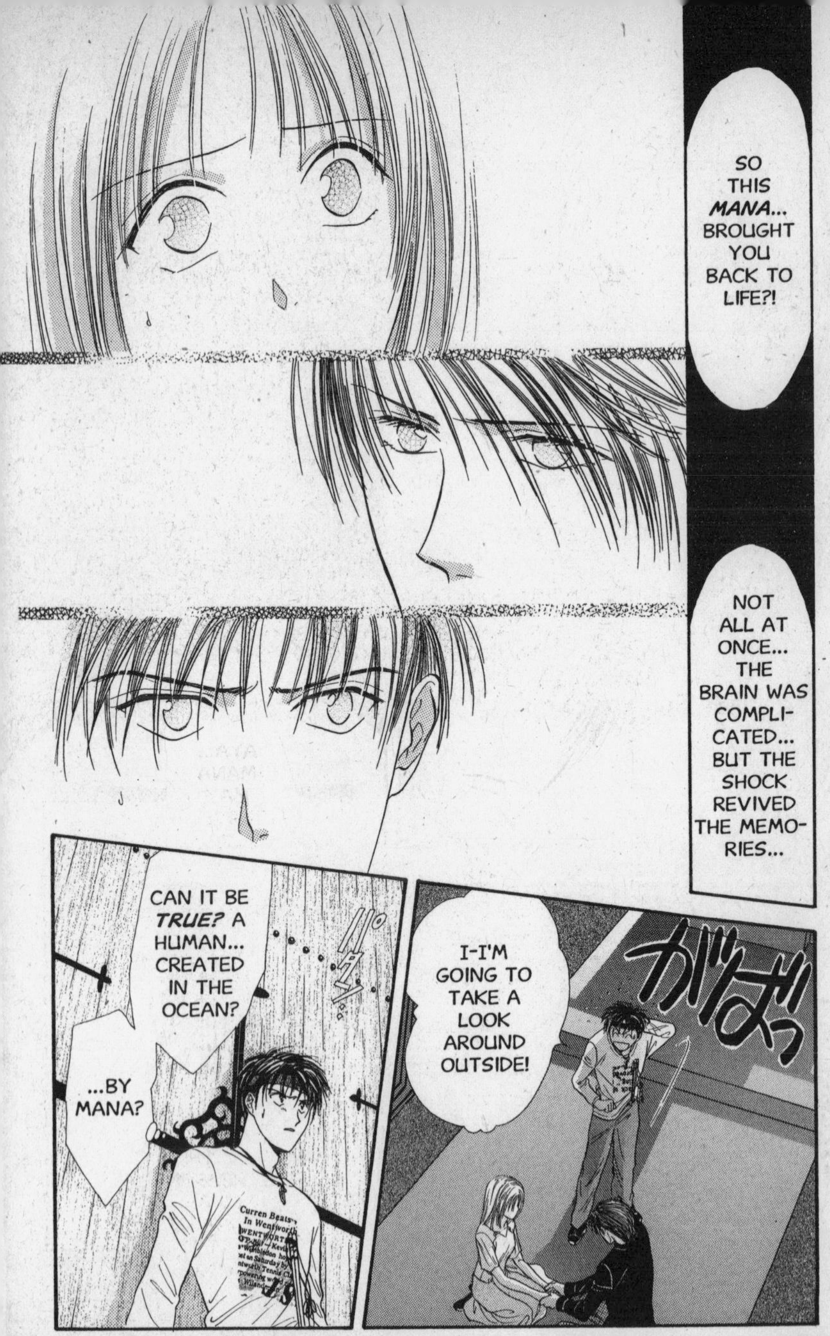
SO THIS *MANA*... BROUGHT YOU BACK TO LIFE?!
NOT ALL AT ONCE... THE BRAIN WAS COMPLI-CATED... BUT THE SHOCK REVIVED THE MEMO-RIES...
がばっ
I-I'M GOING TO TAKE A LOOK AROUND OUTSIDE!
パタン
CAN IT BE ***TRUE?*** A HUMAN... CREATED IN THE OCEAN?
...BY MANA?

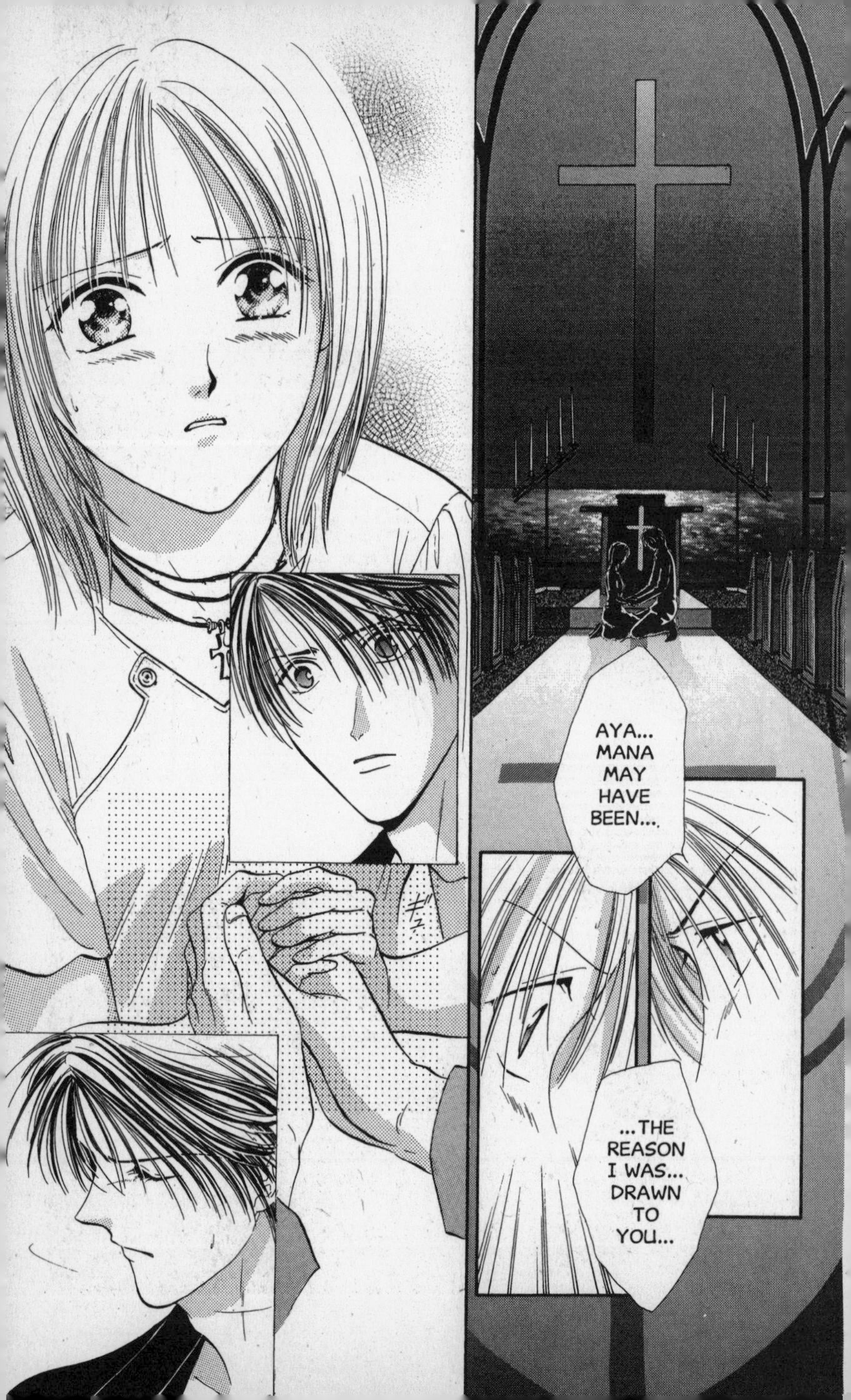
AYA... MANA MAY HAVE BEEN...
...THE REASON I WAS... DRAWN TO YOU...

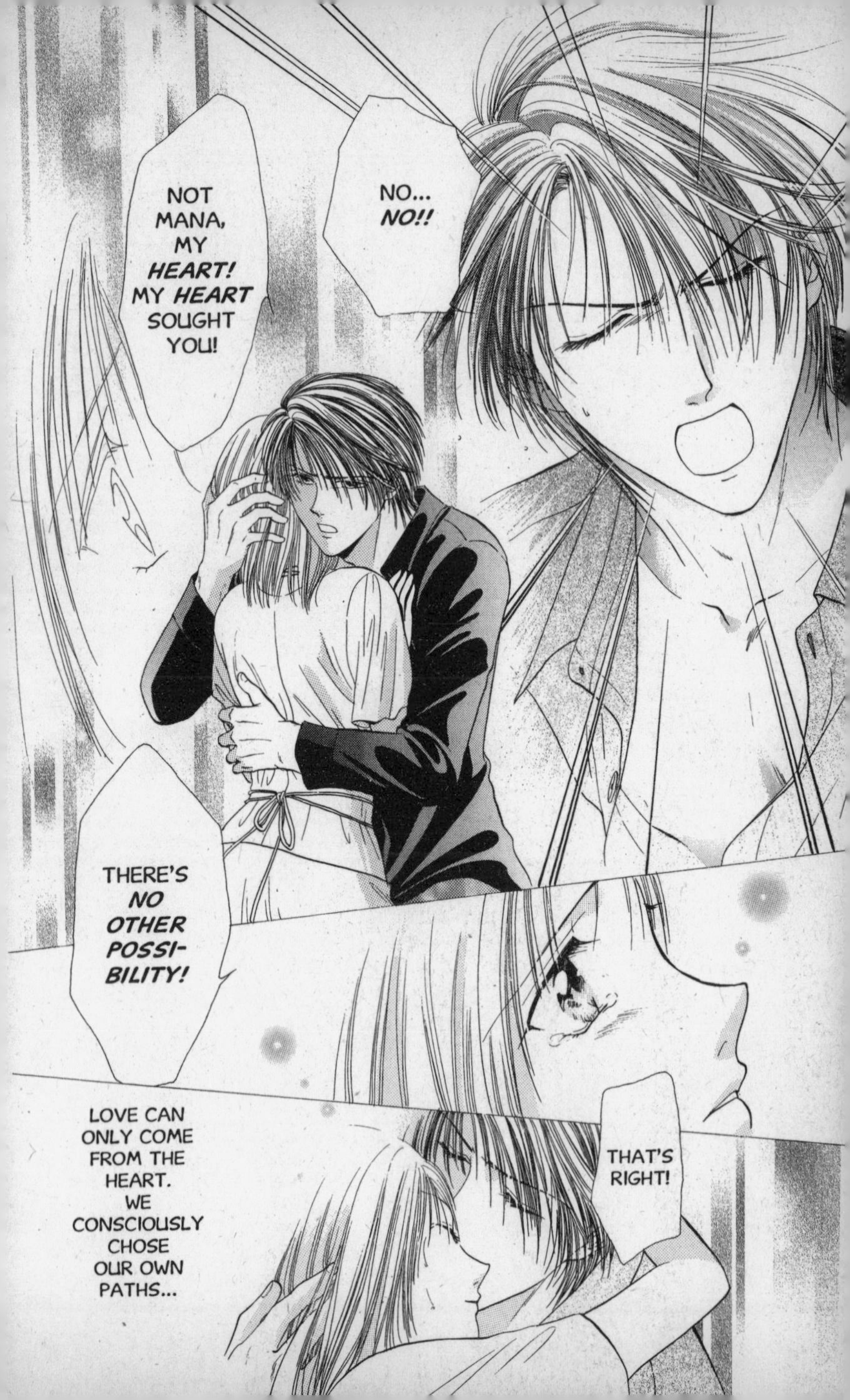
NO... *NO!!*
NOT MANA, MY *HEART!* MY *HEART* SOUGHT YOU!
THERE'S *NO OTHER POSSIBILITY!*
THAT'S RIGHT!
LOVE CAN ONLY COME FROM THE HEART. WE CONSCIOUSLY CHOSE OUR OWN PATHS...

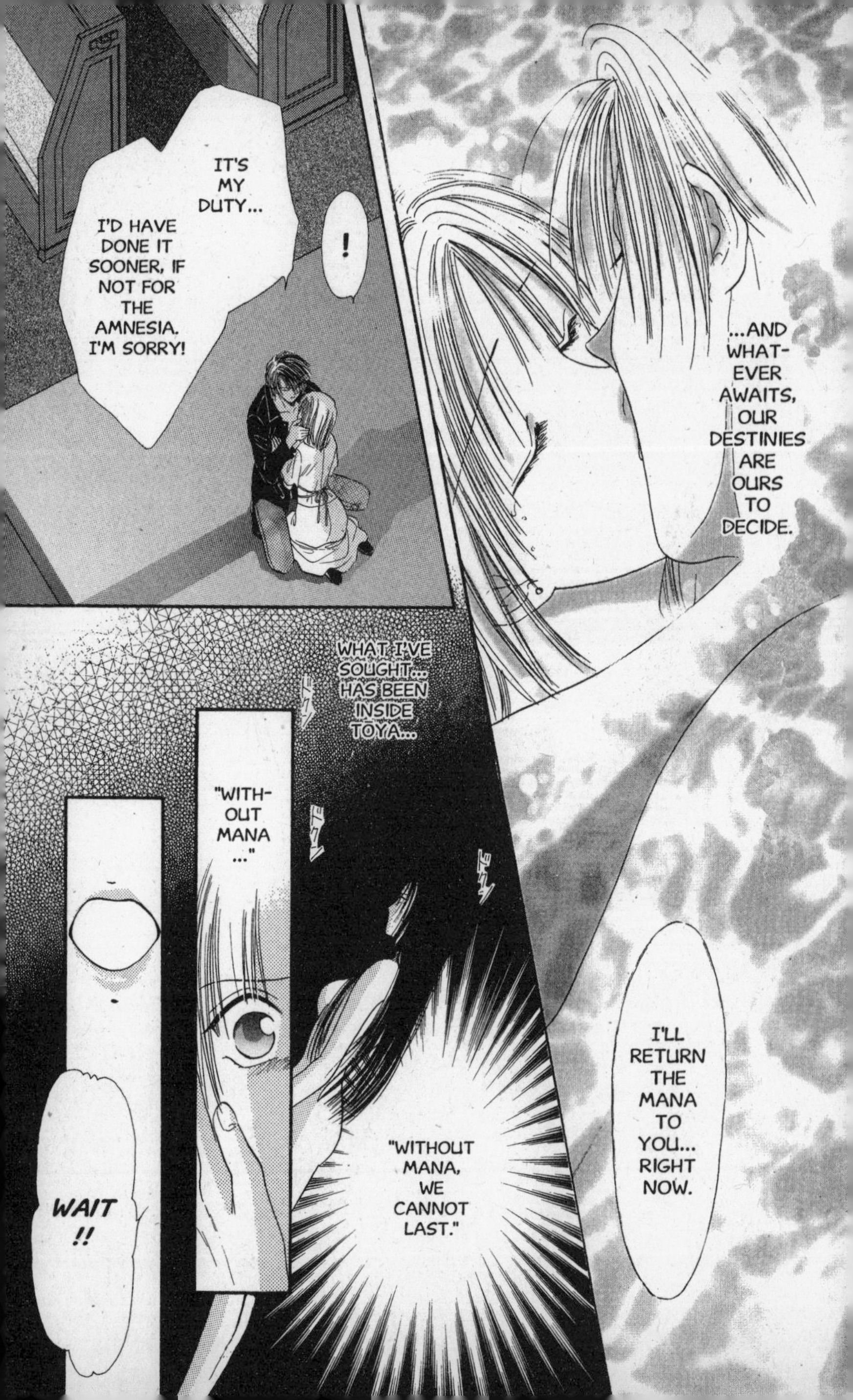
...AND WHATEVER AWAITS, OUR DESTINIES ARE OURS TO DECIDE.
I'LL RETURN THE MANA TO YOU... RIGHT NOW.
IT'S MY DUTY...
I'D HAVE DONE IT SOONER, IF NOT FOR THE AMNESIA. I'M SORRY!
!
WHAT I'VE SOUGHT... HAS BEEN INSIDE TOYA...
"WITHOUT MANA, WE CANNOT LAST."
"WITHOUT MANA..."
WAIT!!

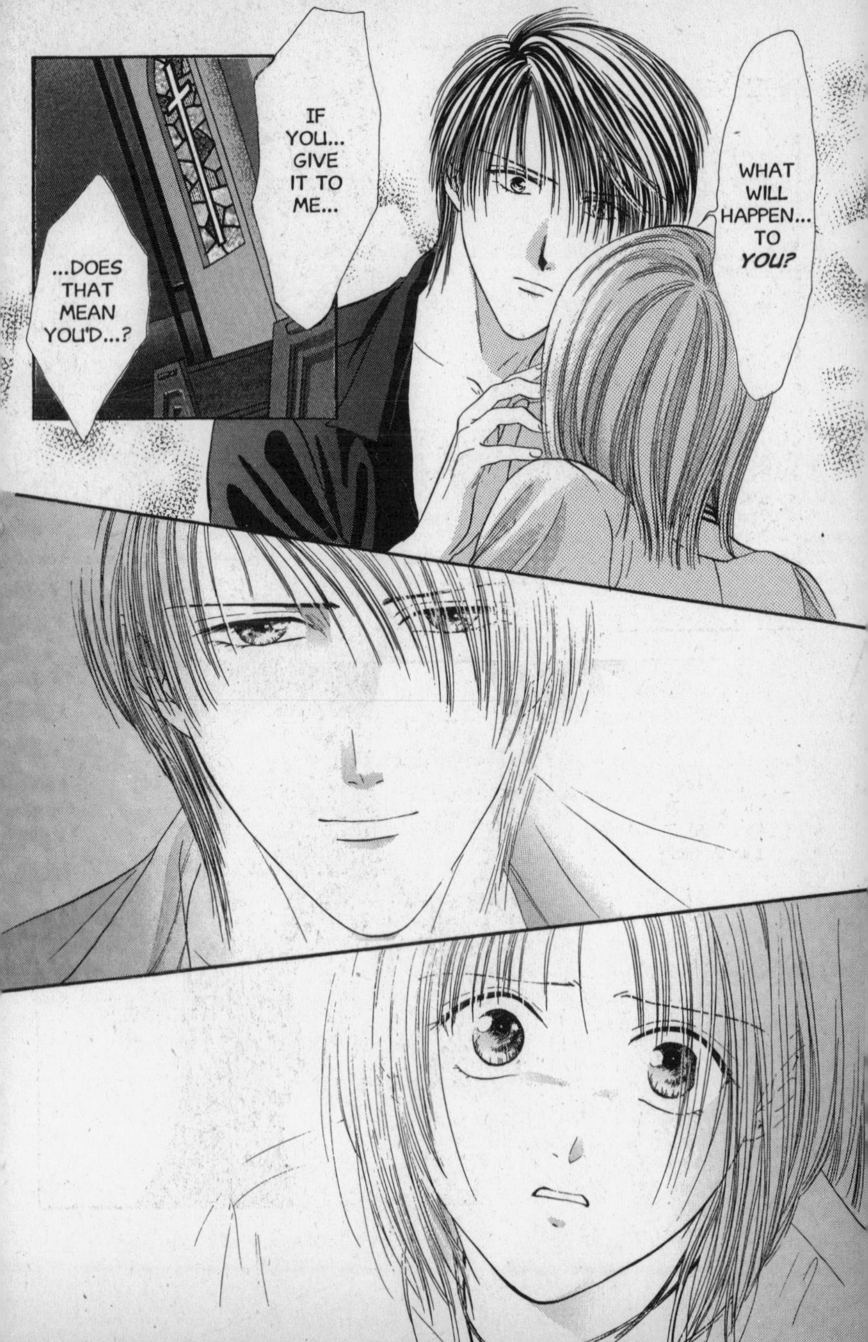
WHAT WILL HAPPEN... TO *YOU?*
IF YOU... GIVE IT TO ME...
...DOES THAT MEAN YOU'D...?

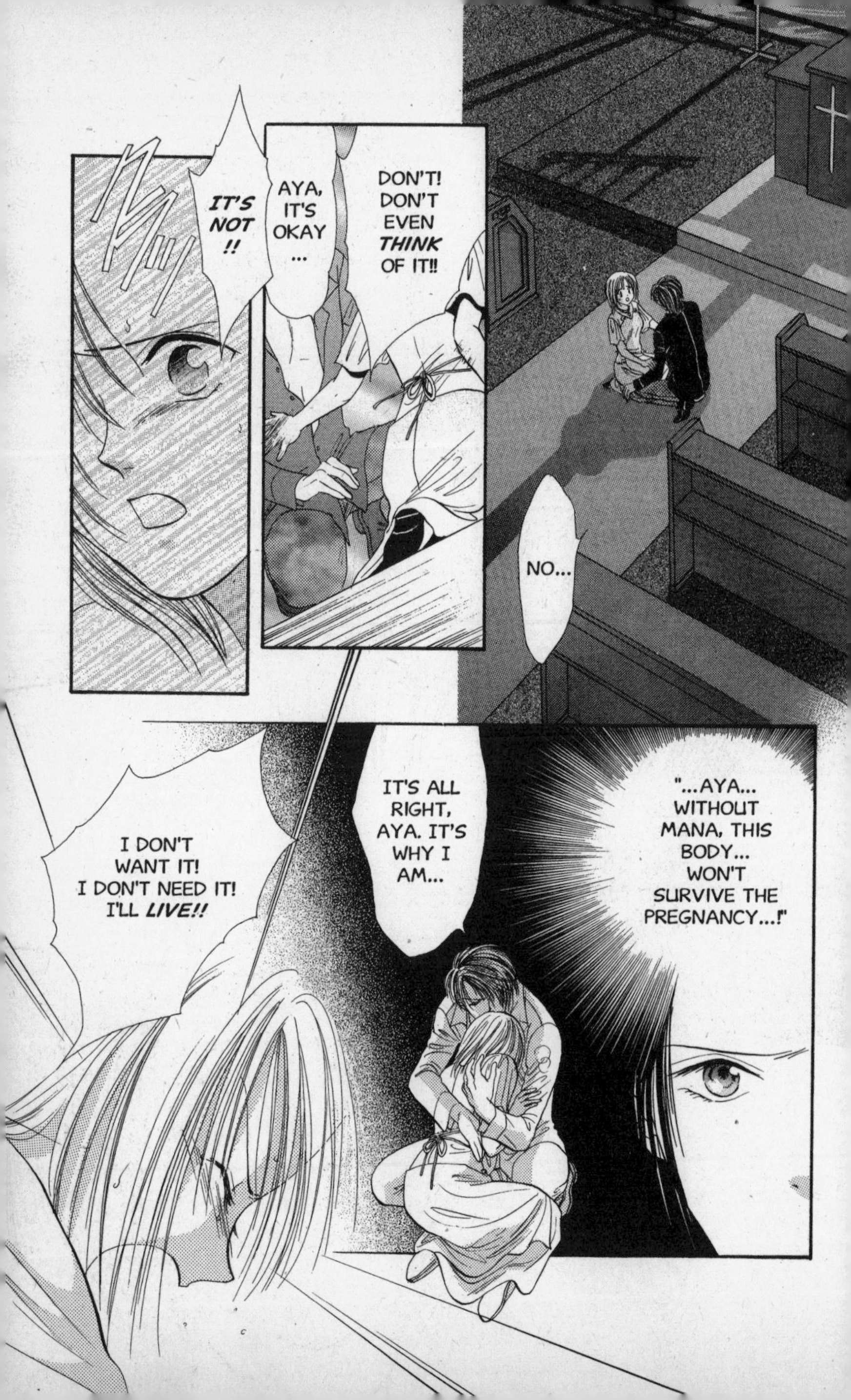
NO...
DON'T! DON'T EVEN *THINK* OF IT!!
AYA, IT'S OKAY ...
IT'S NOT !!
"...AYA... WITHOUT MANA, THIS BODY... WON'T SURVIVE THE PREGNANCY...!"
IT'S ALL RIGHT, AYA. IT'S WHY I AM...
I DON'T WANT IT! I DON'T NEED IT! I'LL *LIVE!!*

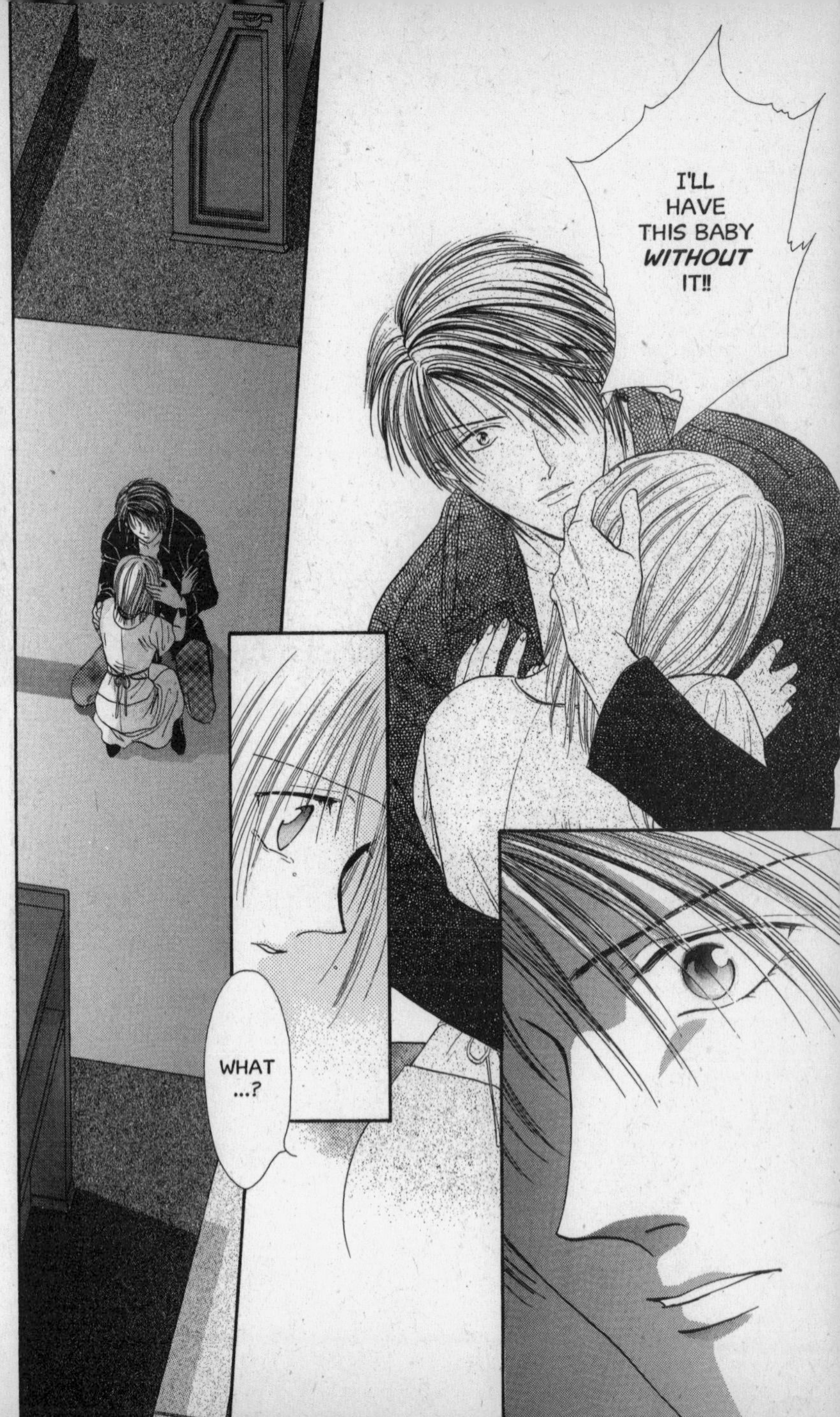
I'LL HAVE THIS BABY WITHOUT IT!!
WHAT ...?

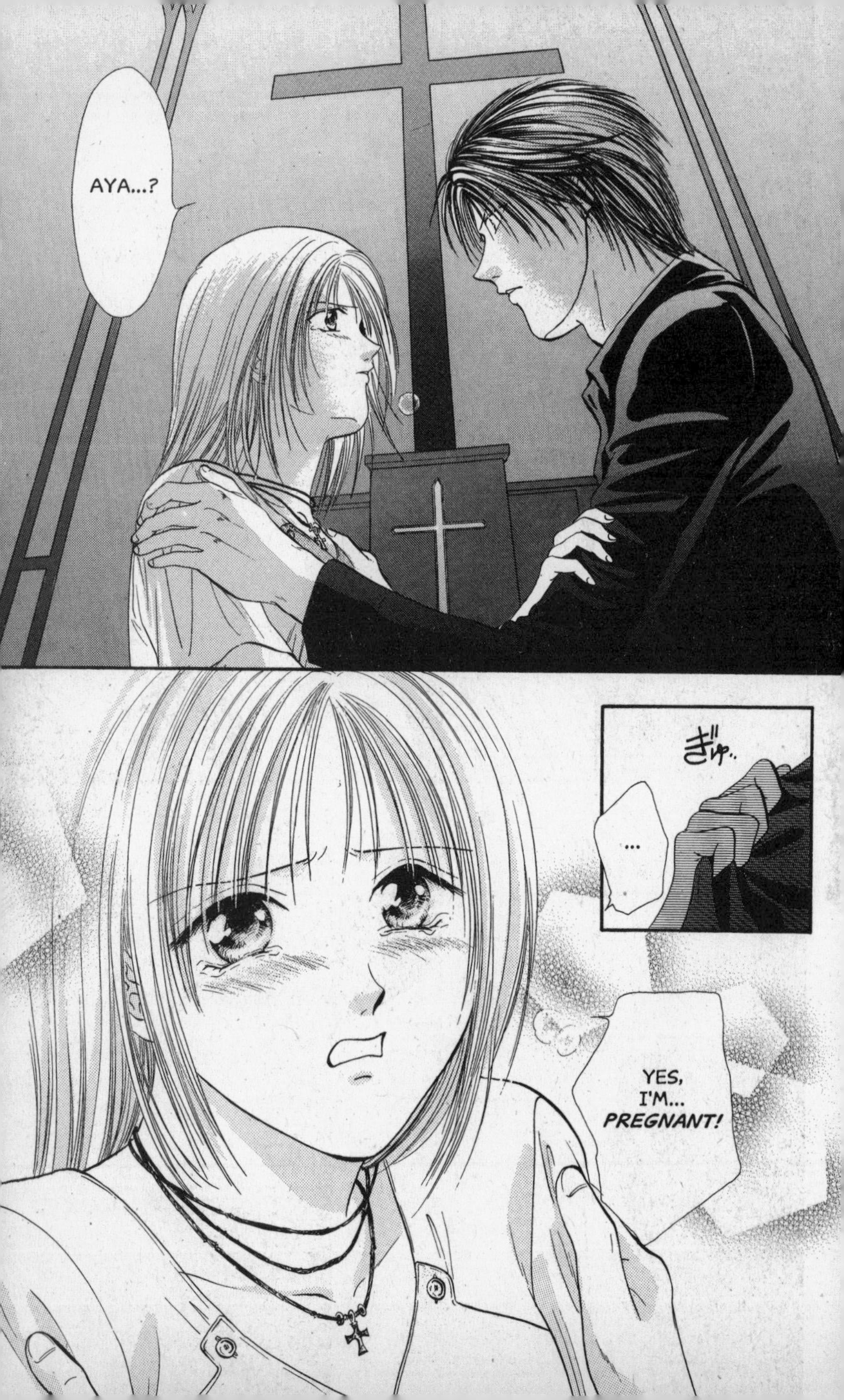
AYA...?
ぎゅ..
...
YES, I'M... PREGNANT!

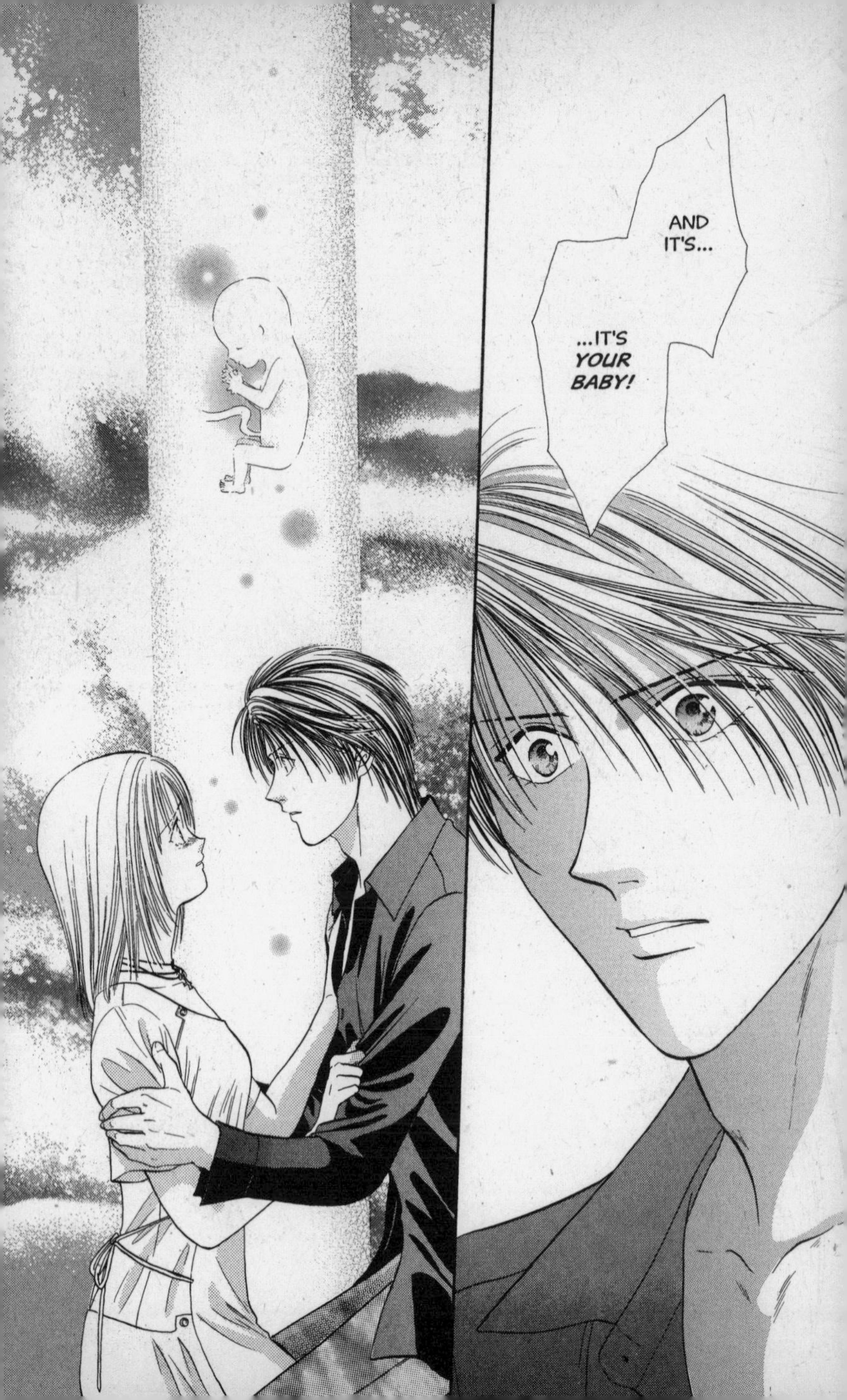
AND IT'S...
...IT'S *YOUR* BABY!

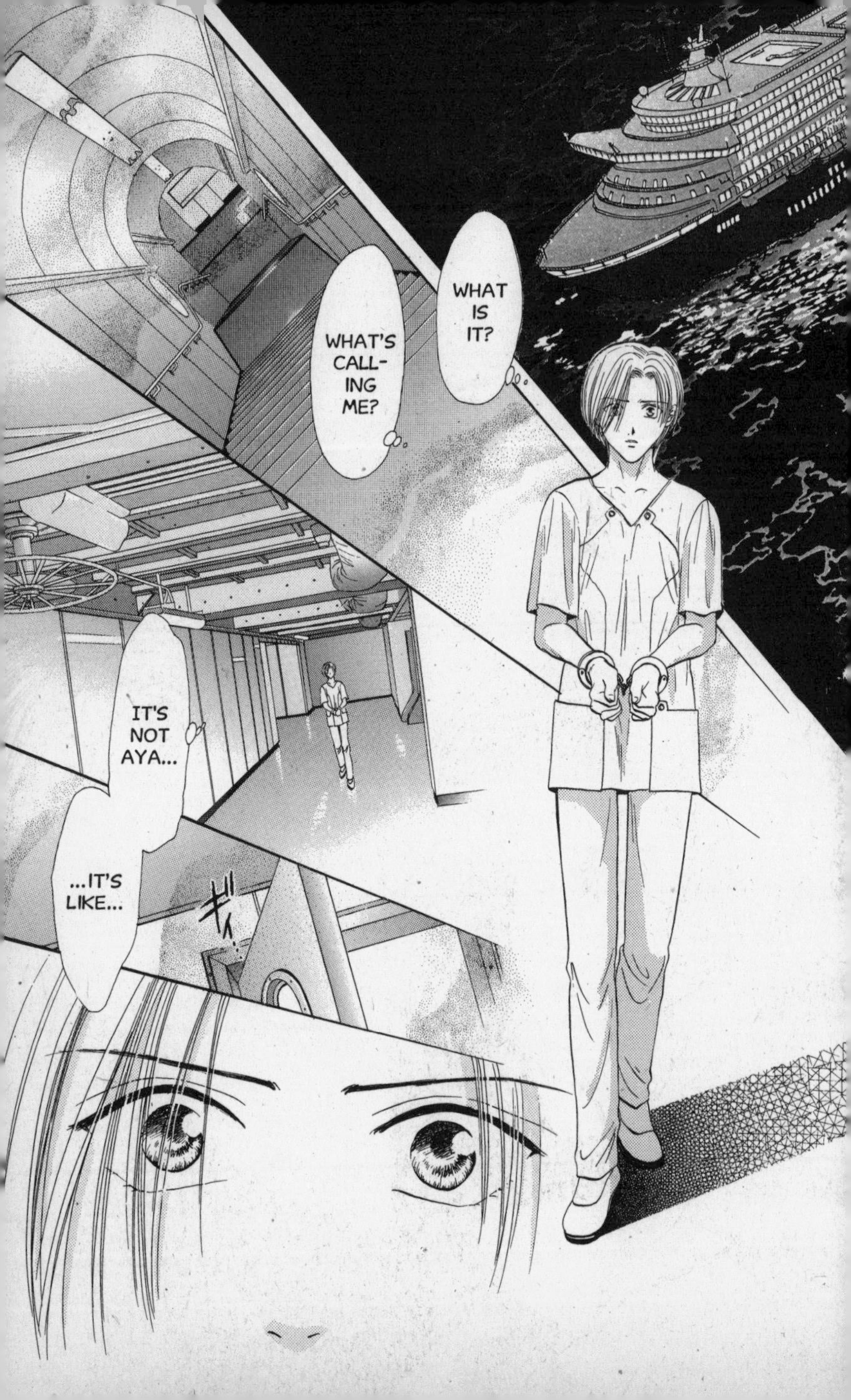
WHAT IS IT?
WHAT'S CALL-ING ME?
IT'S NOT AYA...
...IT'S LIKE...
ギィ

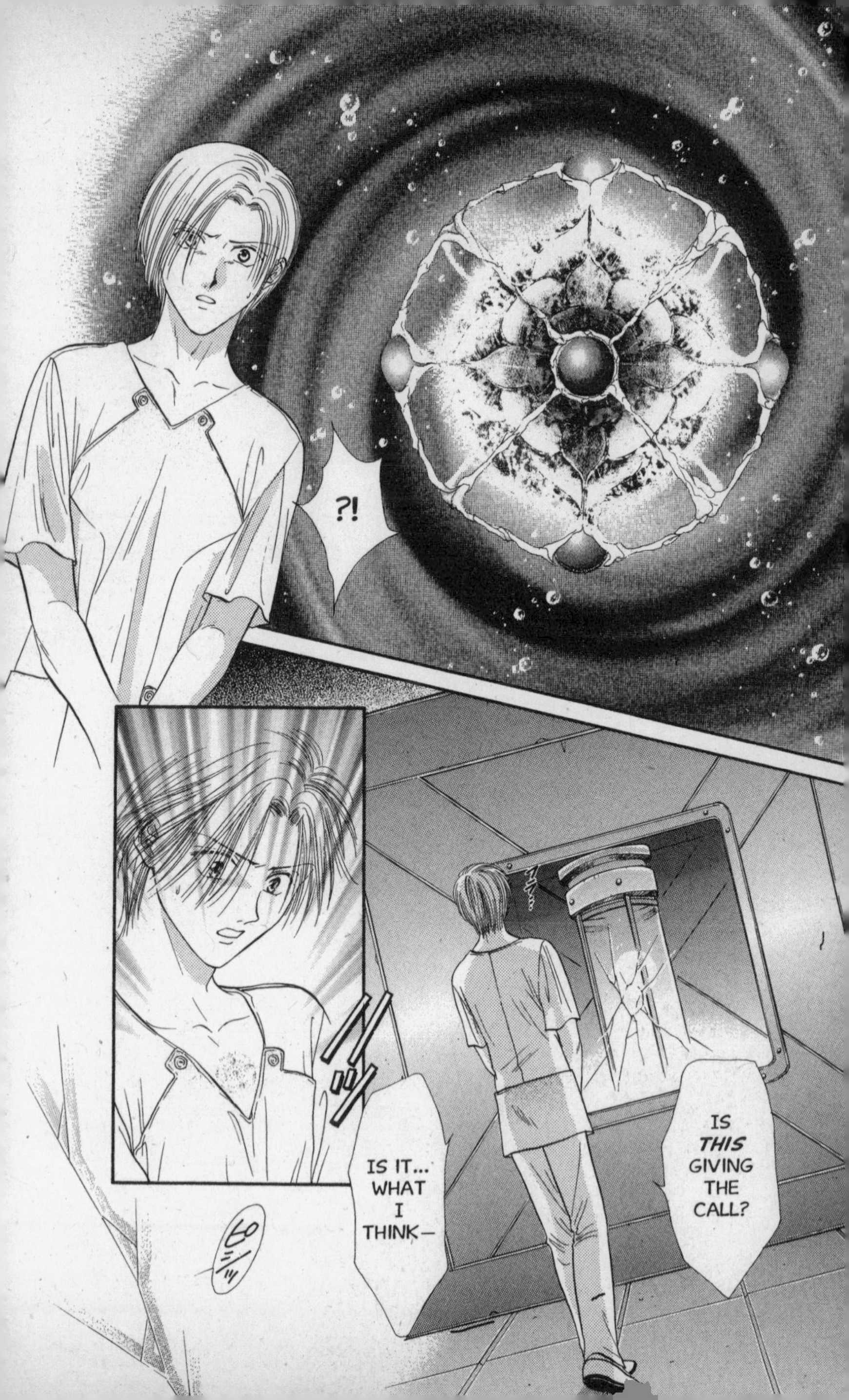
?!
IS *THIS* GIVING THE CALL?
IS IT... WHAT I THINK—

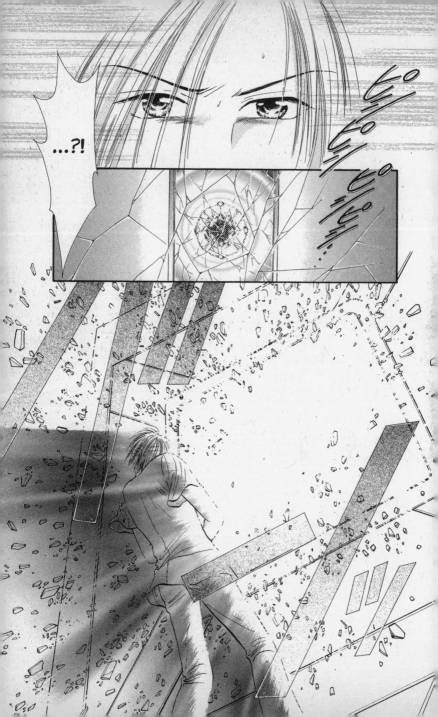

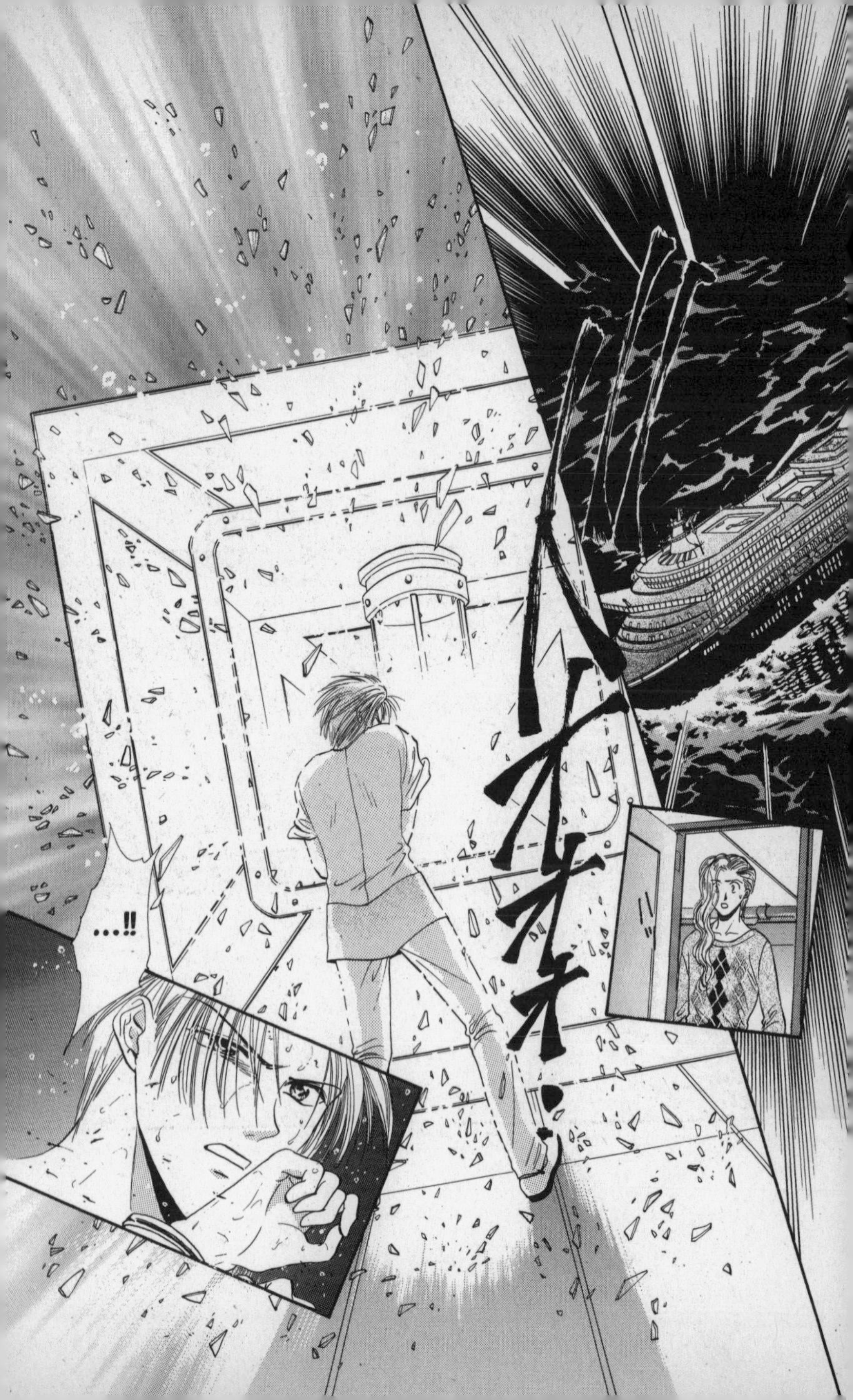
!!
...!!

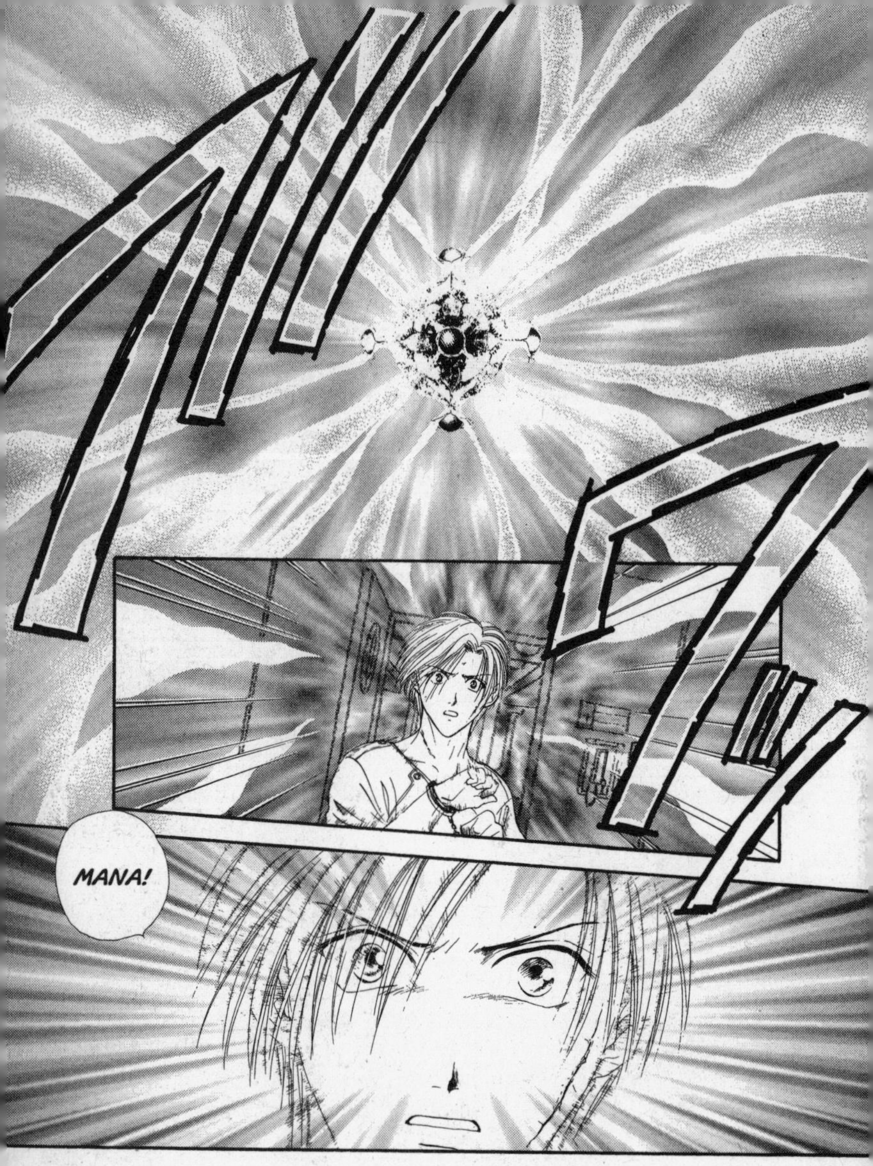
MANA!

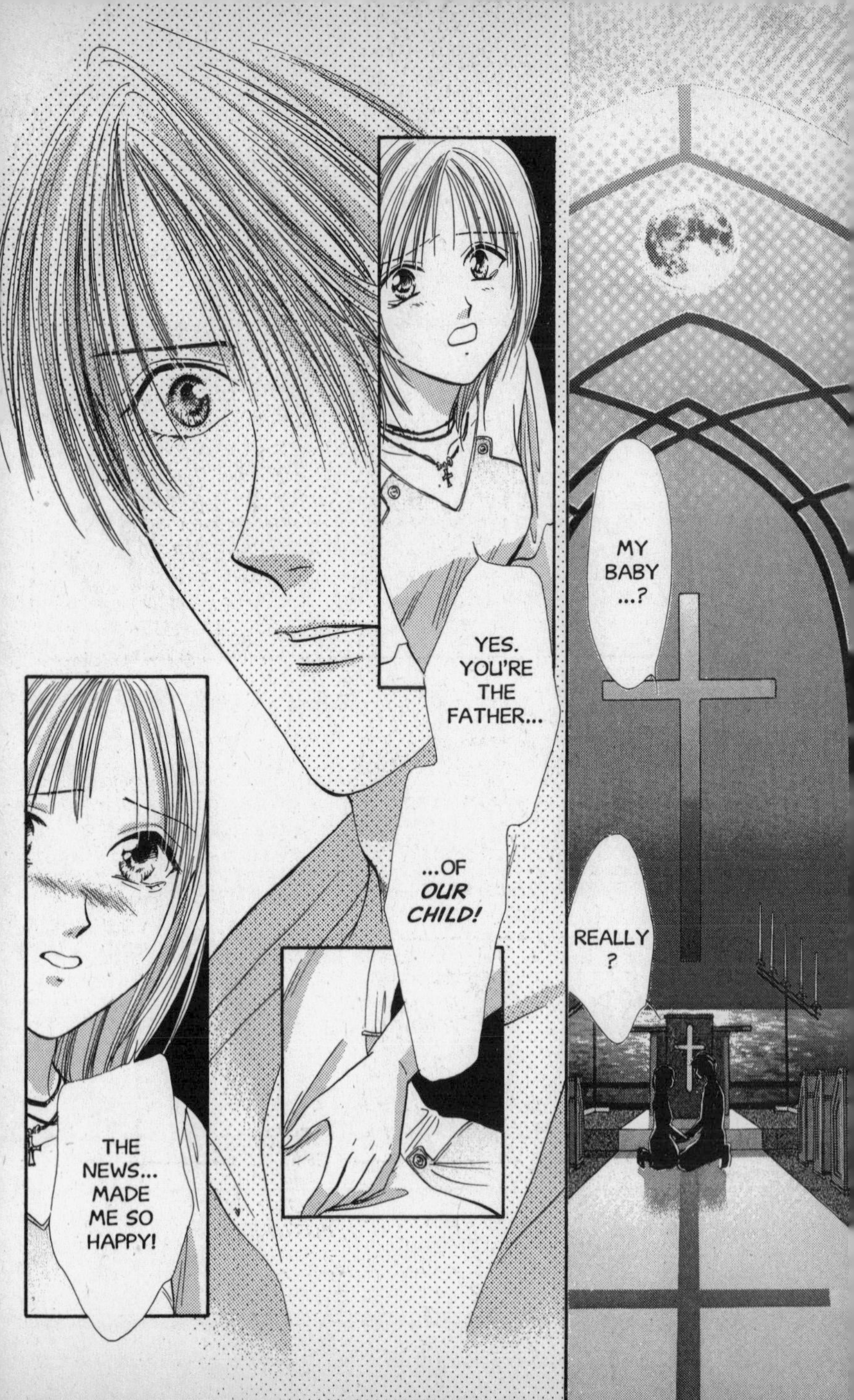
MY BABY ...?
REALLY ?
YES. YOU'RE THE FATHER...
...OF *OUR CHILD!*
THE NEWS... MADE ME SO HAPPY!

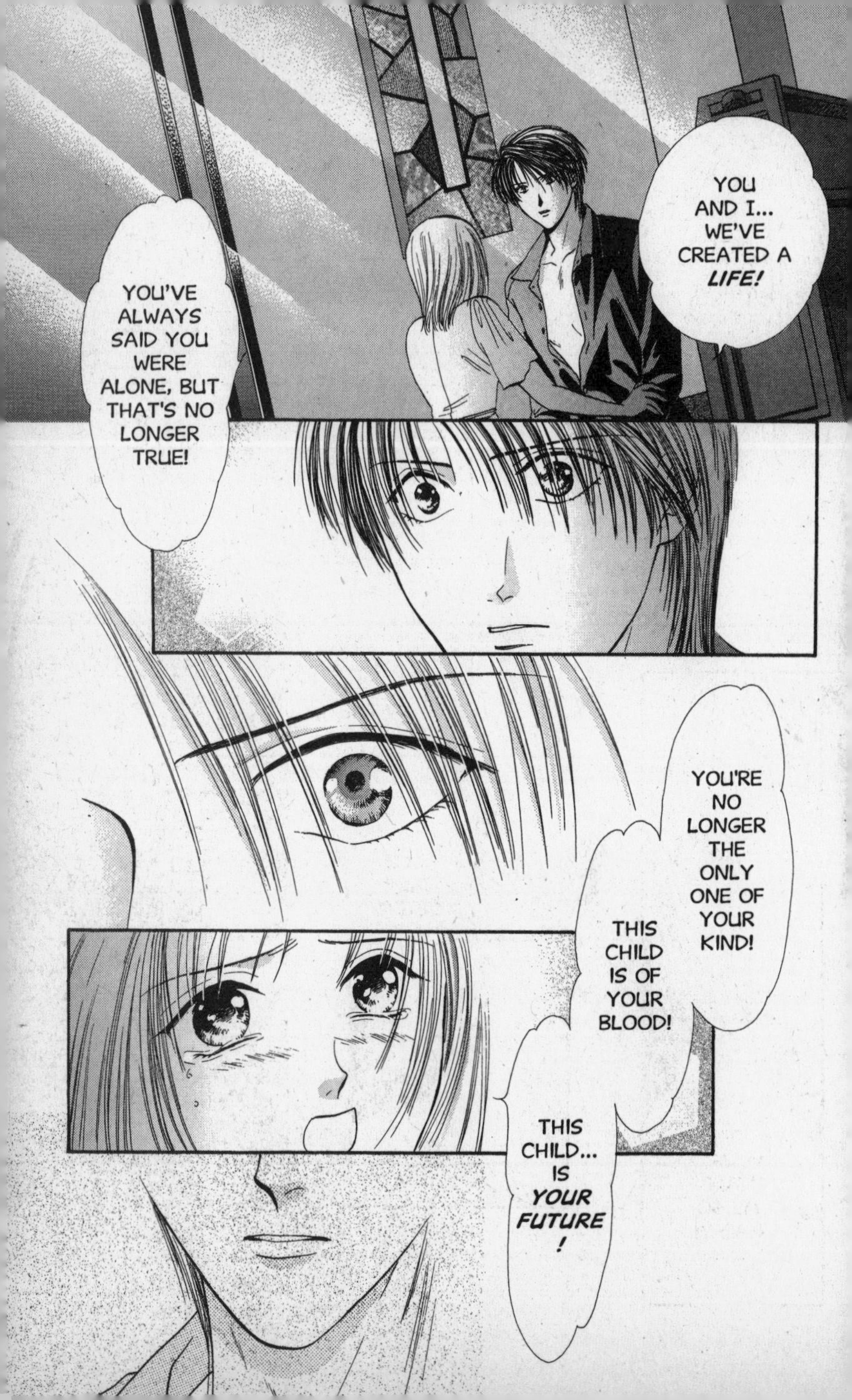
YOU AND I... WE'VE CREATED A *LIFE!*
YOU'VE ALWAYS SAID YOU WERE ALONE, BUT THAT'S NO LONGER TRUE!
YOU'RE NO LONGER THE ONLY ONE OF YOUR KIND!
THIS CHILD IS OF YOUR BLOOD!
THIS CHILD... IS *YOUR FUTURE!*

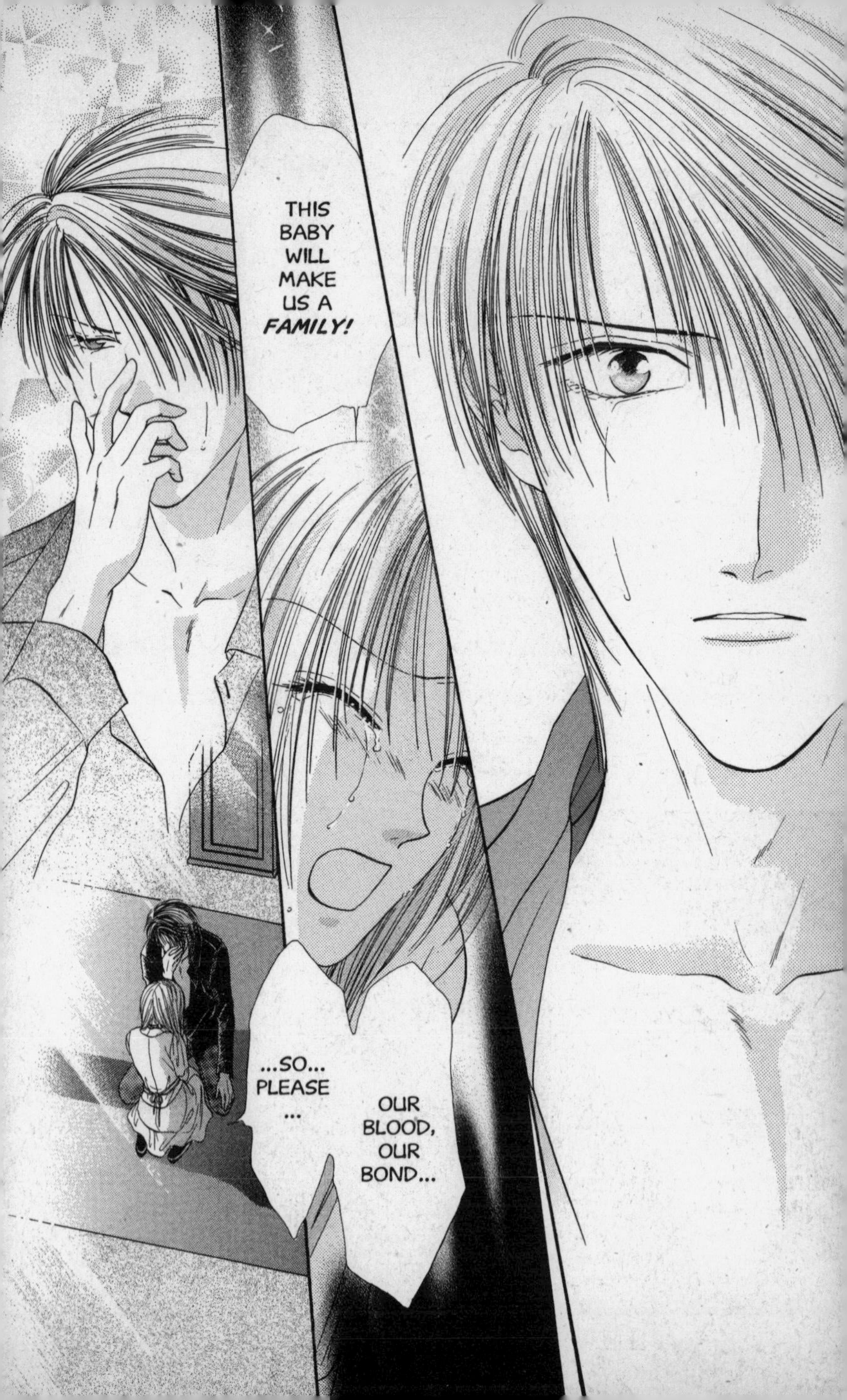
THIS BABY WILL MAKE US A *FAMILY!*
OUR BLOOD, OUR BOND...
...SO... PLEASE ...

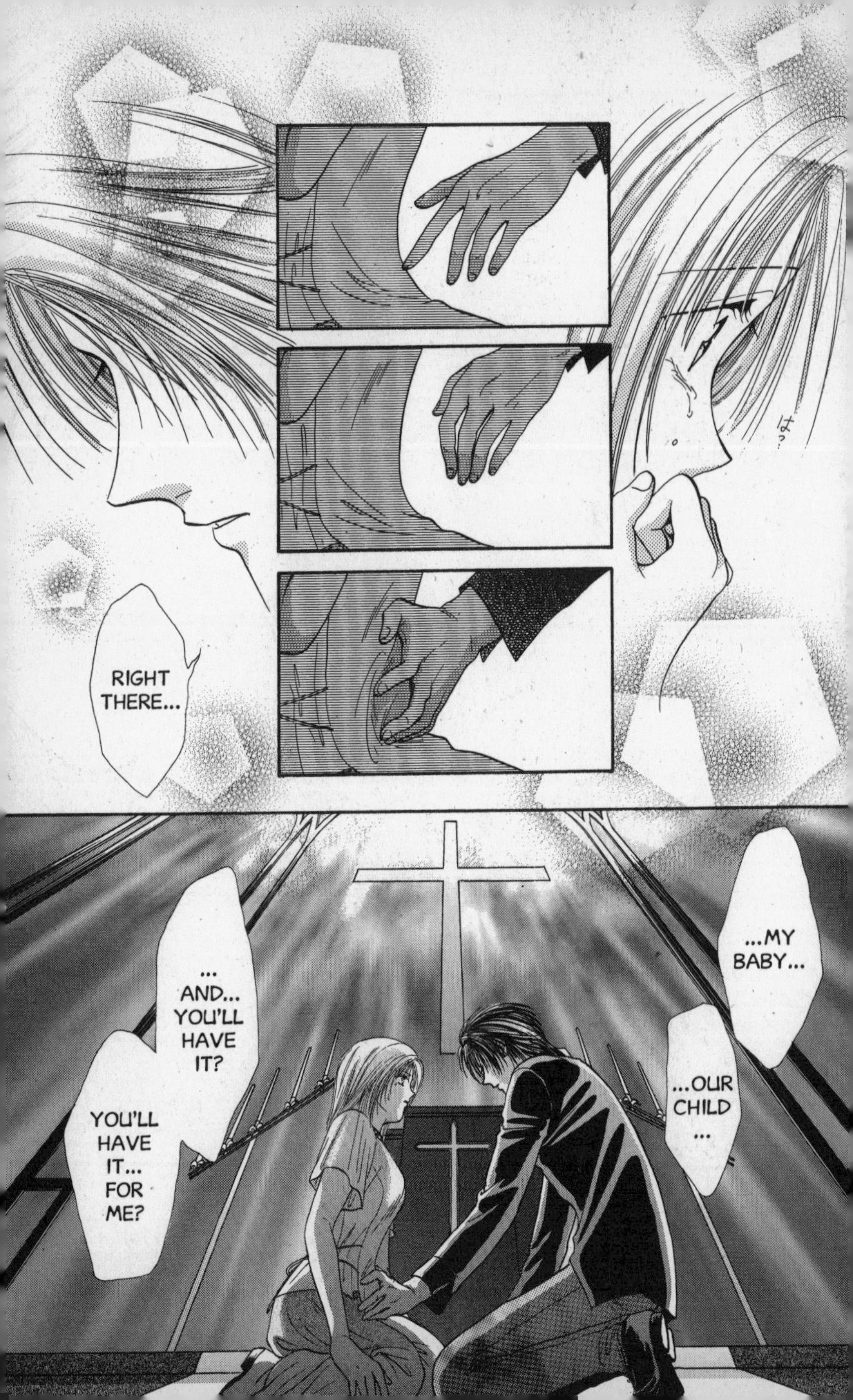
はっ
RIGHT THERE...
...MY BABY...
...OUR CHILD ...
... AND... YOU'LL HAVE IT?
YOU'LL HAVE IT... FOR ME?

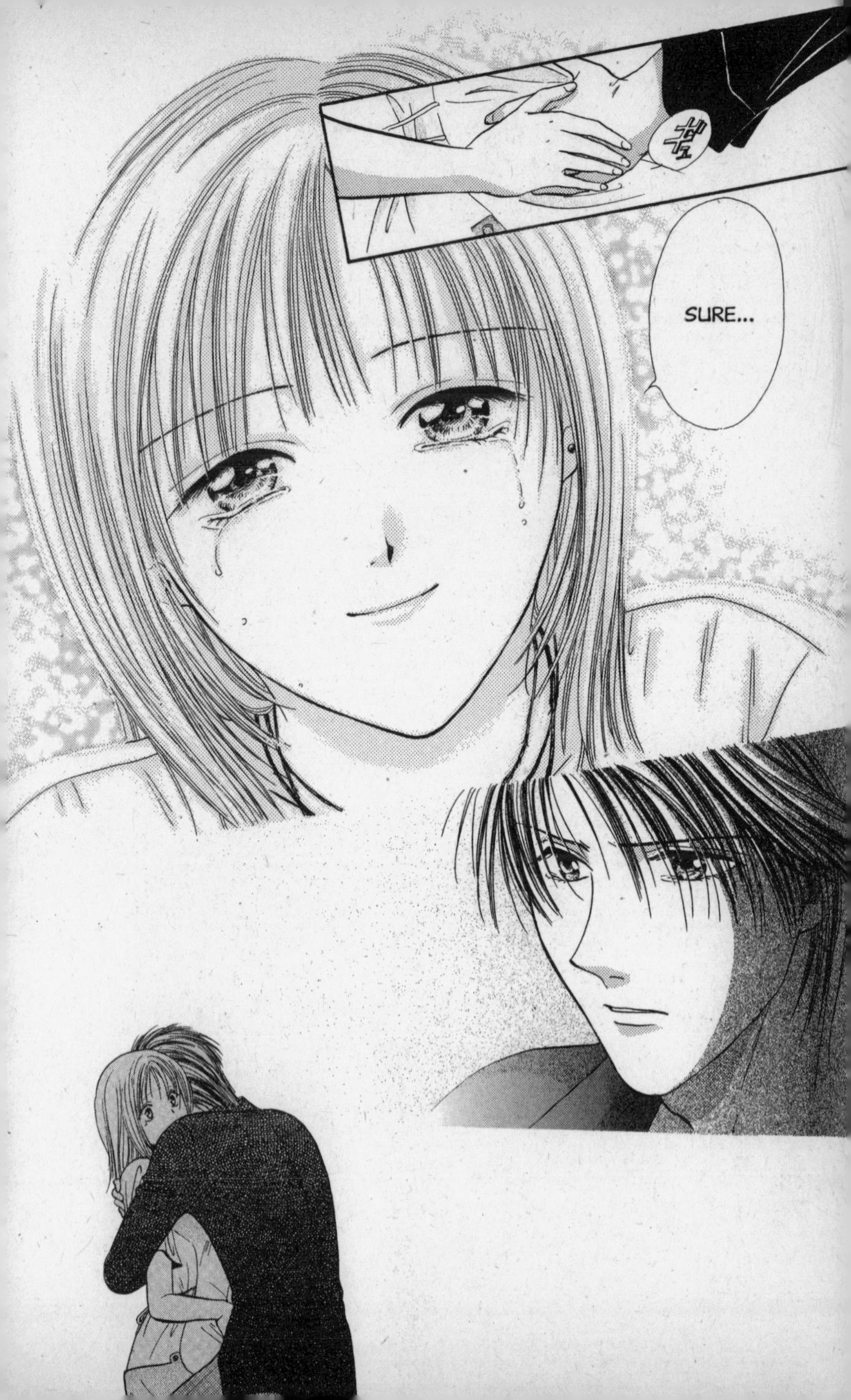
ギュ
SURE...

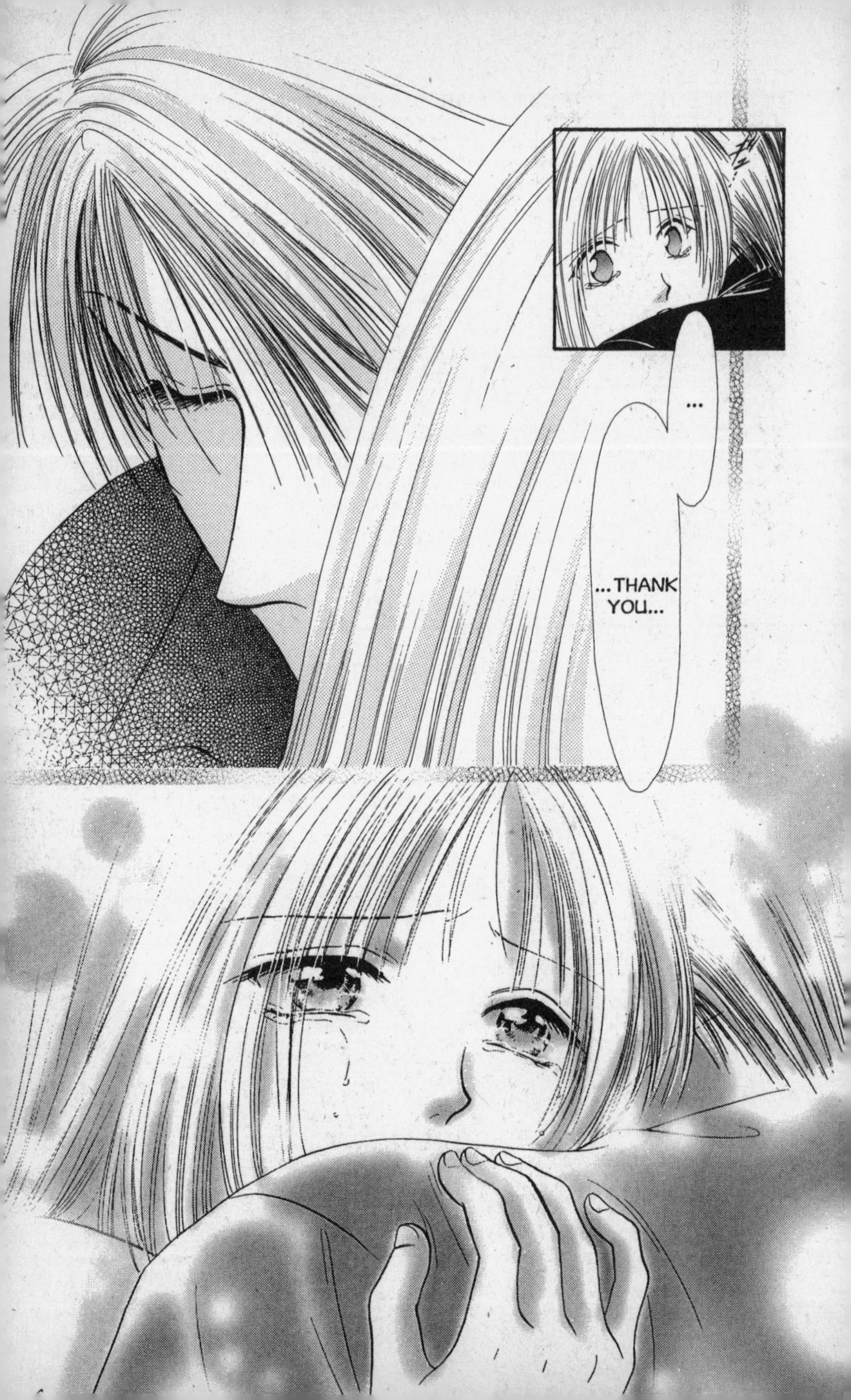
...
...THANK YOU...

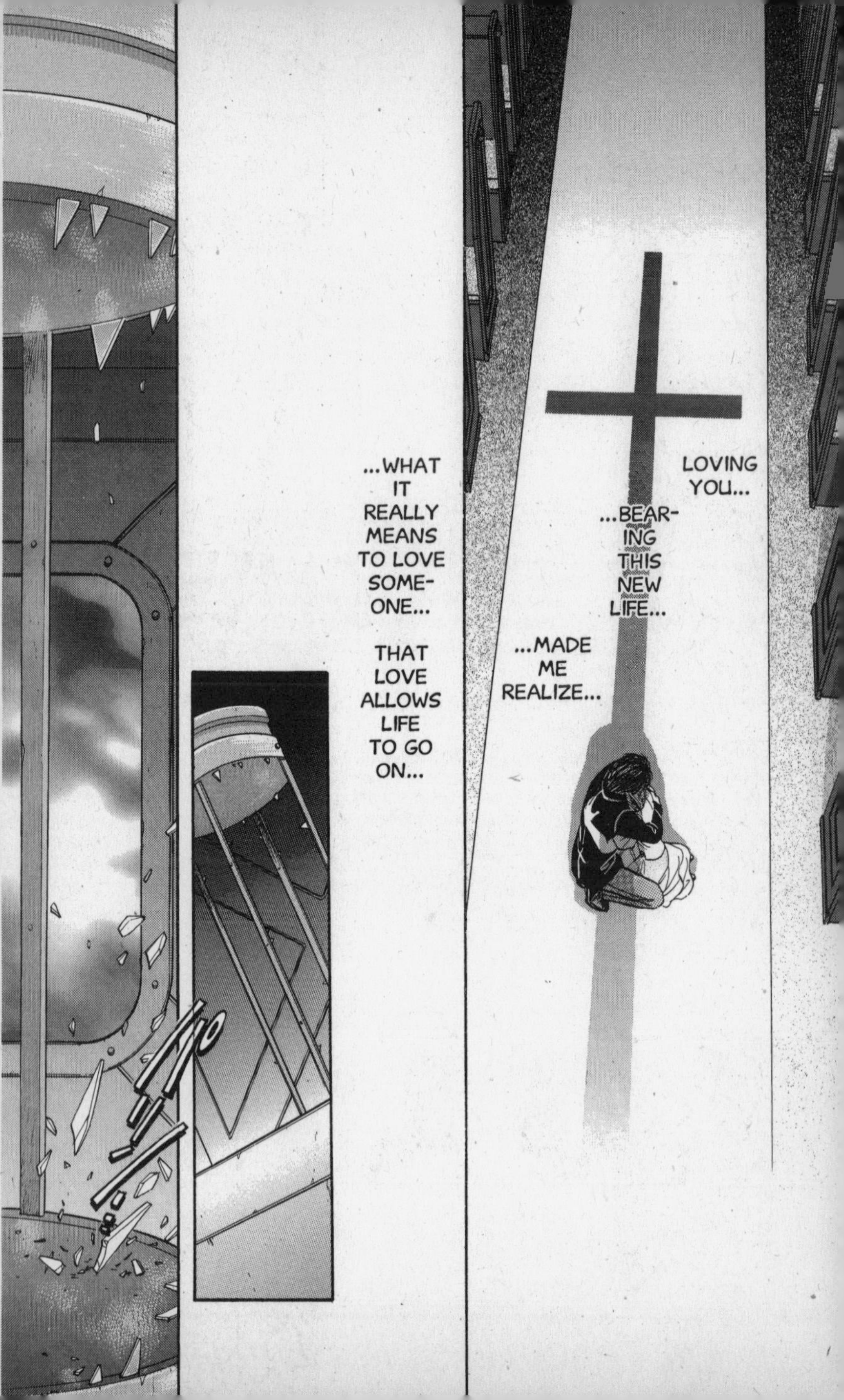
LOVING YOU...
...BEARING THIS NEW LIFE...
...MADE ME REALIZE...
...WHAT IT REALLY MEANS TO LOVE SOMEONE...
THAT LOVE ALLOWS LIFE TO GO ON...

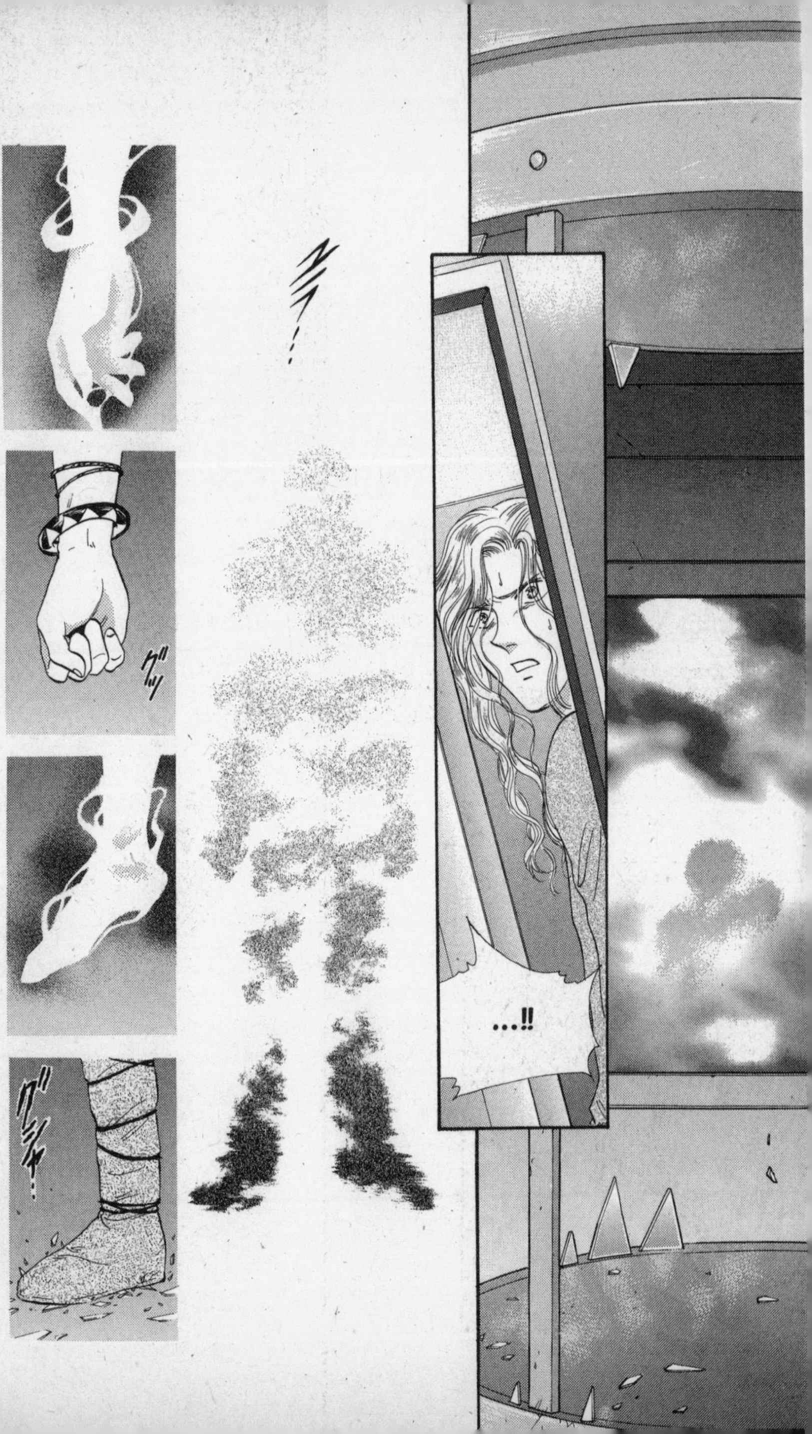
...!!

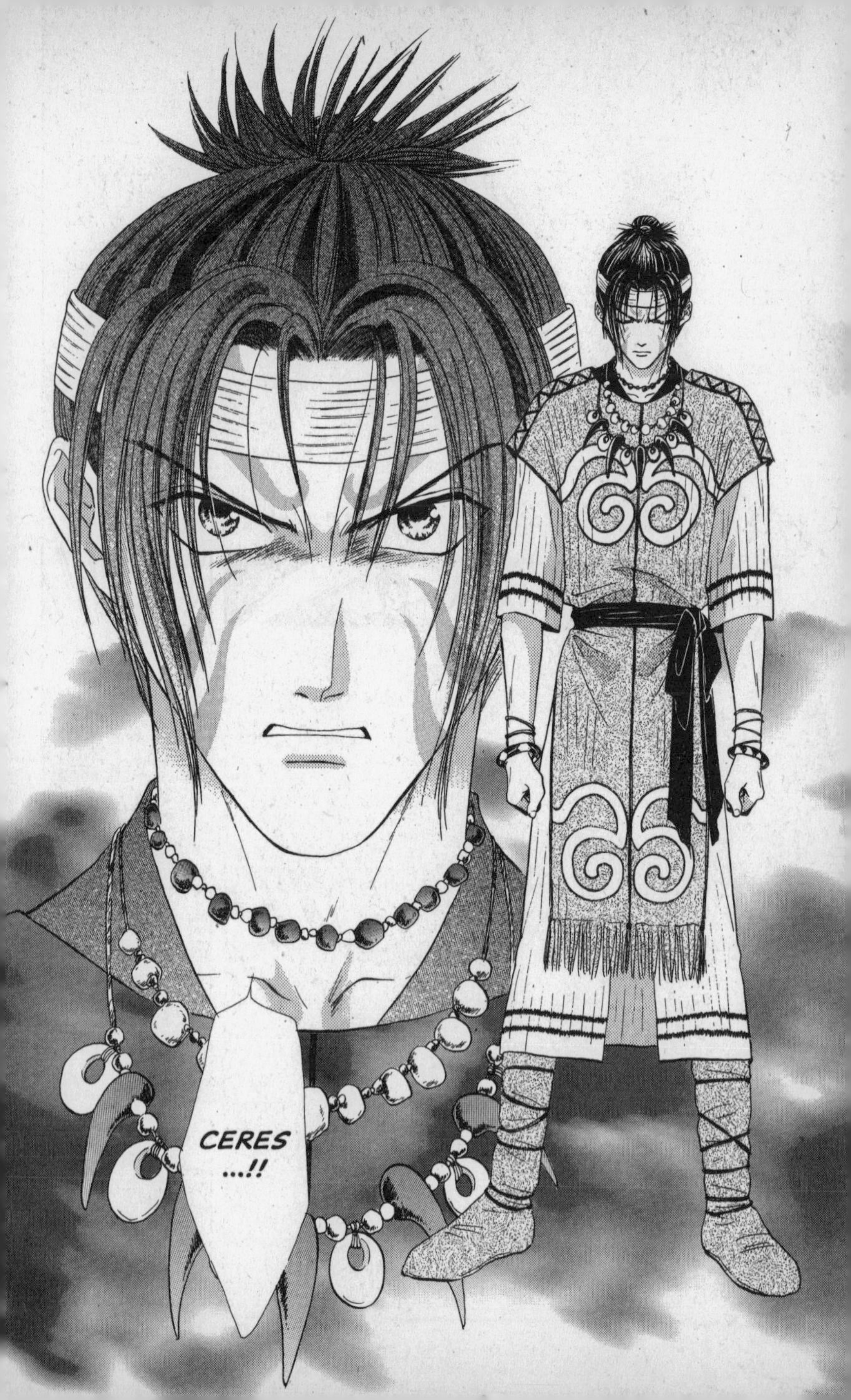
CERES ...!!

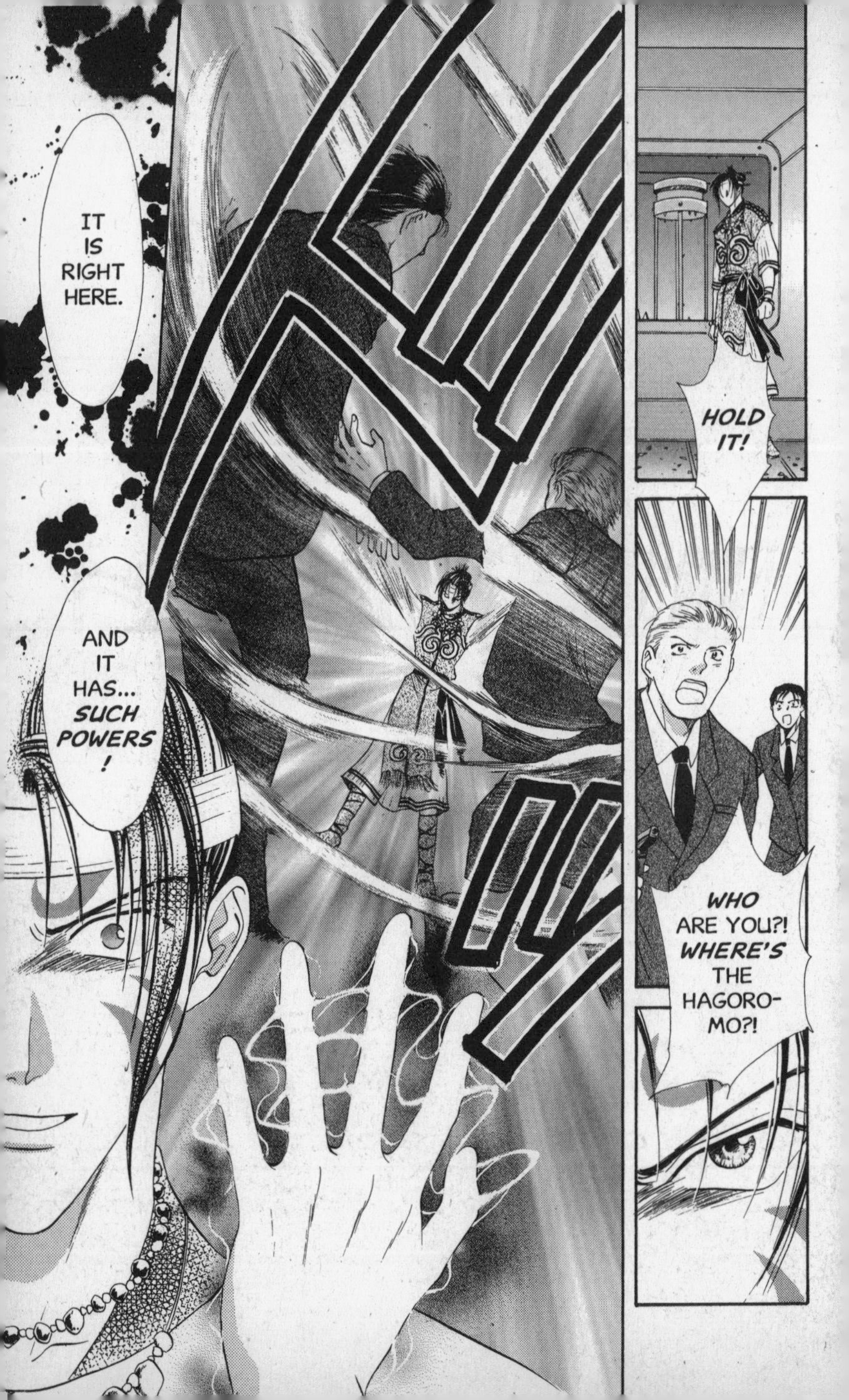
HOLD IT!
WHO ARE YOU?! WHERE'S THE HAGORO-MO?!
IT IS RIGHT HERE.
AND IT HAS... SUCH POWERS!

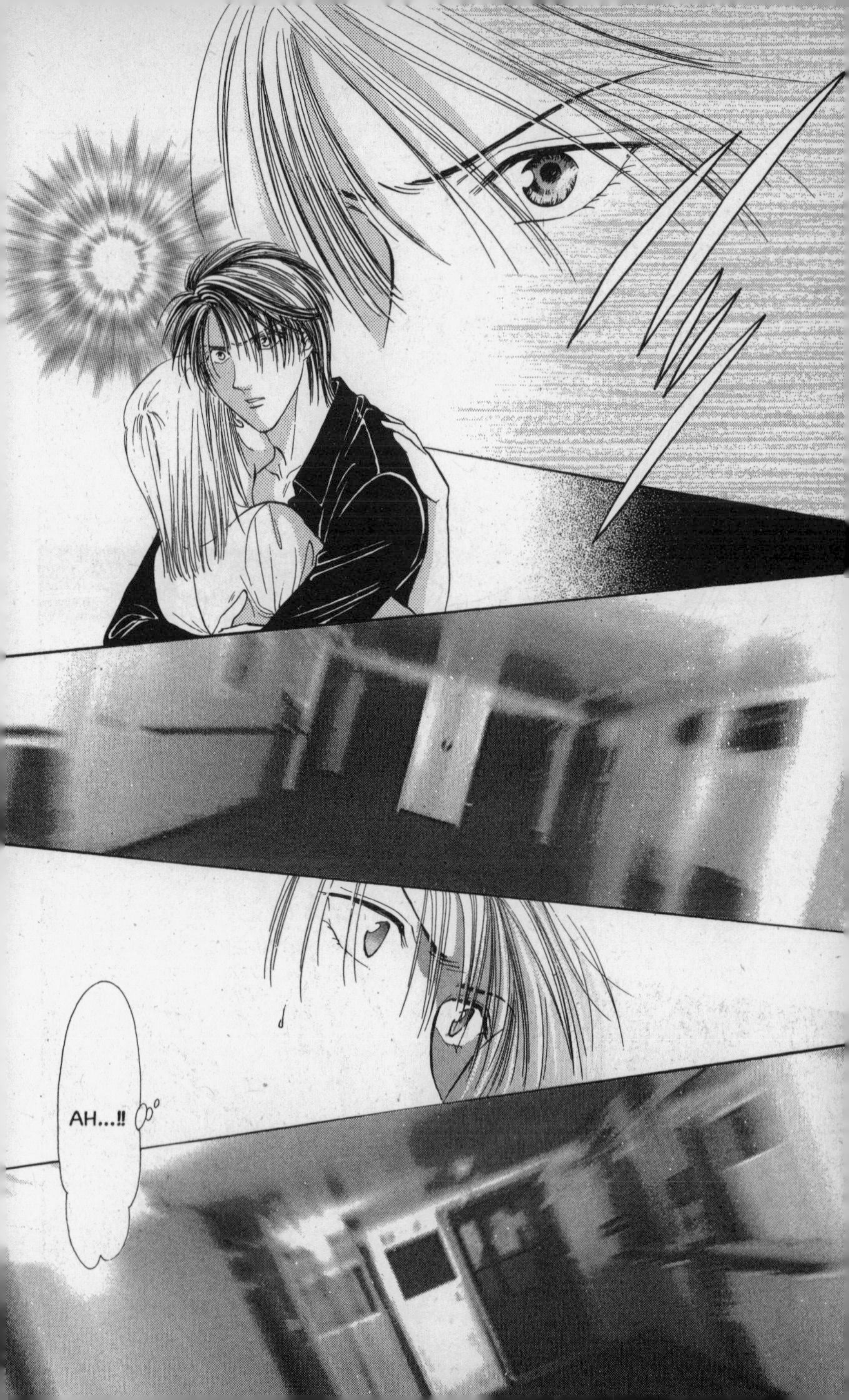
AH...!!

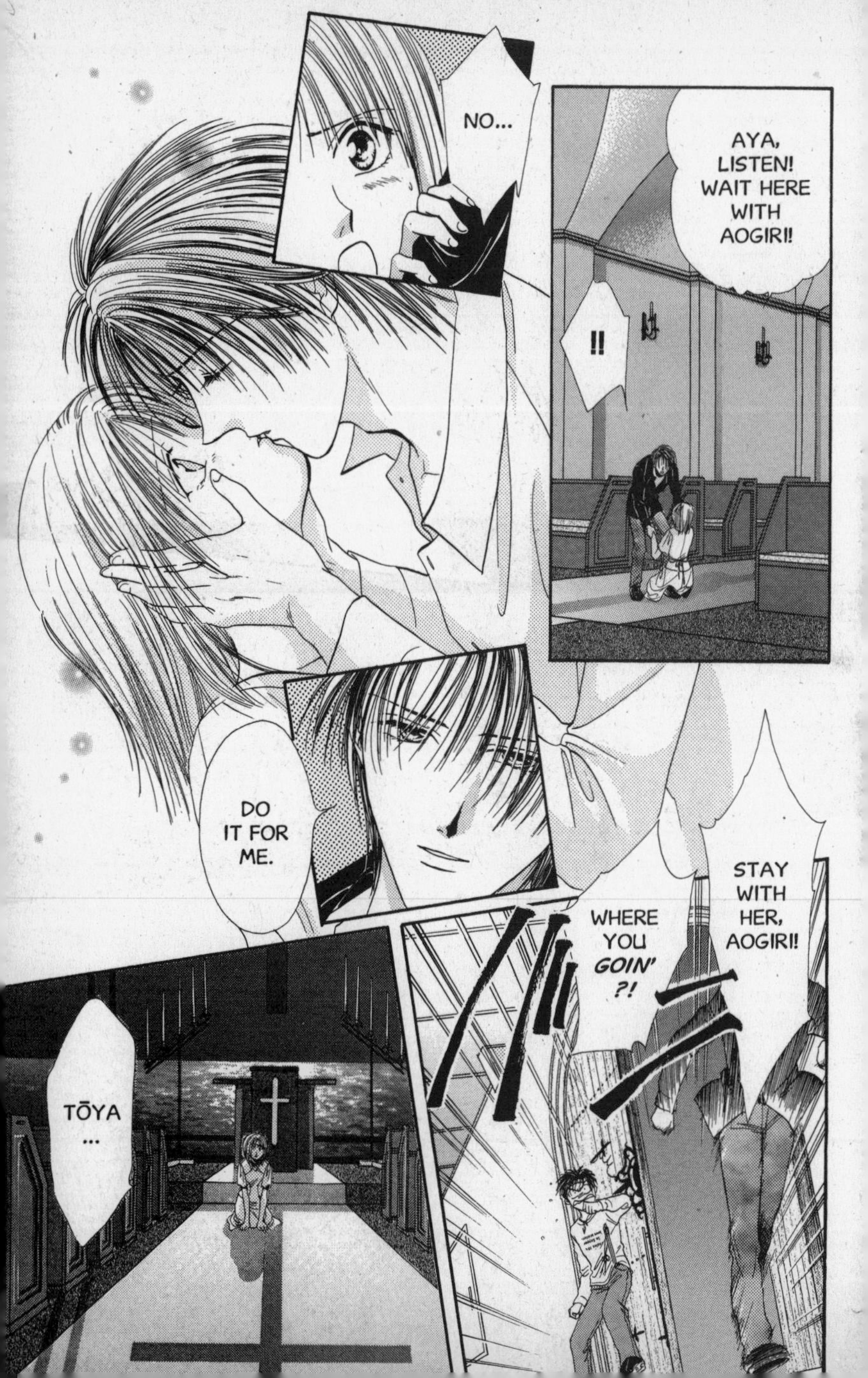
AYA, LISTEN! WAIT HERE WITH AOGIRI!
!!
NO...
DO IT FOR ME.
STAY WITH HER, AOGIRI!
WHERE YOU GOIN'?!
TŌYA ...

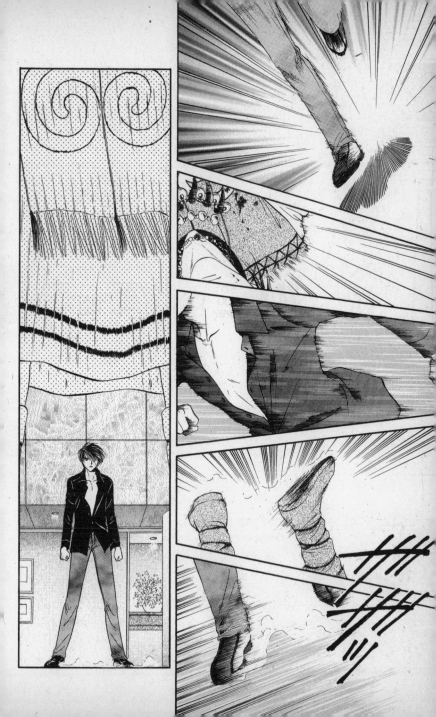

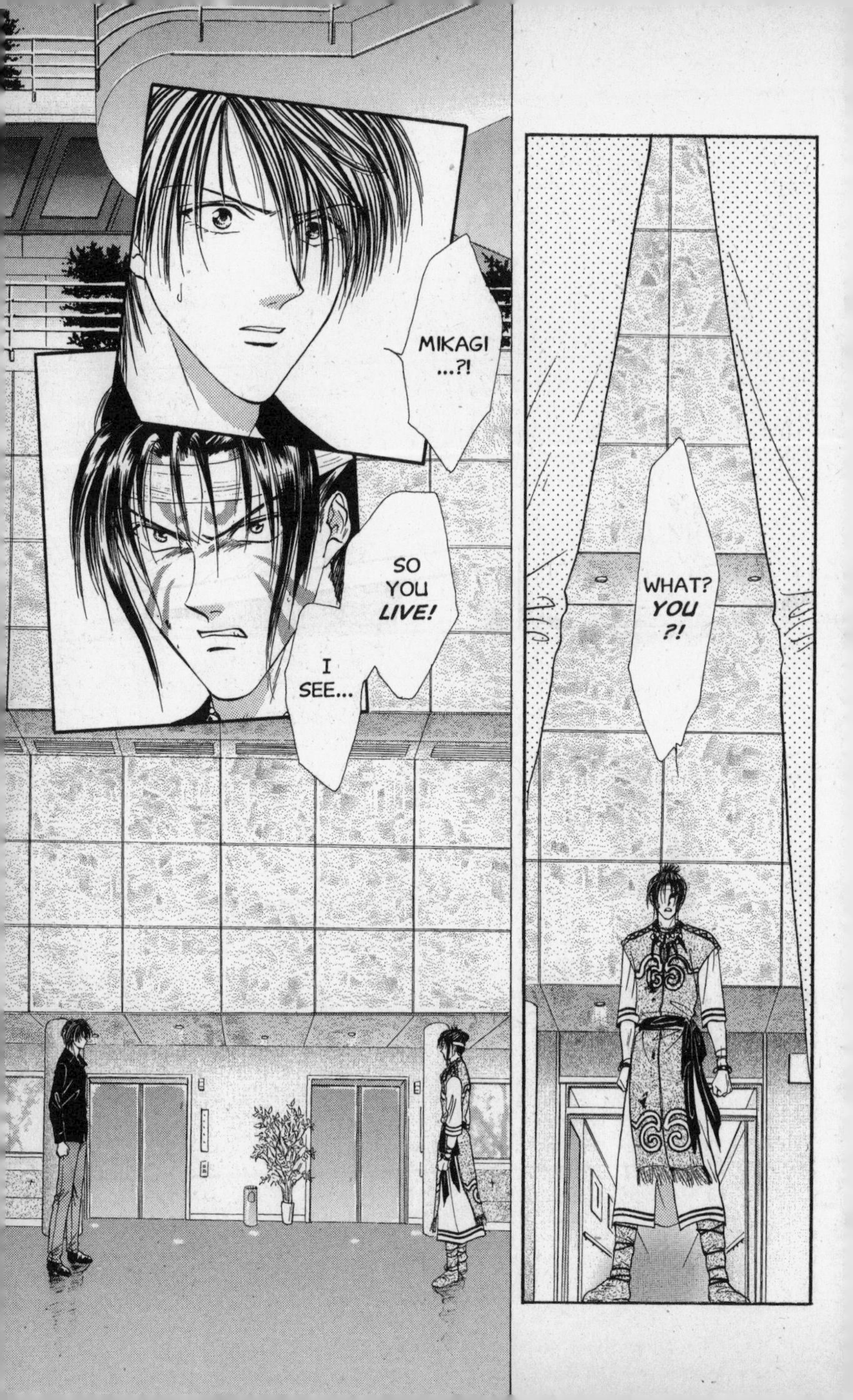
WHAT? YOU ?!
MIKAGI ...?!
SO YOU LIVE!
I SEE...

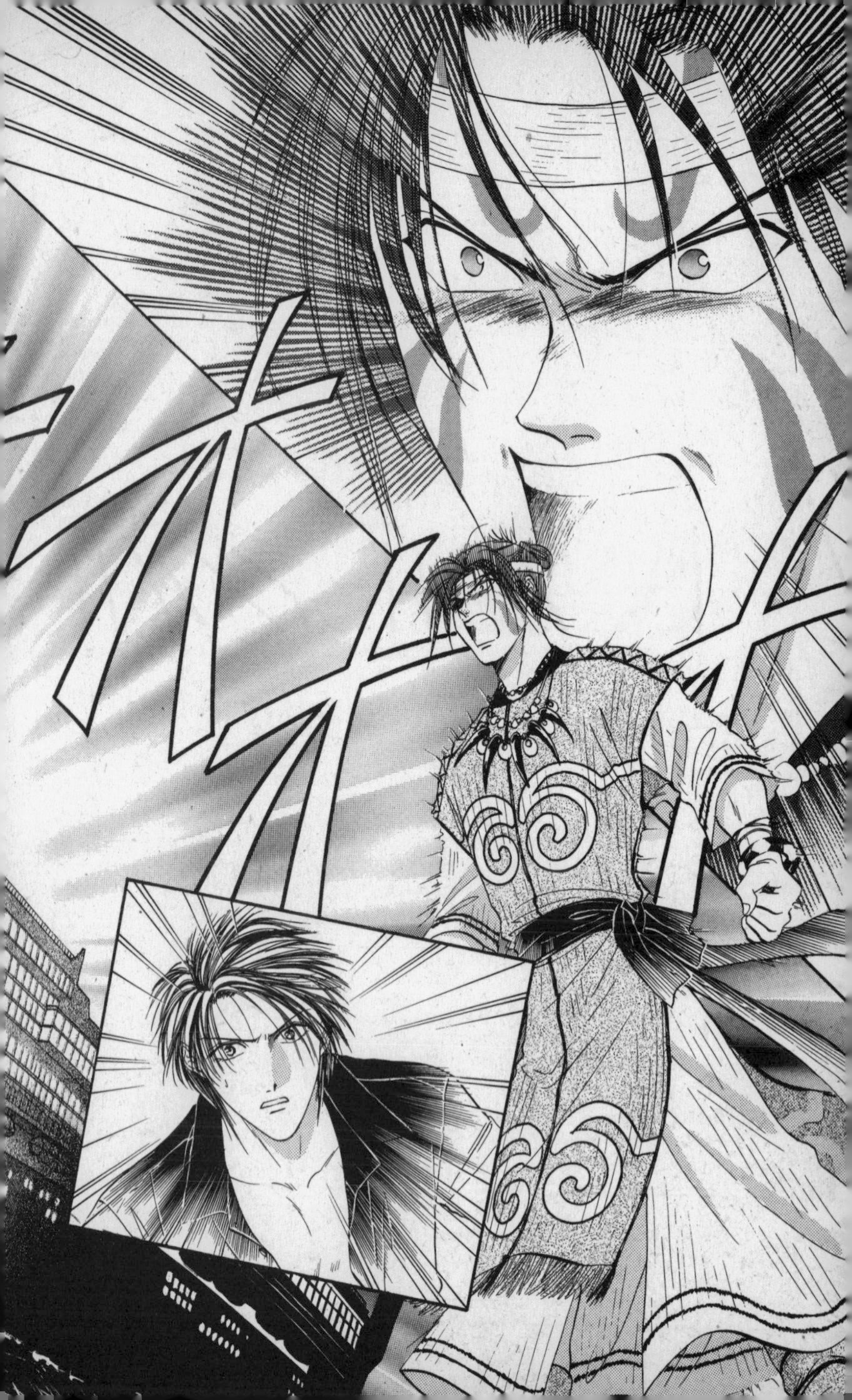

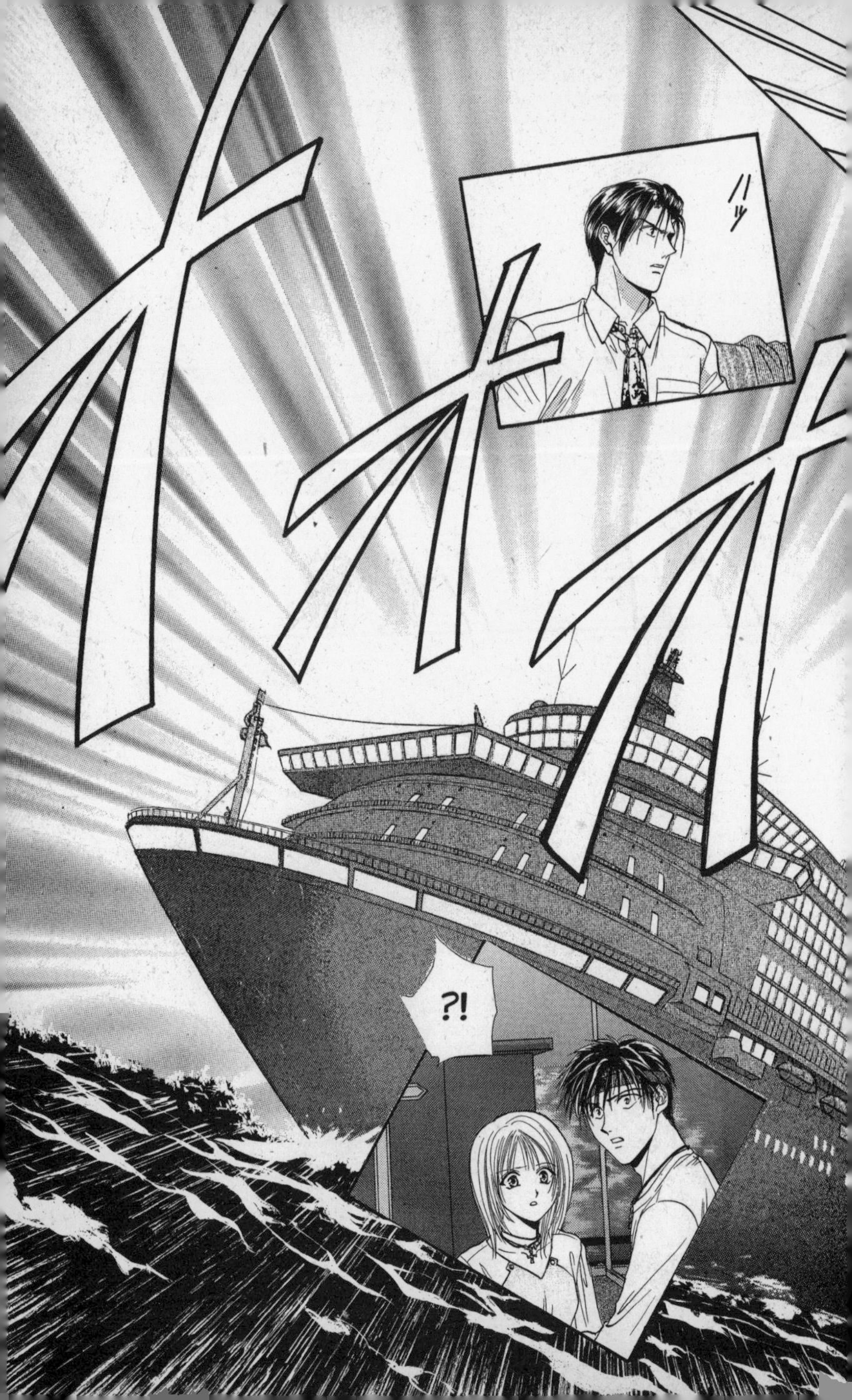
ハッ
オオオ
?!

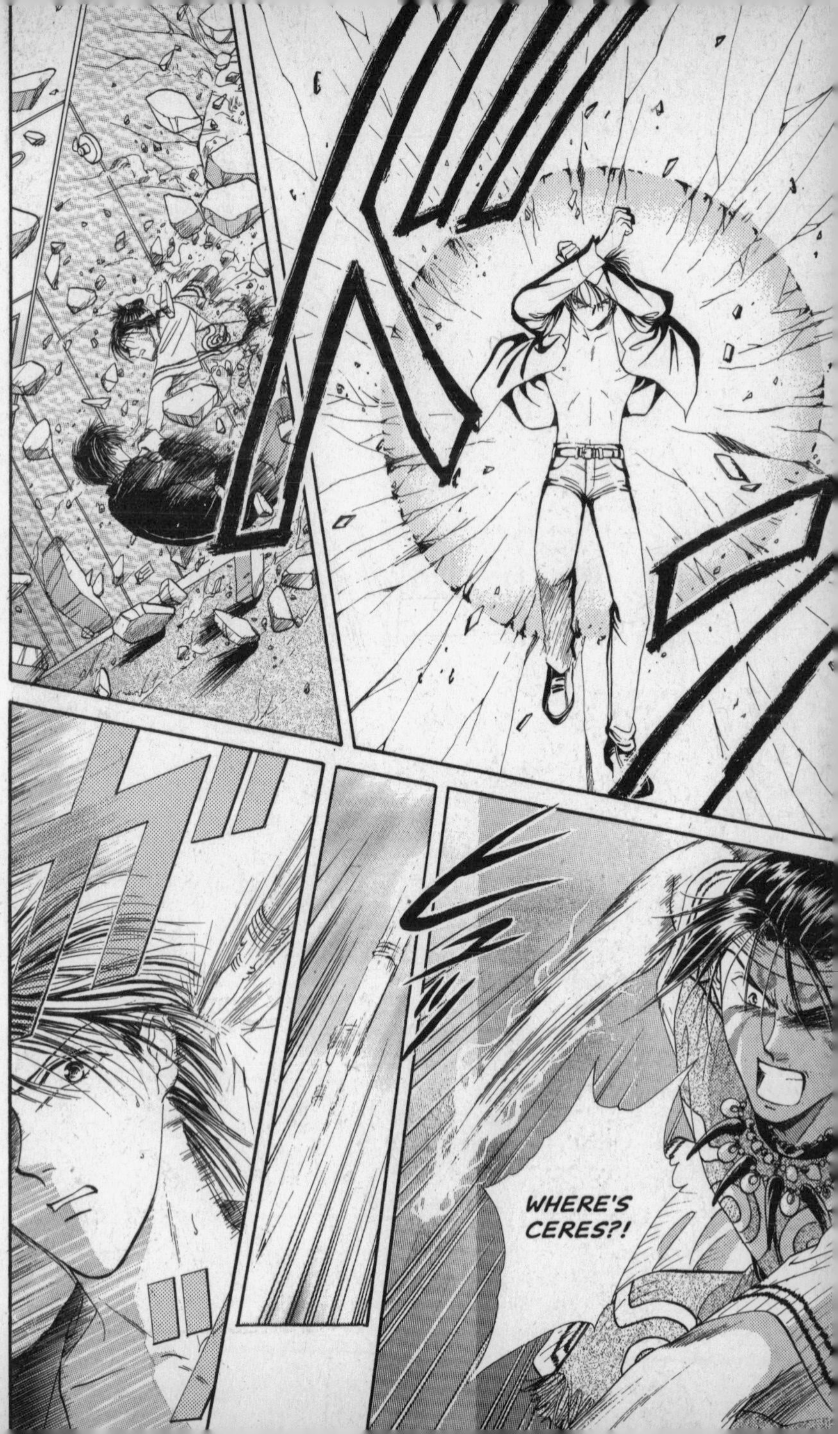
WHERE'S CERES?!

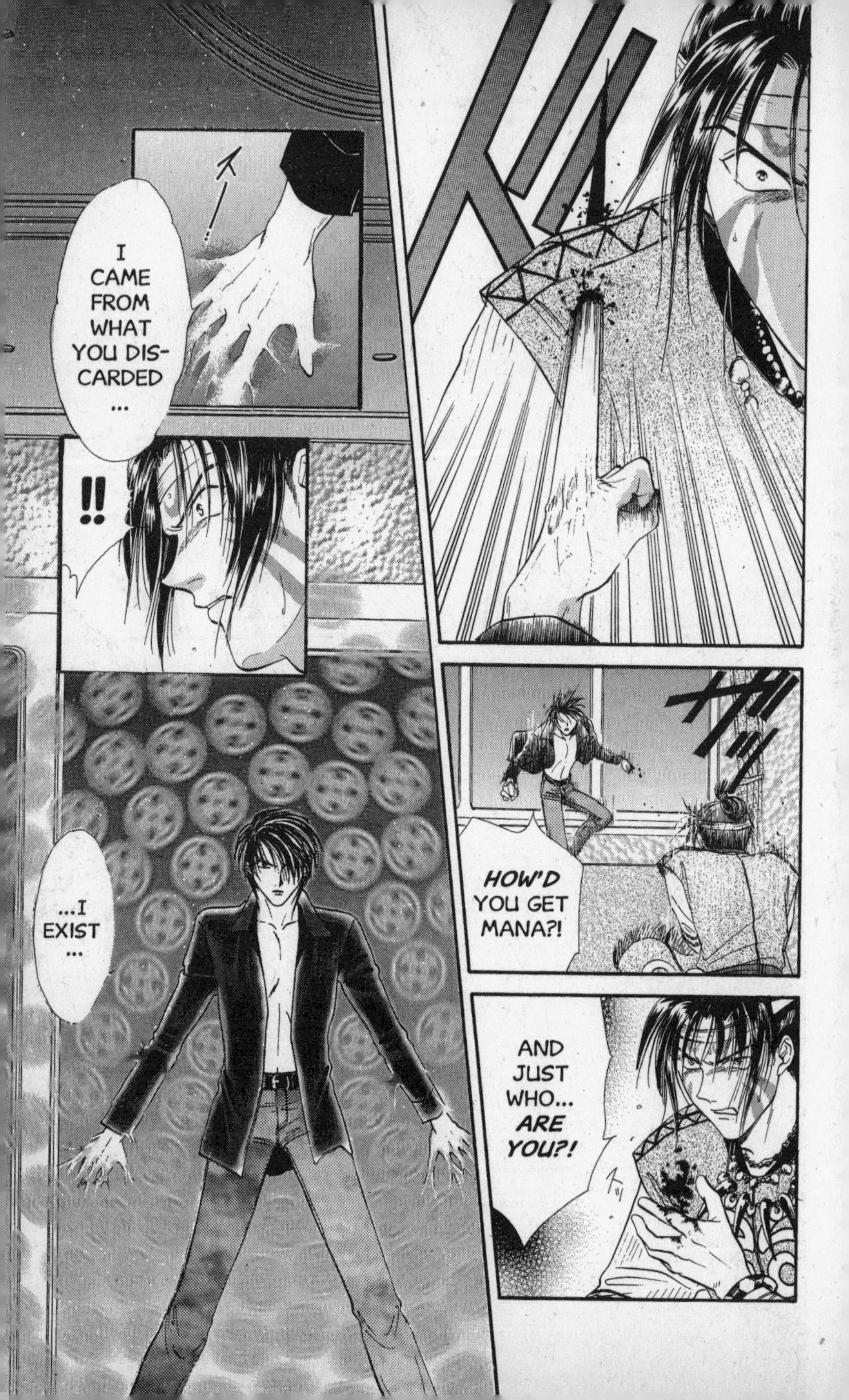
HOW'D YOU GET MANA?!
AND JUST WHO... ARE YOU?!
I CAME FROM WHAT YOU DIS-CARDED ...
!!
...I EXIST ...

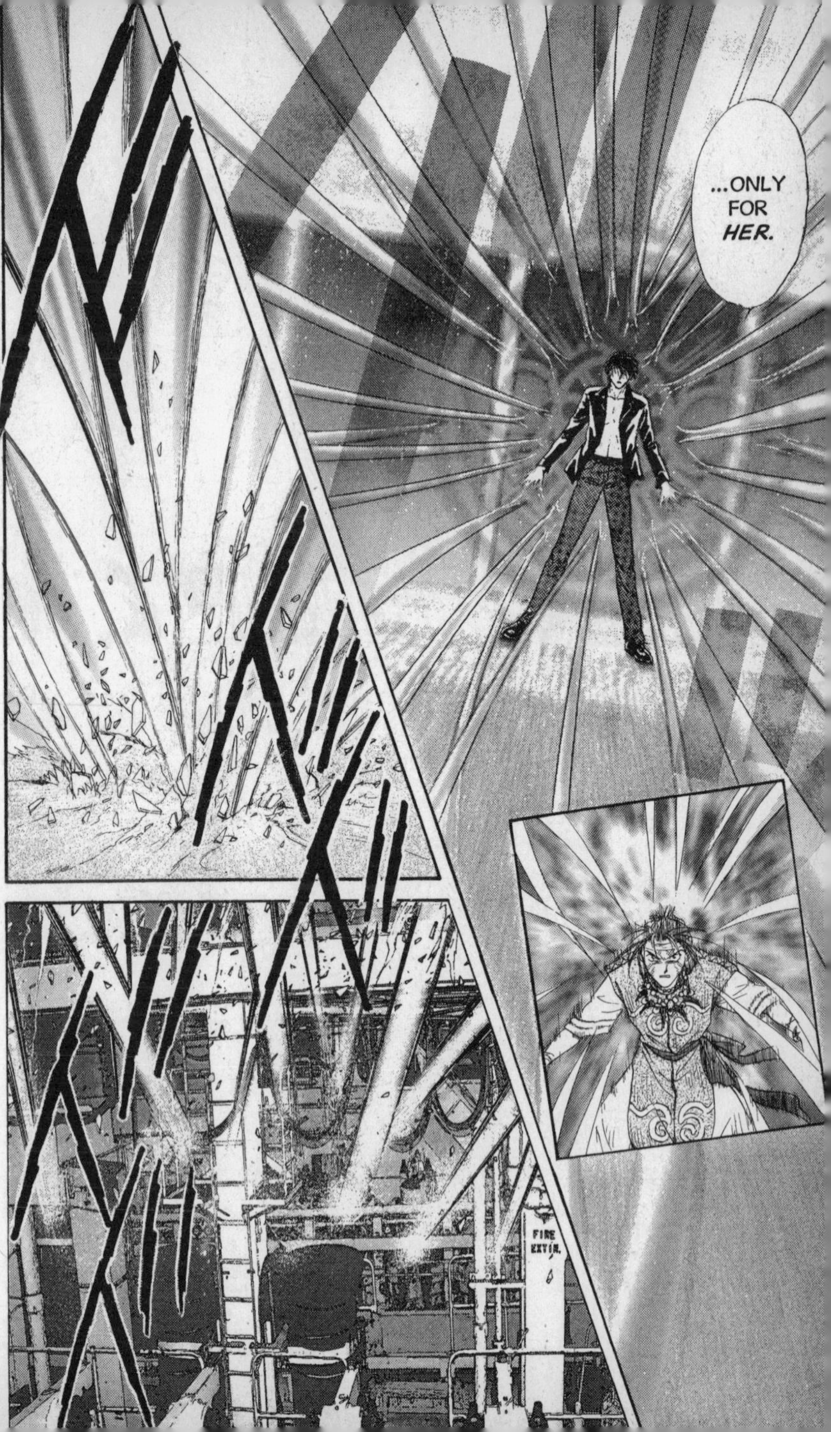
...ONLY FOR HER.
FIRE EXTIN.

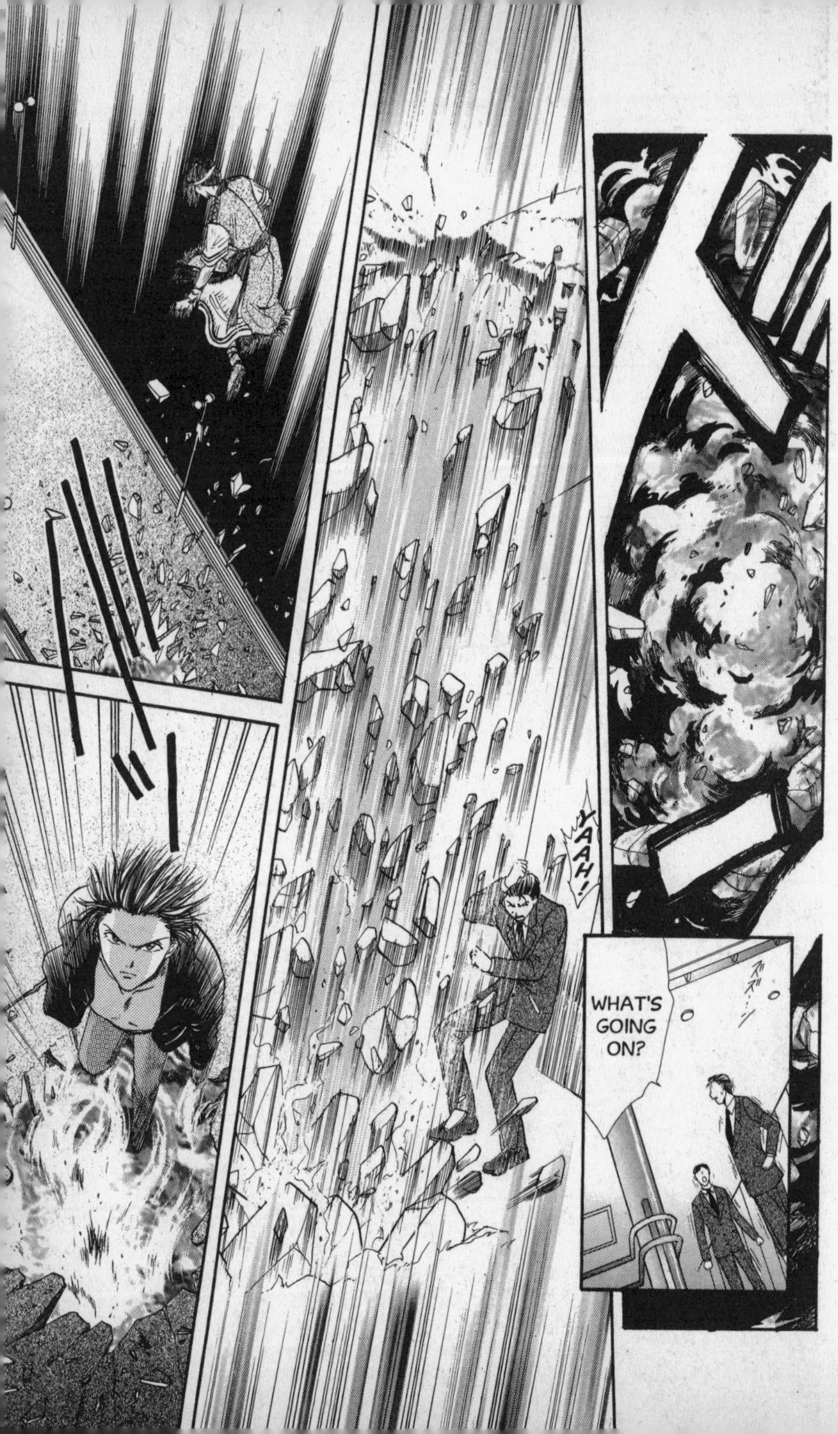
WHAT'S GOING ON?
ズズ…ン
YAAAH!

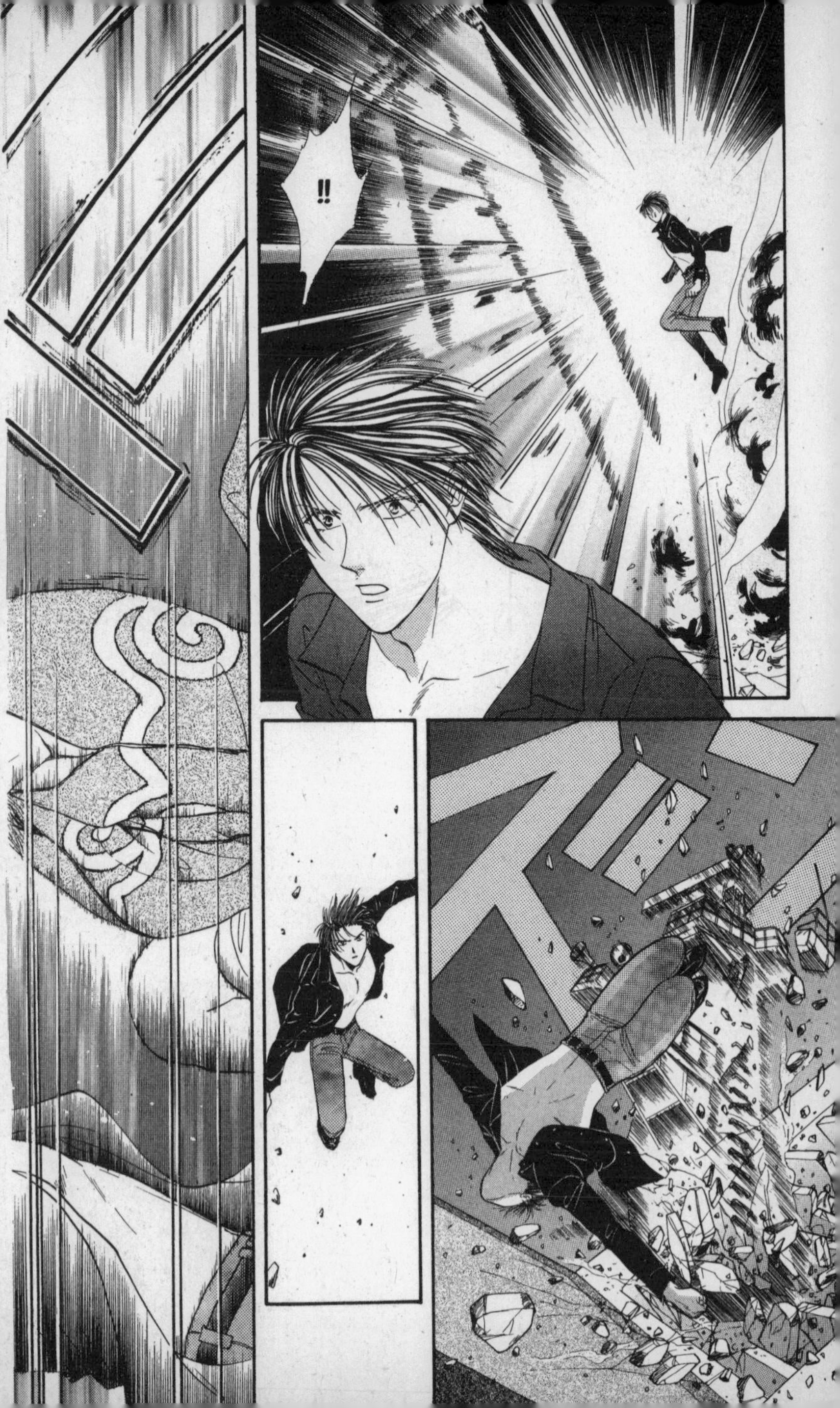
!!

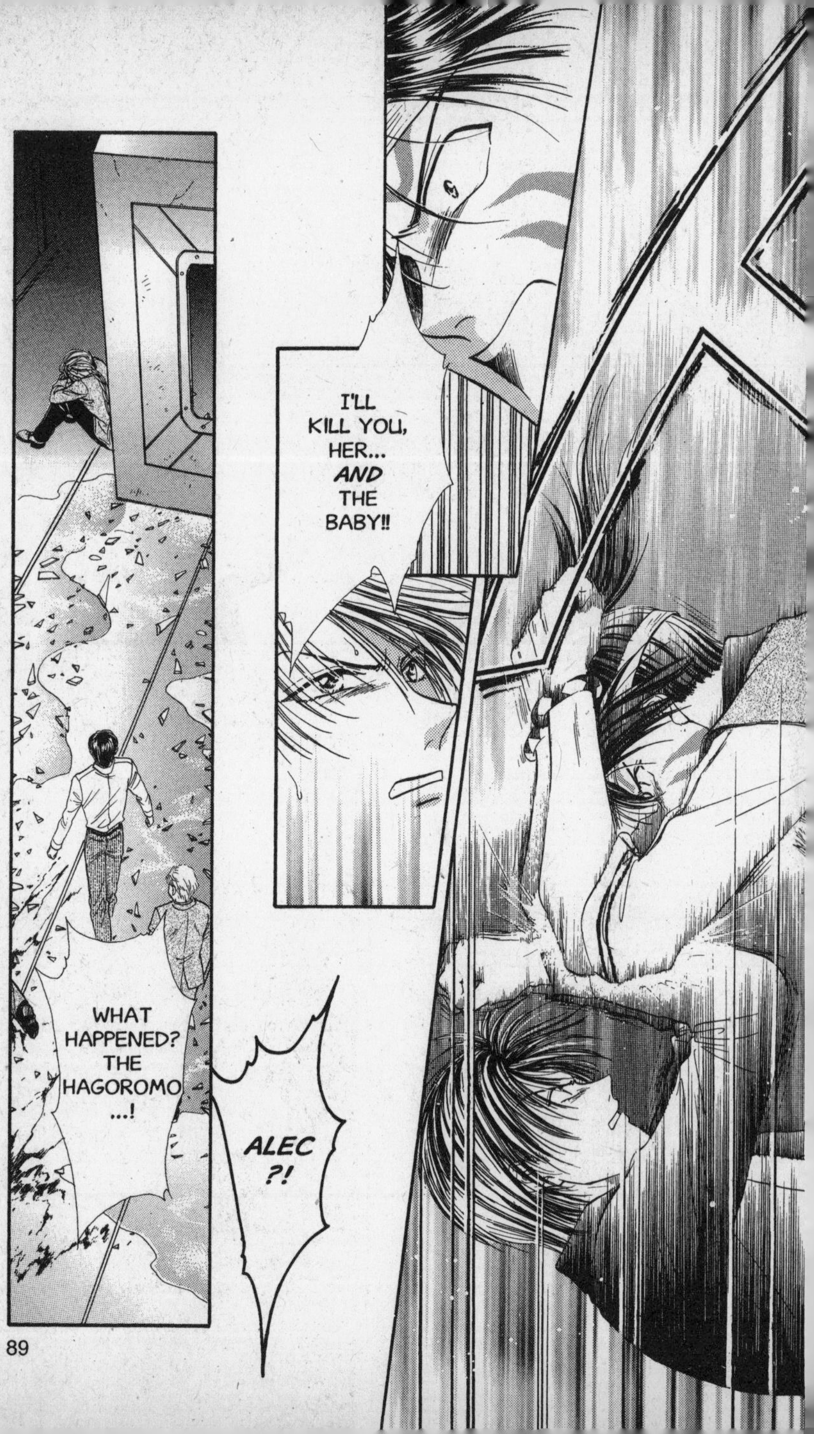
I'LL KILL YOU, HER... AND THE BABY!!
ALEC ?!
WHAT HAPPENED? THE HAGOROMO ...!

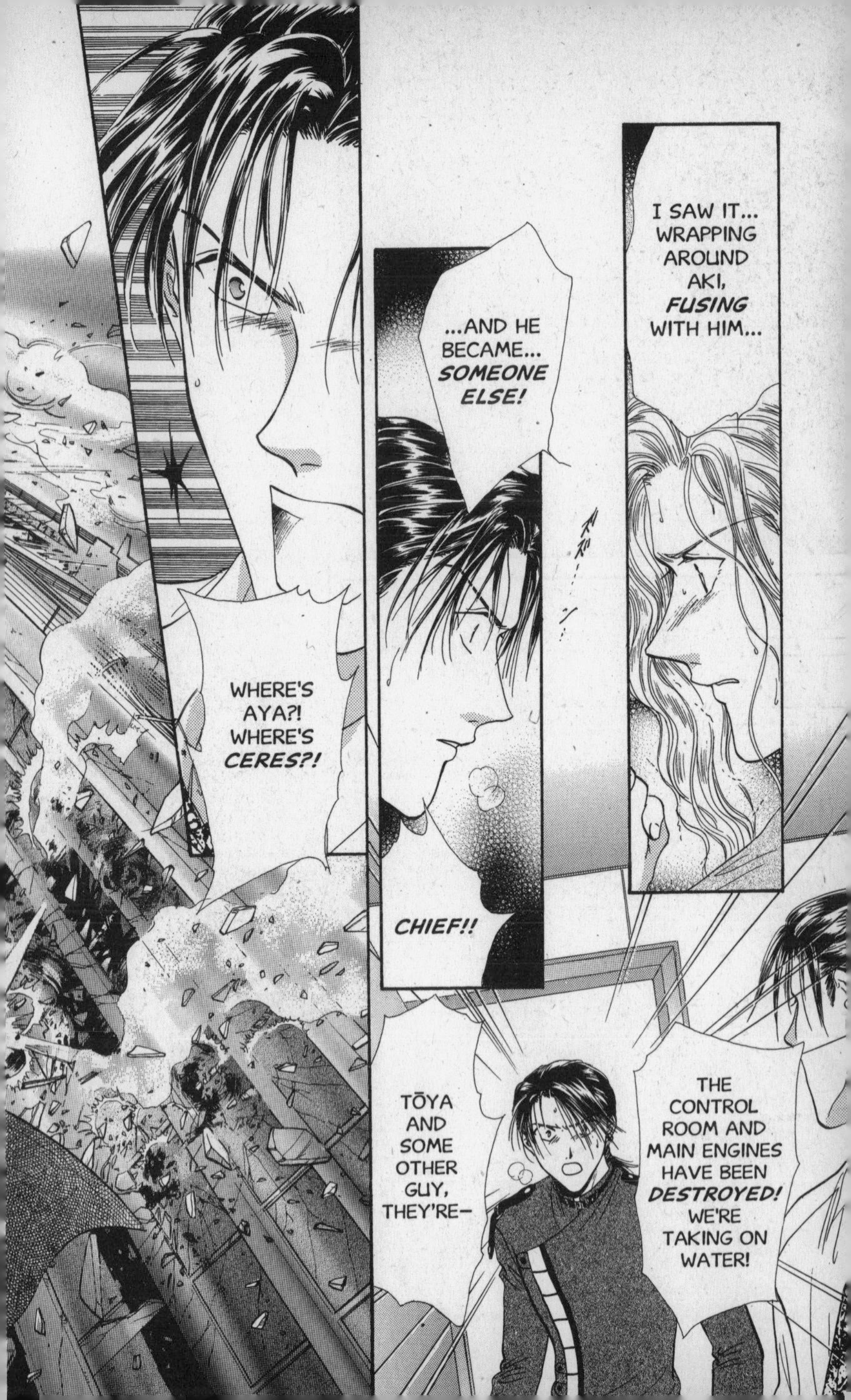
I SAW IT... WRAPPING AROUND AKI, *FUSING* WITH HIM...
...AND HE BECAME... *SOMEONE ELSE!*
CHIEF!!
THE CONTROL ROOM AND MAIN ENGINES HAVE BEEN *DESTROYED!* WE'RE TAKING ON WATER!
TŌYA AND SOME OTHER GUY, THEY'RE–
WHERE'S AYA?! WHERE'S *CERES?!*

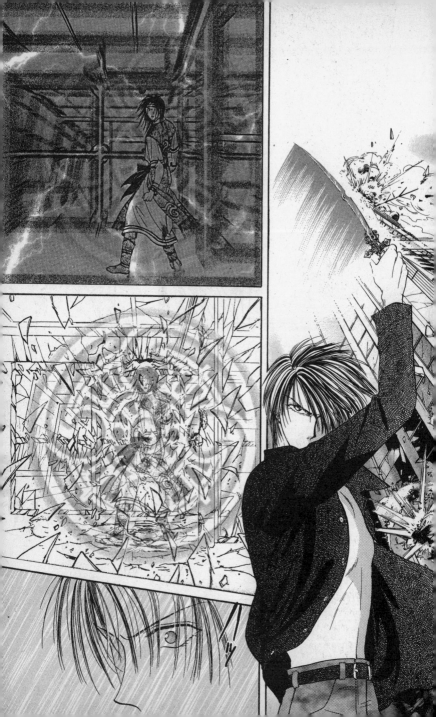

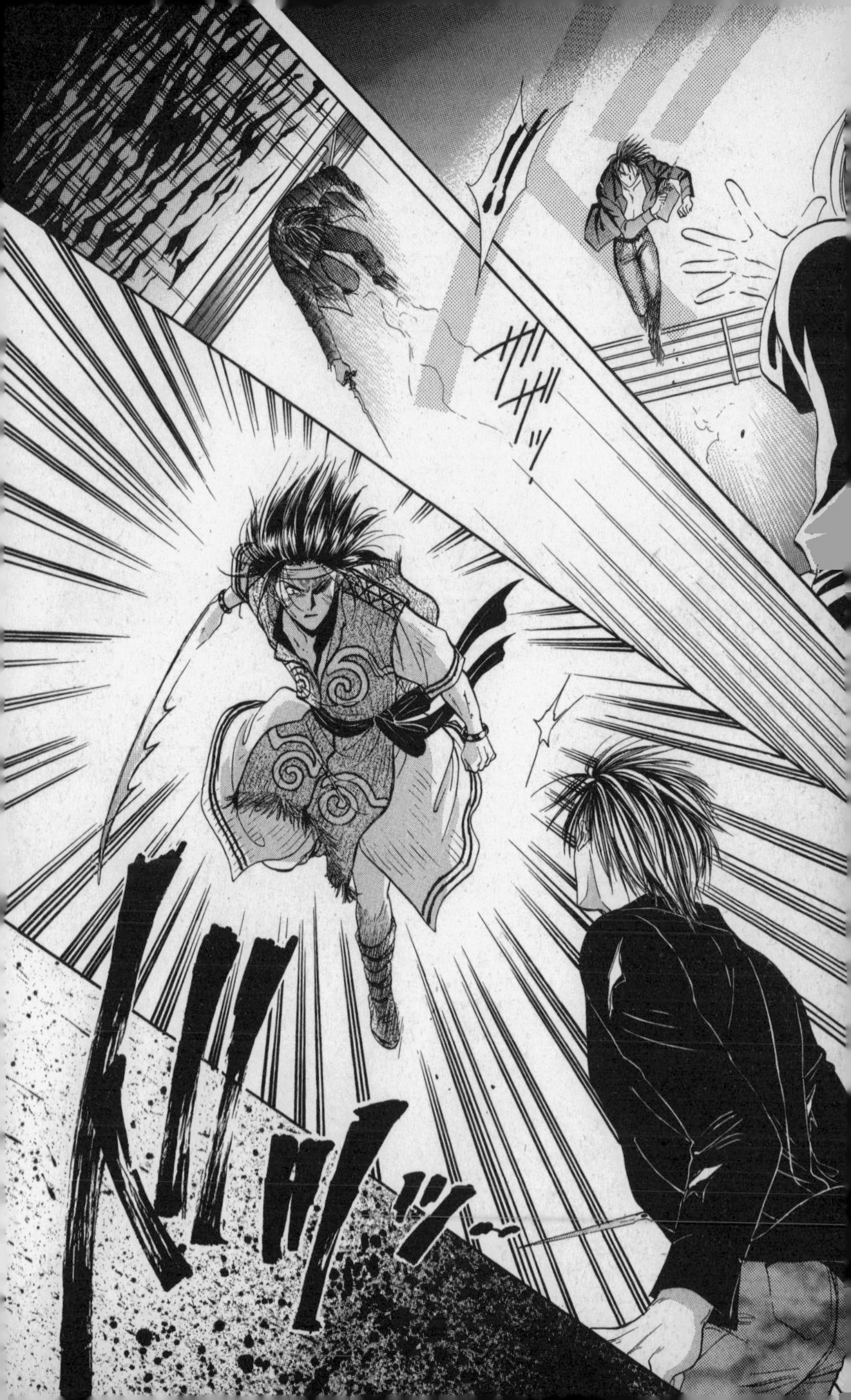
ガガッ

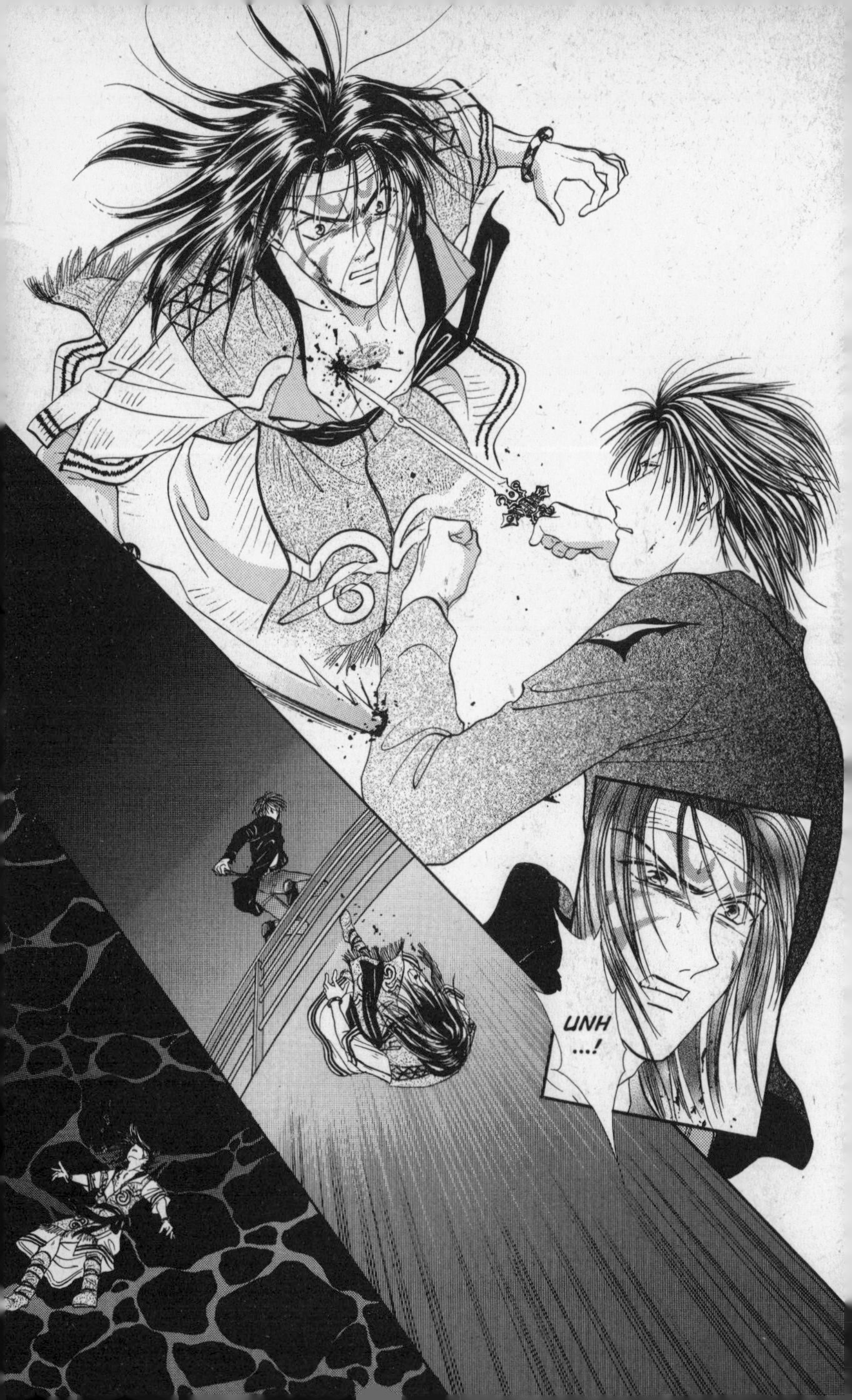
UNH ...!

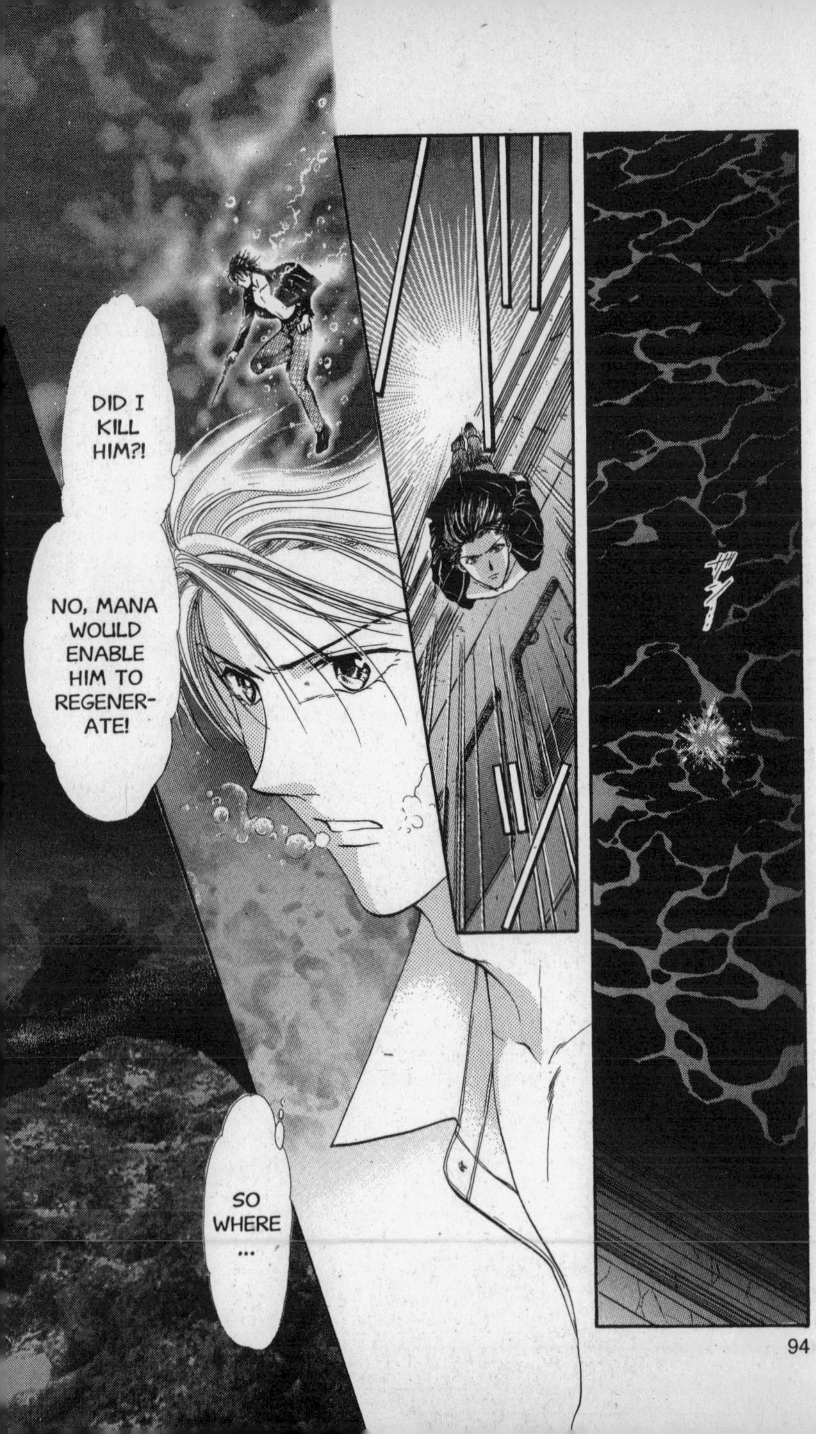
DID I KILL HIM?!
NO, MANA WOULD ENABLE HIM TO REGENER-ATE!
SO WHERE ...

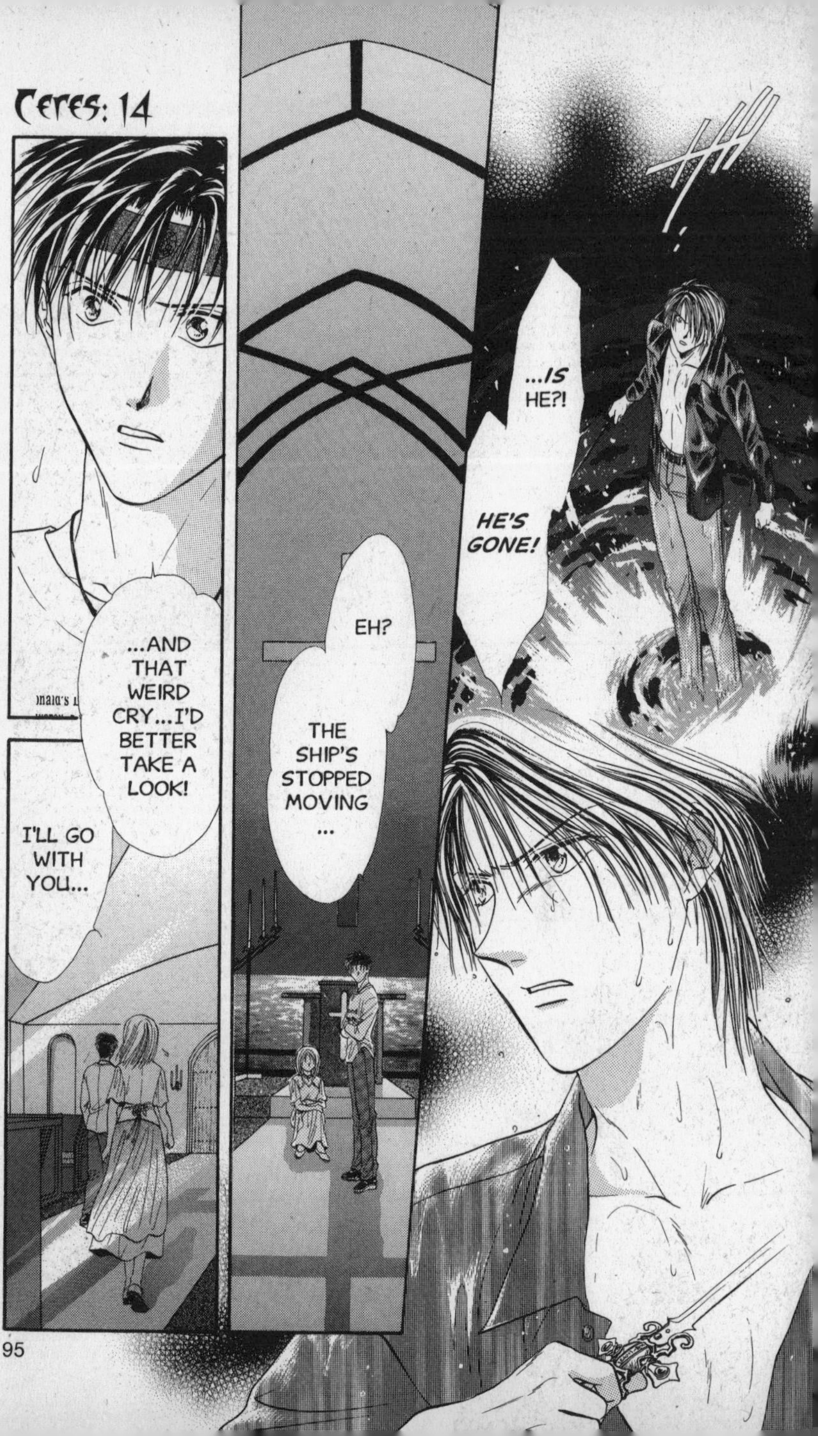
...IS HE?!
HE'S GONE!
EH?
THE SHIP'S STOPPED MOVING ...
...AND THAT WEIRD CRY...I'D BETTER TAKE A LOOK!
I'LL GO WITH YOU...

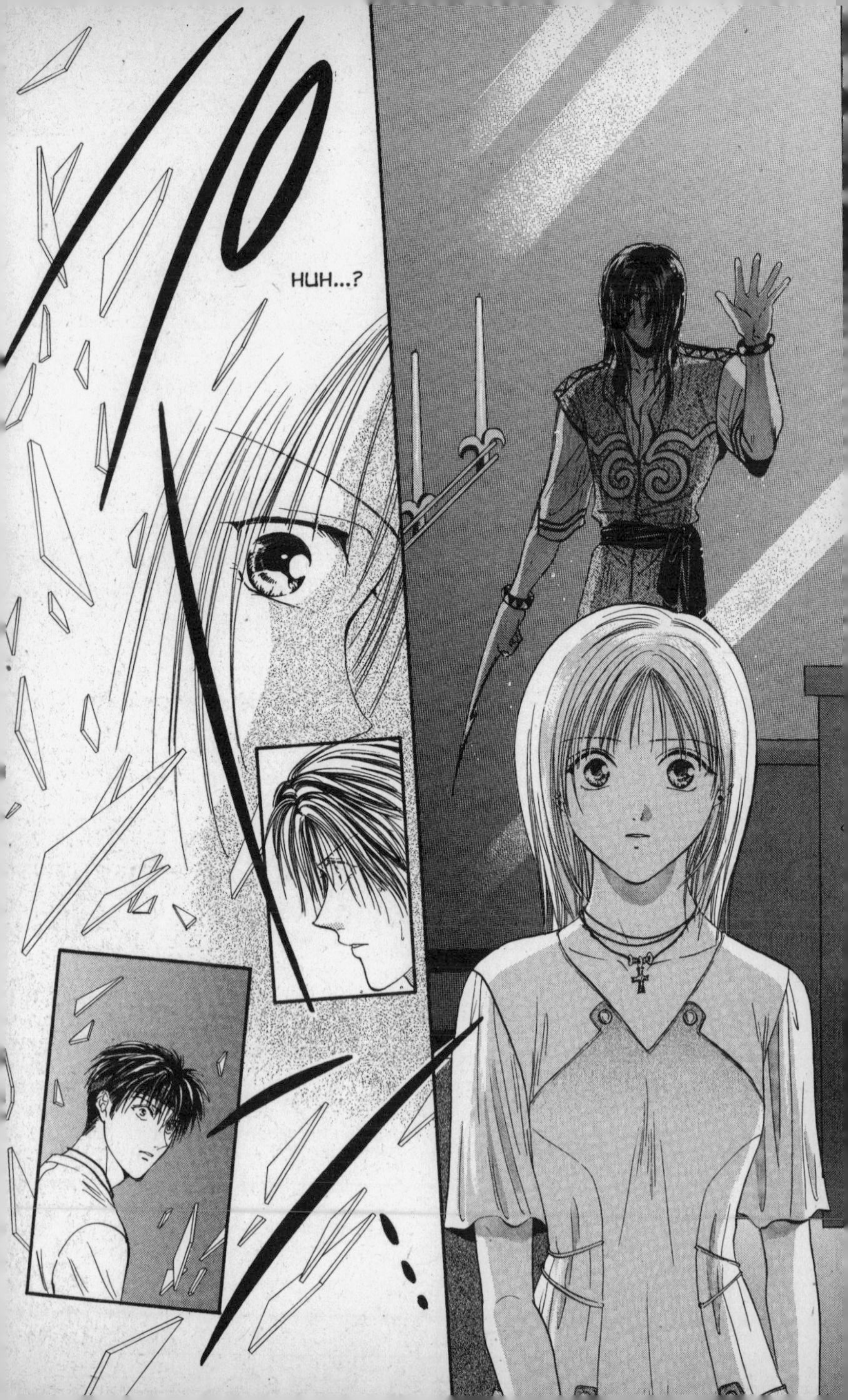
HUH...?

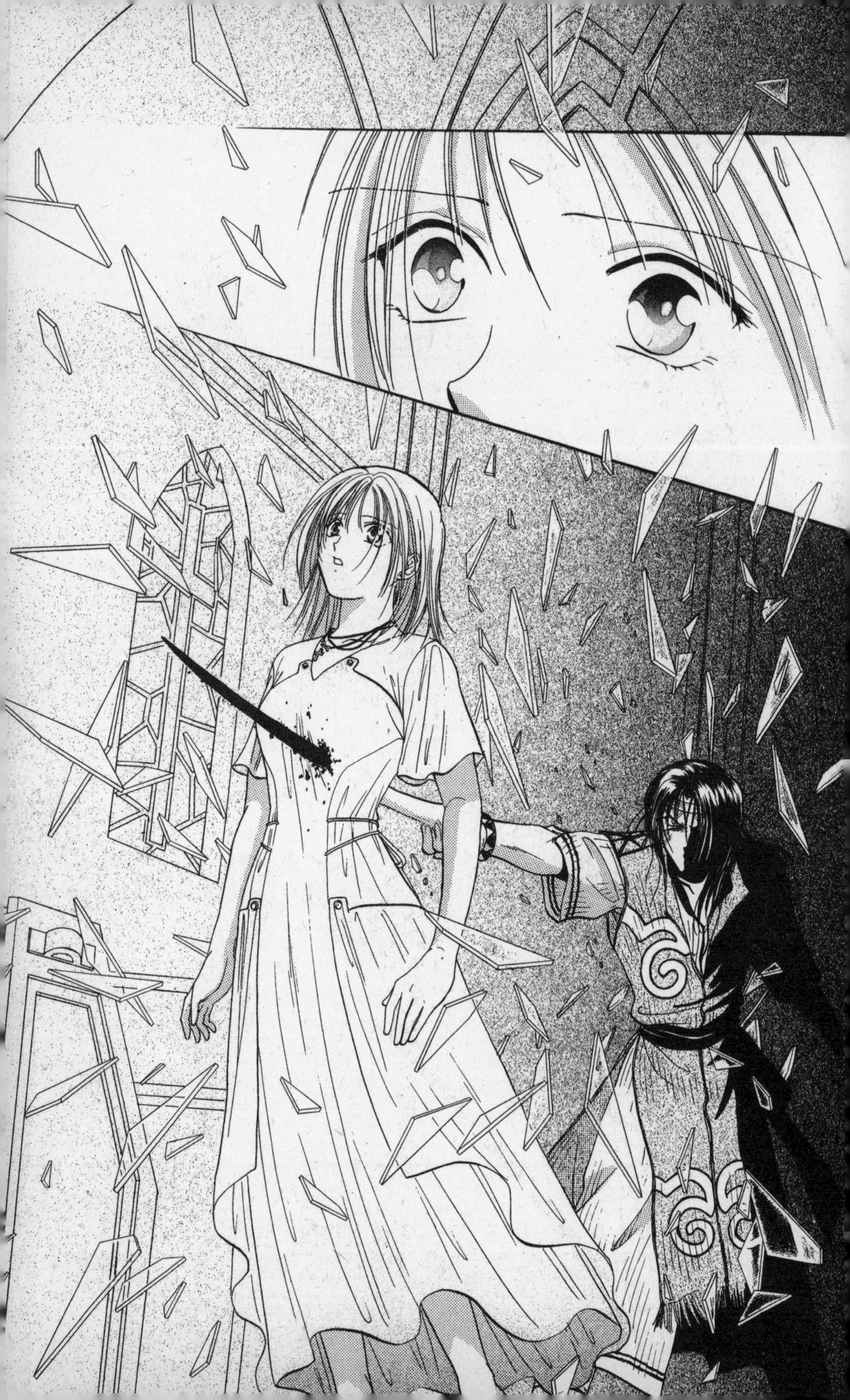

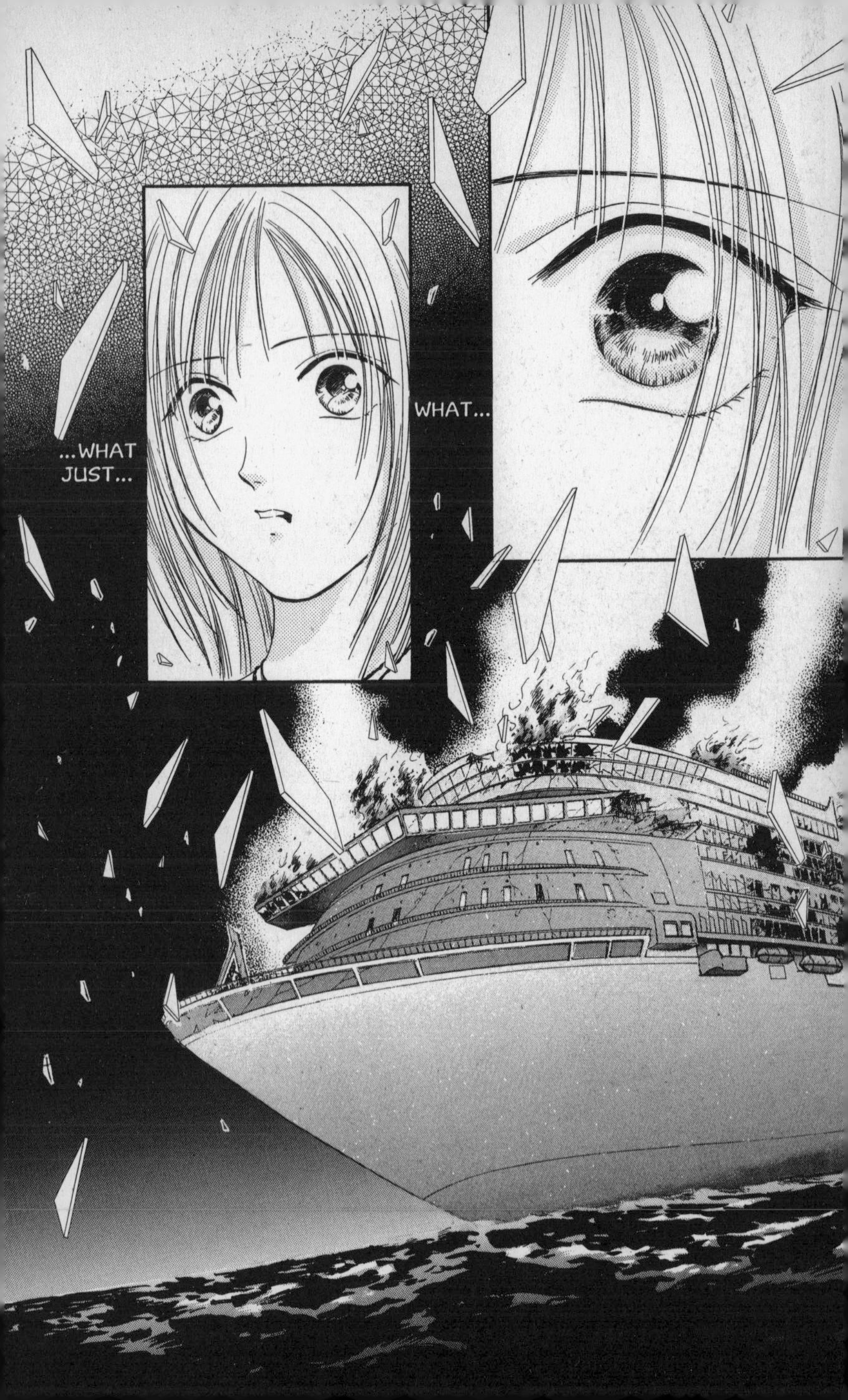
WHAT...
...WHAT JUST...

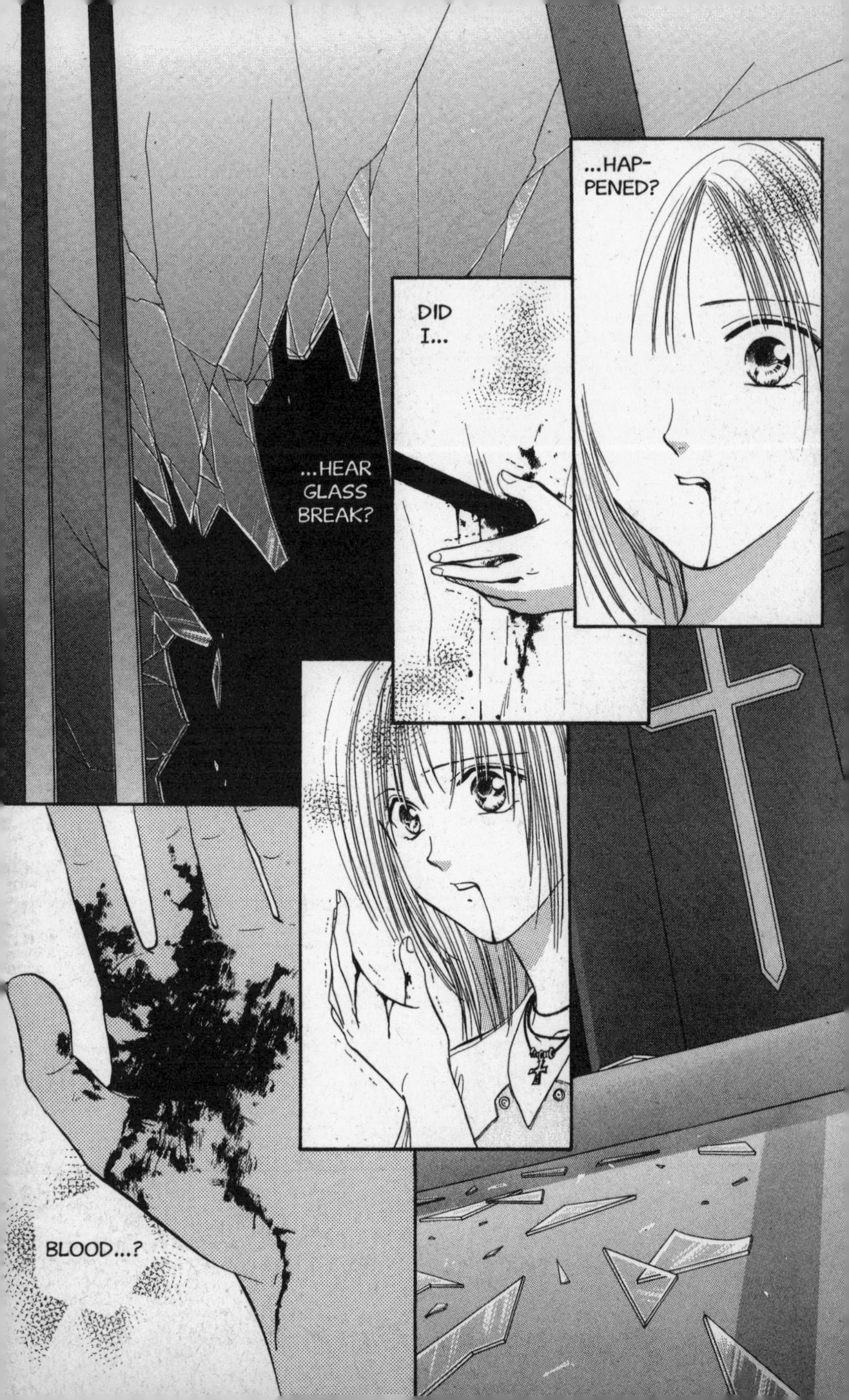
...HAP-PENED?
DID I...
...HEAR GLASS BREAK?
BLOOD...?

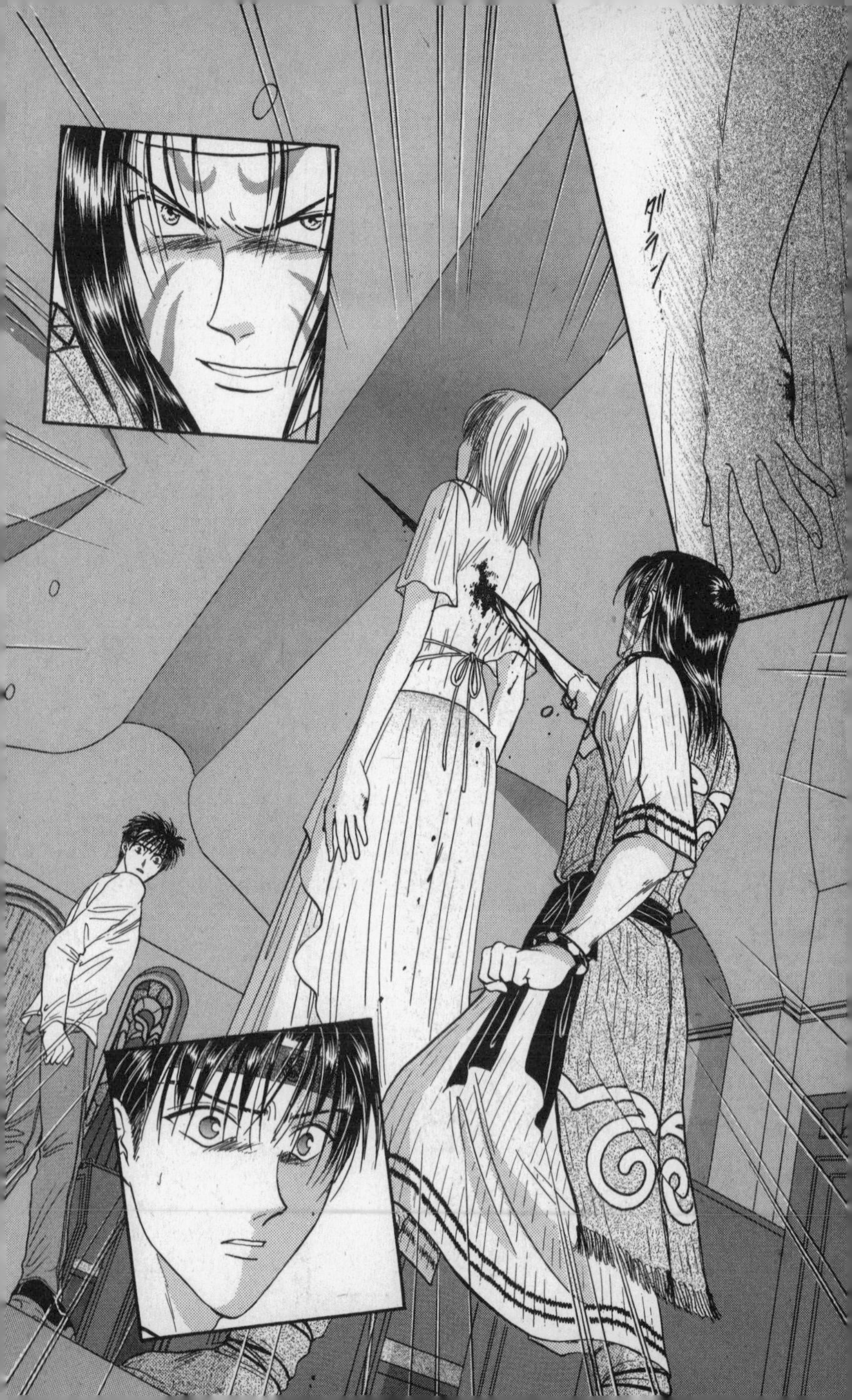
ダラン…

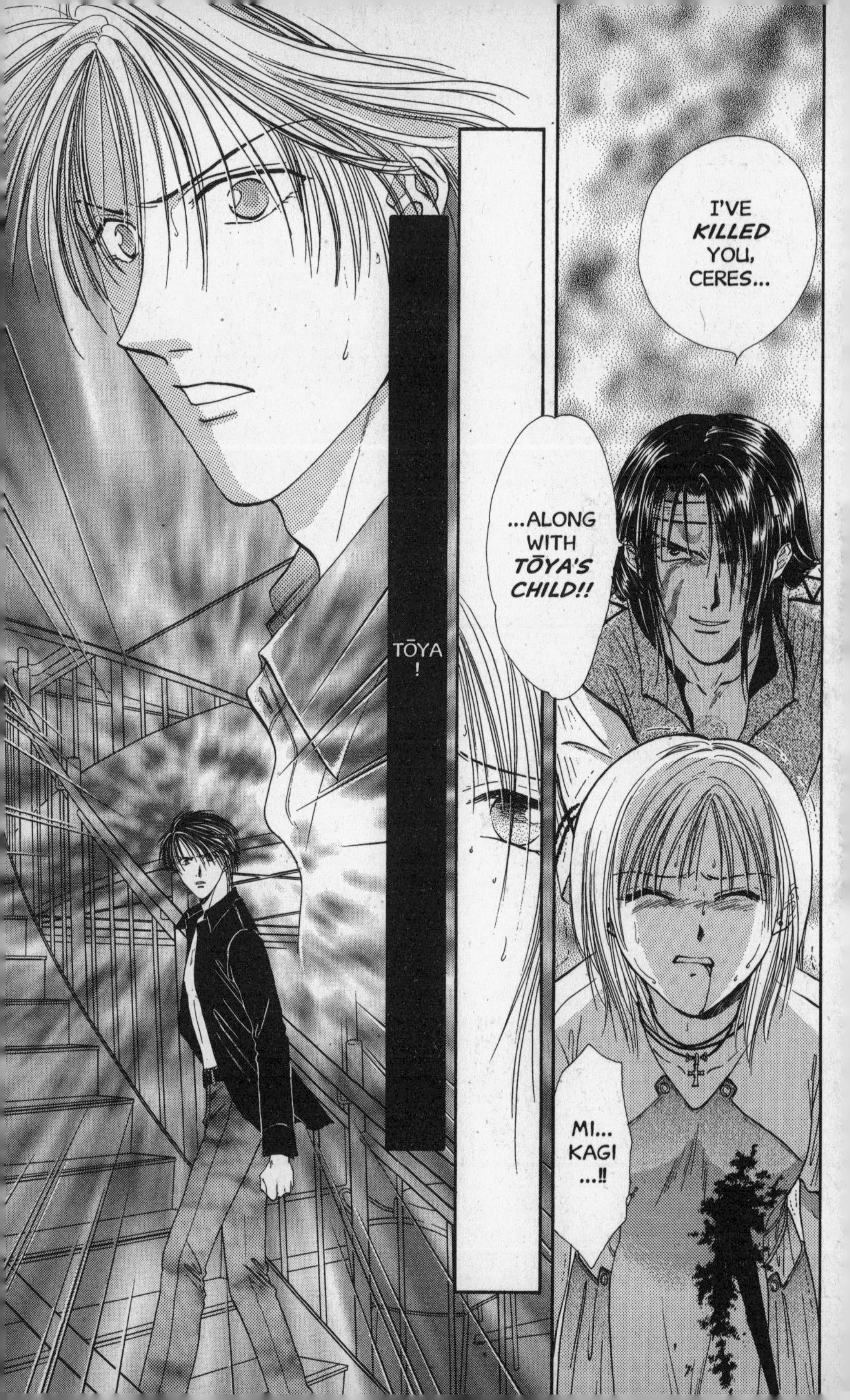
I'VE *KILLED* YOU, CERES...
...ALONG WITH *TŌYA'S CHILD!!*
MI... KAGI ...!!
TŌYA !

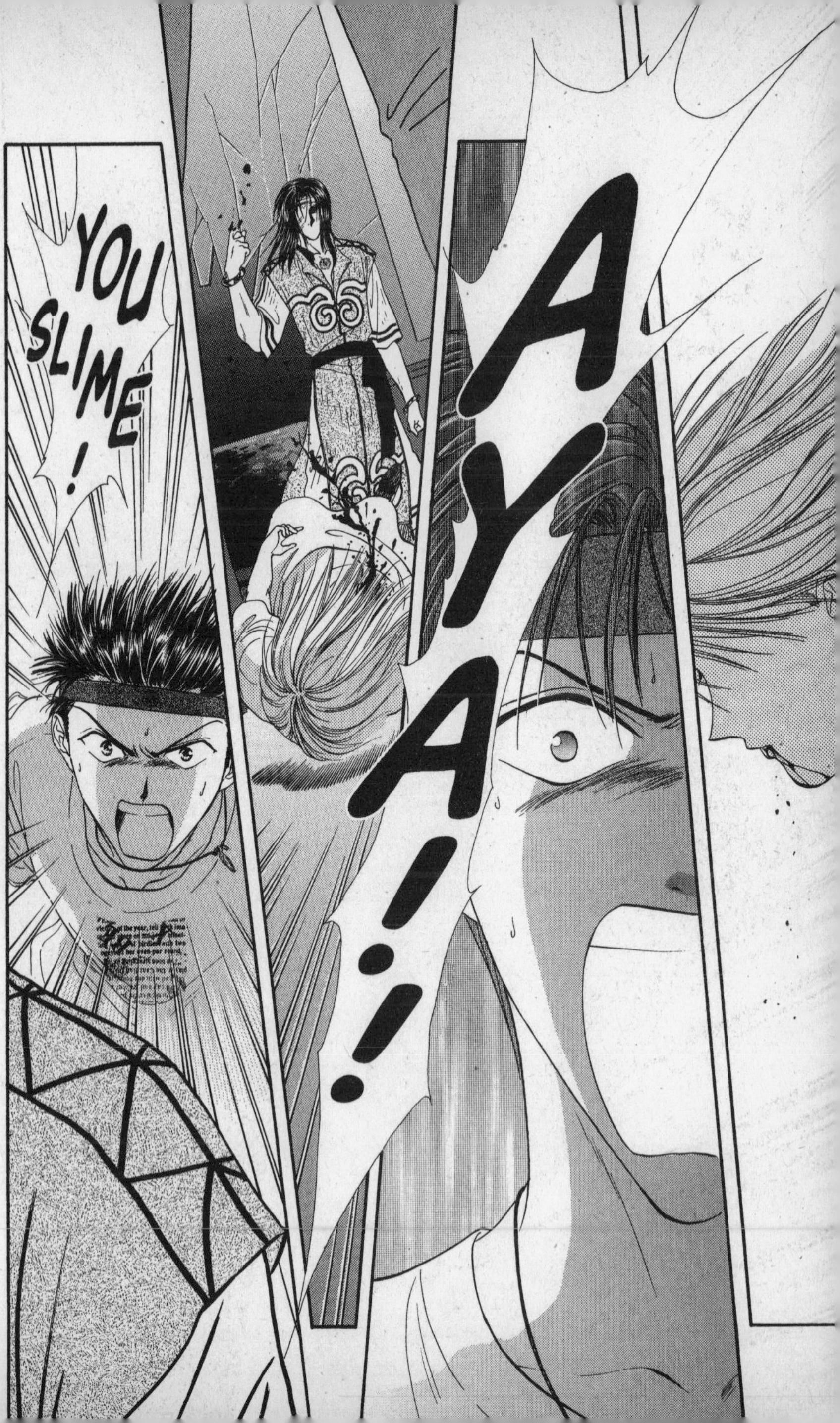
AYA!!!
YOU SLIME!

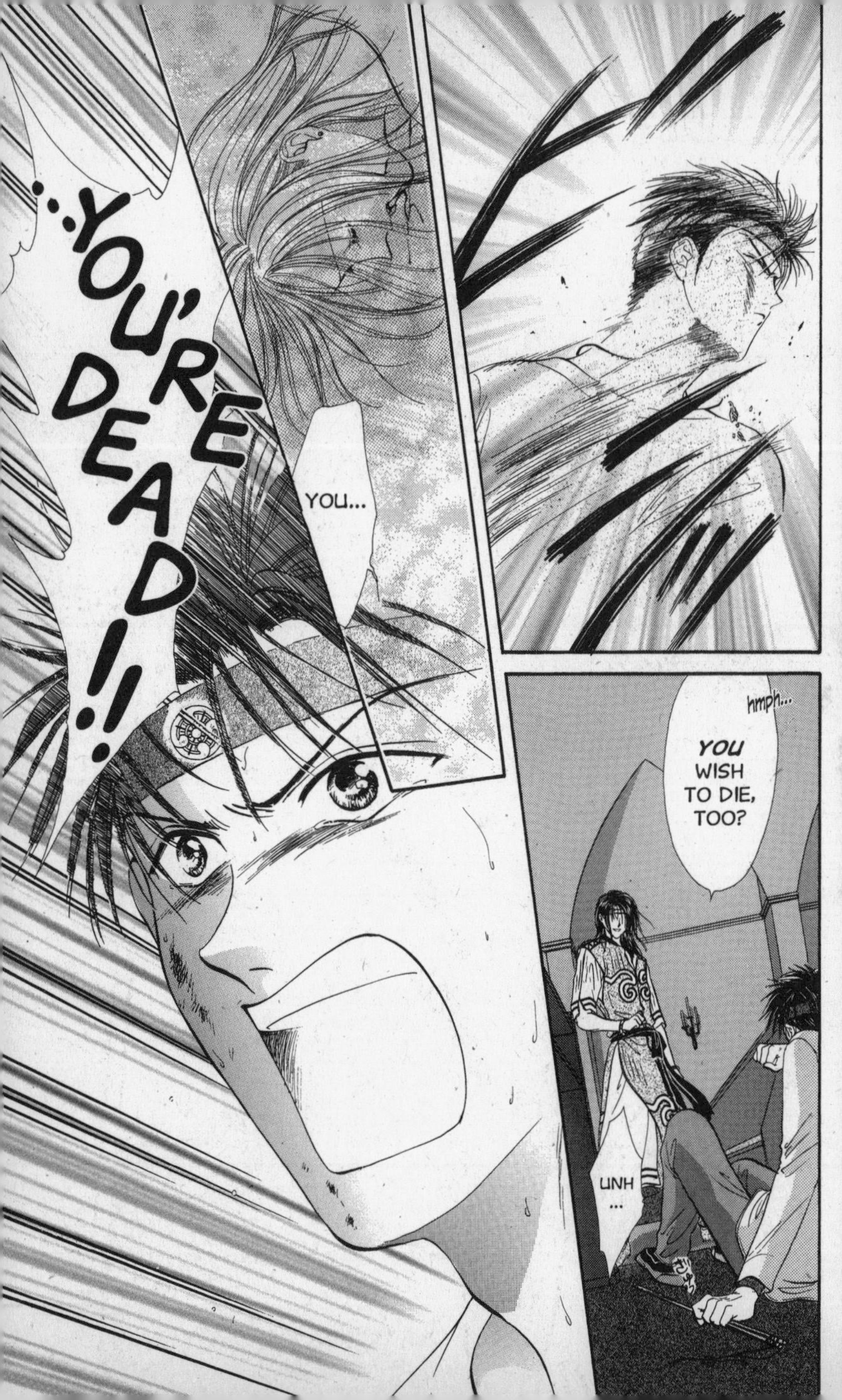
YOU...
hmph...
YOU WISH TO DIE, TOO?
UNH ...
...YOU'RE DEAD!!!

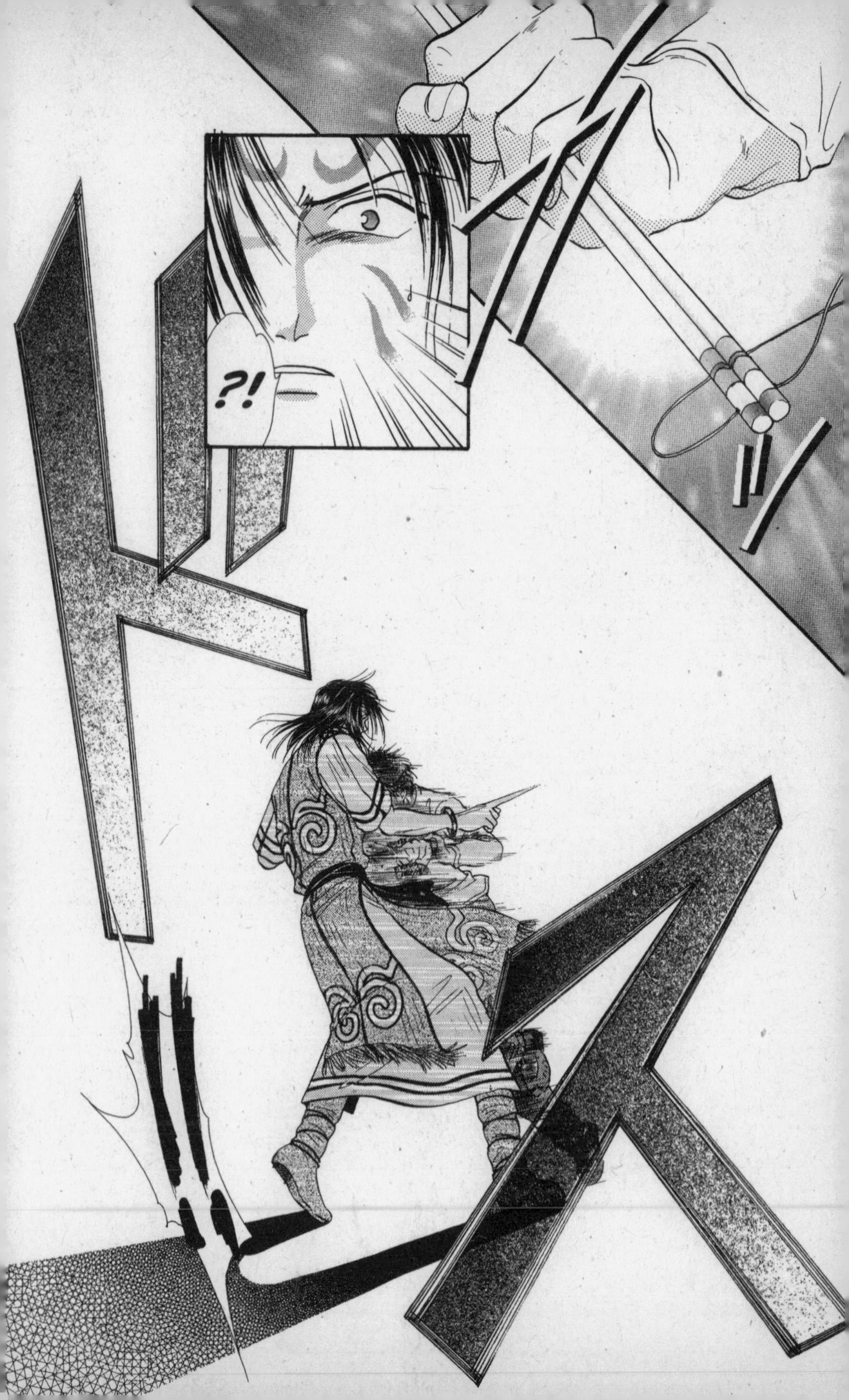
?!
ドン

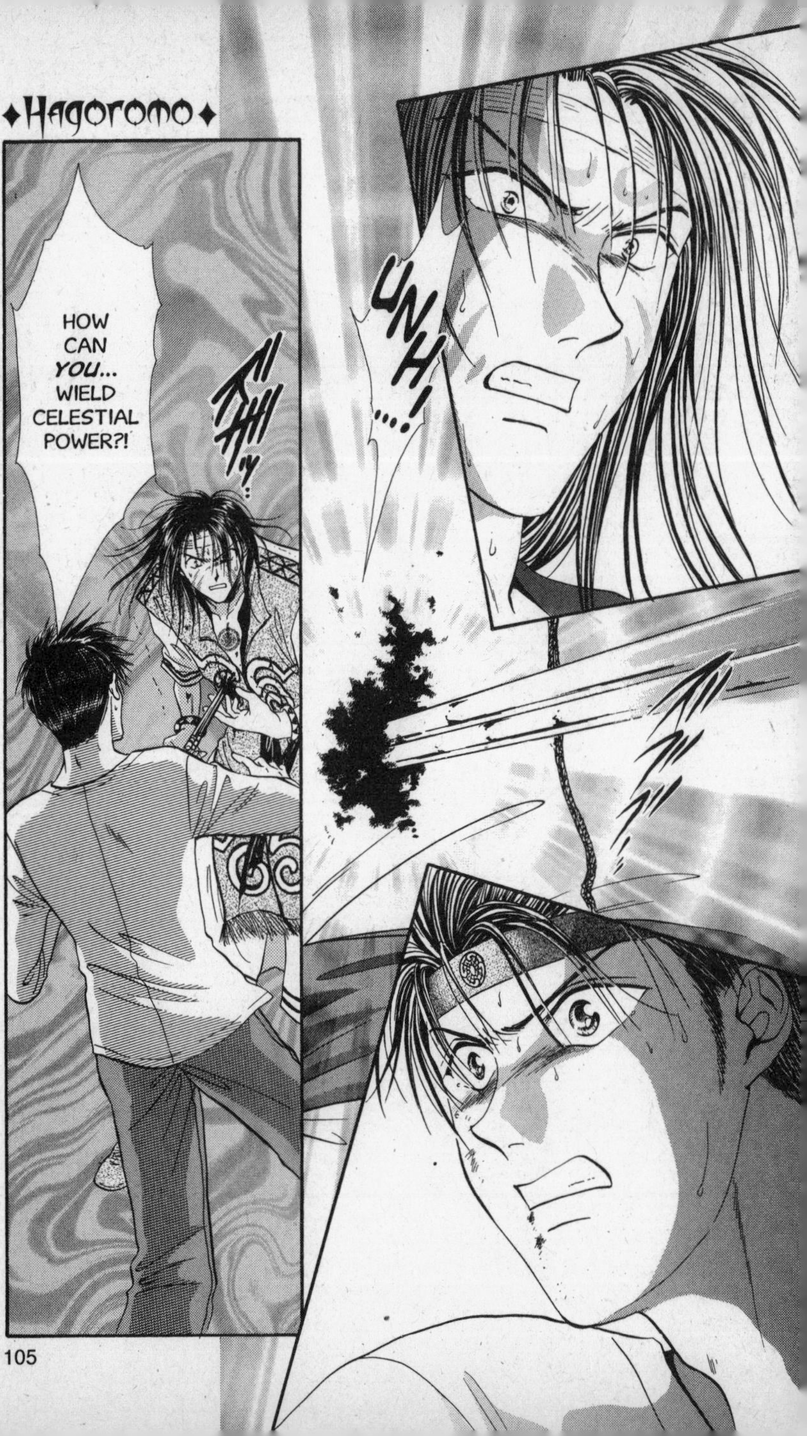
UNH...!
HOW CAN *YOU*... WIELD CELESTIAL POWER?!

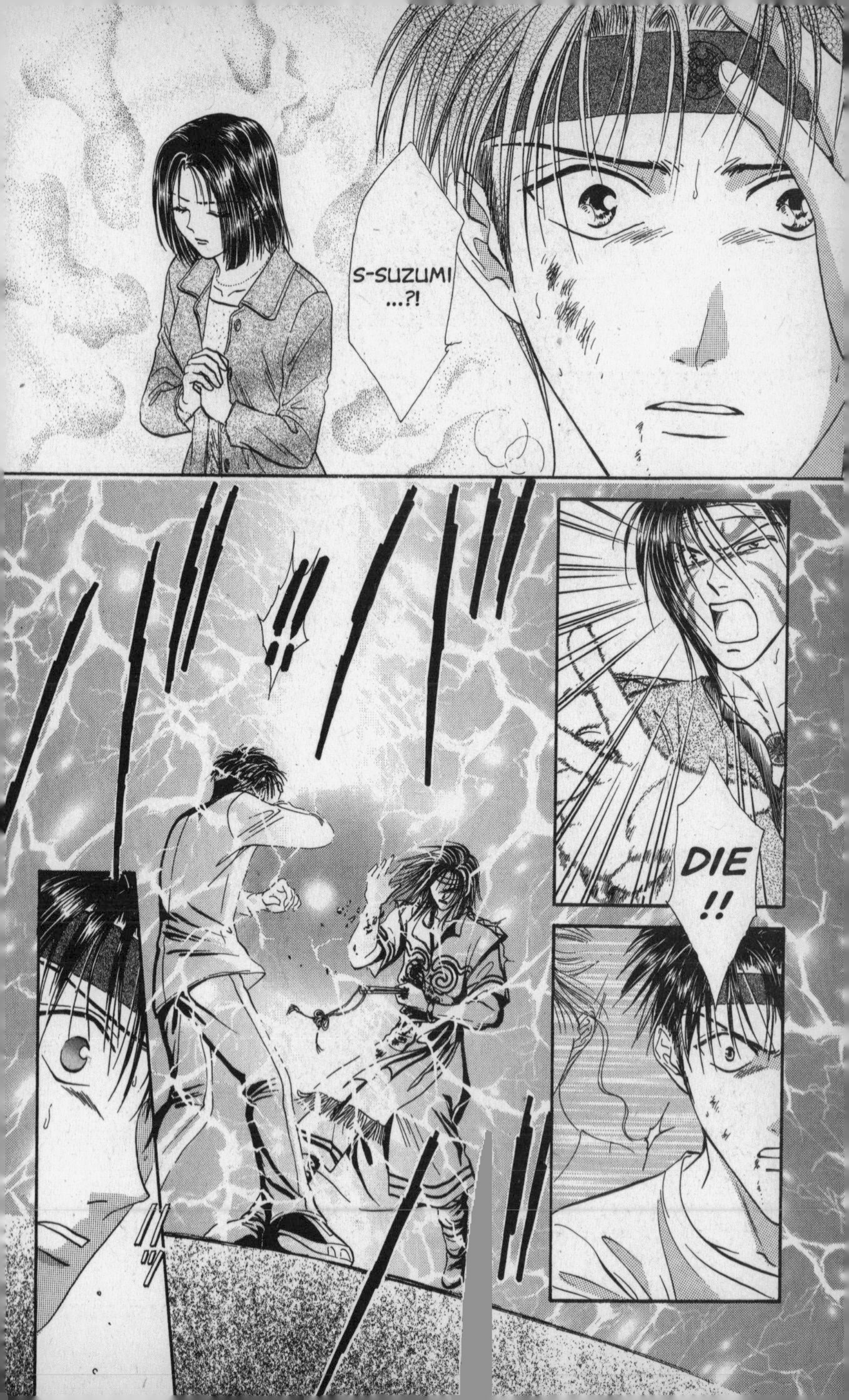
S-SUZUMI ...?!
DIE !!

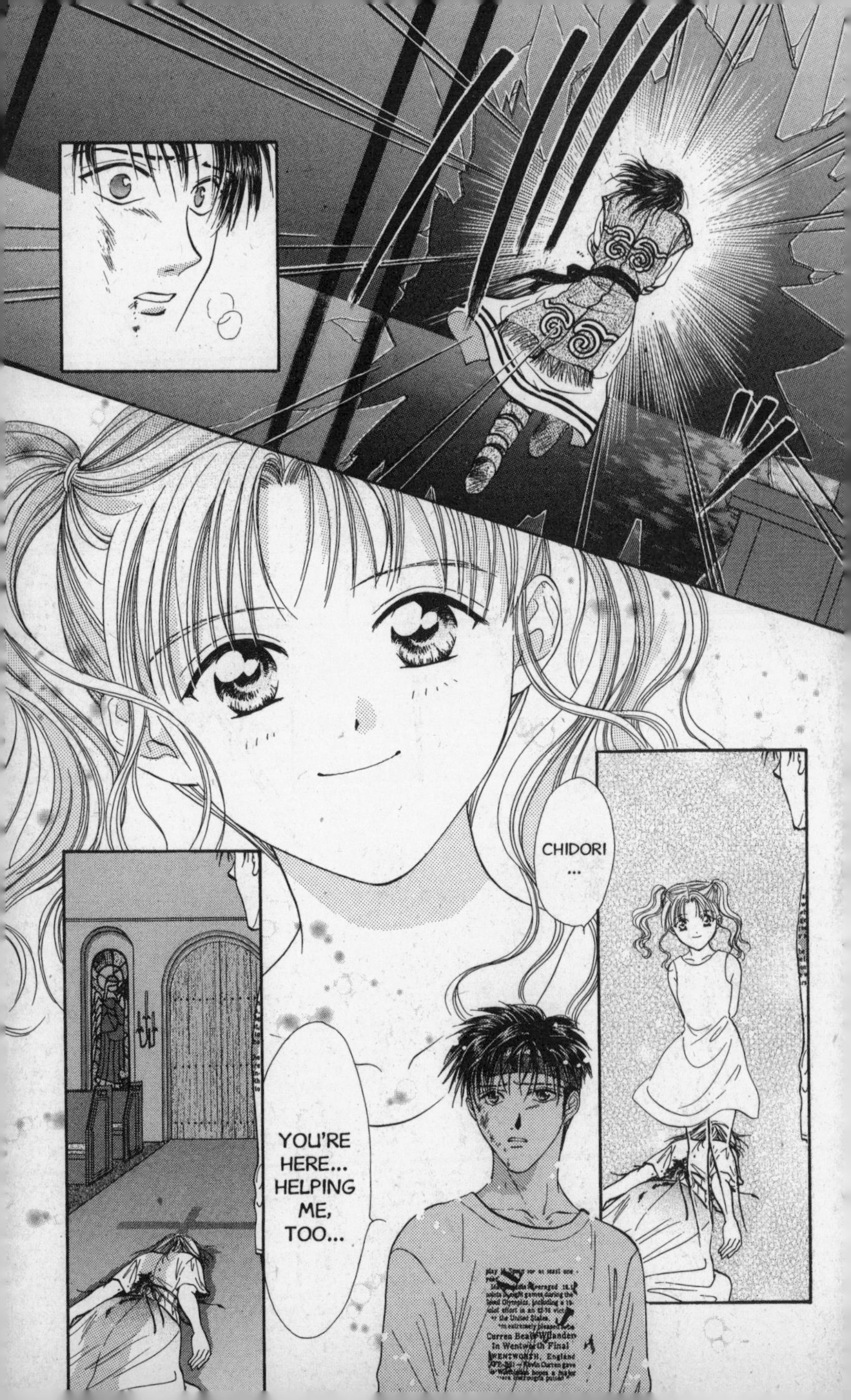
CHIDORI...
YOU'RE HERE... HELPING ME, TOO...

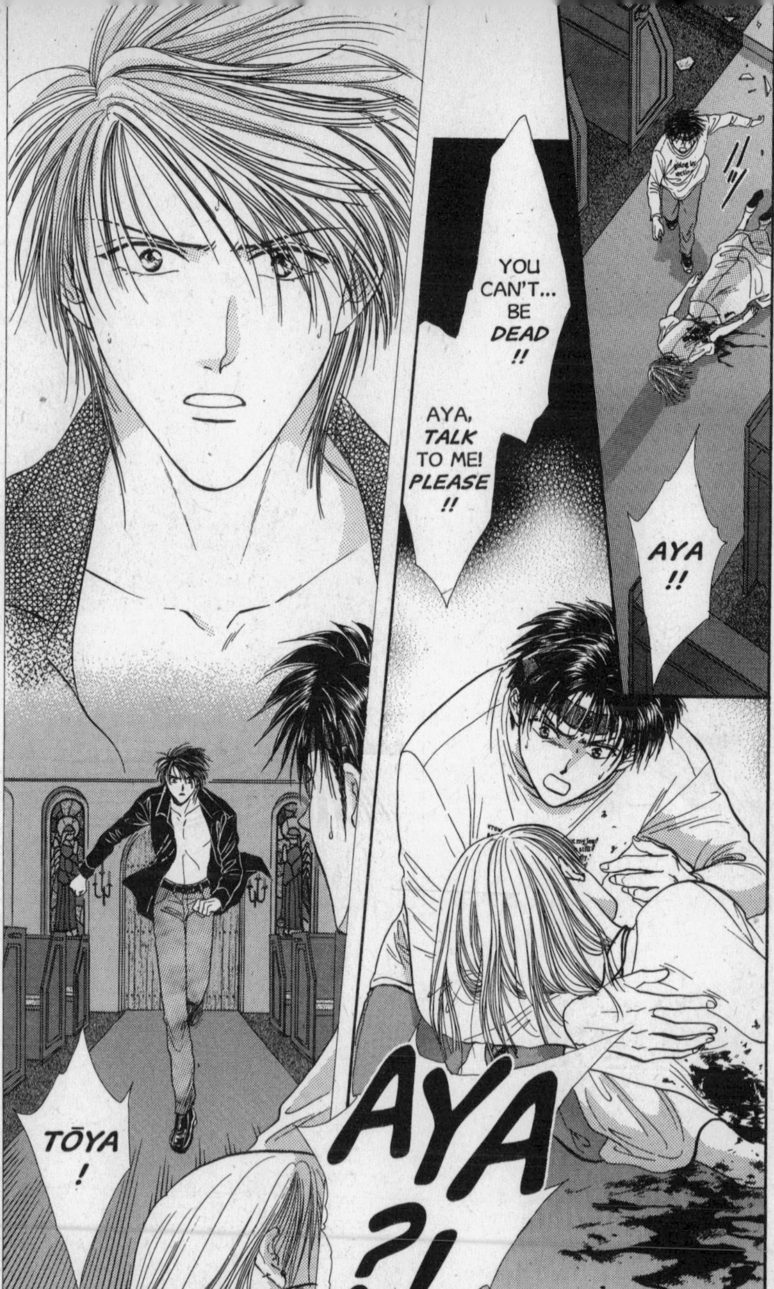
AYA !!
YOU CAN'T... BE DEAD !!
AYA, TALK TO ME! PLEASE !!
AYA ?!
TŌYA !

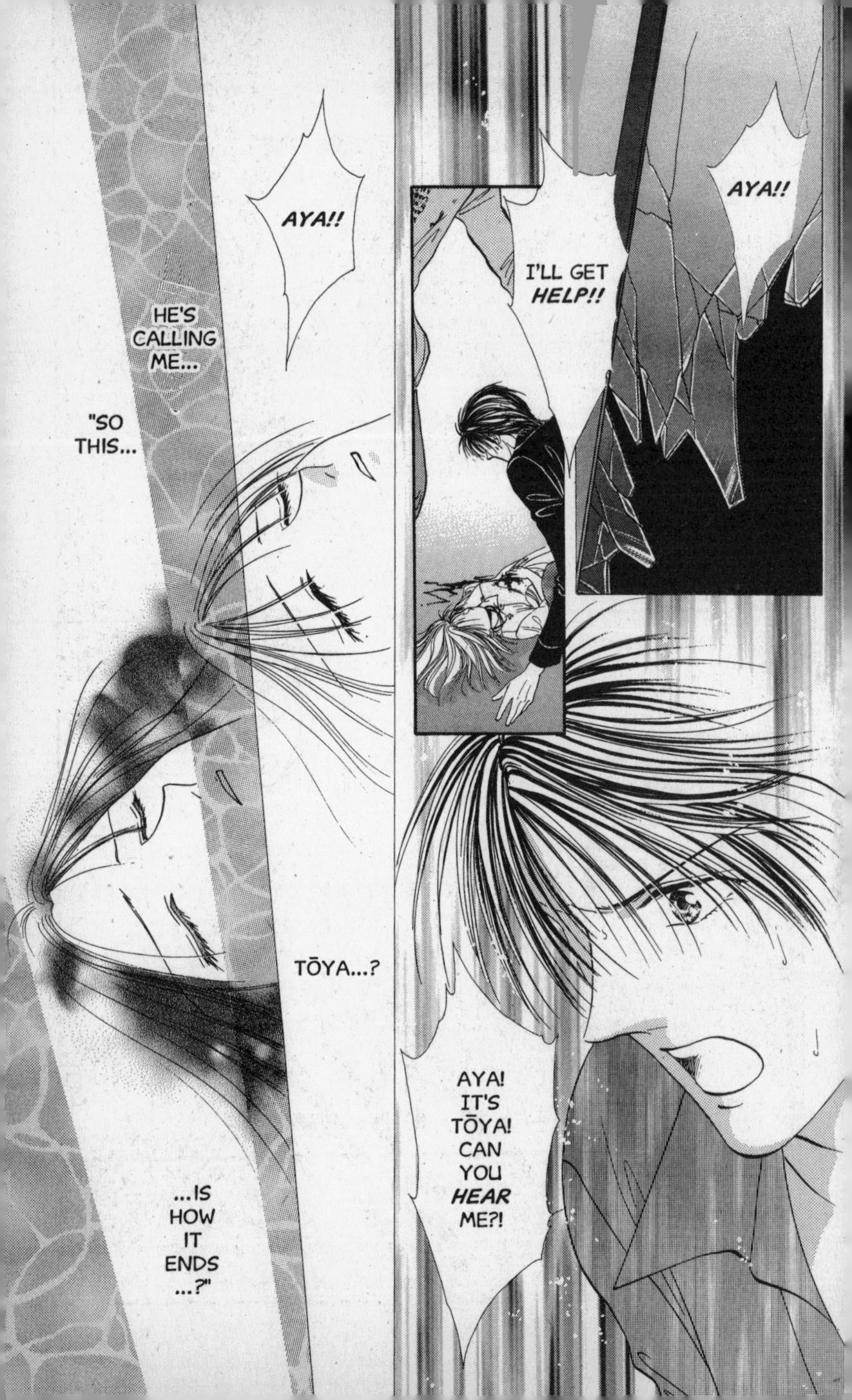
AYA!!
I'LL GET HELP!!
AYA! IT'S TŌYA! CAN YOU HEAR ME?!
AYA!!
HE'S CALLING ME...
"SO THIS...
TŌYA...?
...IS HOW IT ENDS ...?"

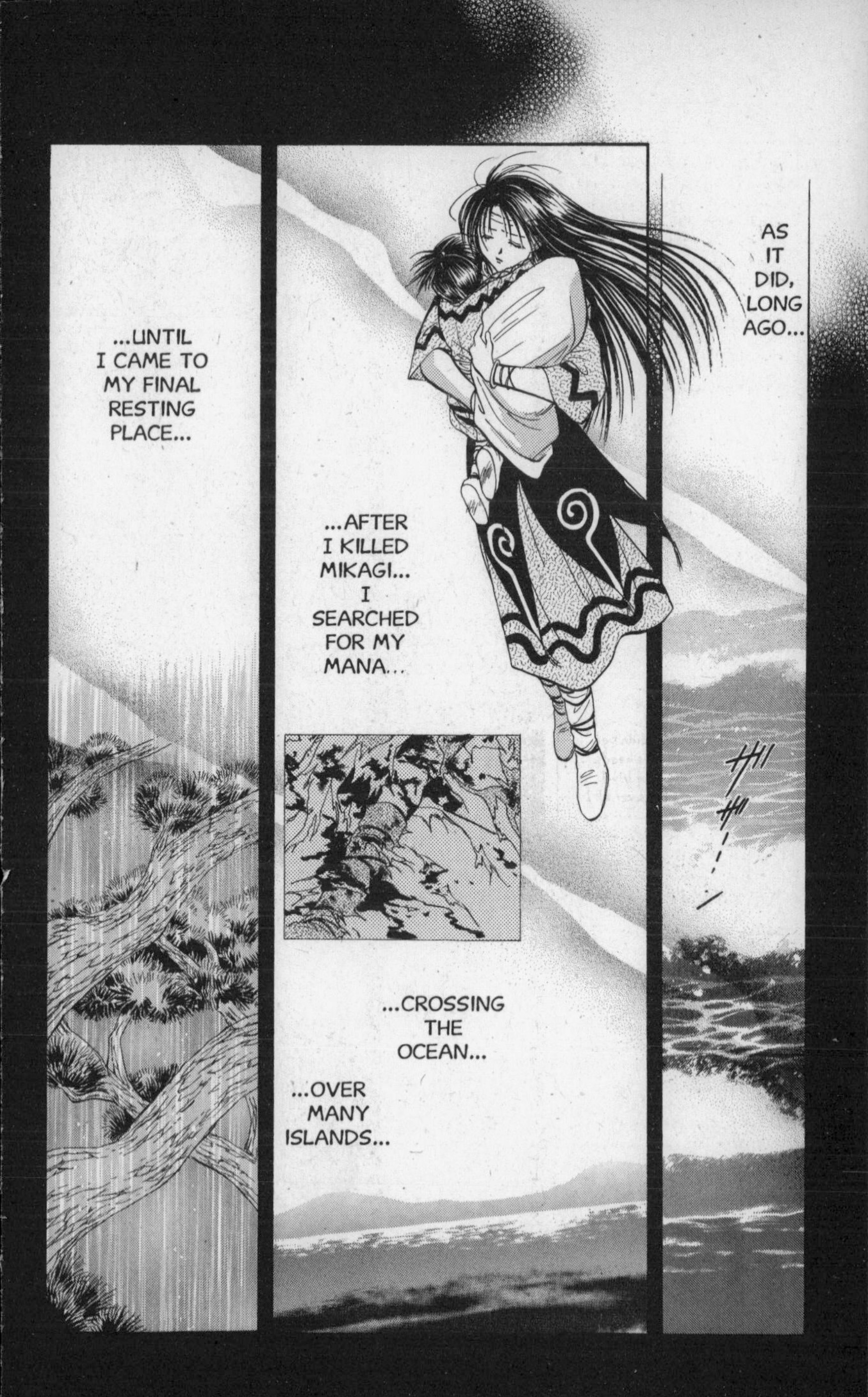
AS IT DID, LONG AGO...
...AFTER I KILLED MIKAGI... I SEARCHED FOR MY MANA...
...CROSSING THE OCEAN...
...OVER MANY ISLANDS...
...UNTIL I CAME TO MY FINAL RESTING PLACE...

Oh, before I forget!! My friend started a website. Everyone kept asking me if I was ever going to make my own homepage. I have no time! The prospect was too daunting (?)! Then my friend kindly offered the use of her page to promote my stuff!! Thanks so much!! I contribute news, so you can get the quickest updates about me there! ☺

http://homepage2.nifty.com/nankou/

Please check it out! I often write on the bulletin boards, too. ☺ I think all my friends have visited the site...so I contributed a doodle of Tōya. ☺ There are links to other **Ceres** sites in Japan and abroad, and you should be able to follow them to get **Ceres** and **FY** info. We're also running a petition to have the **FY** novels animated into an OVA, so if you want to see more **FY**, please participate! Just be sure to observe proper netiquette.

× × ×

I owe everything to the readers, and I hope this story didn't go over too many people's heads. ^^; [that's a sweating face btw] I think I was able to cover all I wanted to draw, theme-wise. I got more and more letters as the story progressed about how "**Ceres** is a manga that makes you think". I was surprised that Ceres & Mikagi's story in vol. 13 was so well received. Ceres was more like an "animal" [in that she was motivated purely out of her biological needs], but she tried to become more "human" when she fell in love for the first time. (The same with Tōya.) Kagami's assertions were never necessarily "wrong", but they don't show much improvement over caveman days. Mikagi was the embodiment of everything negative about men and humanity in general. But then again maybe he was the most "human" because of it. Oh, the pine tree on the next page is the same tree on the Mikage property! This is where she tried to protect her descendants... ;_; [that's a crying face]

I HAD TO LEAVE...

I NEVER FOUND MY MANA...

...AND SO I FACED... DEATH.

...MY CHILDREN BEHIND...

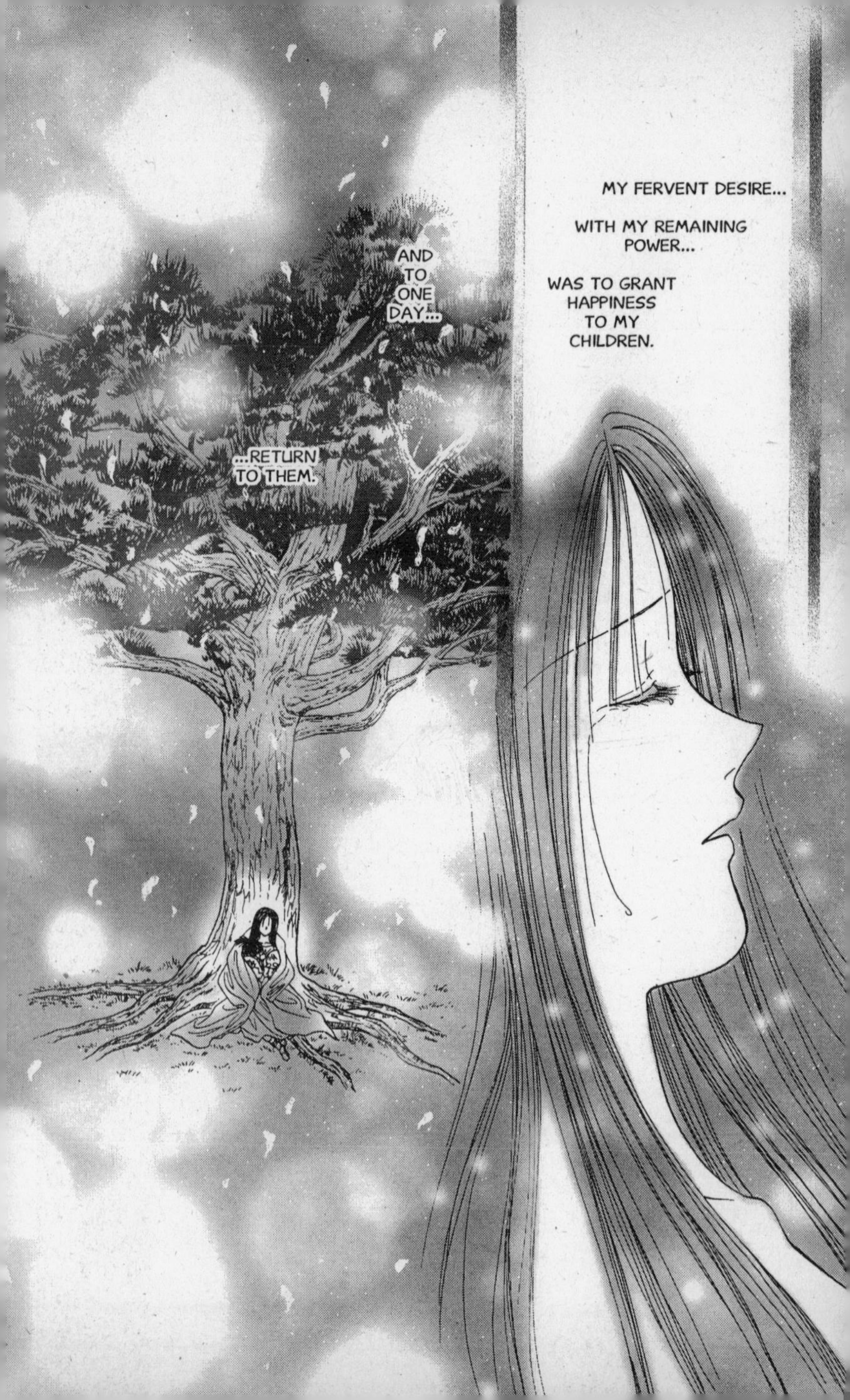
MY FERVENT DESIRE...
WITH MY REMAINING POWER...
WAS TO GRANT HAPPINESS TO MY CHILDREN.
AND TO ONE DAY...
...RETURN TO THEM.

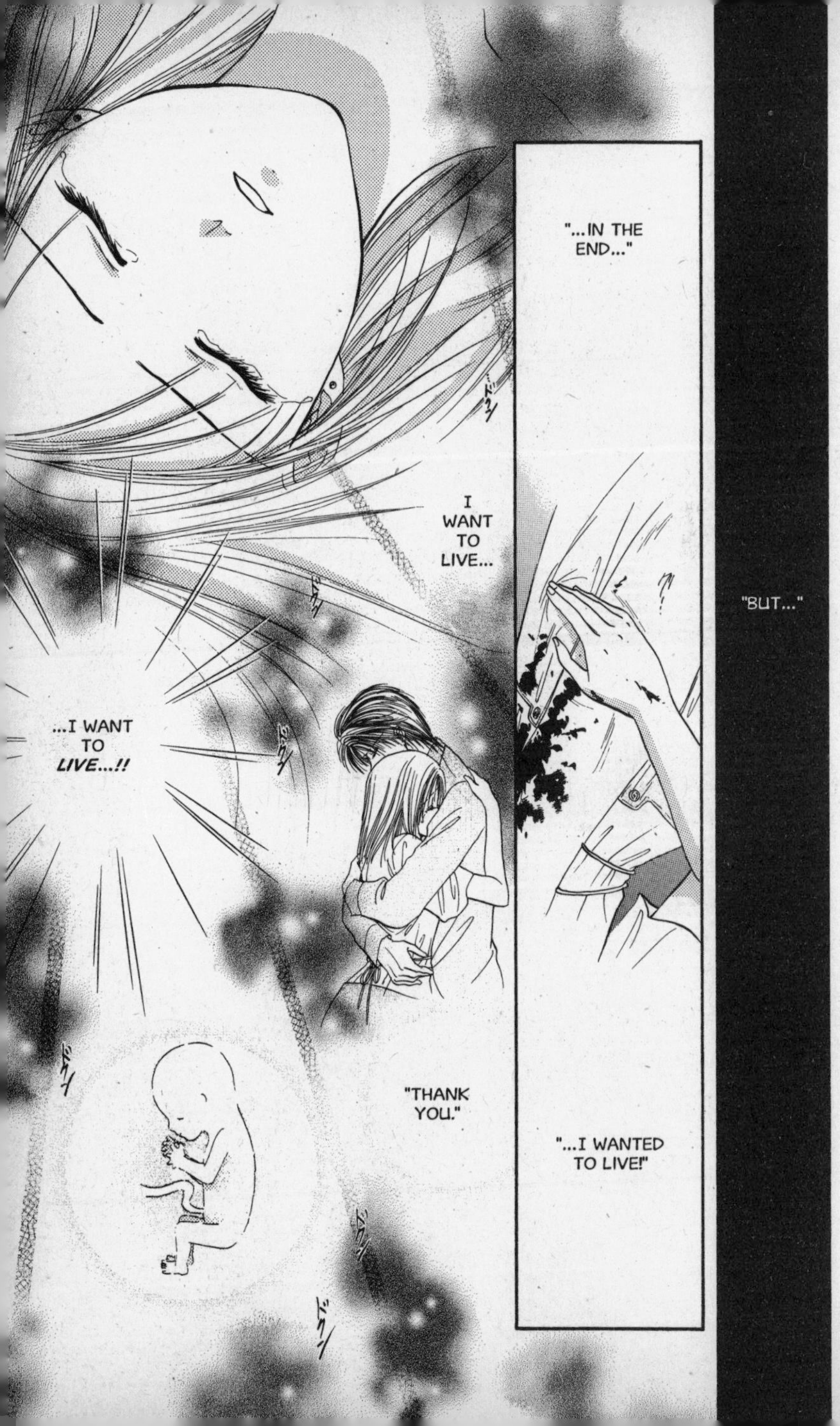
"BUT..."
"...IN THE END..."
"...I WANTED TO LIVE!"
I WANT TO LIVE...
...I WANT TO LIVE...!!
"THANK YOU."

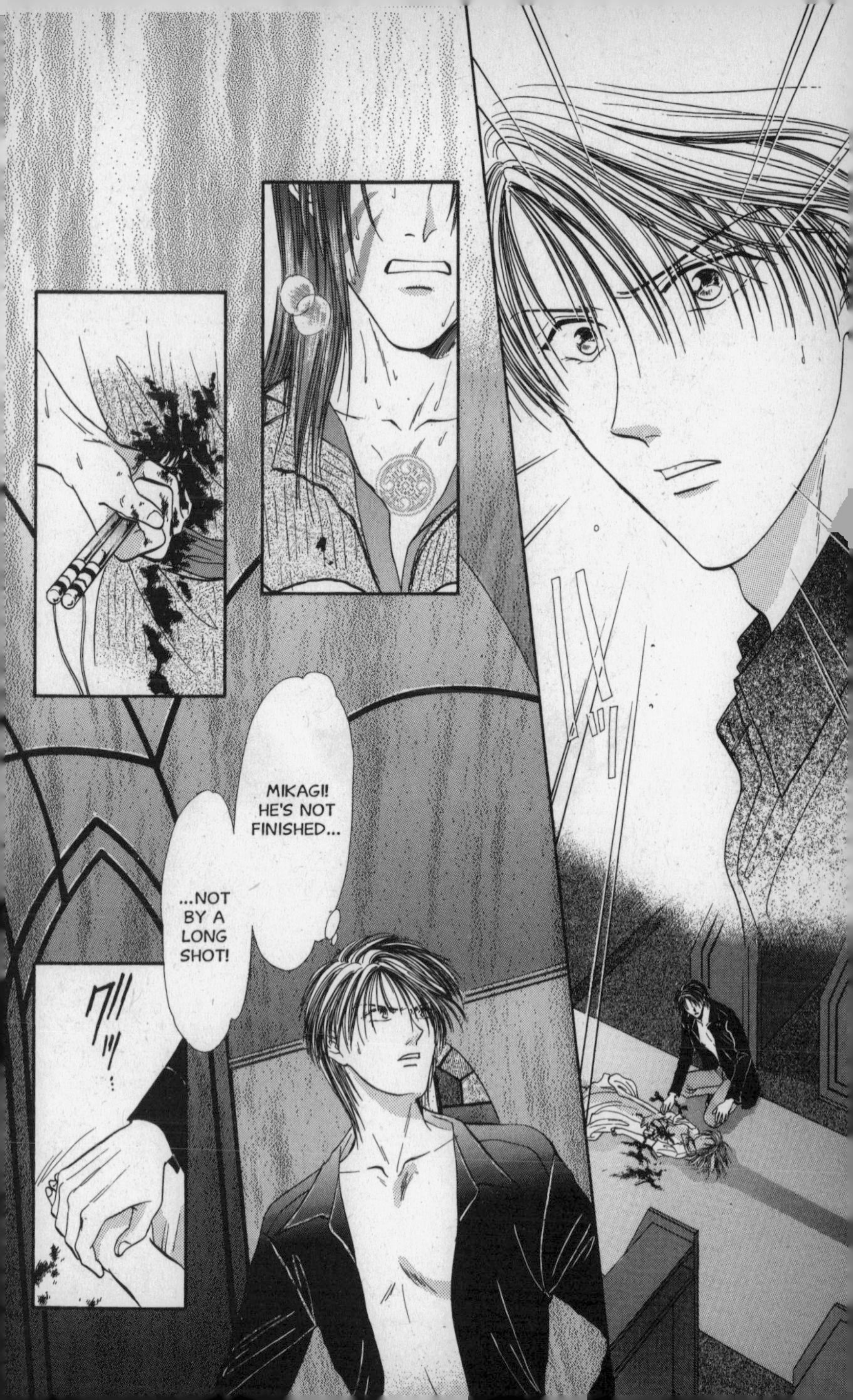
MIKAGI! HE'S NOT FINISHED...
...NOT BY A LONG SHOT!
グッ

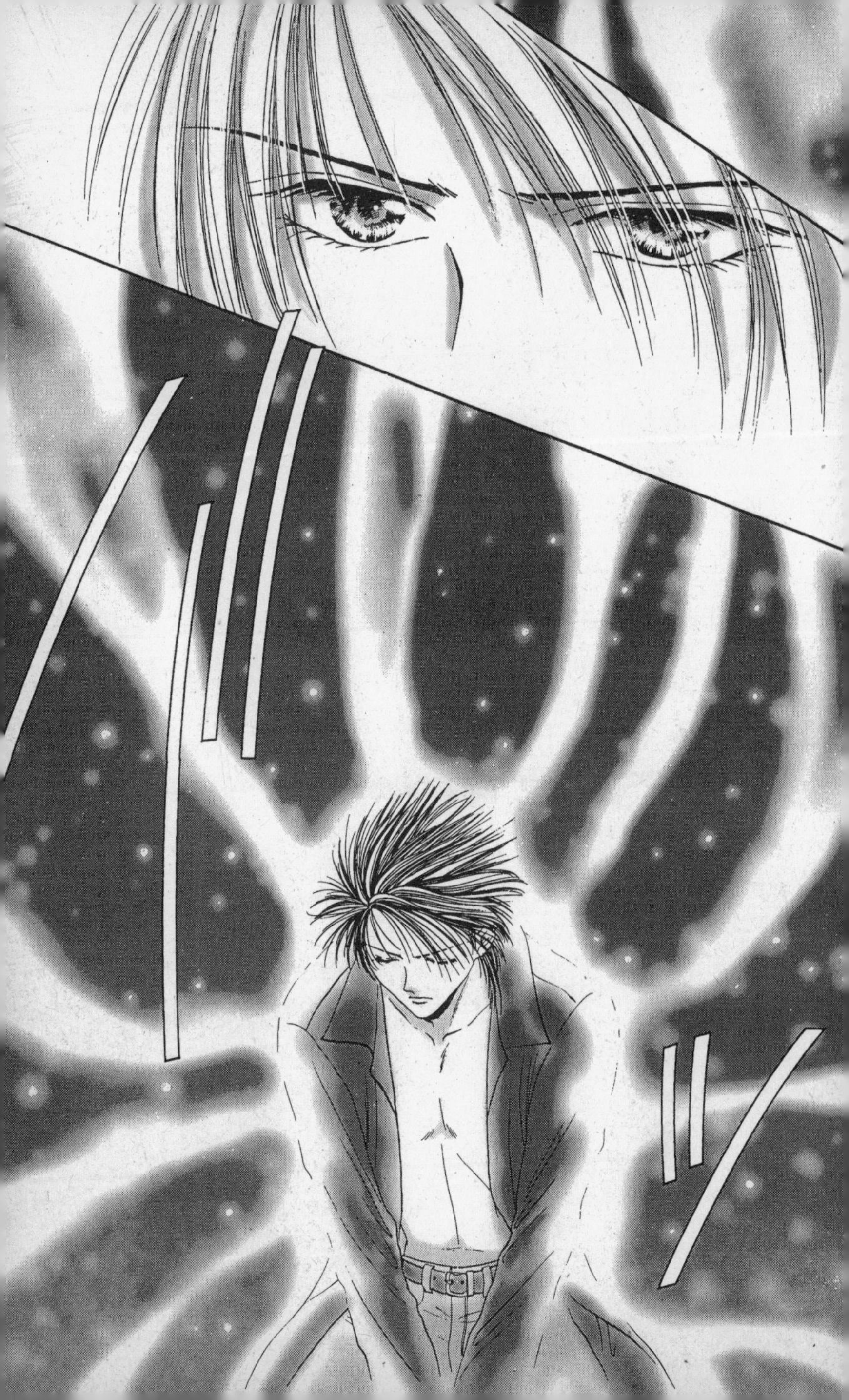

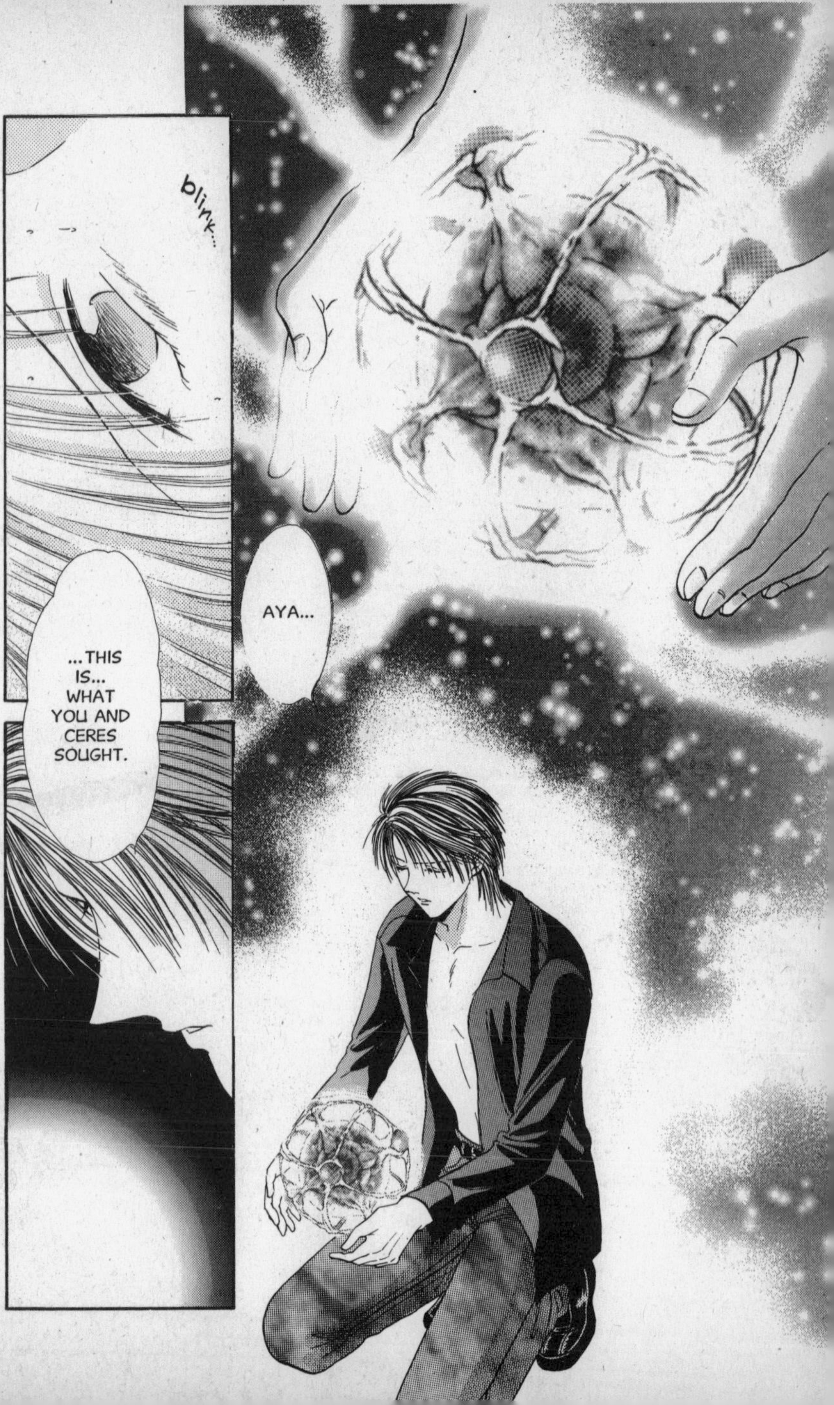
AYA...
blink...
...THIS IS... WHAT YOU AND CERES SOUGHT.

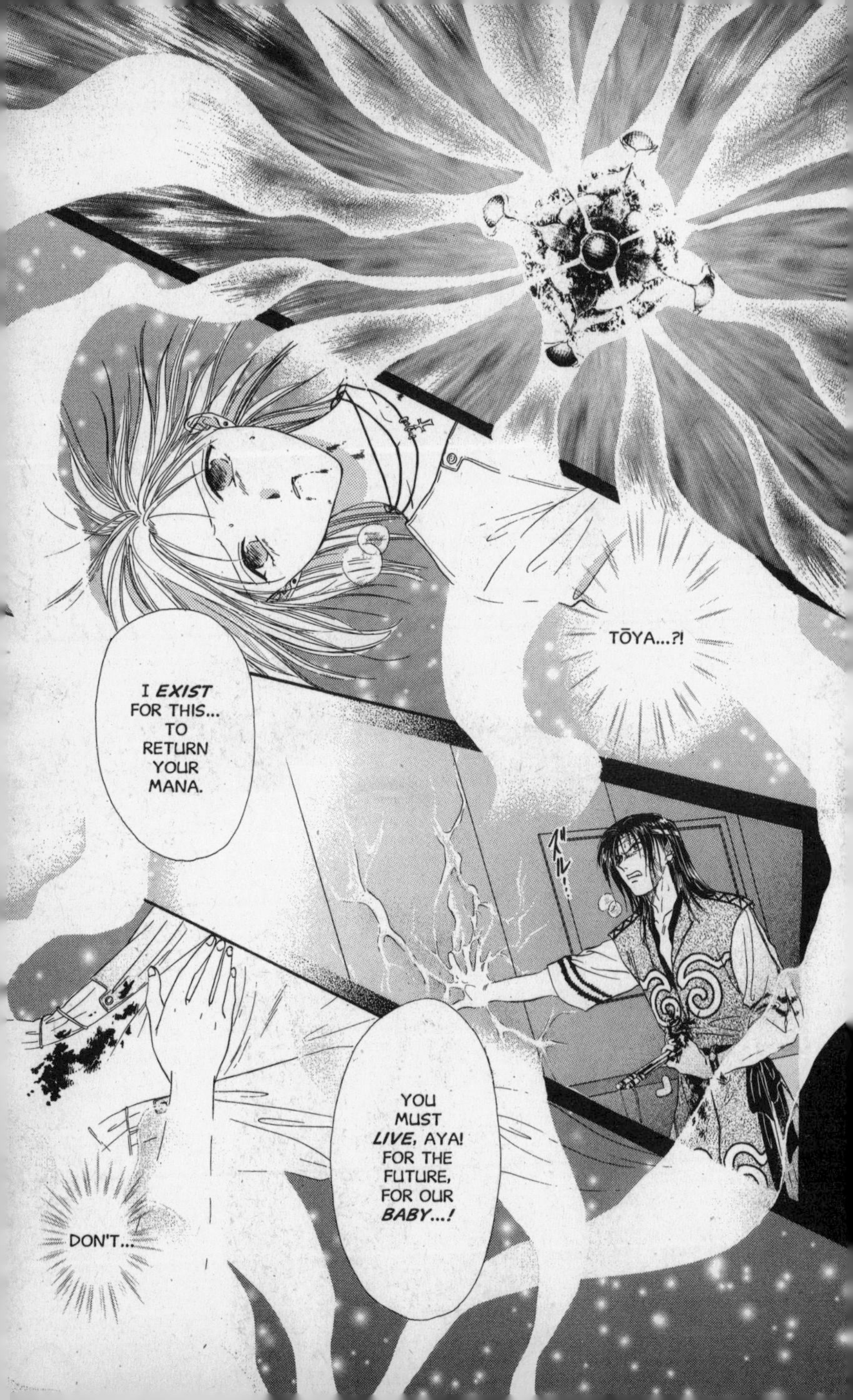

TŌYA...?!
I EXIST FOR THIS... TO RETURN YOUR MANA.
YOU MUST LIVE, AYA! FOR THE FUTURE, FOR OUR BABY...!
DON'T...

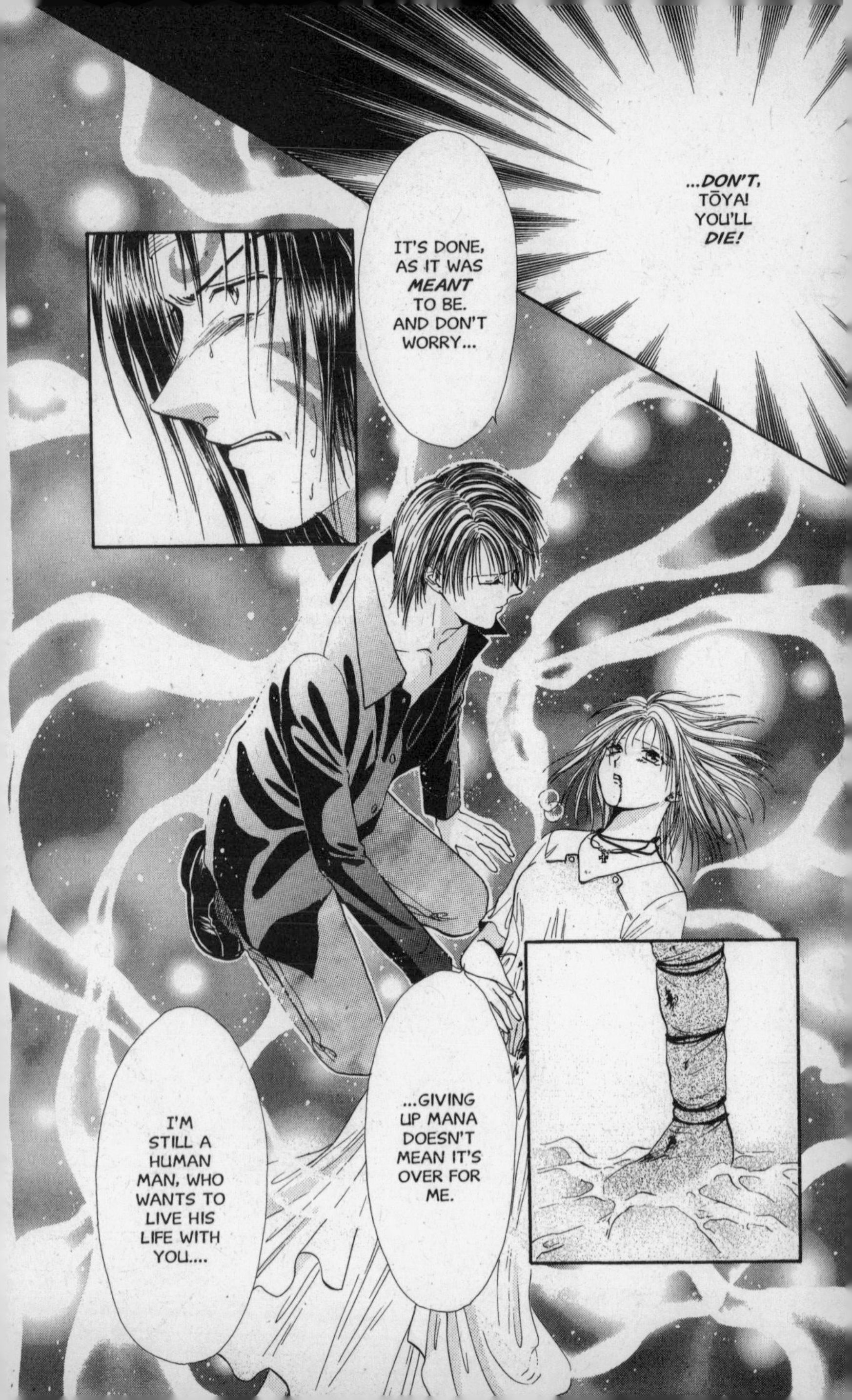
...DON'T, TŌYA! YOU'LL DIE!
IT'S DONE, AS IT WAS MEANT TO BE. AND DON'T WORRY...
...GIVING UP MANA DOESN'T MEAN IT'S OVER FOR ME.
I'M STILL A HUMAN MAN, WHO WANTS TO LIVE HIS LIFE WITH YOU....

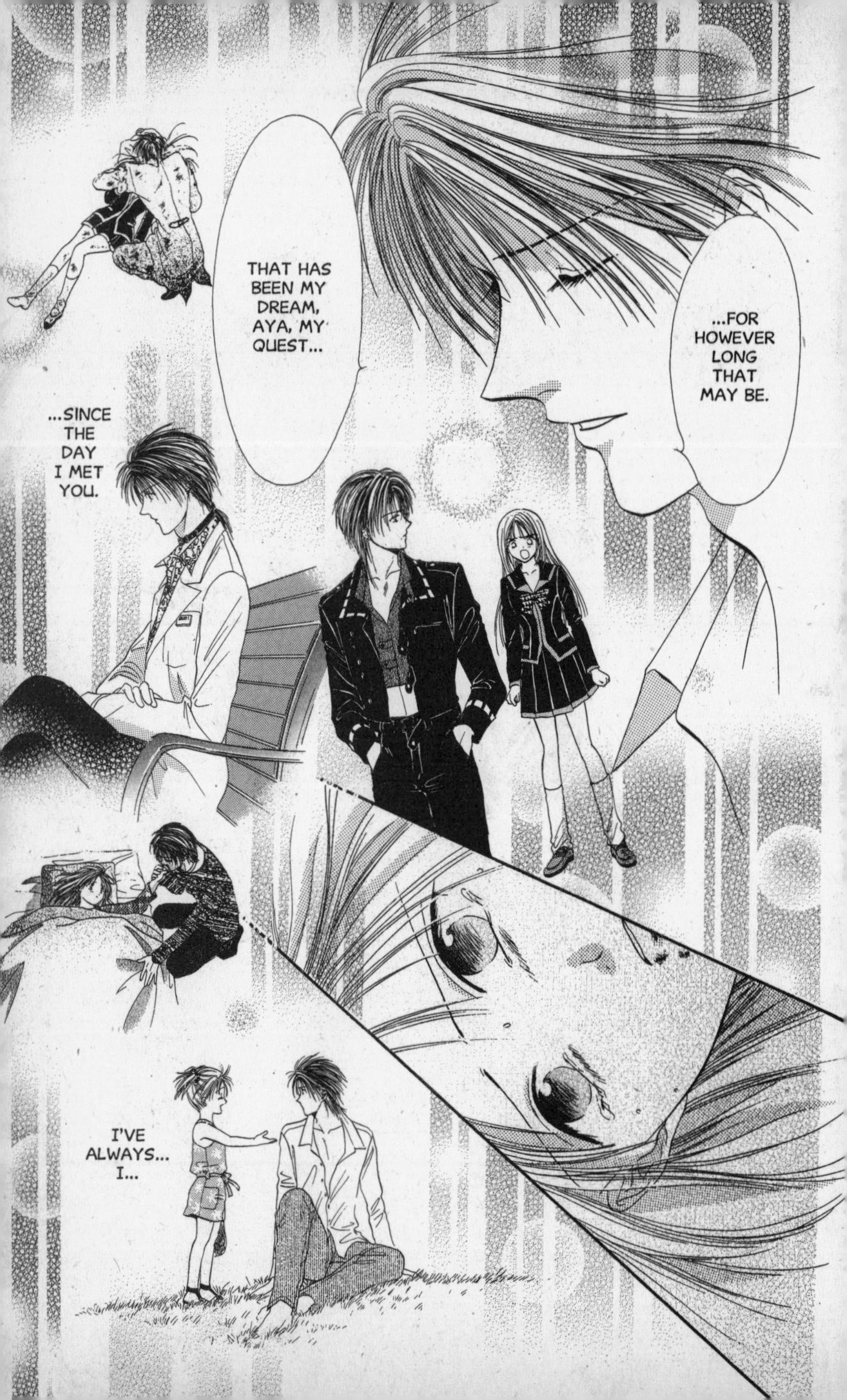
THAT HAS BEEN MY DREAM, AYA, MY QUEST...
...FOR HOWEVER LONG THAT MAY BE.
...SINCE THE DAY I MET YOU.
I'VE ALWAYS... I...

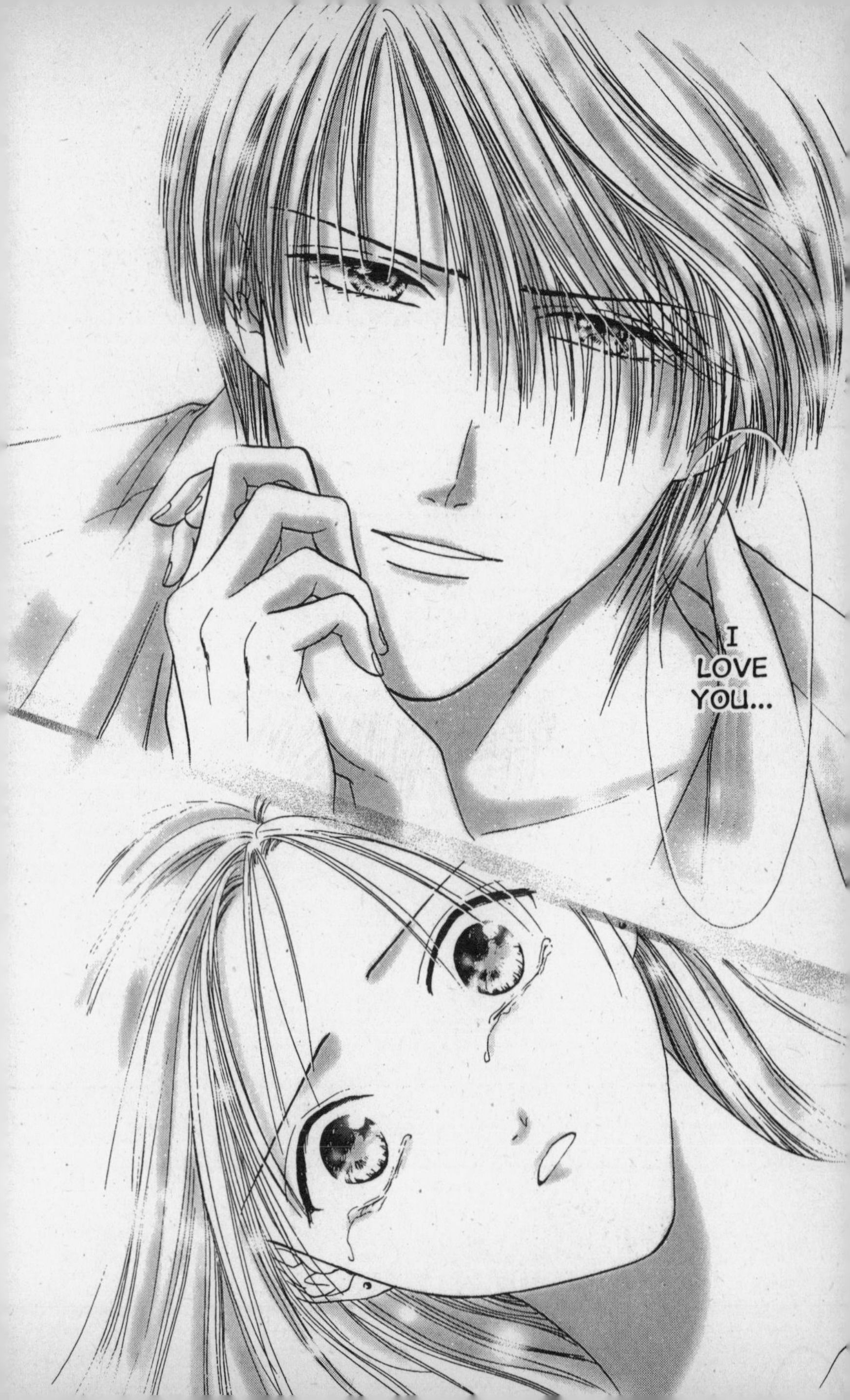
I LOVE YOU...

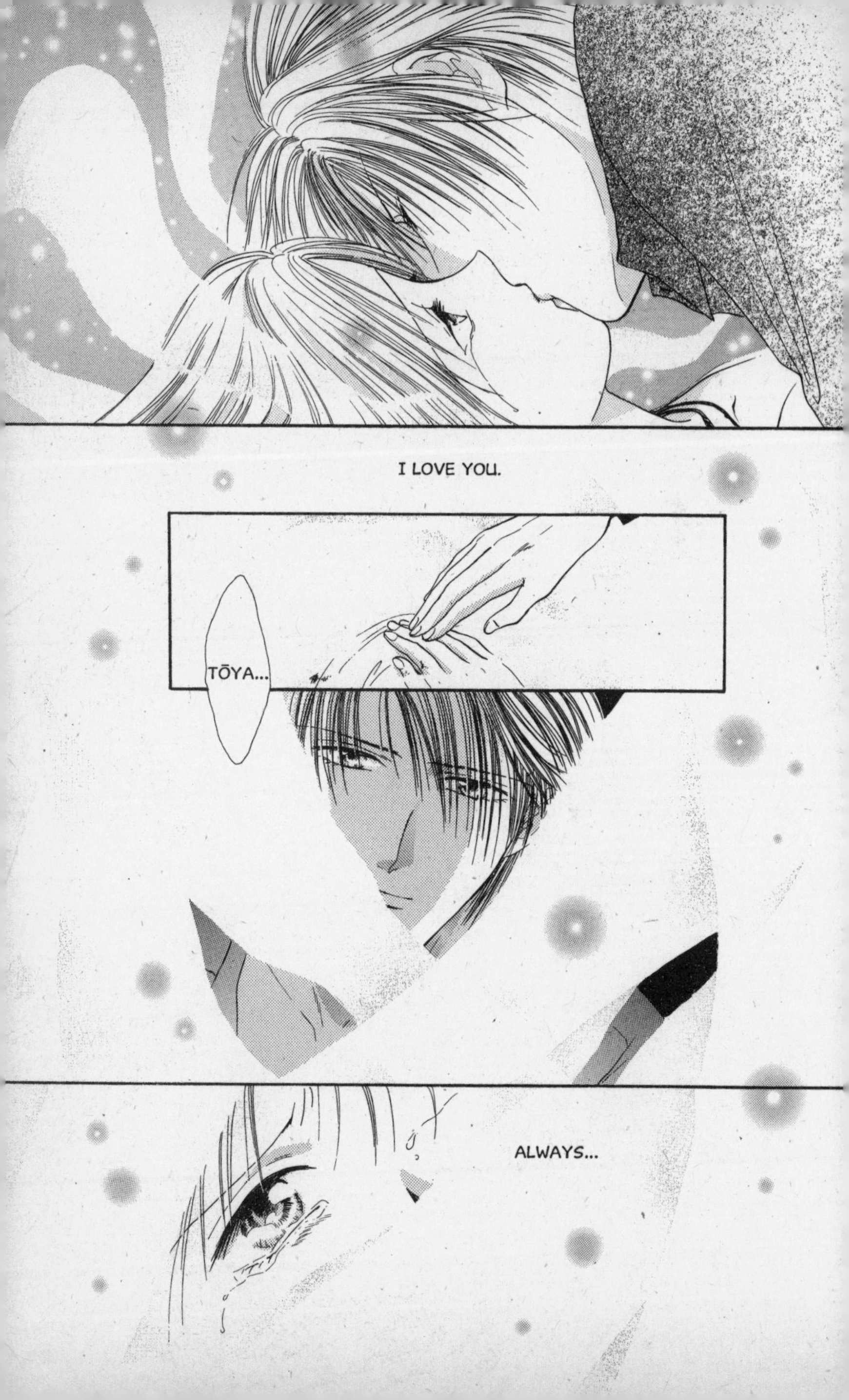
I LOVE YOU.
TŌYA...
ALWAYS...

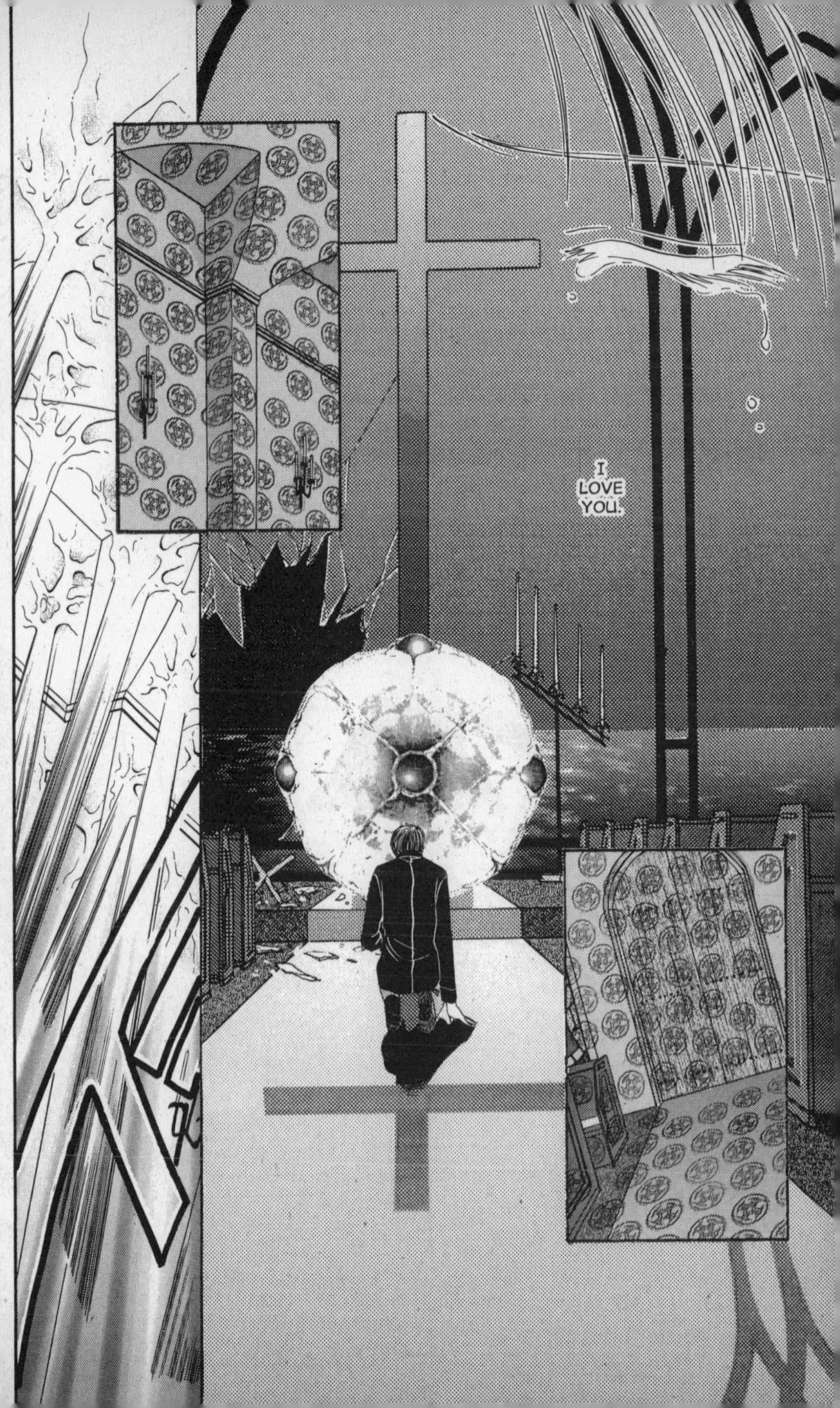
I LOVE YOU.

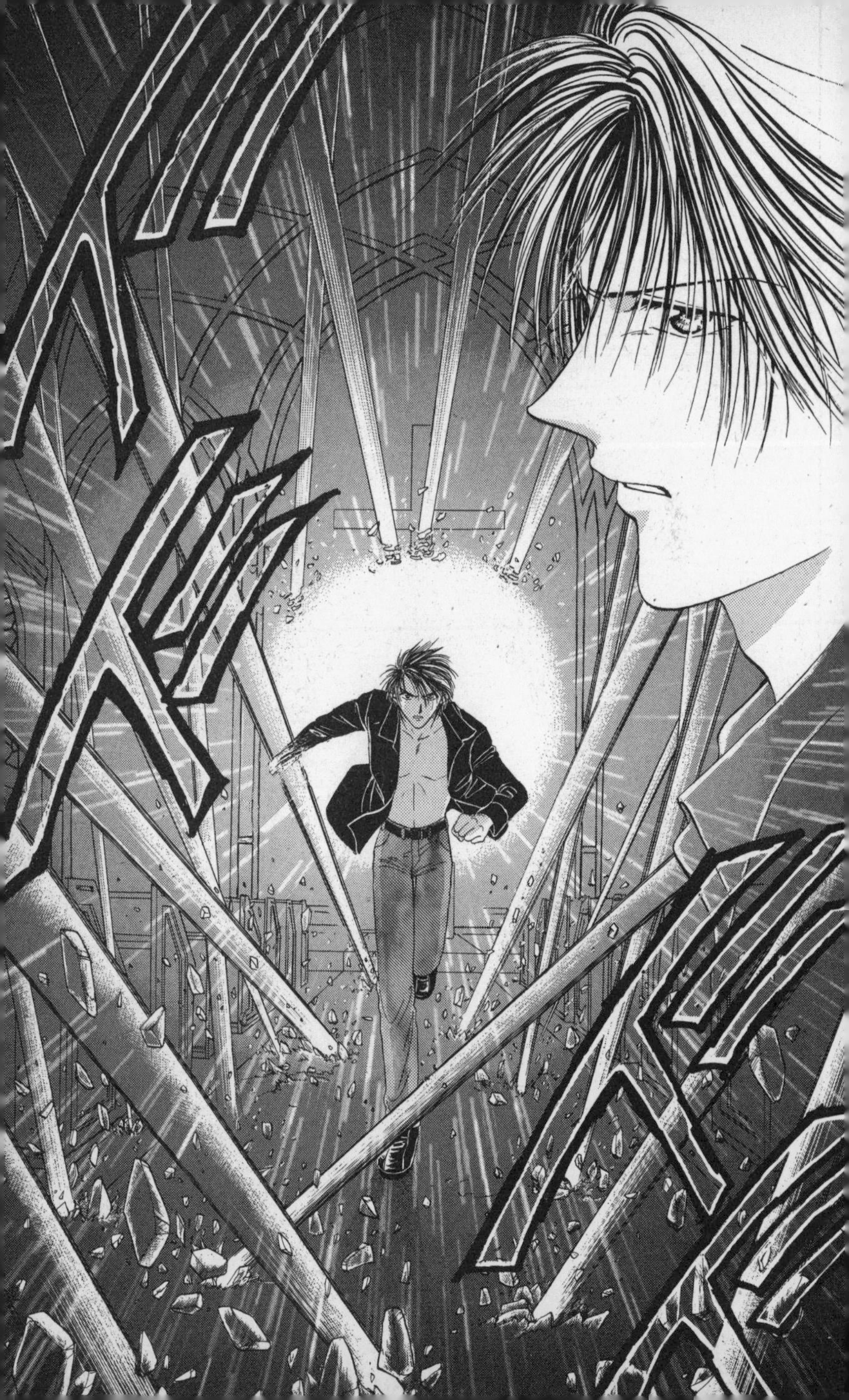

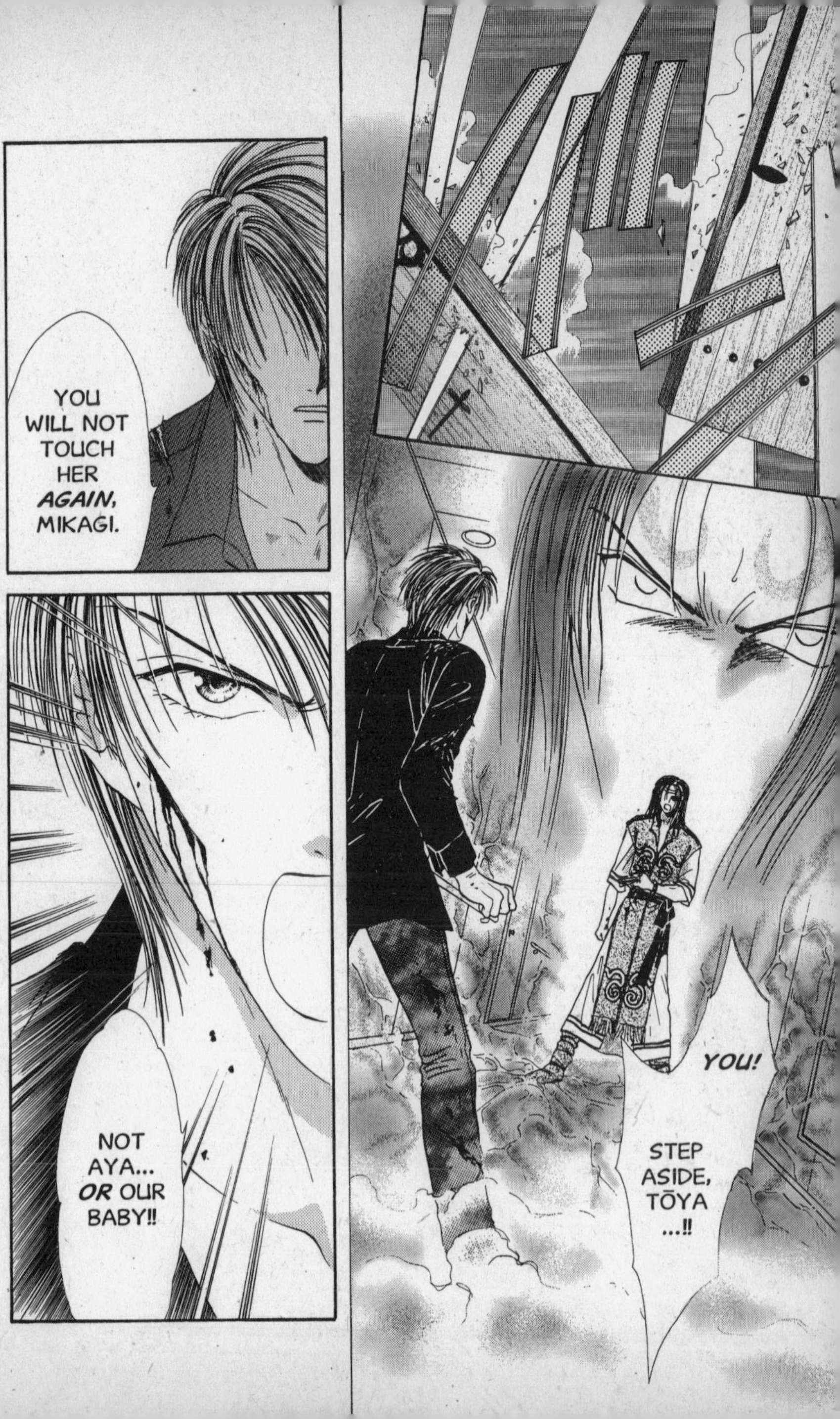
YOU!
STEP ASIDE, TŌYA ...!!
YOU WILL NOT TOUCH HER *AGAIN*, MIKAGI.
NOT AYA... *OR* OUR BABY!!

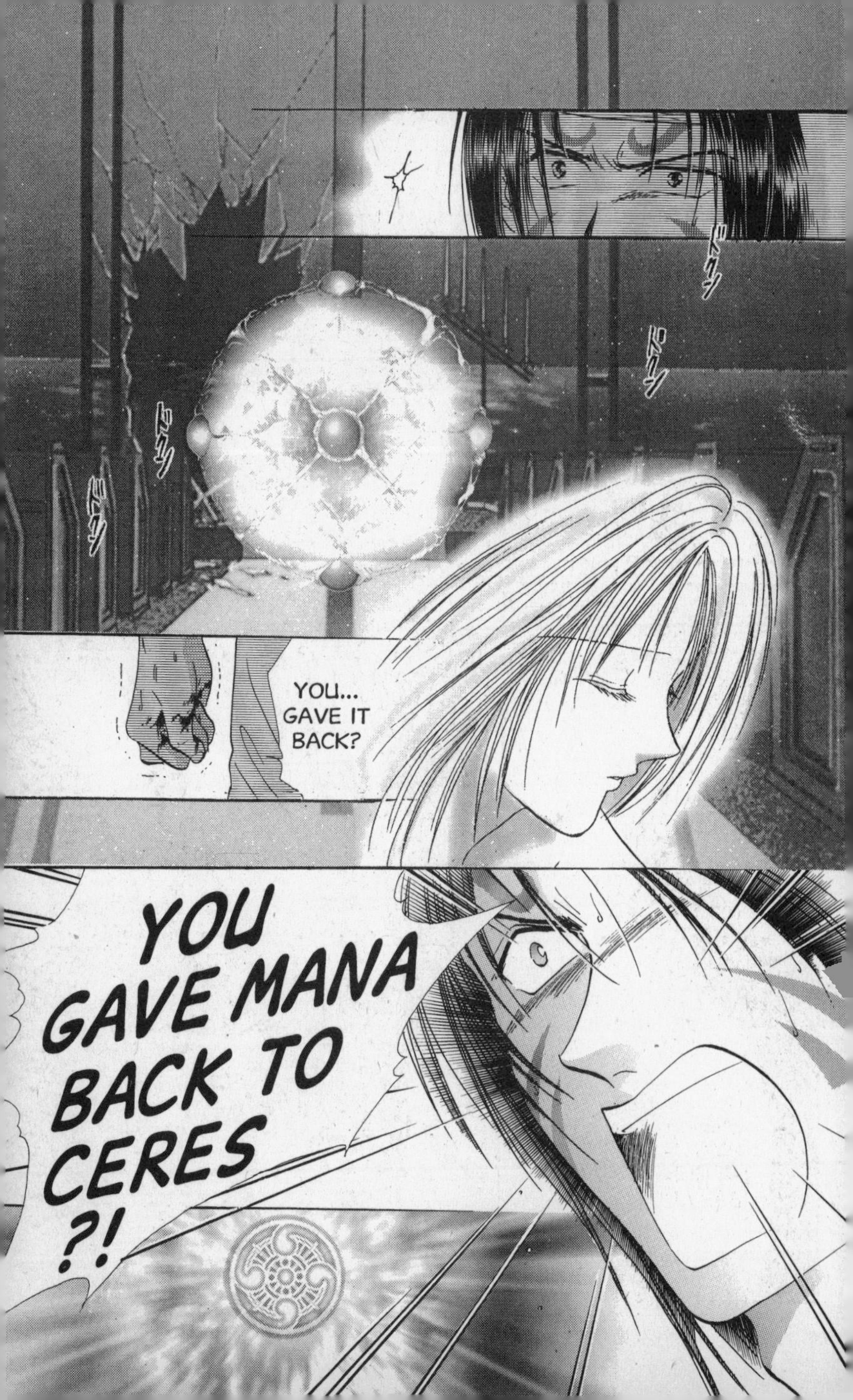
YOU... GAVE IT BACK?
YOU GAVE MANA BACK TO CERES ?!

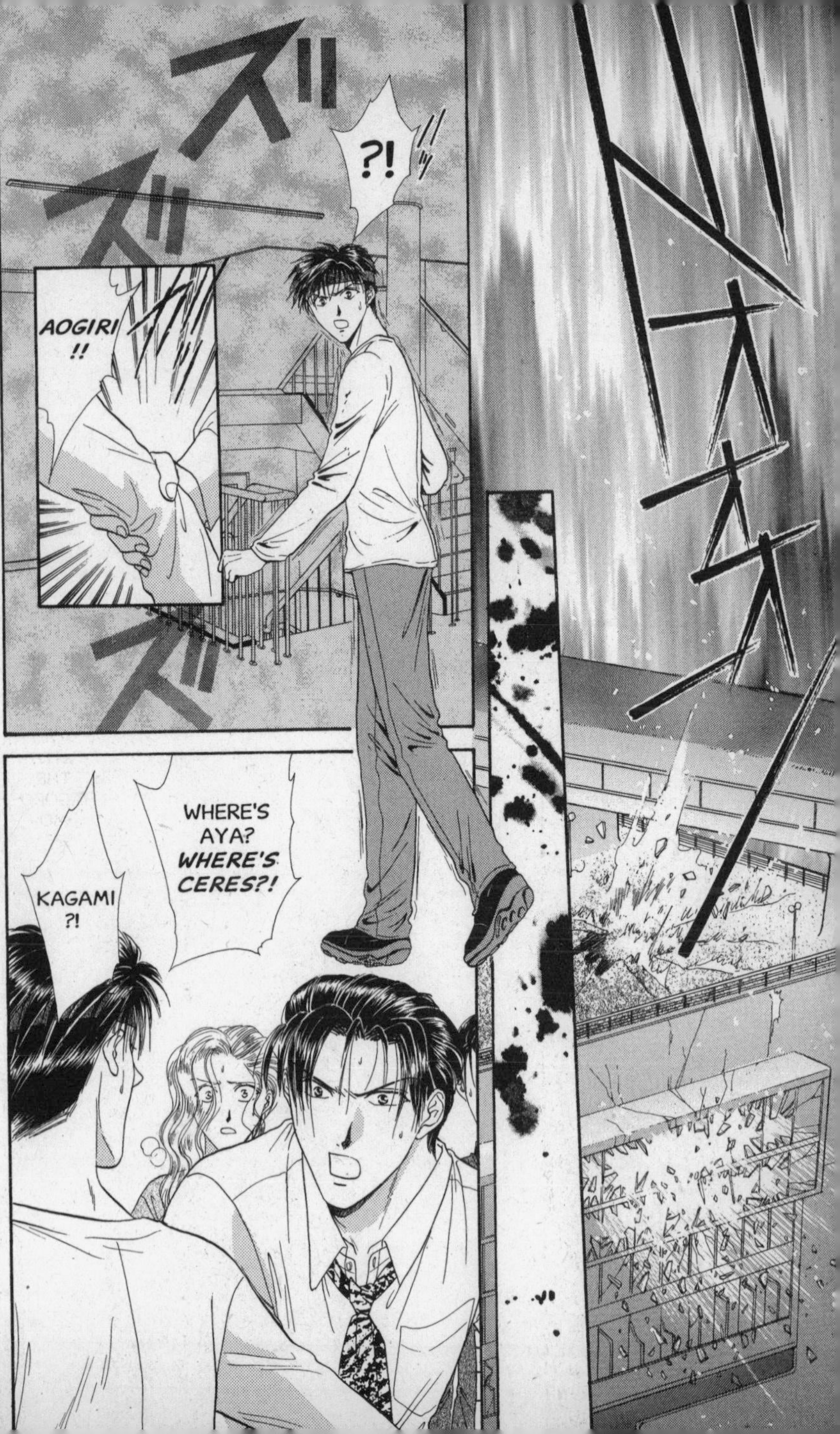
?!
AOGIRI !!
WHERE'S AYA? WHERE'S CERES?!
KAGAMI ?!

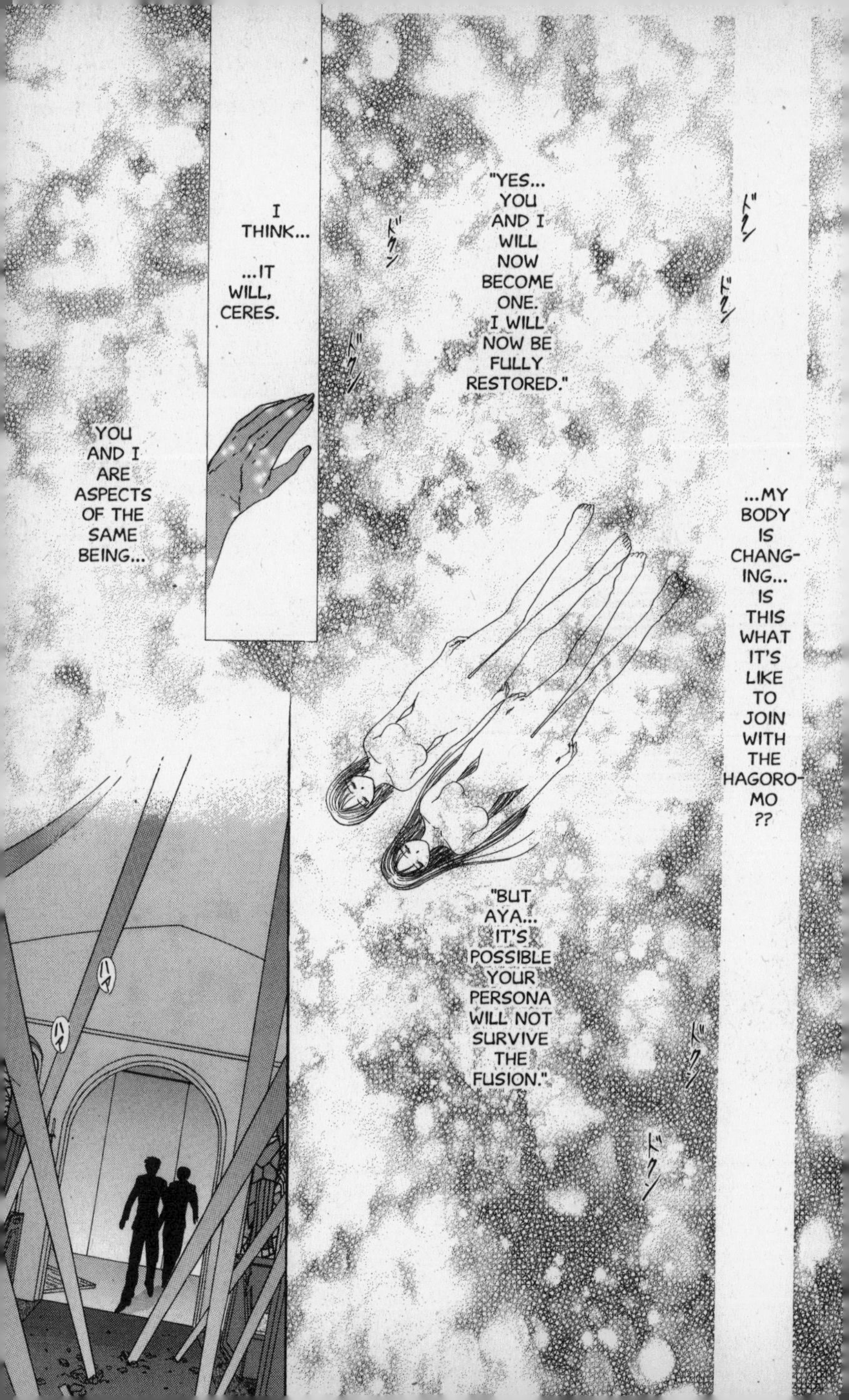
...MY BODY IS CHANGING... IS THIS WHAT IT'S LIKE TO JOIN WITH THE HAGOROMO??
"YES... YOU AND I WILL NOW BECOME ONE. I WILL NOW BE FULLY RESTORED."
"BUT AYA... IT'S POSSIBLE YOUR PERSONA WILL NOT SURVIVE THE FUSION."
I THINK...
...IT WILL, CERES.
YOU AND I ARE ASPECTS OF THE SAME BEING...

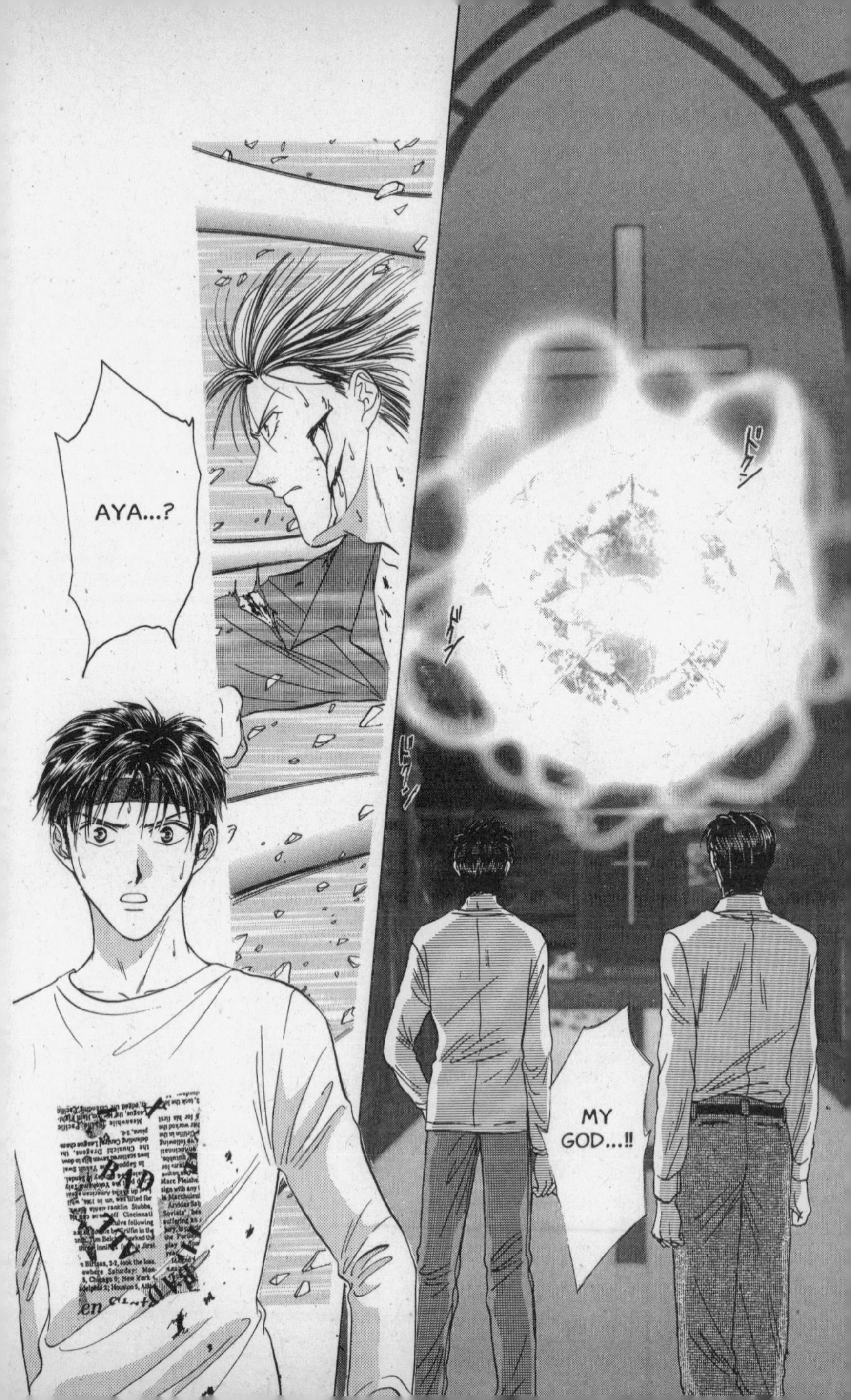
MY GOD...!!
AYA...?

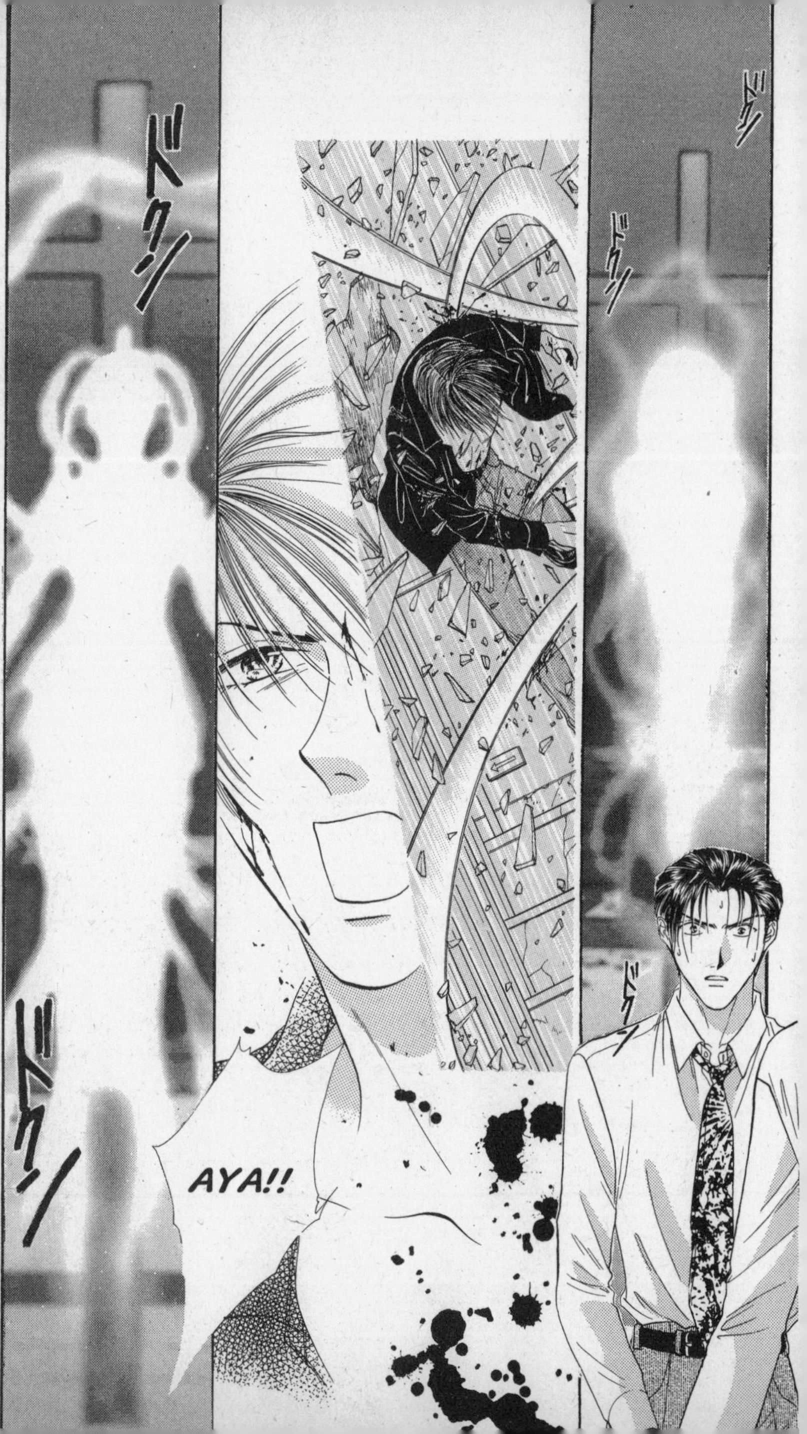
ドクン
ドクン
ドク
AYA!!
ドクン
ドクン

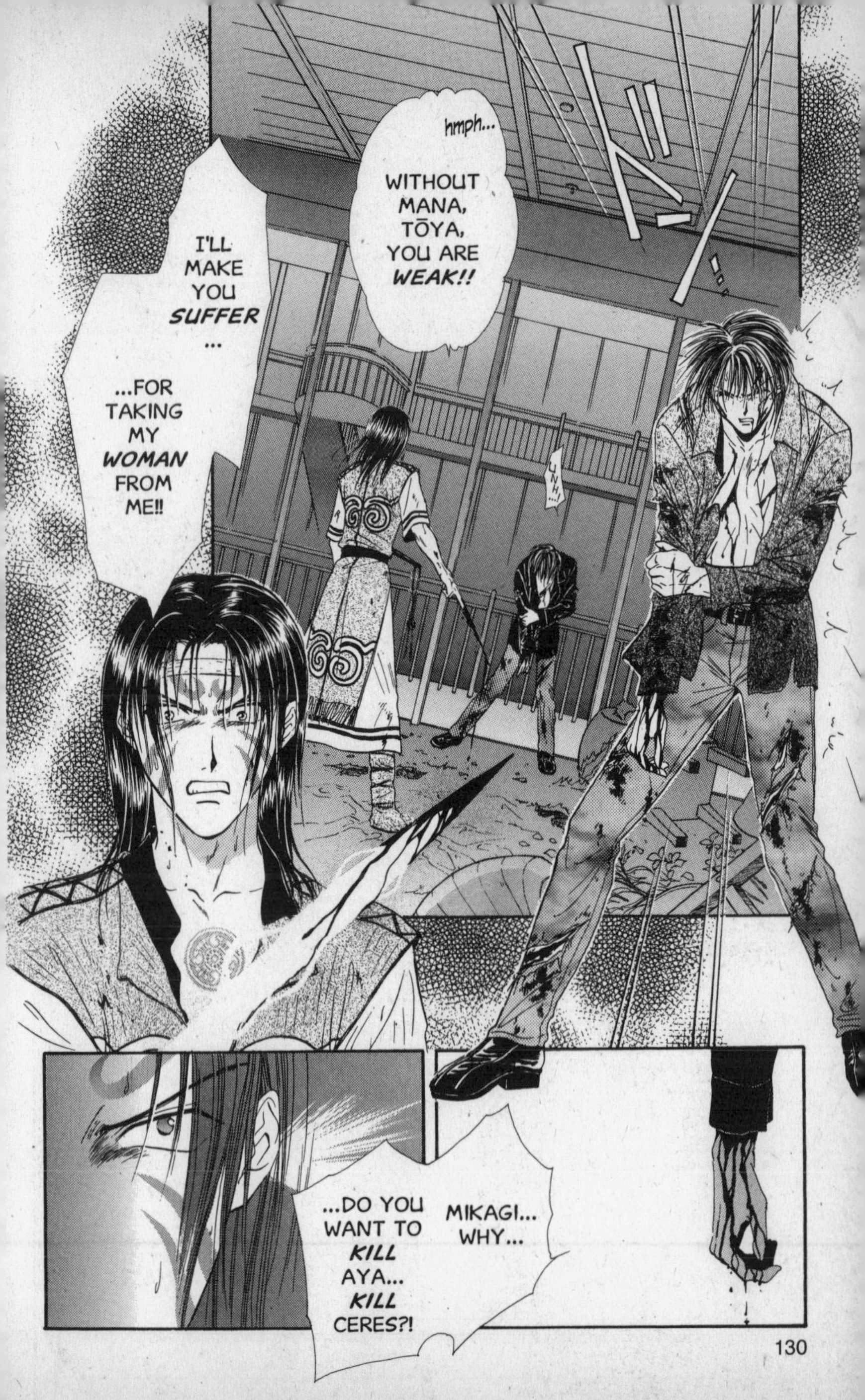
hmph...
WITHOUT MANA, TŌYA, YOU ARE *WEAK!!*
UNH...
I'LL MAKE YOU *SUFFER*...
...FOR TAKING MY *WOMAN* FROM ME!!
MIKAGI... WHY...
...DO YOU WANT TO *KILL* AYA... *KILL* CERES?!

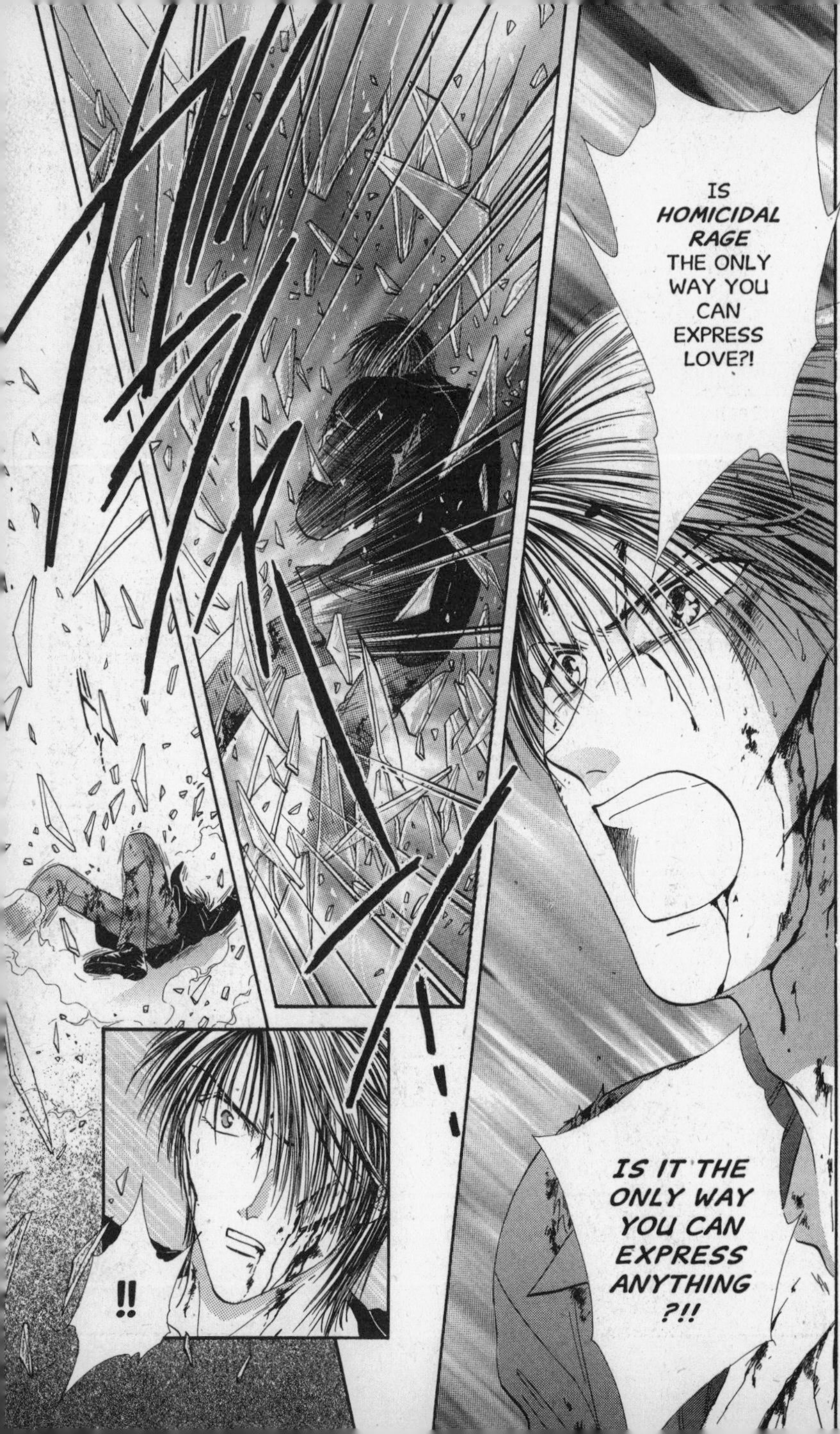
IS *HOMICIDAL RAGE* THE ONLY WAY YOU CAN EXPRESS LOVE?!
IS IT THE ONLY WAY YOU CAN EXPRESS ANYTHING ?!!
!!

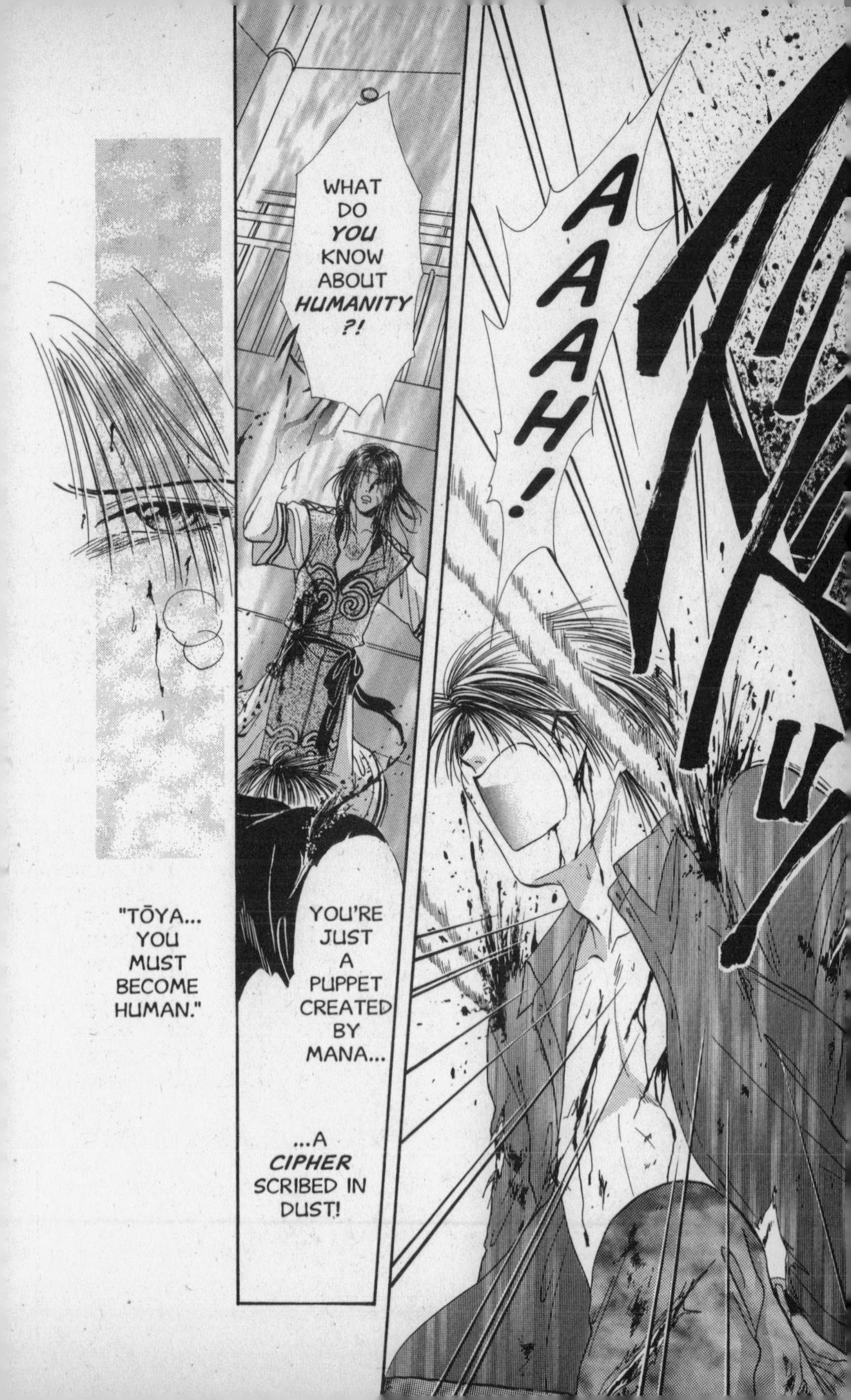
AAAAH!
WHAT DO *YOU* KNOW ABOUT *HUMANITY* ?!
YOU'RE JUST A PUPPET CREATED BY MANA...
...A *CIPHER* SCRIBED IN DUST!
"TŌYA... YOU MUST BECOME HUMAN."

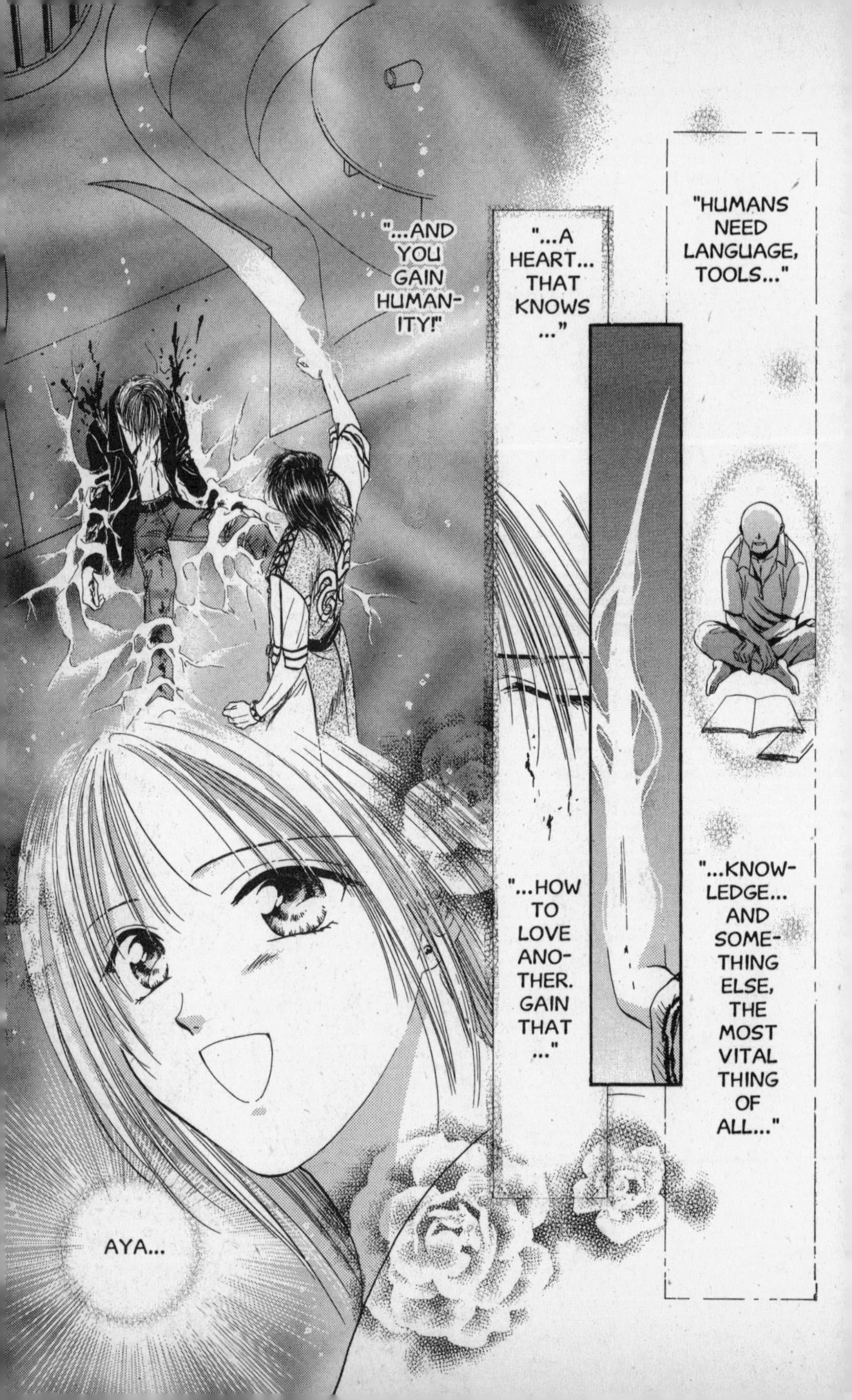
"HUMANS NEED LANGUAGE, TOOLS..."
"...KNOW-LEDGE... AND SOME-THING ELSE, THE MOST VITAL THING OF ALL..."
"...A HEART... THAT KNOWS..."
"...HOW TO LOVE ANO-THER. GAIN THAT..."
"...AND YOU GAIN HUMAN-ITY!"
AYA...

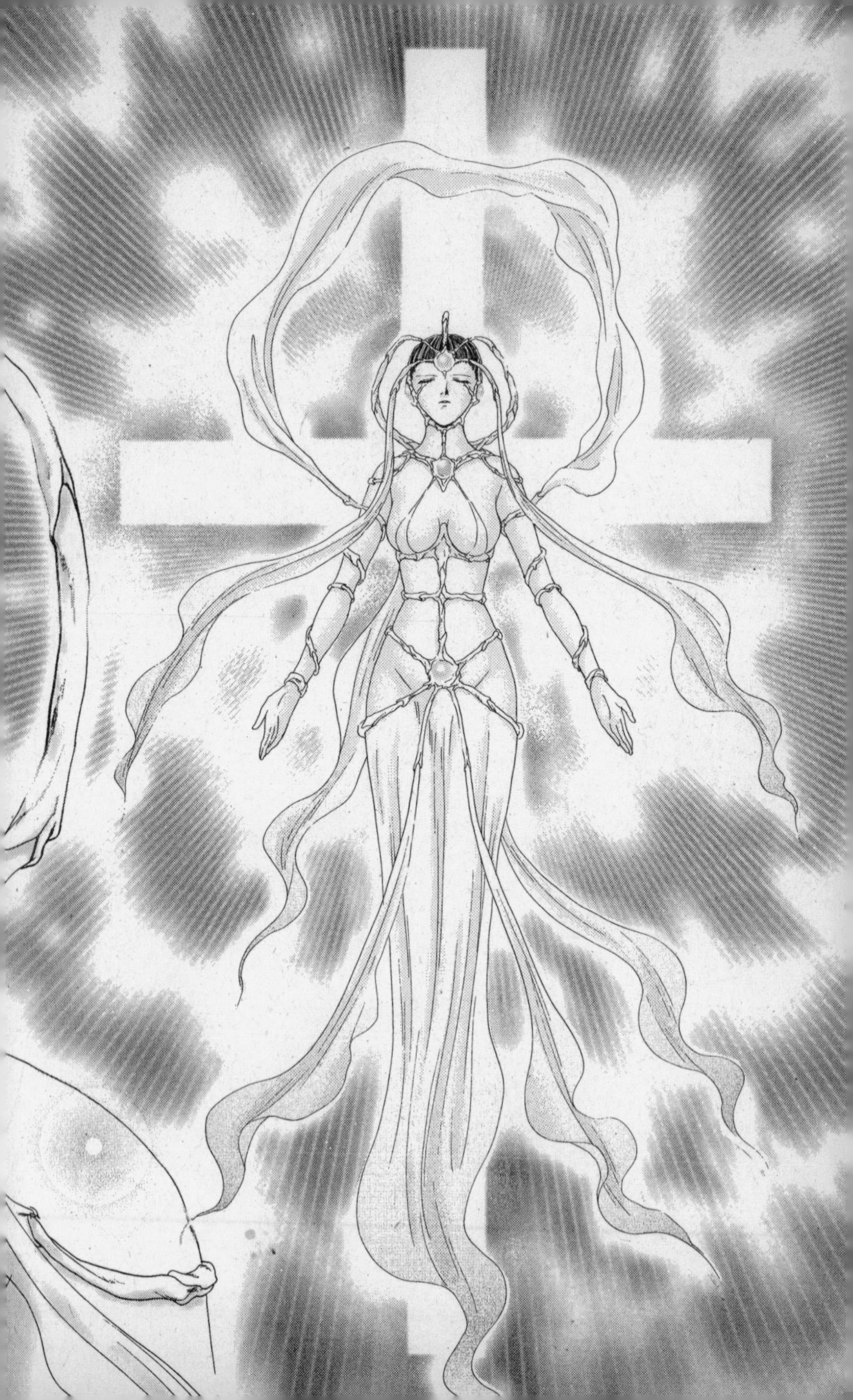

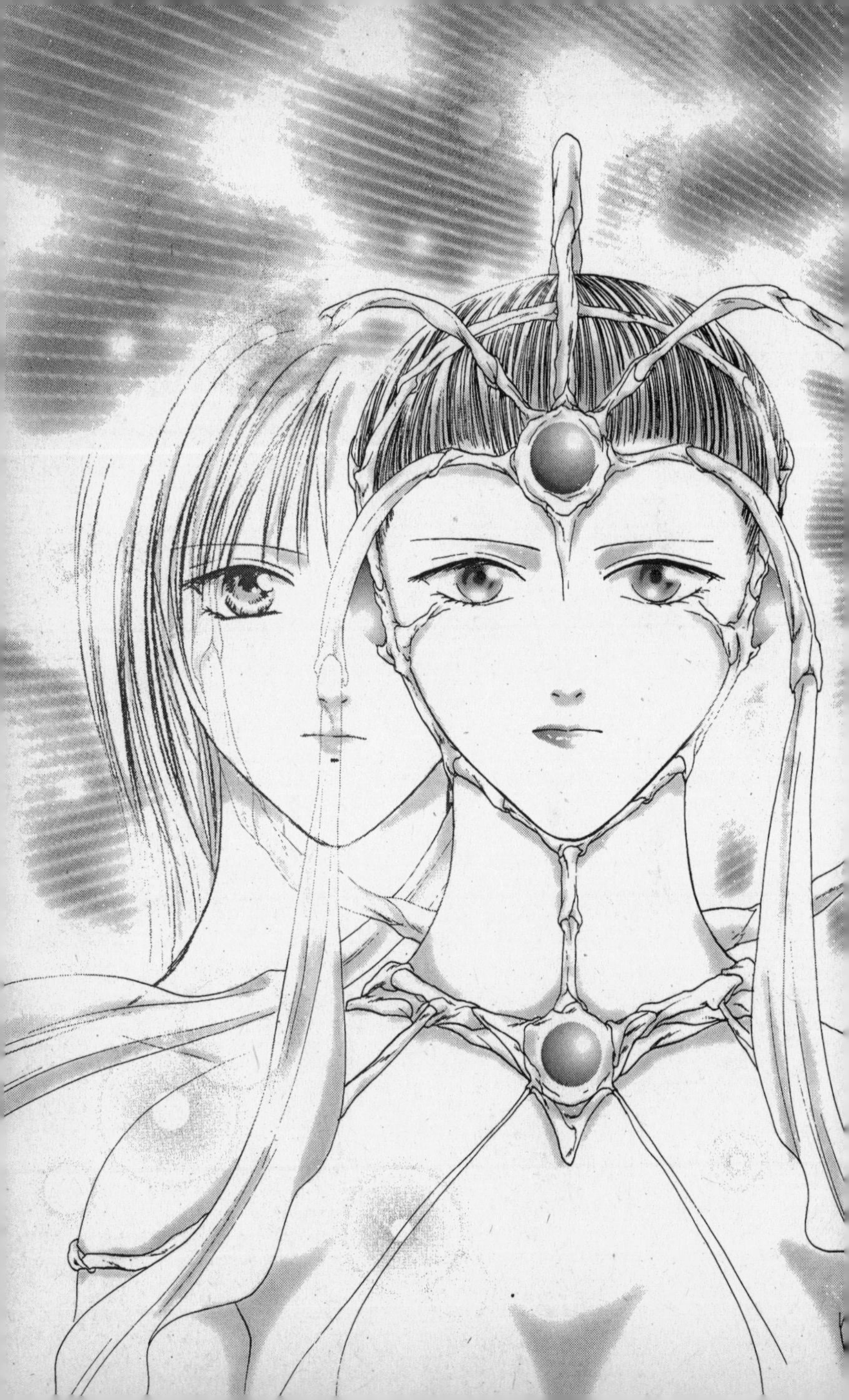

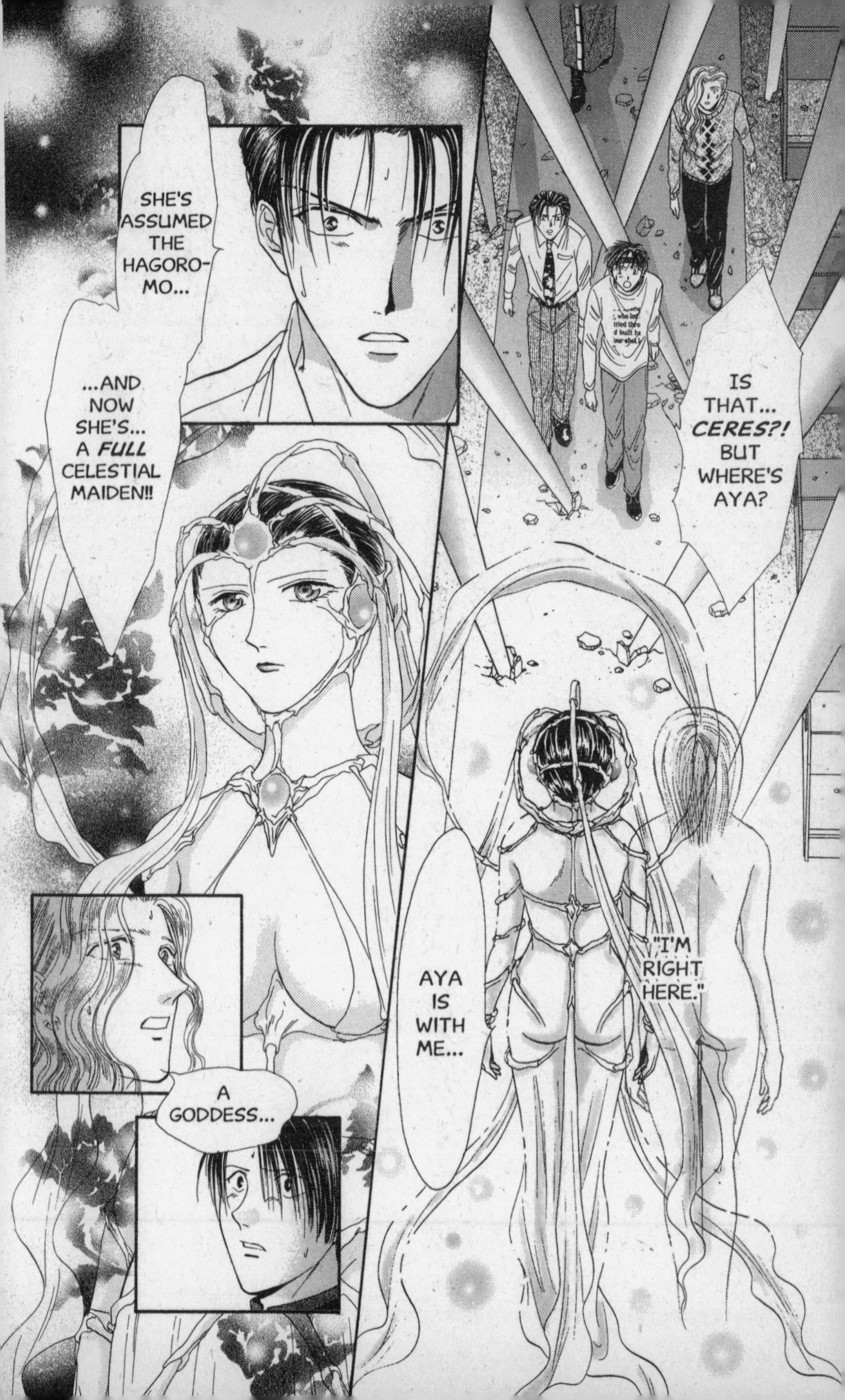
IS THAT... CERES?! BUT WHERE'S AYA?
AYA IS WITH ME...
"I'M RIGHT HERE."
SHE'S ASSUMED THE HAGORO-MO...
...AND NOW SHE'S... A FULL CELESTIAL MAIDEN!!
A GODDESS...

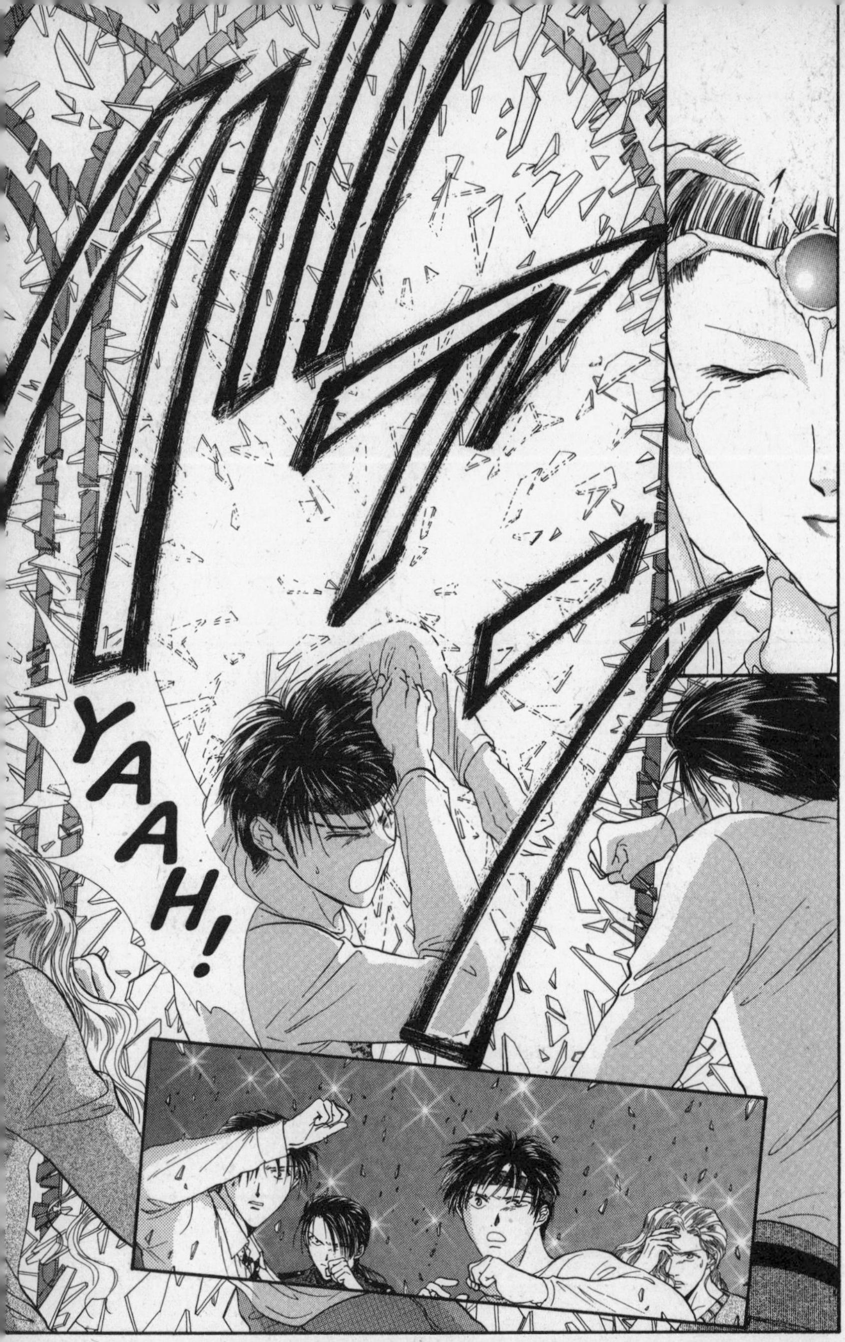
YAAH!

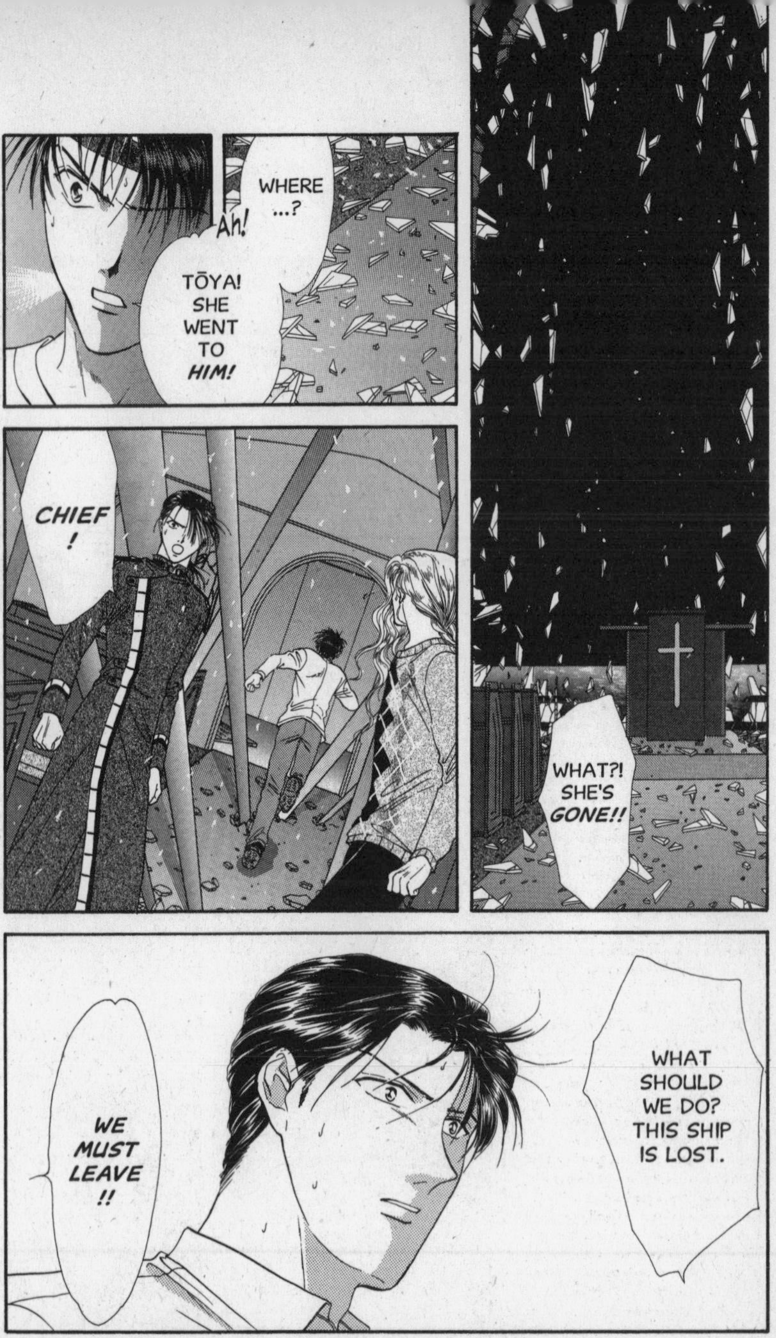
WHAT?! SHE'S GONE!!
WHERE ...?
Ah!
TŌYA! SHE WENT TO HIM!
CHIEF!
WHAT SHOULD WE DO? THIS SHIP IS LOST.
WE MUST LEAVE!!

I made my final comments on **Ceres** in the artbook, so please refer to that for more in-depth thoughts...(Only people who have read the end of the manga should read beyond this point.)

I didn't make a perfectly happy ending this time...though the end feels like there could be more. ◡ Well, if I were asked to make more, the enemy would be Ragnarok, and it would be a global battle to contend for Aya and Tōya's child. What is this, a Hollywood movie?! I don't work for a seinen magazine [an anthology for mature adults], so I won't go that far. It won't be "Aya's story" anymore...(Maybe it could happen in the novels?)

Tōya and Ceres (and celestial maidens) are ultimately weak. Creatures that don't arise from the union of a male and a female — through sexual reproduction — are "weaker" as a species because they don't have the benefit of genetic diversification. I kept the true origins of the celestial maidens ambiguous, because I wanted to leave that to the readers' imaginations. Which came first: mana or the celestial maidens? That's also a mystery.

I went back and forth on Tōya's origins, but I kept the idea that he was created in the ocean, and that the "evolutionary path" that led to him was different from other human beings. Mana allows transformation by utilizing the genetic memories of evolution. Tōya is an "imitation"...created from the genetic data of the finest of the men with whom Ceres was "intimate." ◡ So I guess he contains information from Mikagi, too! When the episode of Tōya's webbed fingers came out, virtually all my readers exclaimed, "is he a kappa (water goblin)?!" ◡ Ah, you see, the journey all fetuses take during the nine months we spend in our mothers' wombs reflects **one billion years of evolution!** (We start as an egg, a tail and webs on our hands and feet grow and recede, and we are finally born as human beings!!) Tōya and the celestial maidens could use that information at will. But human beings were the greatest (?) product of evolution.

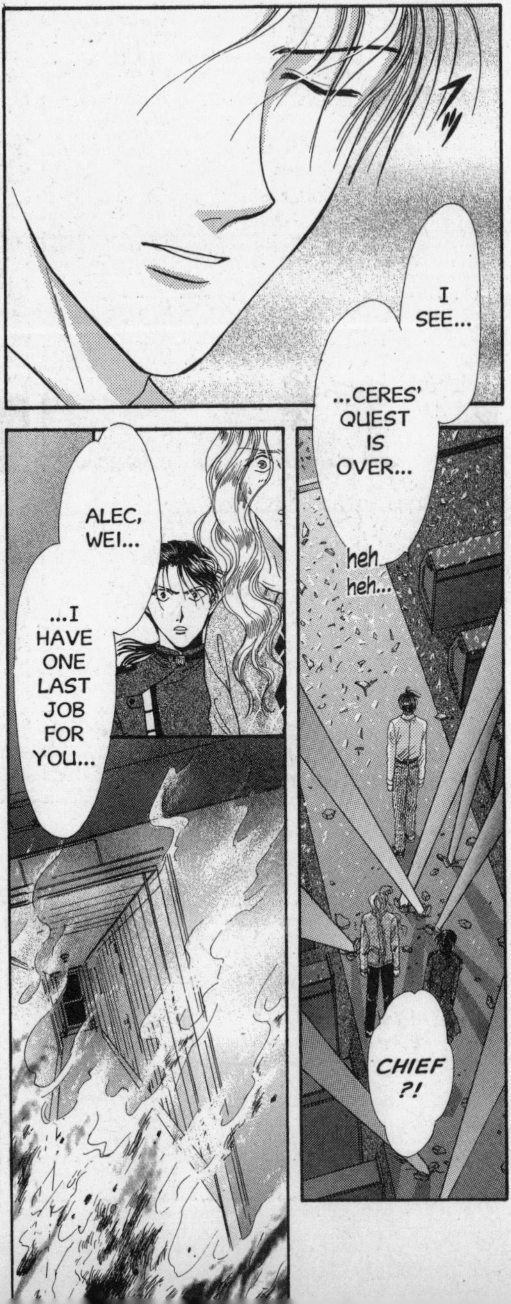
I SEE...
...CERES' QUEST IS OVER...
heh heh...
CHIEF?!
ALEC, WEI...
...I HAVE ONE LAST JOB FOR YOU...

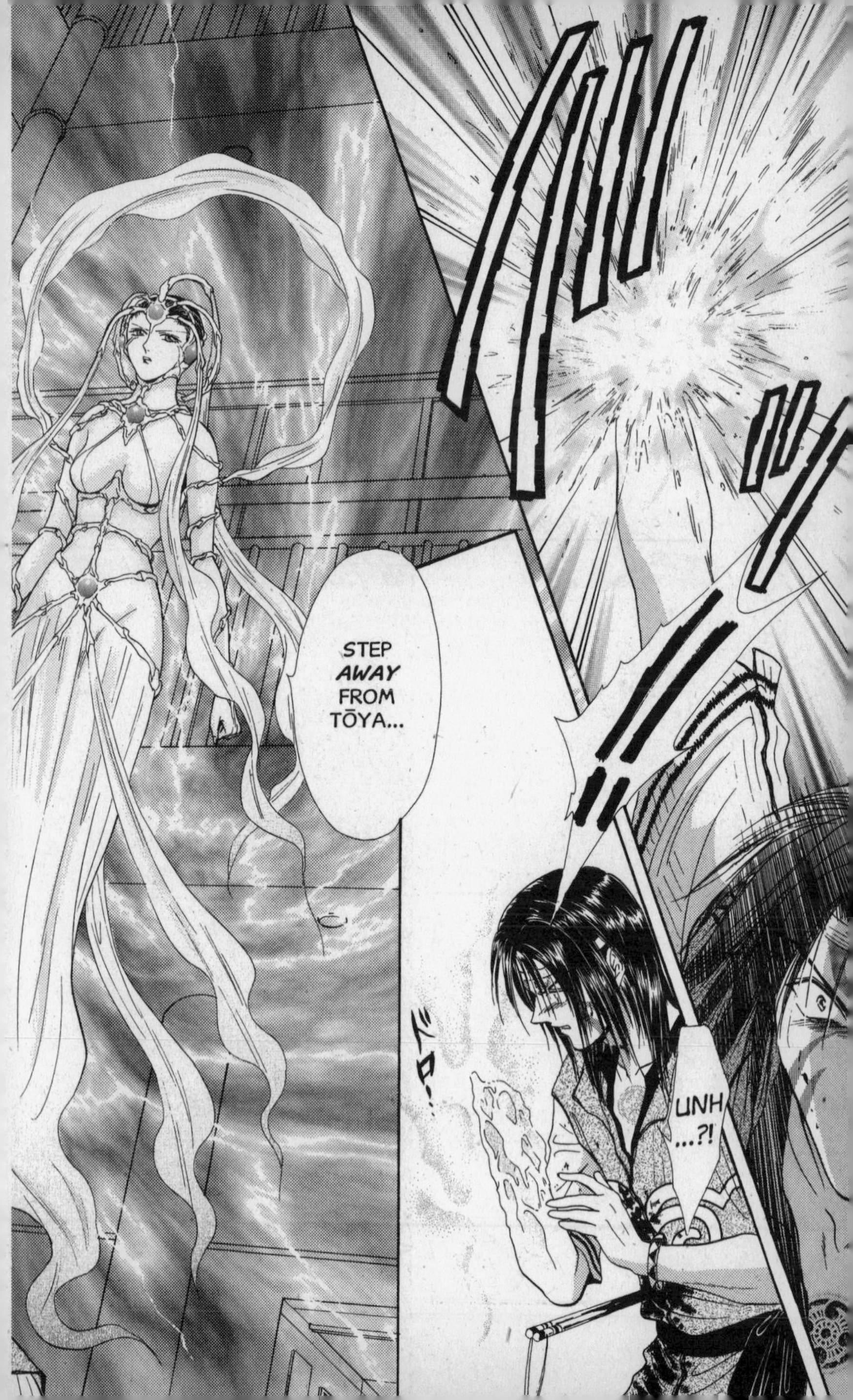

ドロ‥
UNH ...?!
STEP *AWAY* FROM TŌYA...

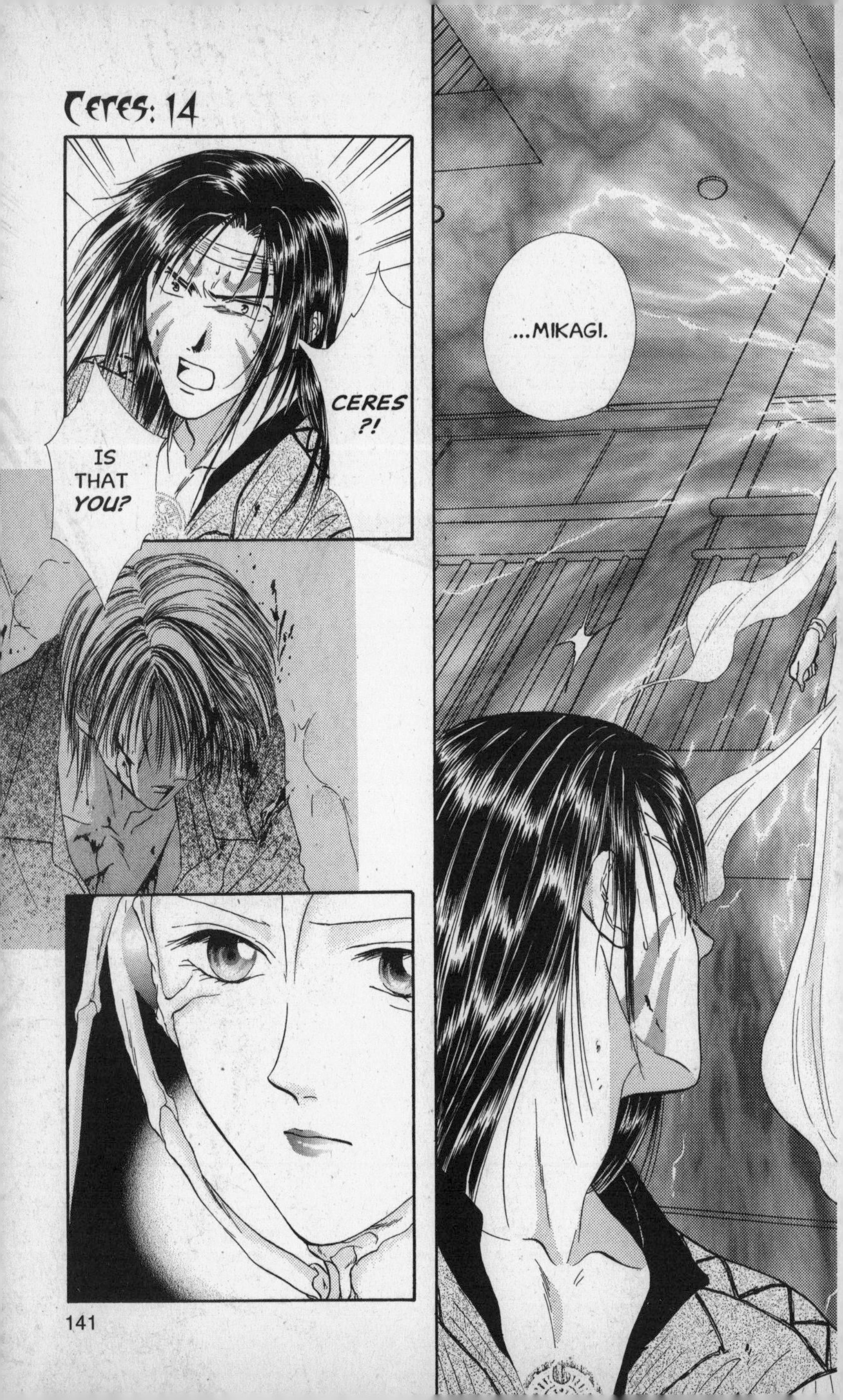
...MIKAGI.
CERES ?!
IS THAT *YOU?*

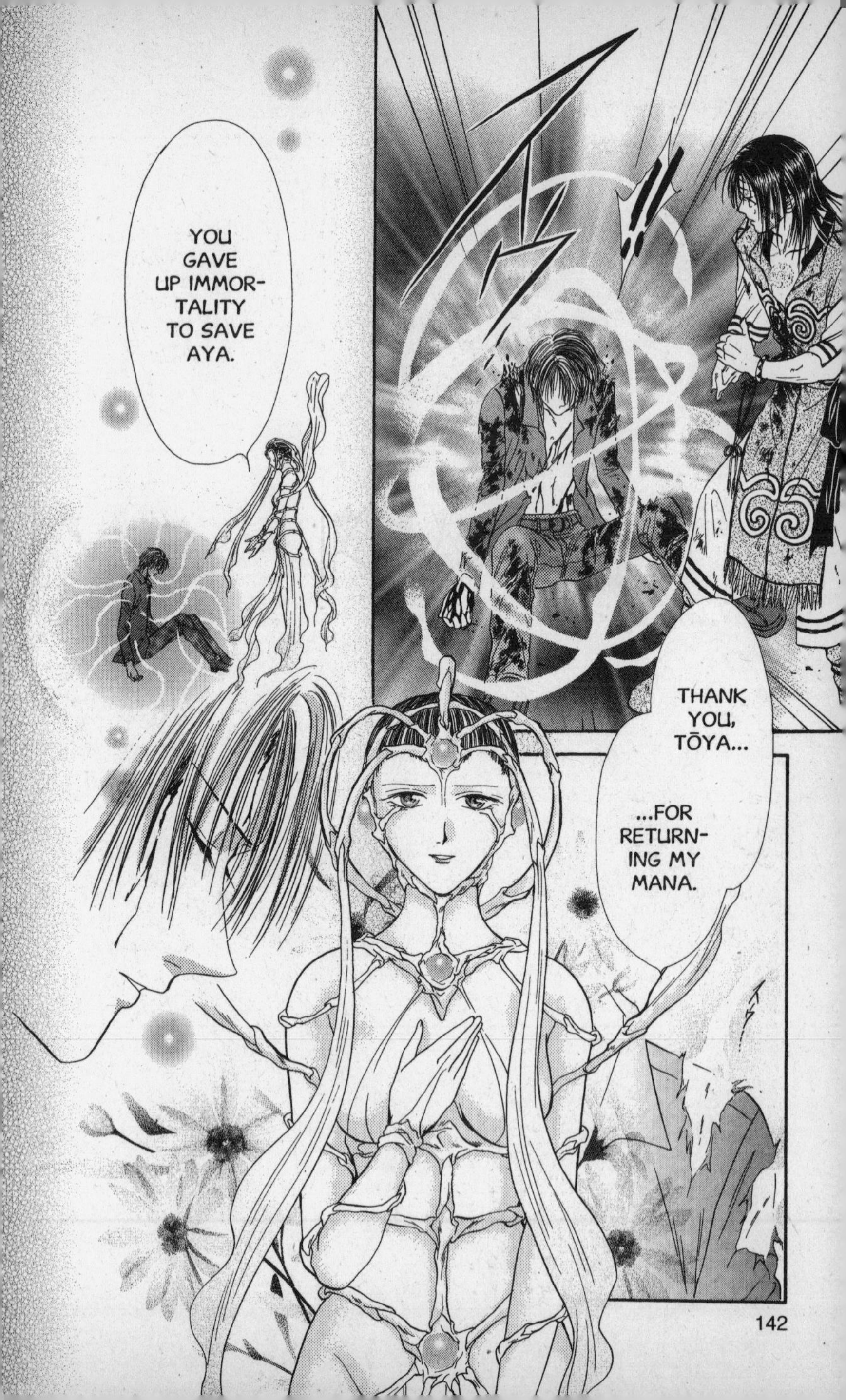
THANK YOU, TŌYA...
...FOR RETURNING MY MANA.
YOU GAVE UP IMMORTALITY TO SAVE AYA.

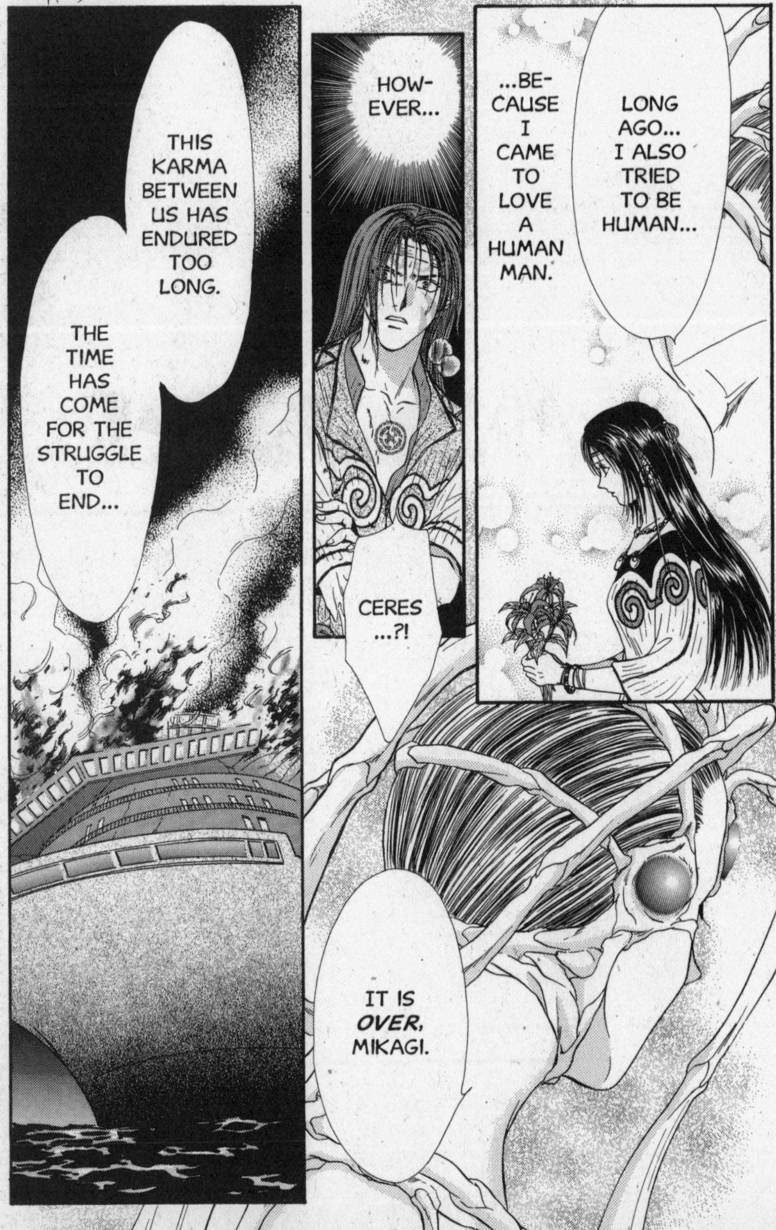
LONG AGO... I ALSO TRIED TO BE HUMAN...
...BE-CAUSE I CAME TO LOVE A HUMAN MAN.
HOW-EVER...
CERES ...?!
IT IS *OVER,* MIKAGI.
THIS KARMA BETWEEN US HAS ENDURED TOO LONG.
THE TIME HAS COME FOR THE STRUGGLE TO END...

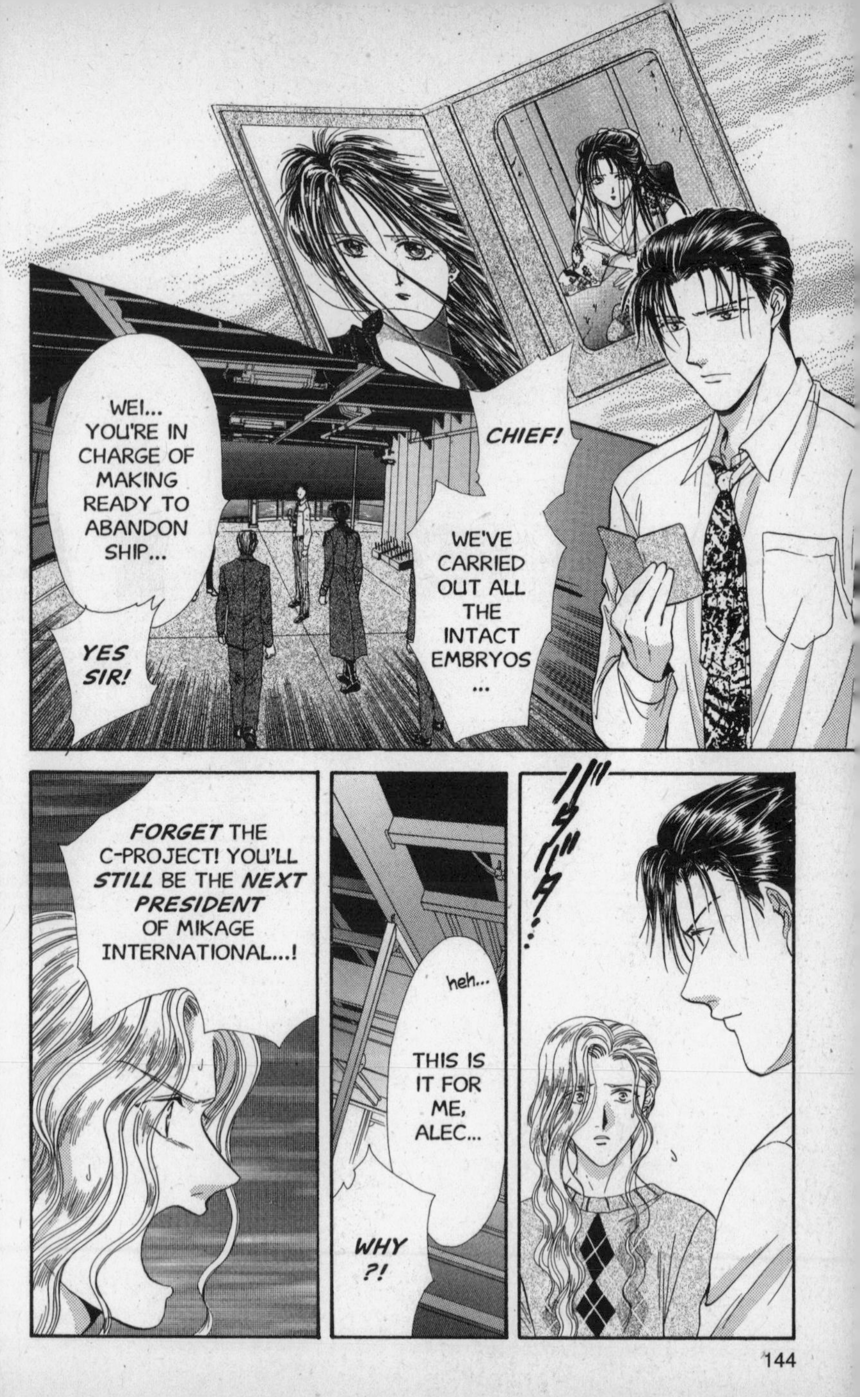
CHIEF!
WE'VE CARRIED OUT ALL THE INTACT EMBRYOS...
WEI... YOU'RE IN CHARGE OF MAKING READY TO ABANDON SHIP...
YES SIR!
heh...
THIS IS IT FOR ME, ALEC...
WHY ?!
FORGET THE C-PROJECT! YOU'LL STILL BE THE NEXT PRESIDENT OF MIKAGE INTERNATIONAL...!

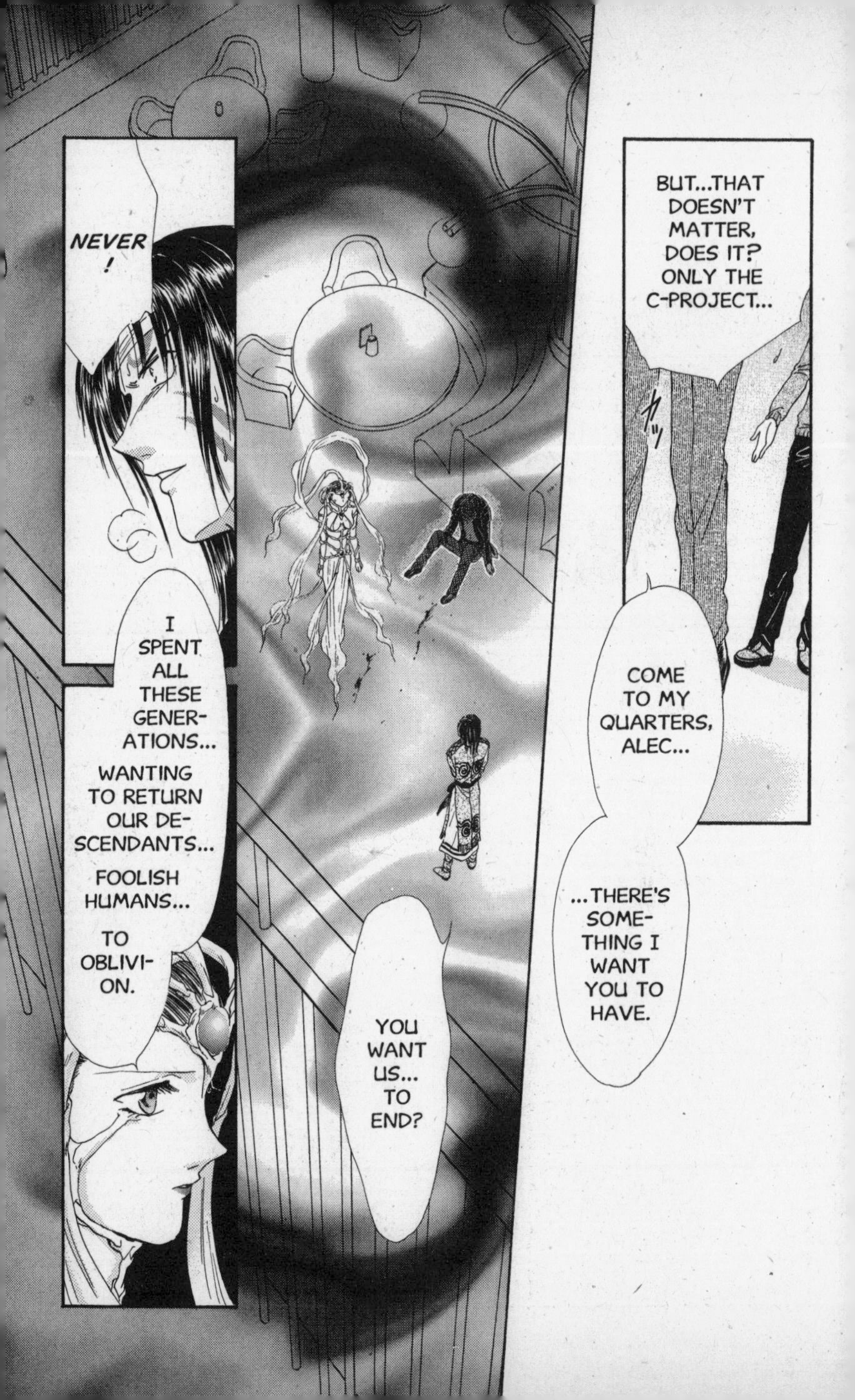
BUT...THAT DOESN'T MATTER, DOES IT? ONLY THE C-PROJECT...
COME TO MY QUARTERS, ALEC...
...THERE'S SOME-THING I WANT YOU TO HAVE.
YOU WANT US... TO END?
NEVER!
I SPENT ALL THESE GENER-ATIONS...
WANTING TO RETURN OUR DE-SCENDANTS...
FOOLISH HUMANS...
TO OBLIVI-ON.

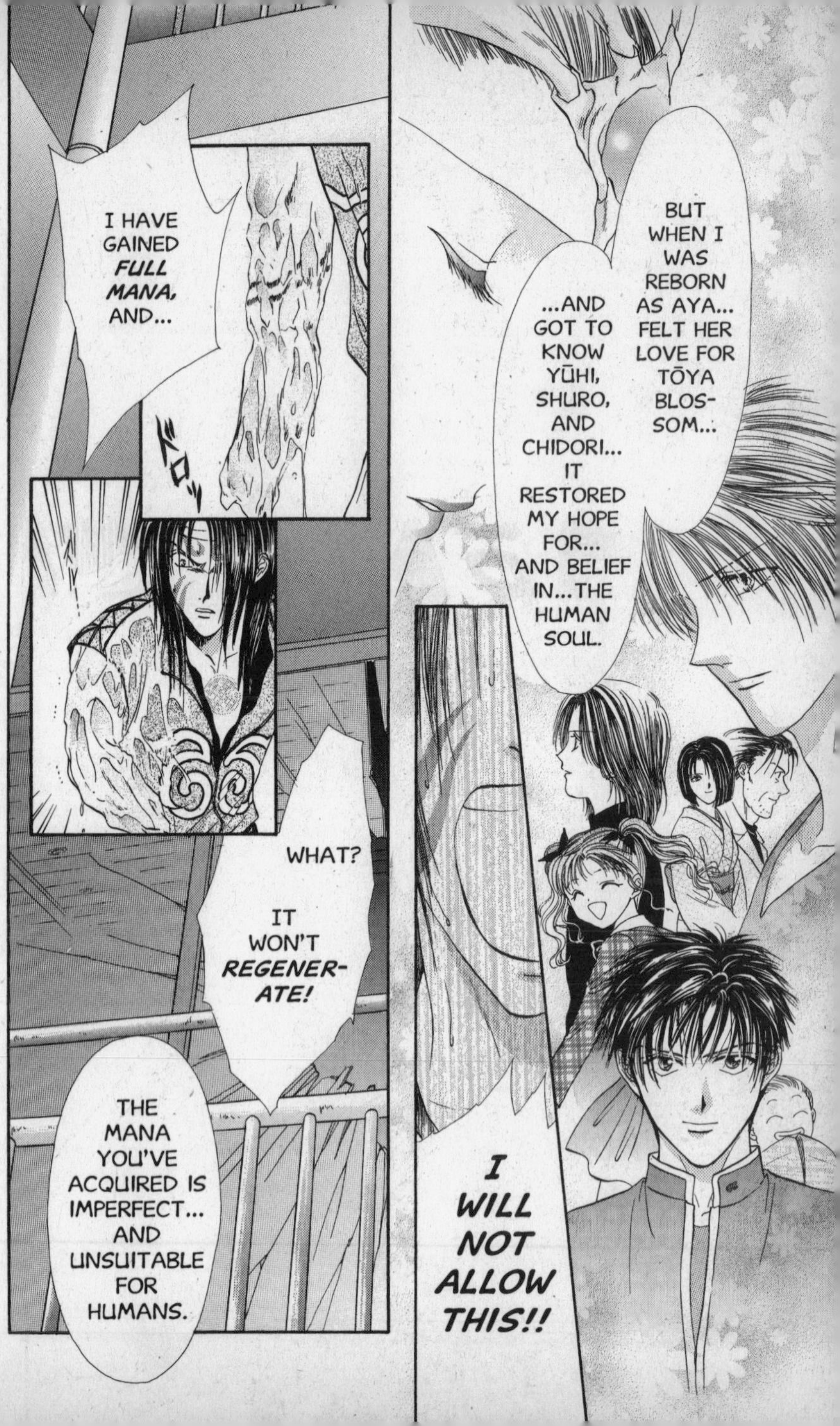

BUT WHEN I WAS REBORN AS AYA... FELT HER LOVE FOR TŌYA BLOSSOM...
...AND GOT TO KNOW YŪHI, SHURO, AND CHIDORI... IT RESTORED MY HOPE FOR... AND BELIEF IN... THE HUMAN SOUL.
I WILL NOT ALLOW THIS!!
I HAVE GAINED *FULL MANA,* AND...
ドロッ
WHAT?
IT WON'T *REGENERATE!*
THE MANA YOU'VE ACQUIRED IS IMPERFECT... AND UNSUITABLE FOR HUMANS.

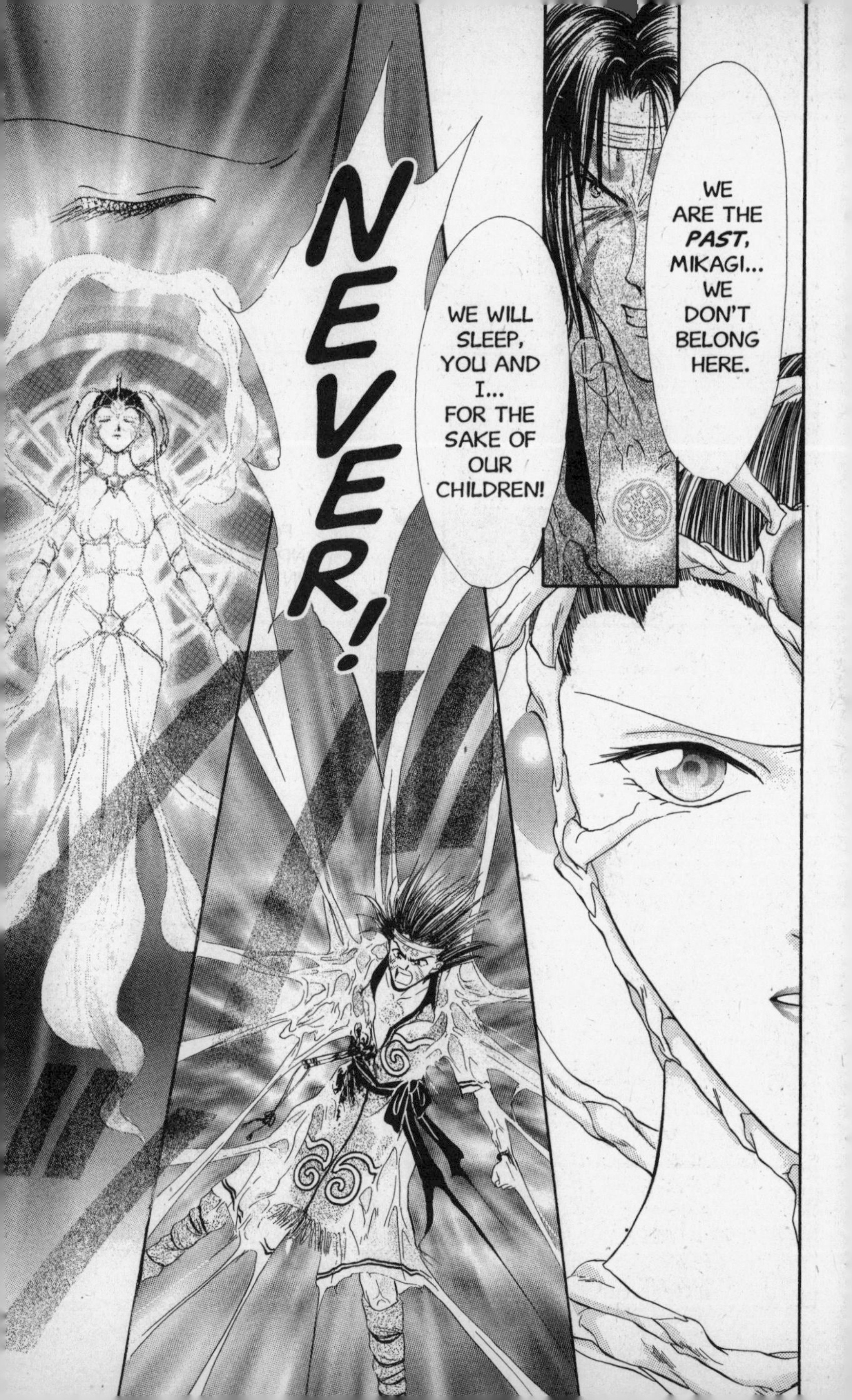
WE ARE THE PAST, MIKAGI... WE DON'T BELONG HERE.
WE WILL SLEEP, YOU AND I... FOR THE SAKE OF OUR CHILDREN!
NEVER!

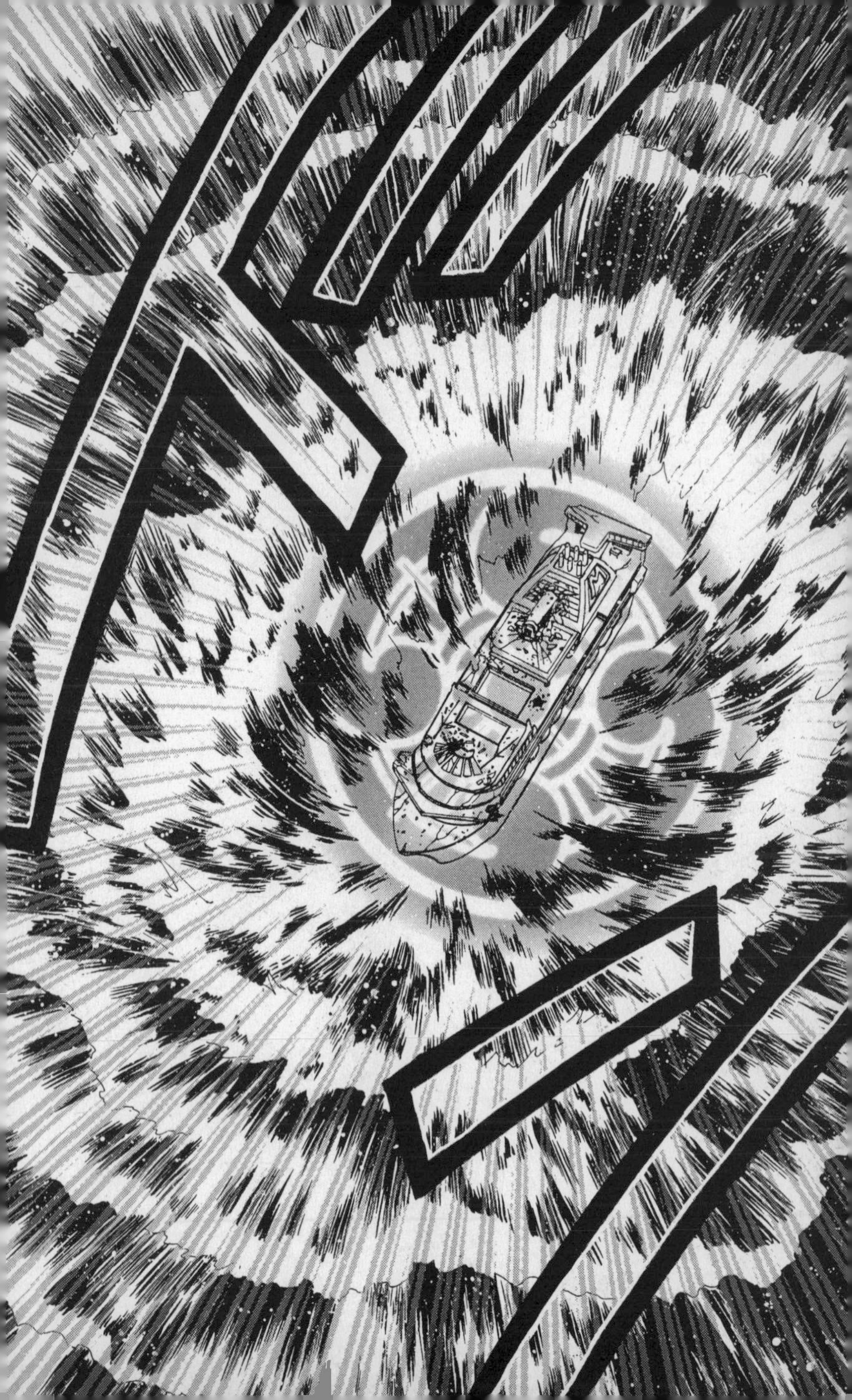

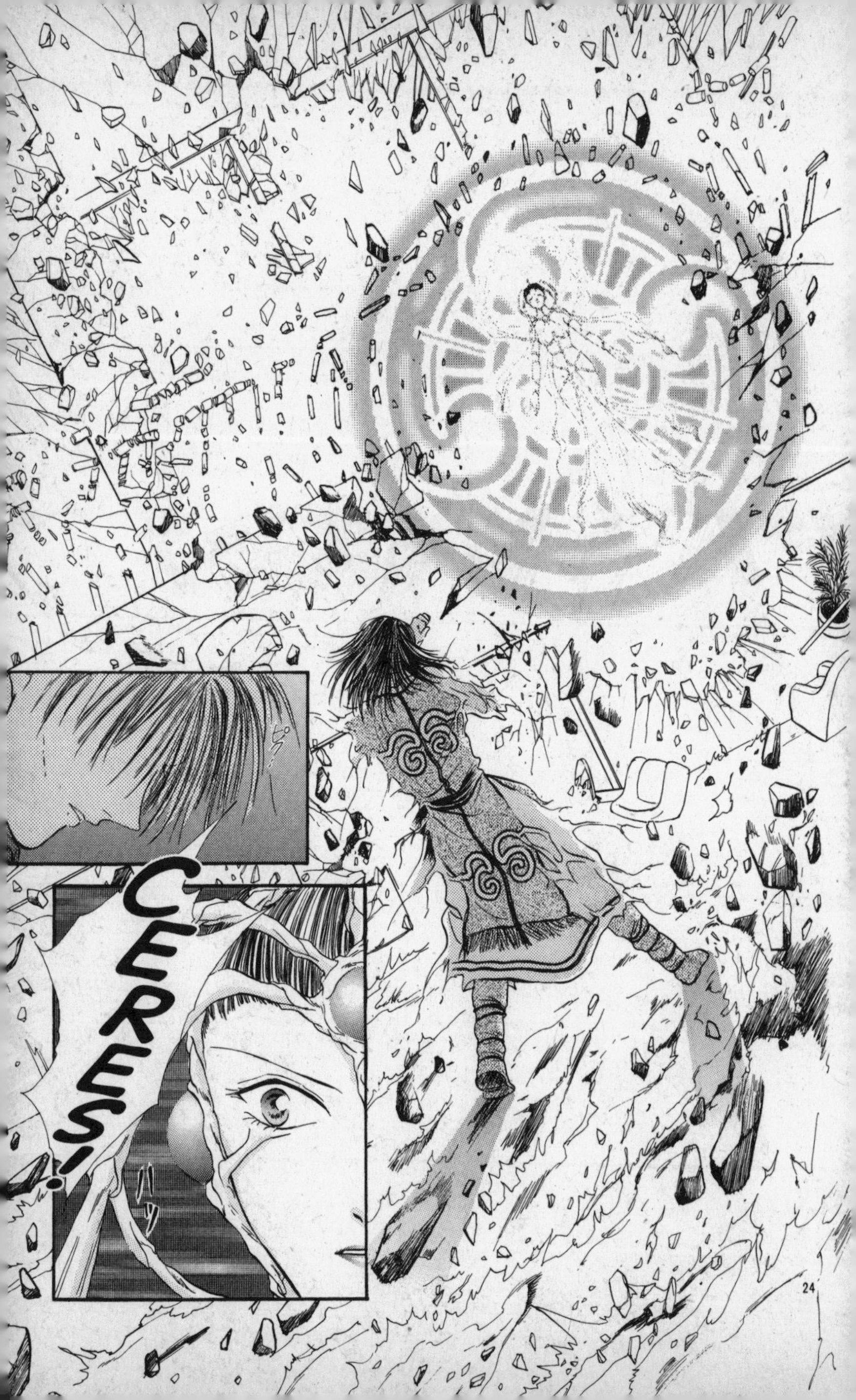
CERES!

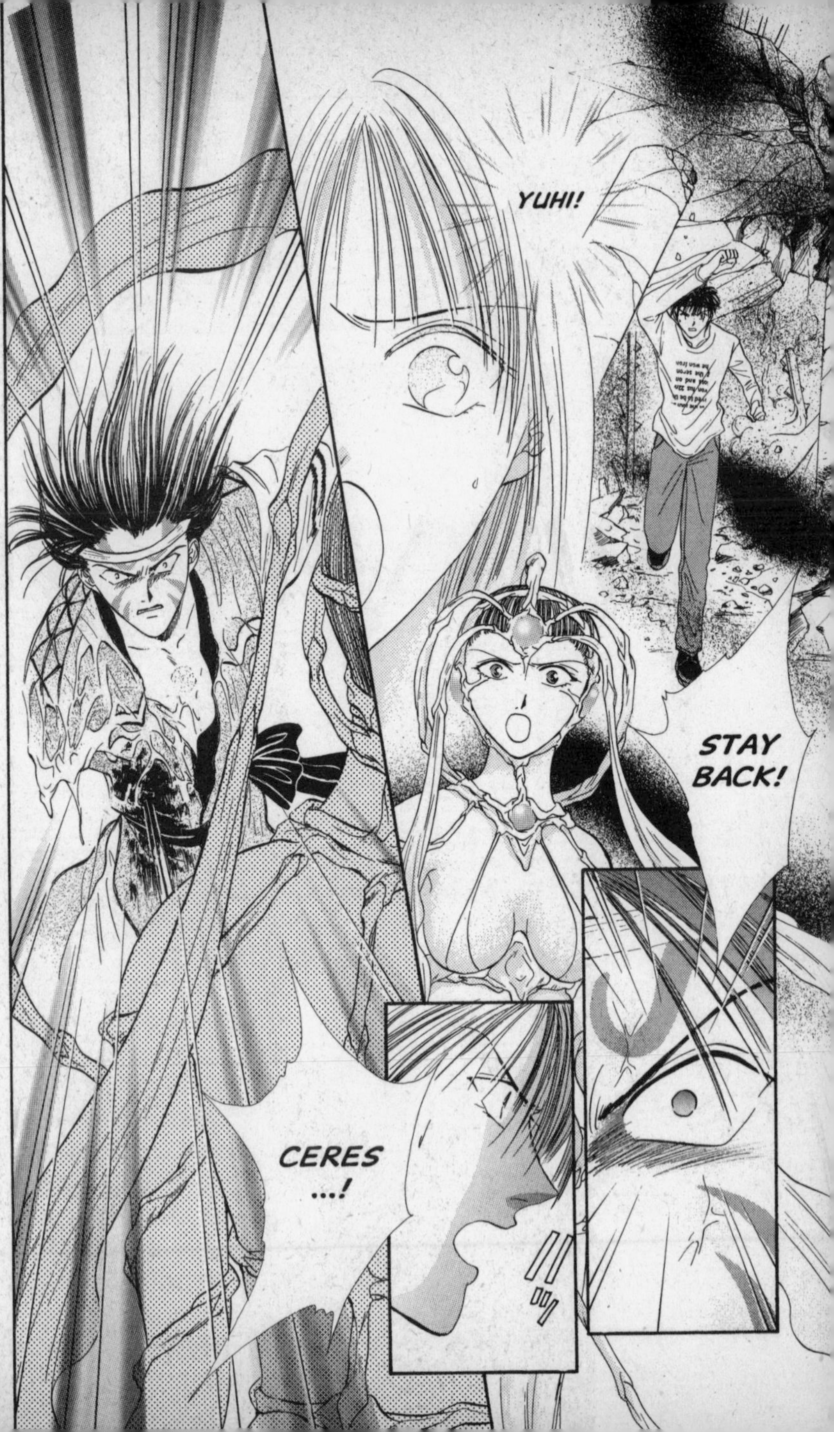
YUHI!
STAY BACK!
CERES ...!

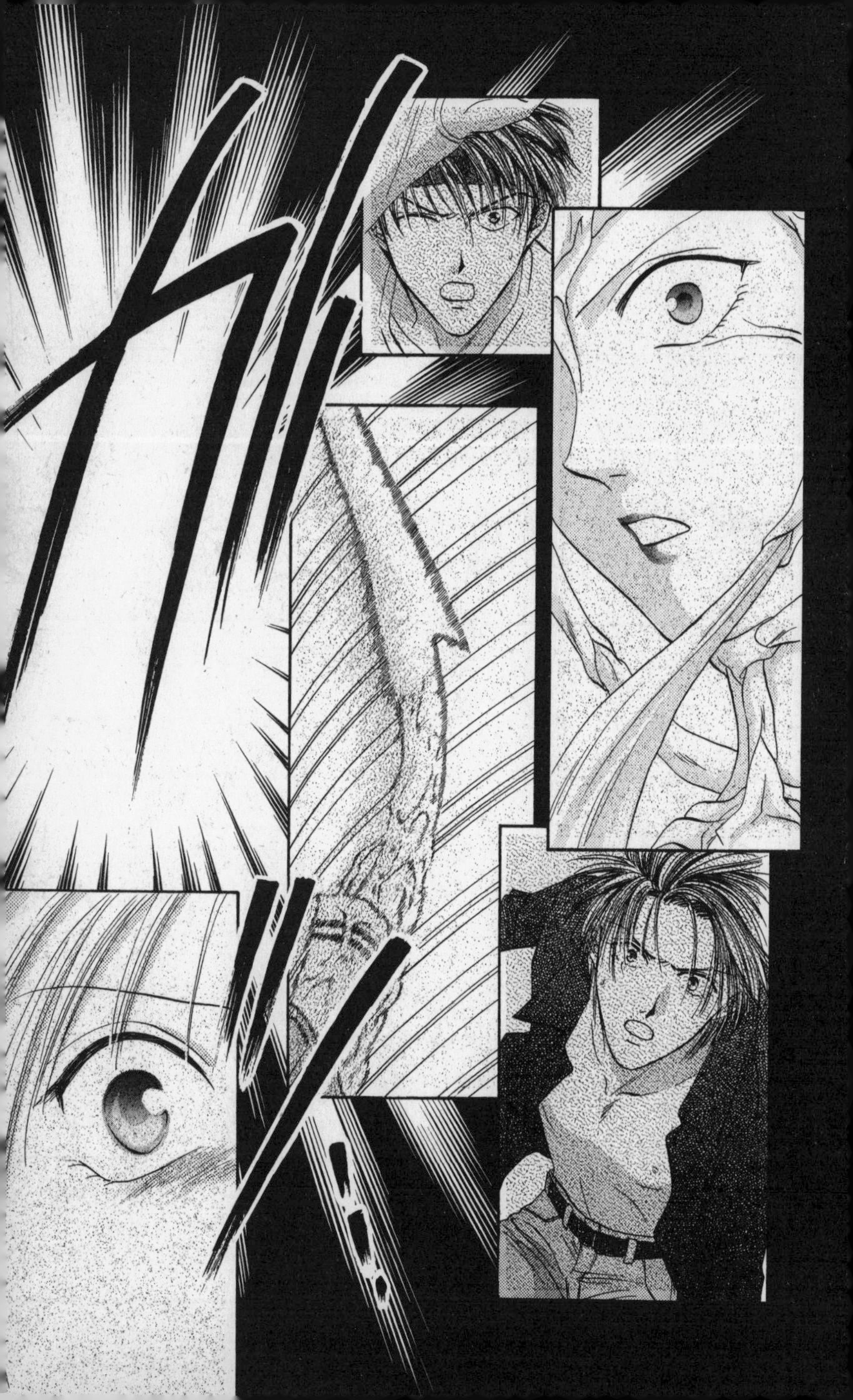

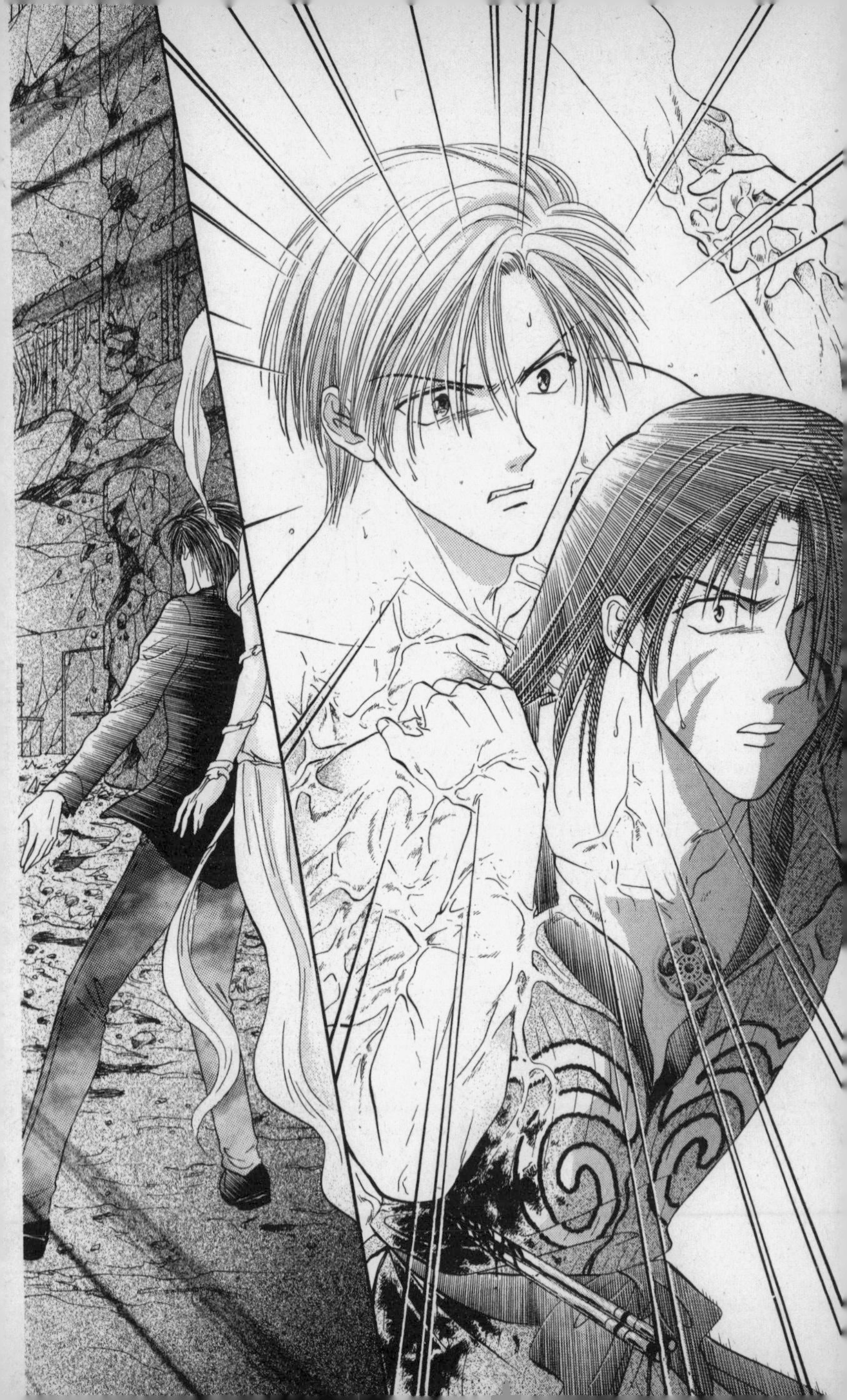

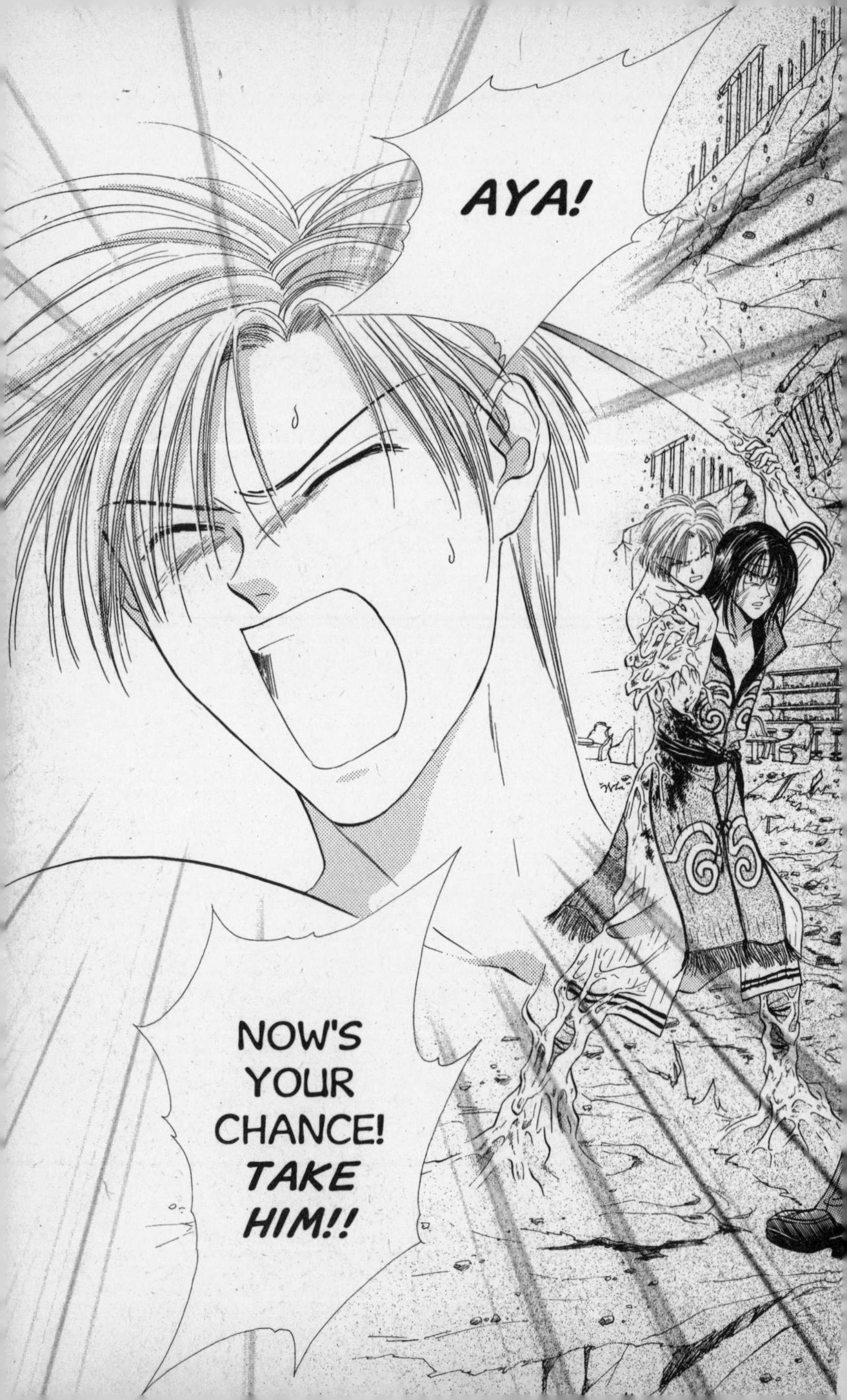
AYA!
NOW'S YOUR CHANCE! TAKE HIM!!

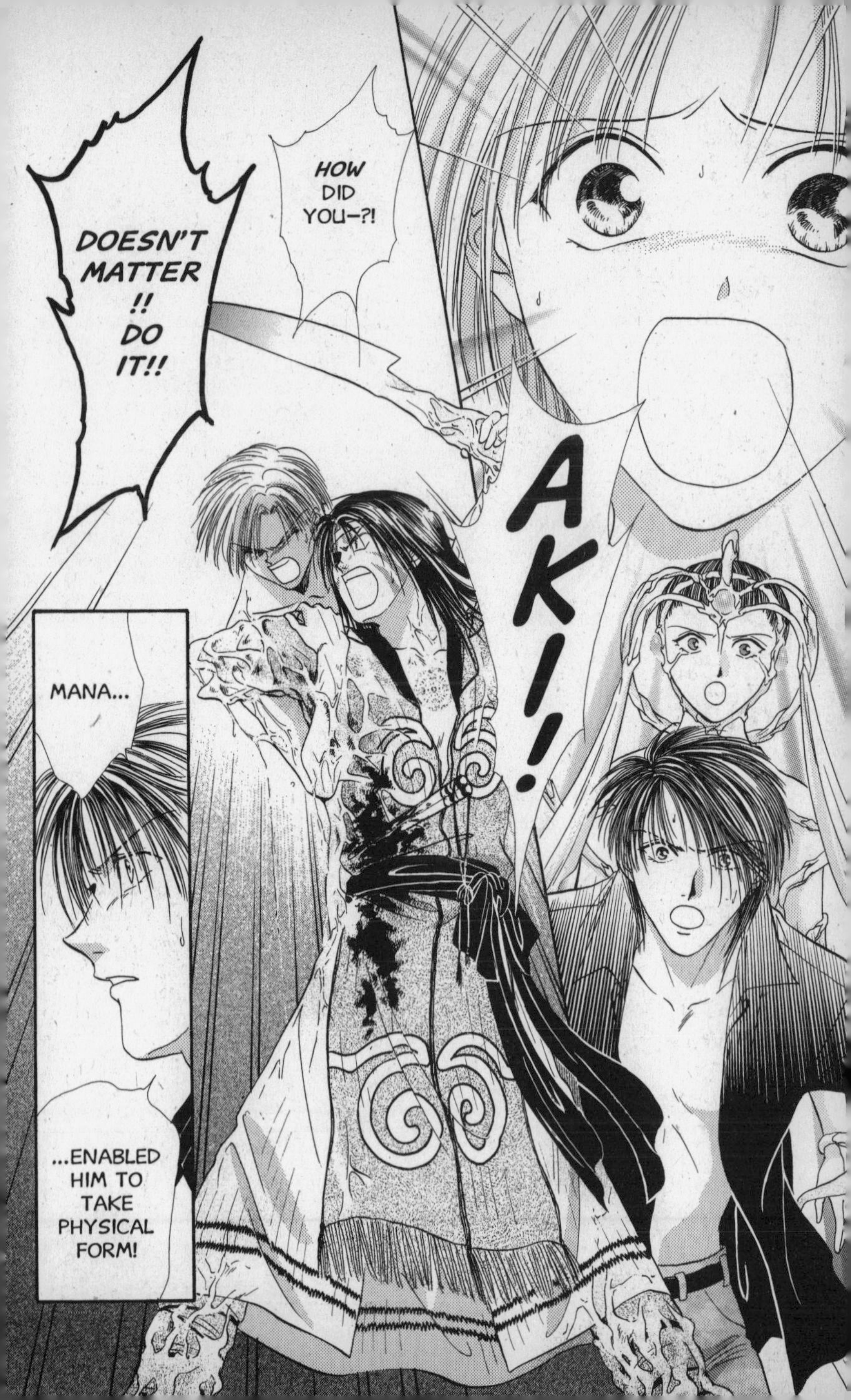
HOW DID YOU–?!
DOESN'T MATTER!! DO IT!!
AKI!!
MANA...
...ENABLED HIM TO TAKE PHYSICAL FORM!

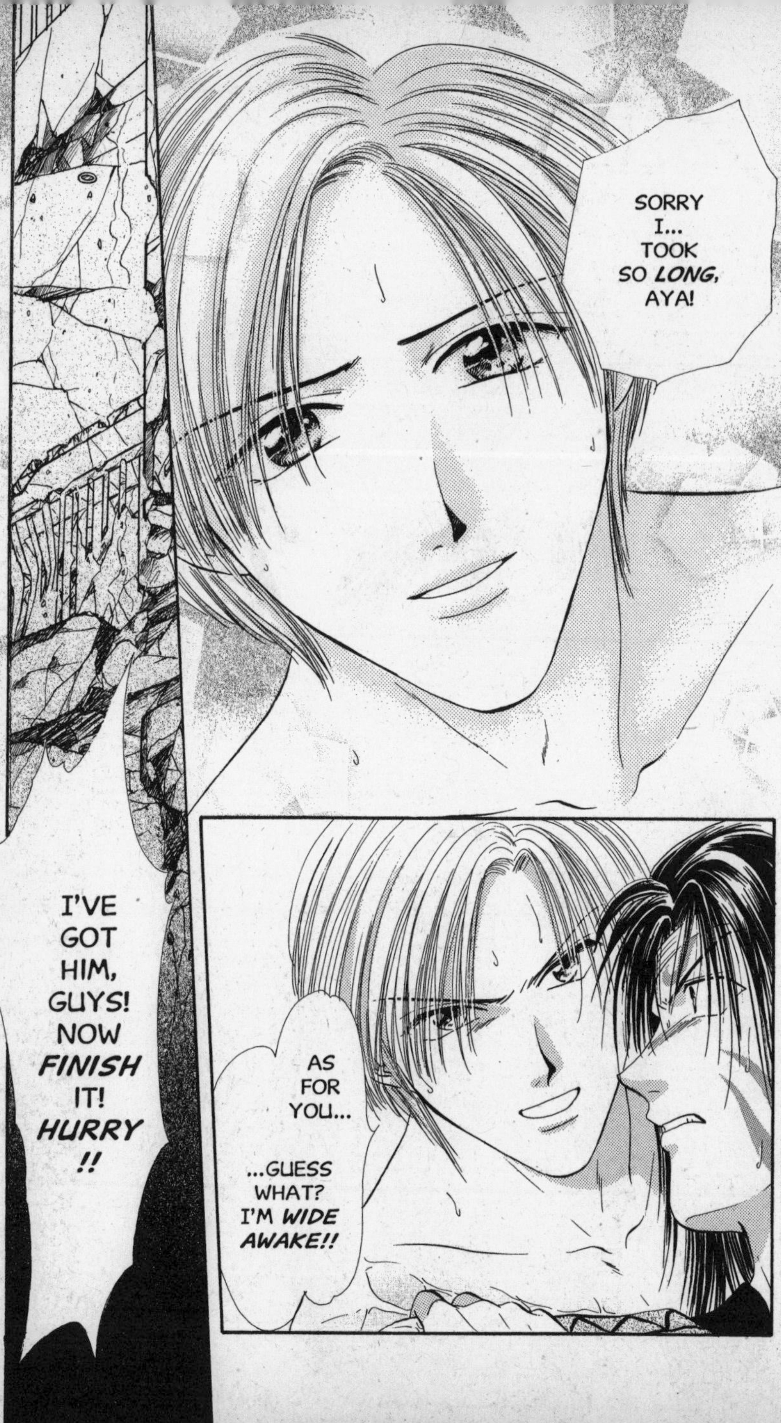
SORRY I... TOOK SO LONG, AYA!
AS FOR YOU...
...GUESS WHAT? I'M WIDE AWAKE!!
I'VE GOT HIM, GUYS! NOW FINISH IT! HURRY !!

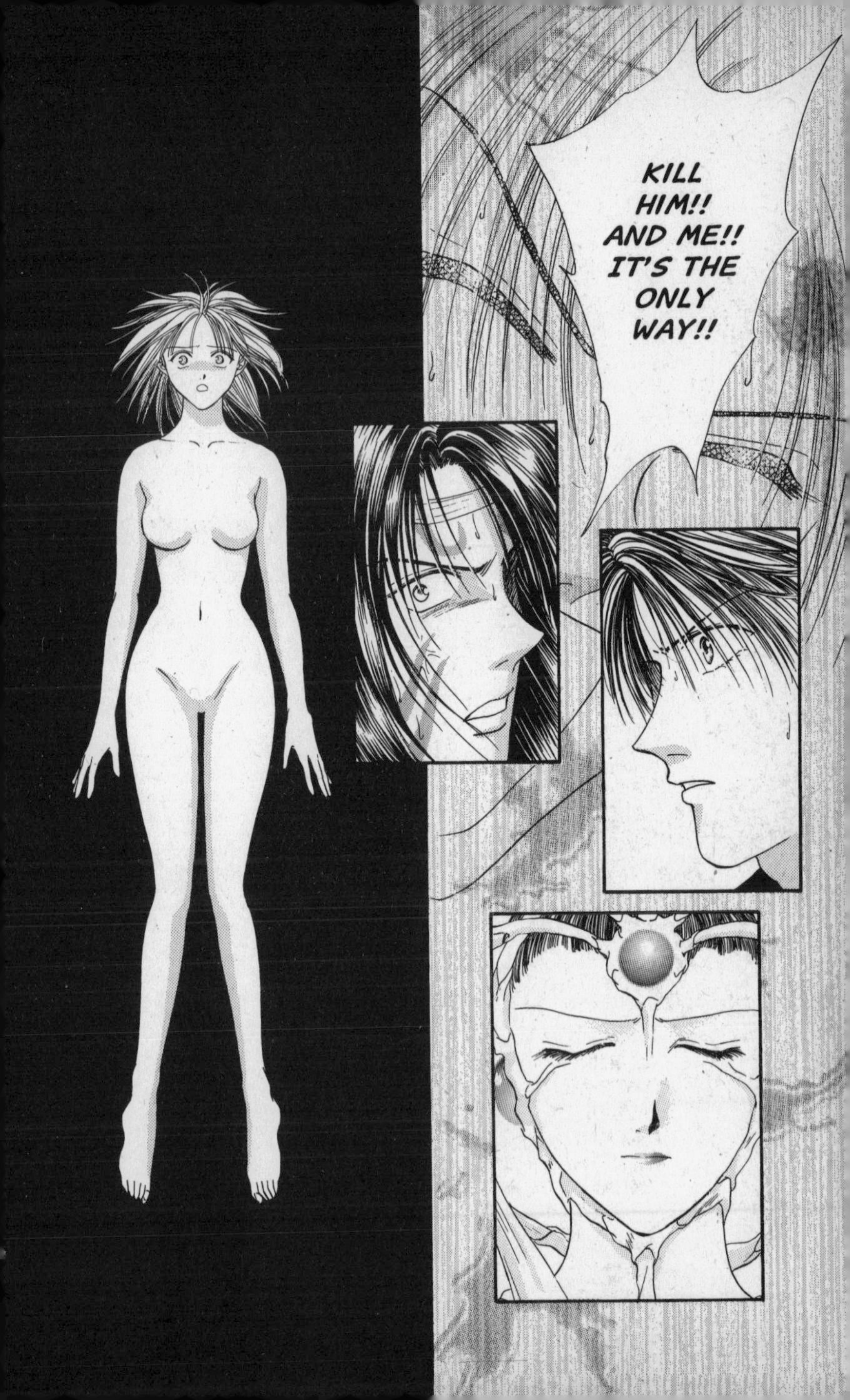
KILL HIM!! AND ME!! IT'S THE ONLY WAY!!

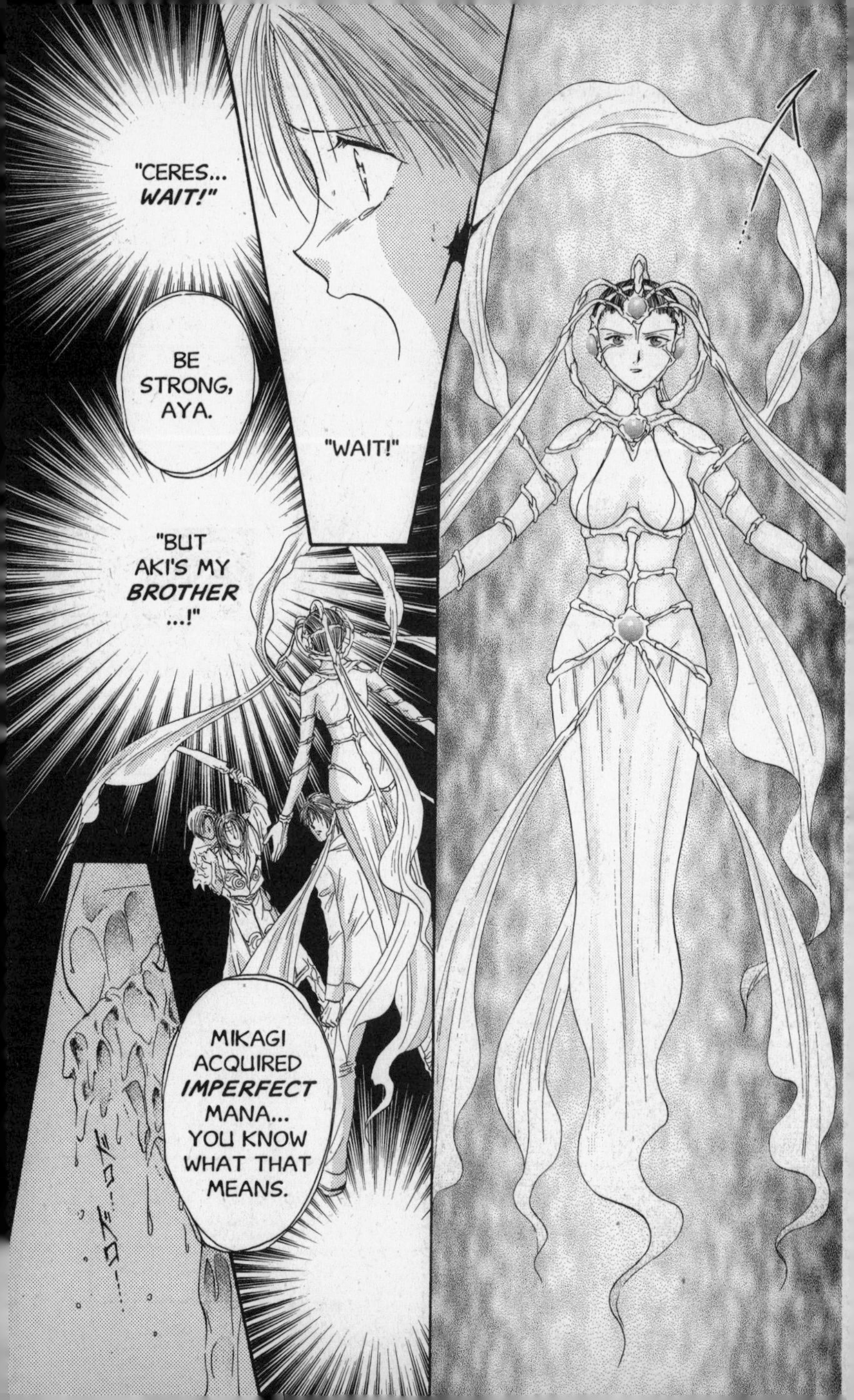
"CERES... WAIT!"
BE STRONG, AYA.
"WAIT!"
"BUT AKI'S MY BROTHER ...!"
MIKAGI ACQUIRED IMPERFECT MANA... YOU KNOW WHAT THAT MEANS.

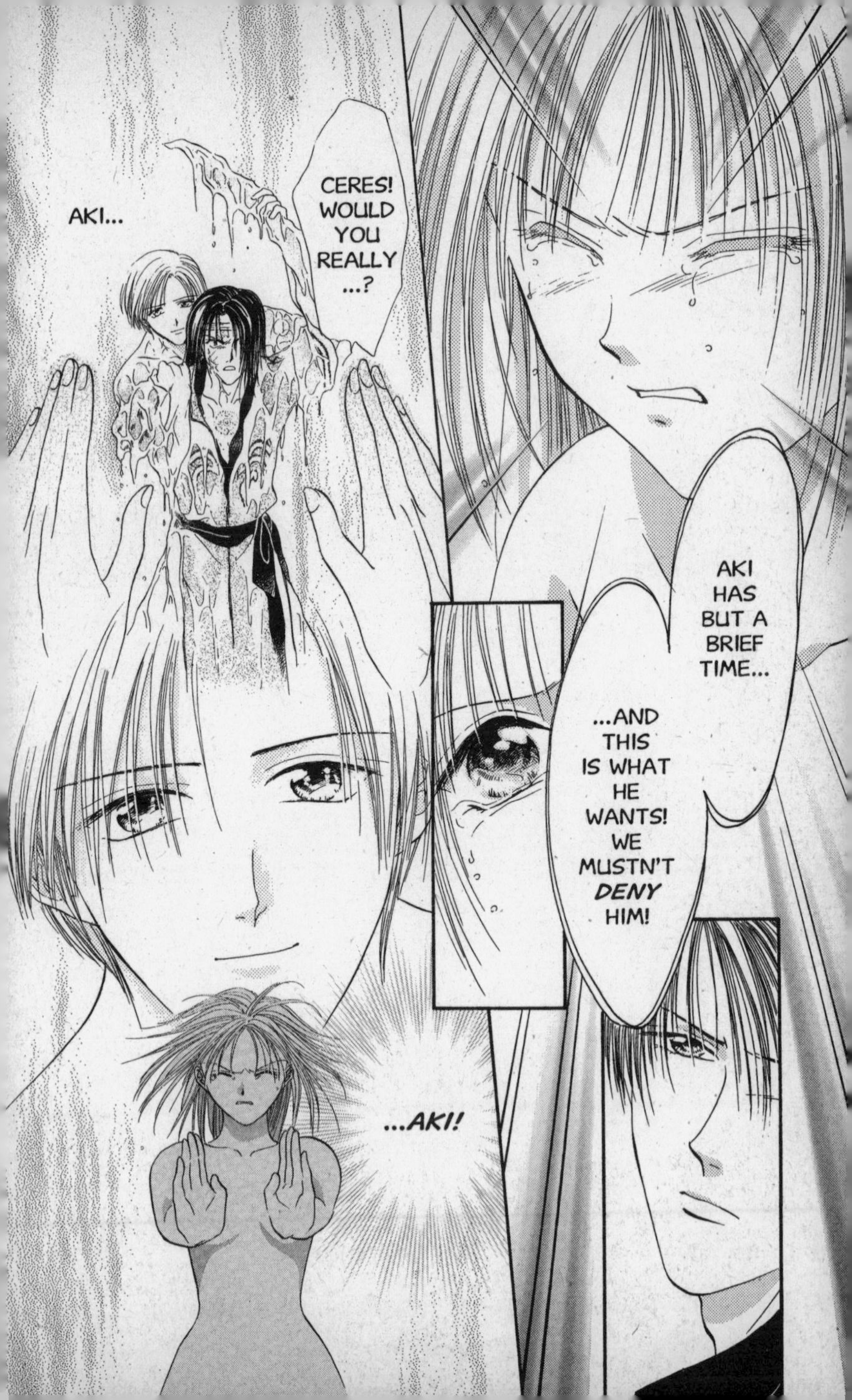
AKI HAS BUT A BRIEF TIME...
...AND THIS IS WHAT HE WANTS! WE MUSTN'T *DENY* HIM!
CERES! WOULD YOU REALLY ...?
AKI...
...AKI!

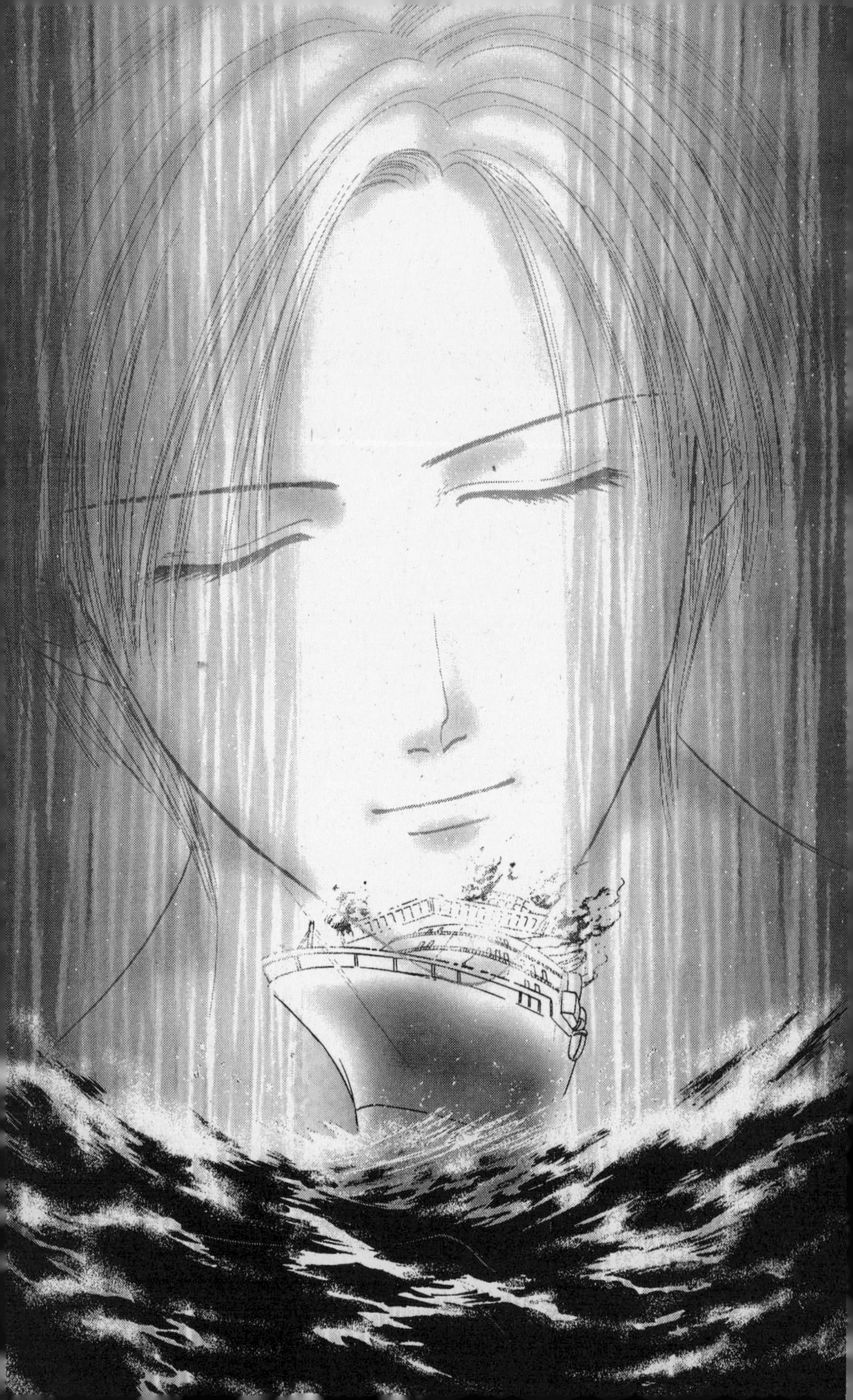

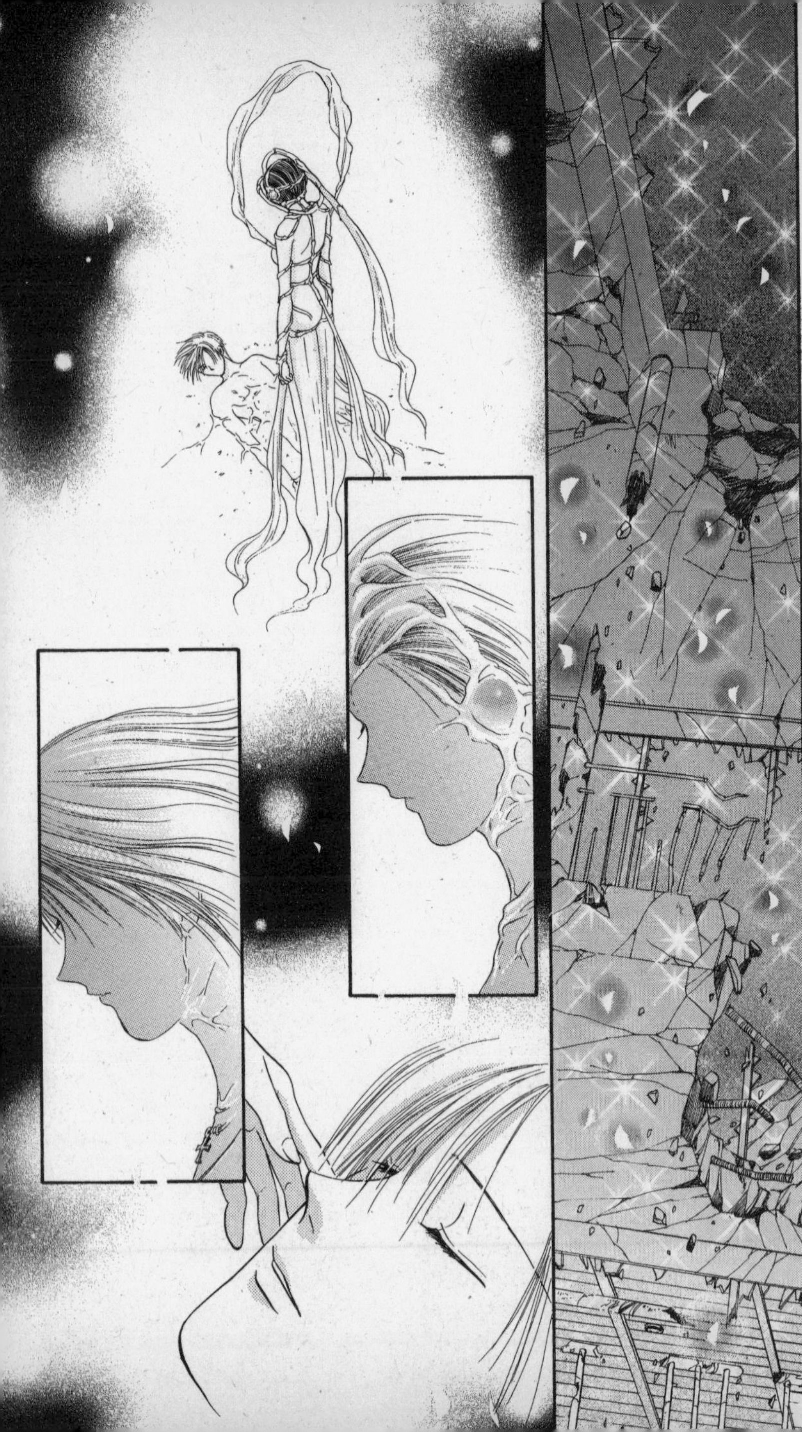

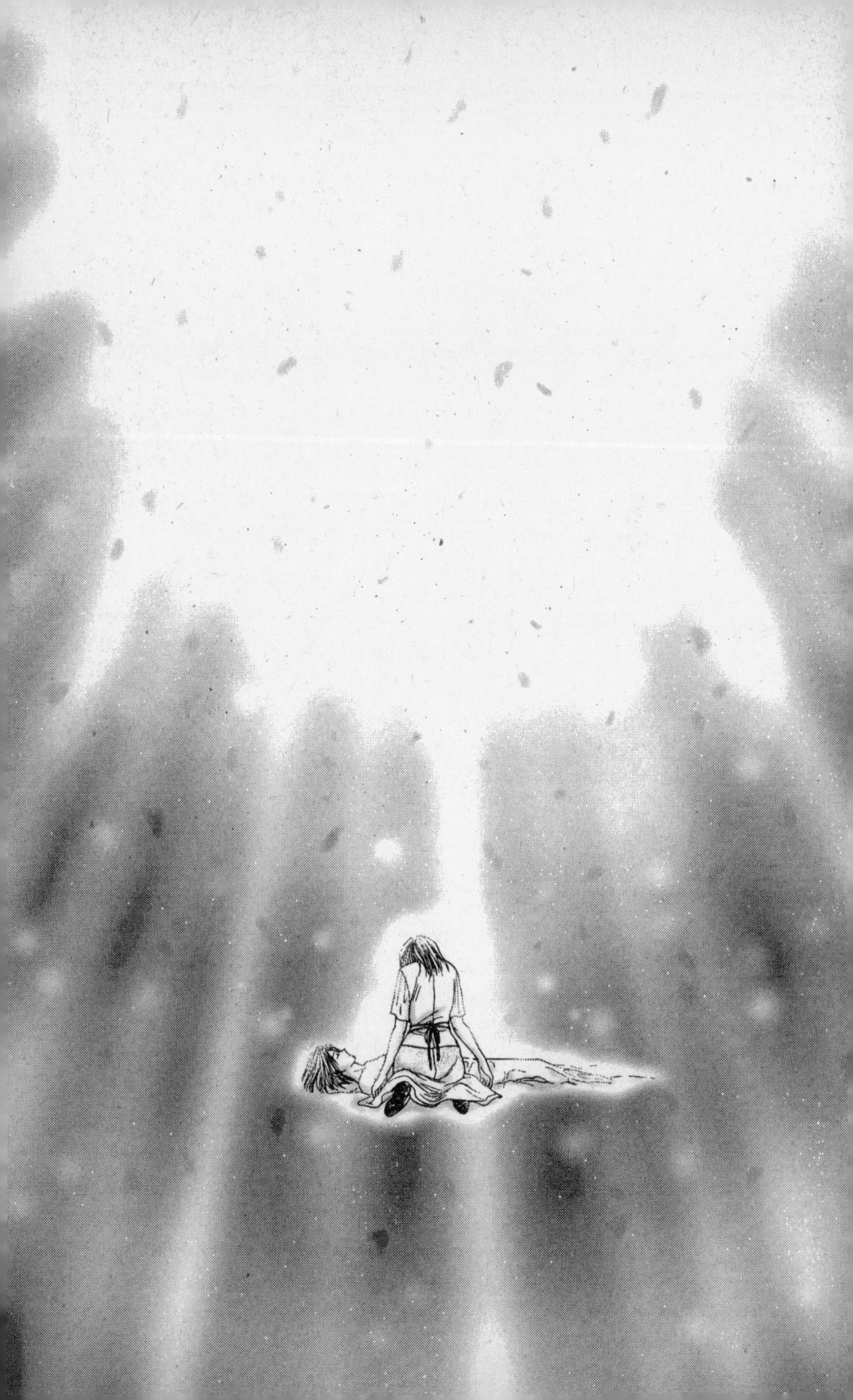

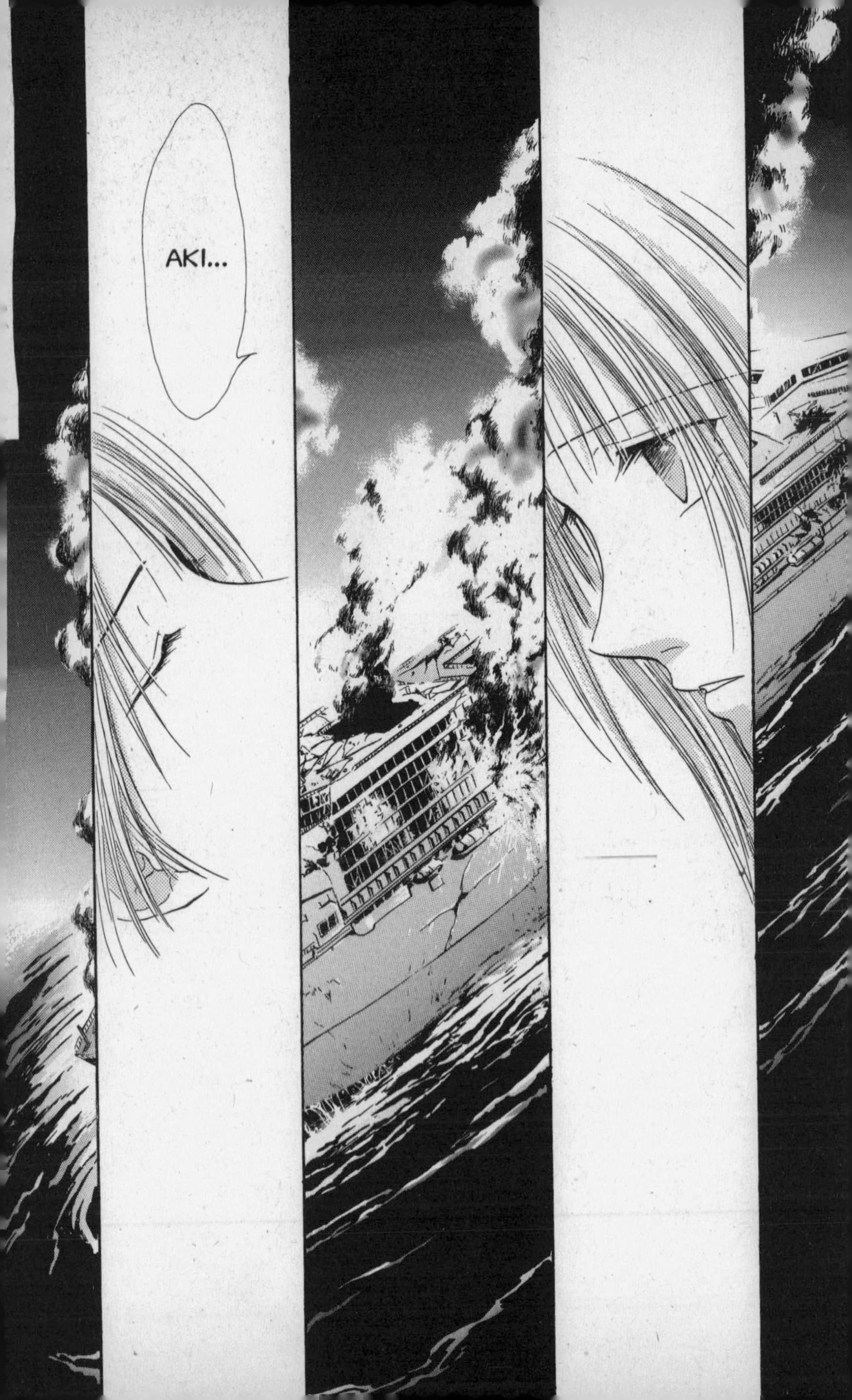
AKI...

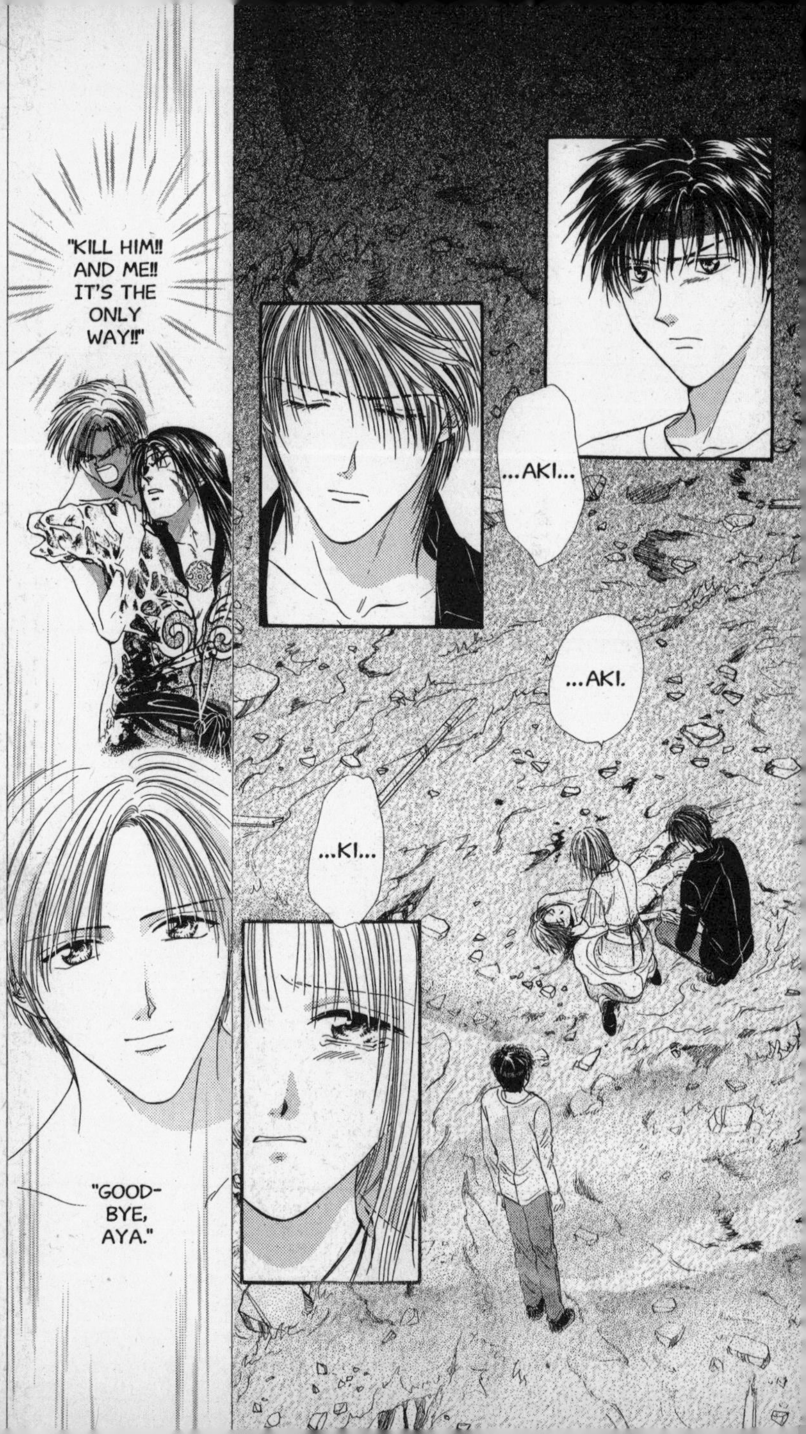
...AKI...
...AKI.
...KI...
"KILL HIM!! AND ME!! IT'S THE ONLY WAY!!"
"GOOD-BYE, AYA."

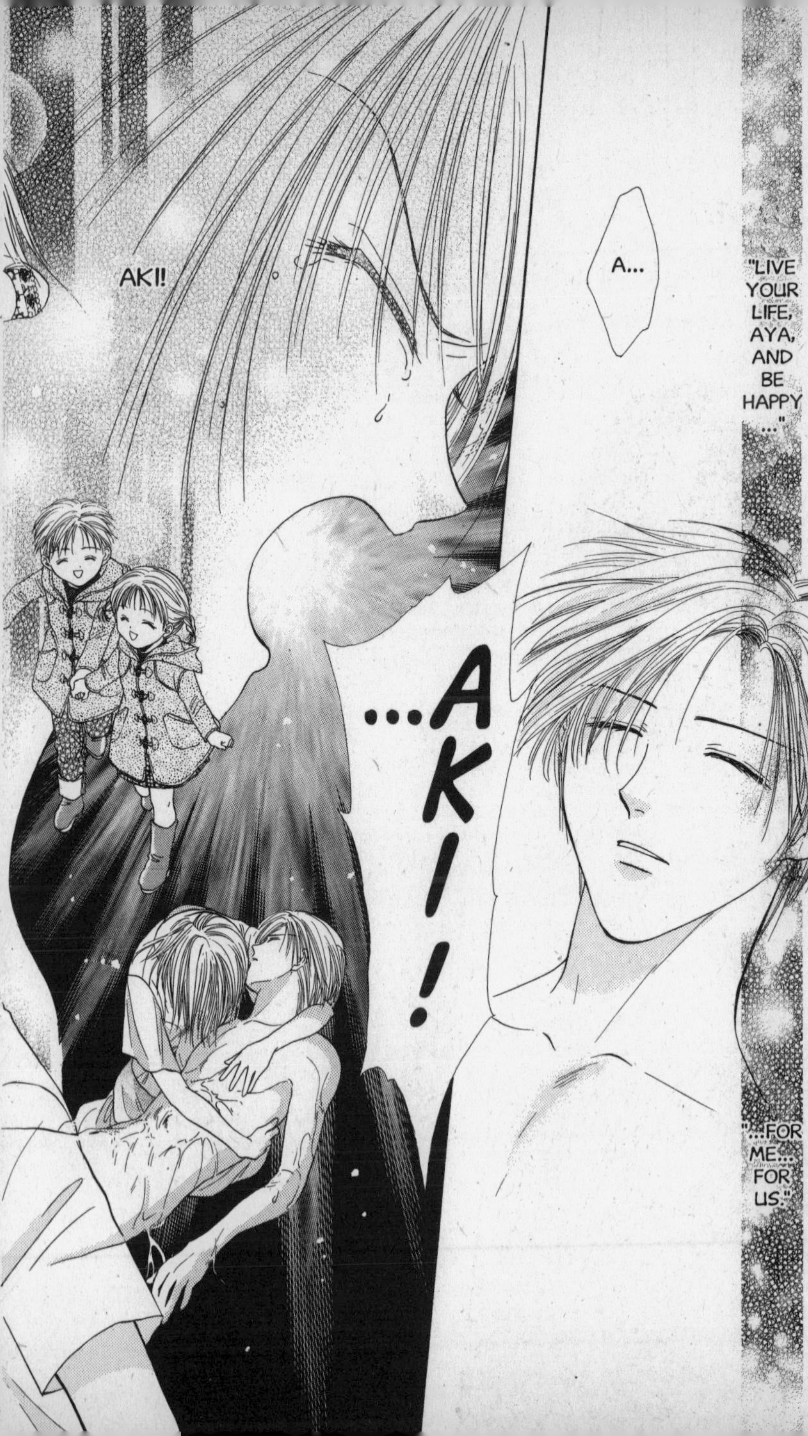
"LIVE YOUR LIFE, AYA, AND BE HAPPY ..."
"...FOR ME... FOR US."
A...
...AKI!
AKI!

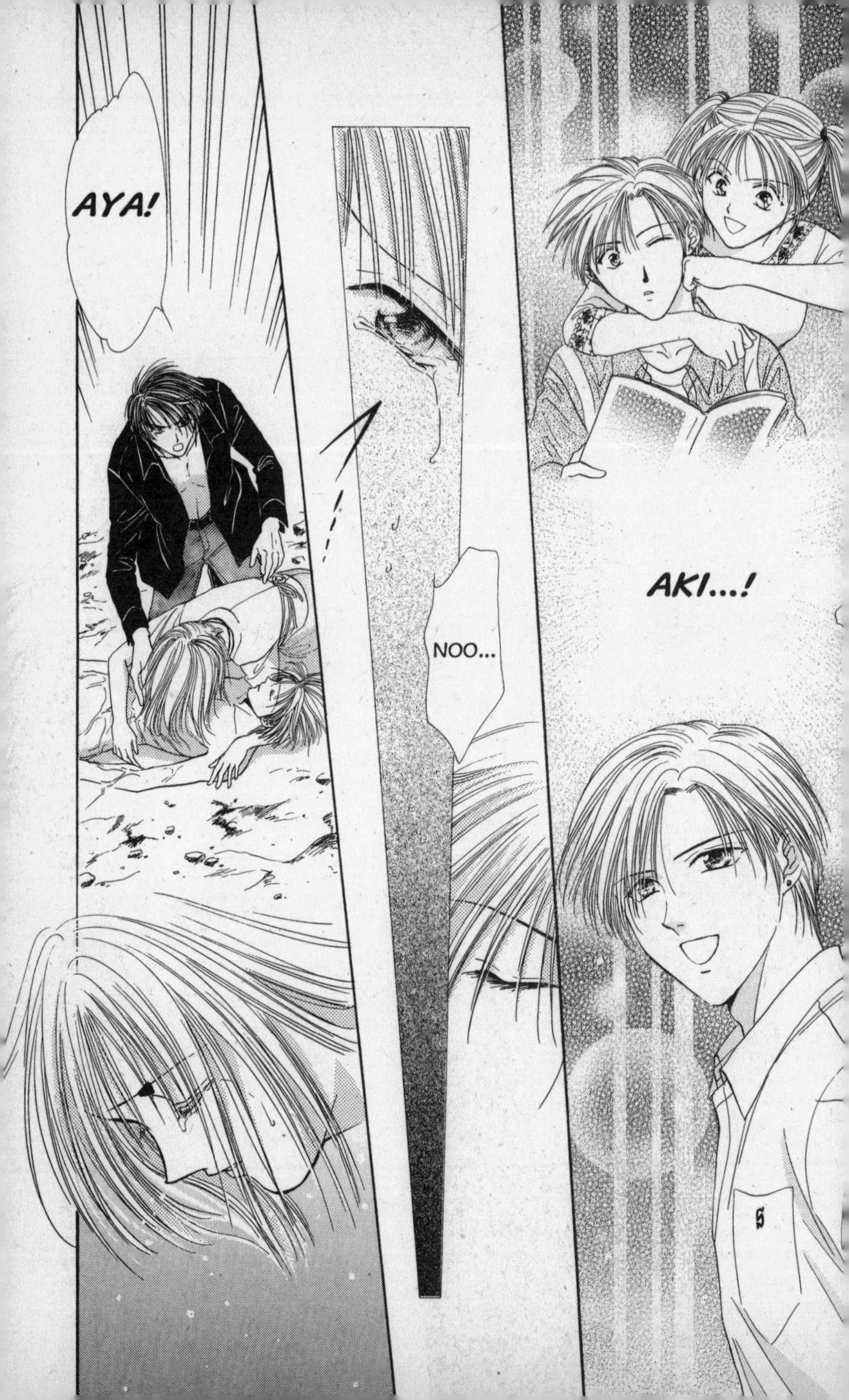
AKI...!
NOO...
AYA!

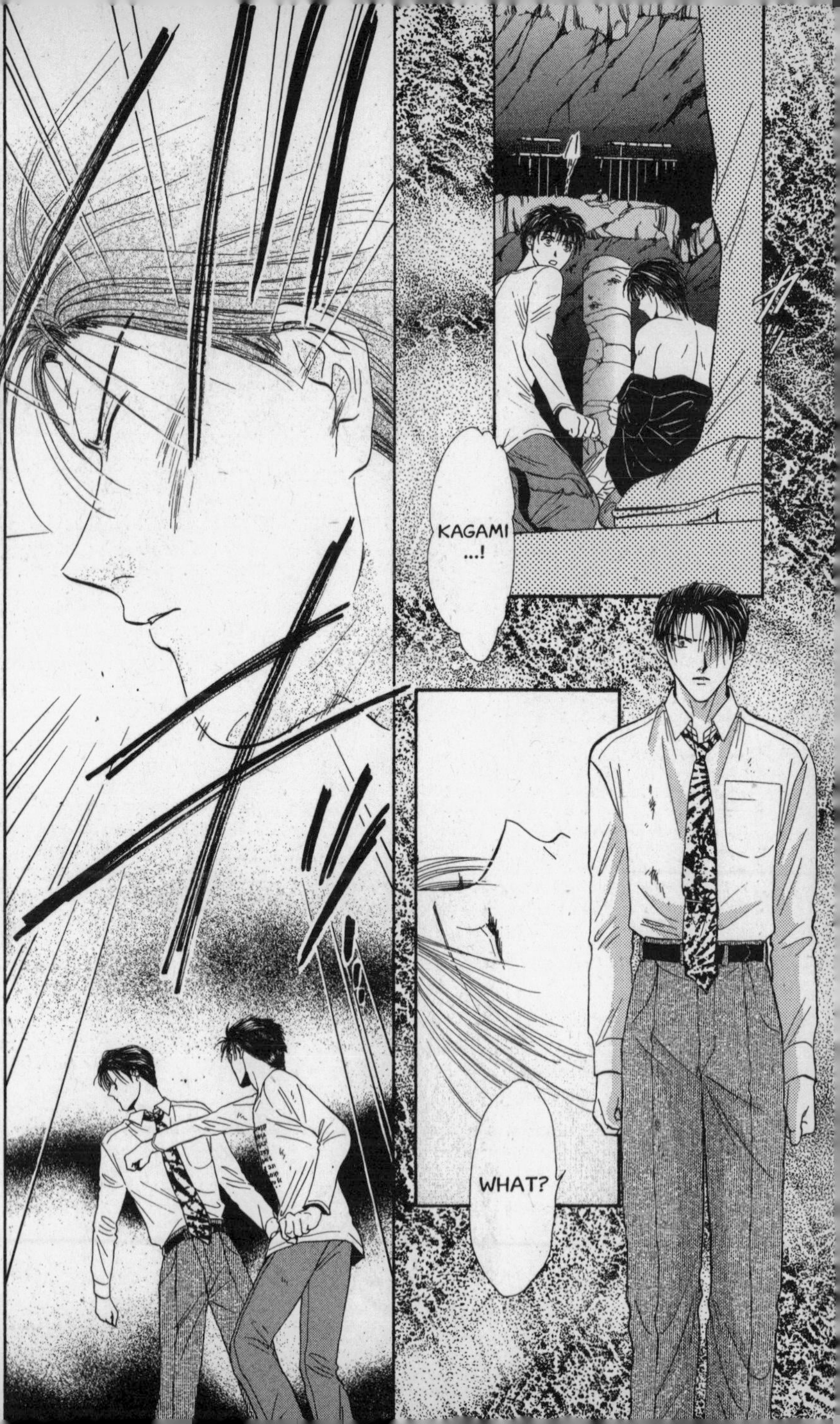
KAGAMI ...!
WHAT?
...

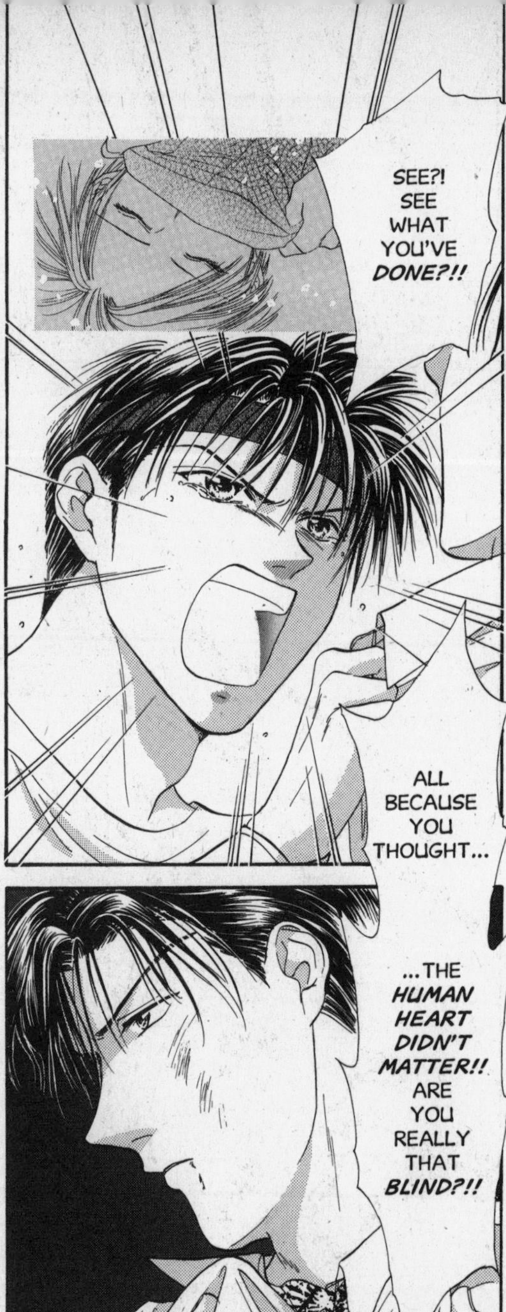
SEE?! SEE WHAT YOU'VE *DONE?!!*
ALL BECAUSE YOU THOUGHT...
...THE *HUMAN HEART DIDN'T MATTER!!* ARE YOU REALLY THAT *BLIND?!!*

I told you Kagami wasn't so evil! ☺ Ceres was like a mother to him...but did he really die in the end? (As I plant the seeds in your mind...) I tried to leave the end of the story with hope and many possibilities (Kagami and the Guardinals' purpose was fulfilled, in a way, by Tōya and Aya's child, after all). Most of the letters I got said it felt bitter-sweet...

I know the story was difficult to understand. There are many things I should've done differently, and I've learned a lot from the process. I tried to include many interpretations, so I hope you can find your own conclusions. Oh, maybe it would help to take some biology classes first...(I read the Shogakukan comic book version of NHK's "Life" for reference, so why not start there?) Life experience helps, too. ☺ I received the most empathic letters from people who have experienced love, had relationships, or had become mothers themselves...I guess it really was geared for a mature audience. ☺ I was happy when my friend told me she liked the theme! (She liked it better than FY.) Many friends who know me well have told me that this series reflects who I am the most...I think so, too. What's most important between men and women, and in turn, for all of humanity? It's basically what Yūhi's saying on this page. It's an important message that should be passed down to future generations! It should be told to the present world, too, of course!! ☺ Okay then...the rest can go in the novels. ☺

Editors: Mr. H, Mr. E, Mr. S, Mr. Y.
Assistants: Yoriko Hiraoka
Shinobu Matsumoto
Naomi Kaji
Kaori Shimada
Akiko Tsuchida

And last but not least, Mr. Toshinobu Kondo, temporary assistant and computer master...and so many more people who helped — thank you so much!

I'd also like to dedicate this volume to the esteemed Mr. [Daisaku] Ikeda, whom I quoted in these columns from his book, "The Way of Youth"!
I'm not worthy...
Thank you so much for reading!!
See you in my next title!

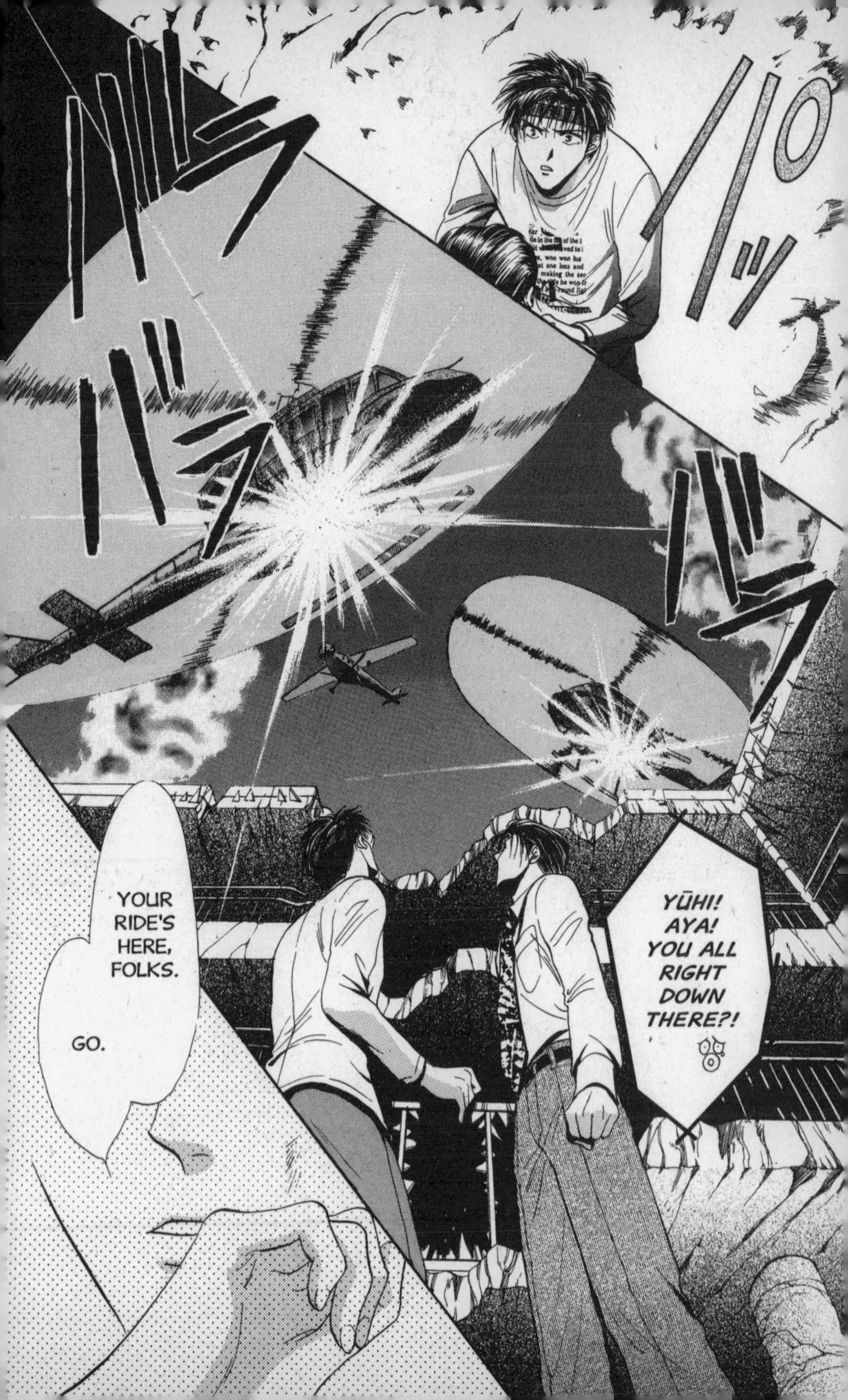
YŪHI! AYA! YOU ALL RIGHT DOWN THERE?!
YOUR RIDE'S HERE, FOLKS.
GO.

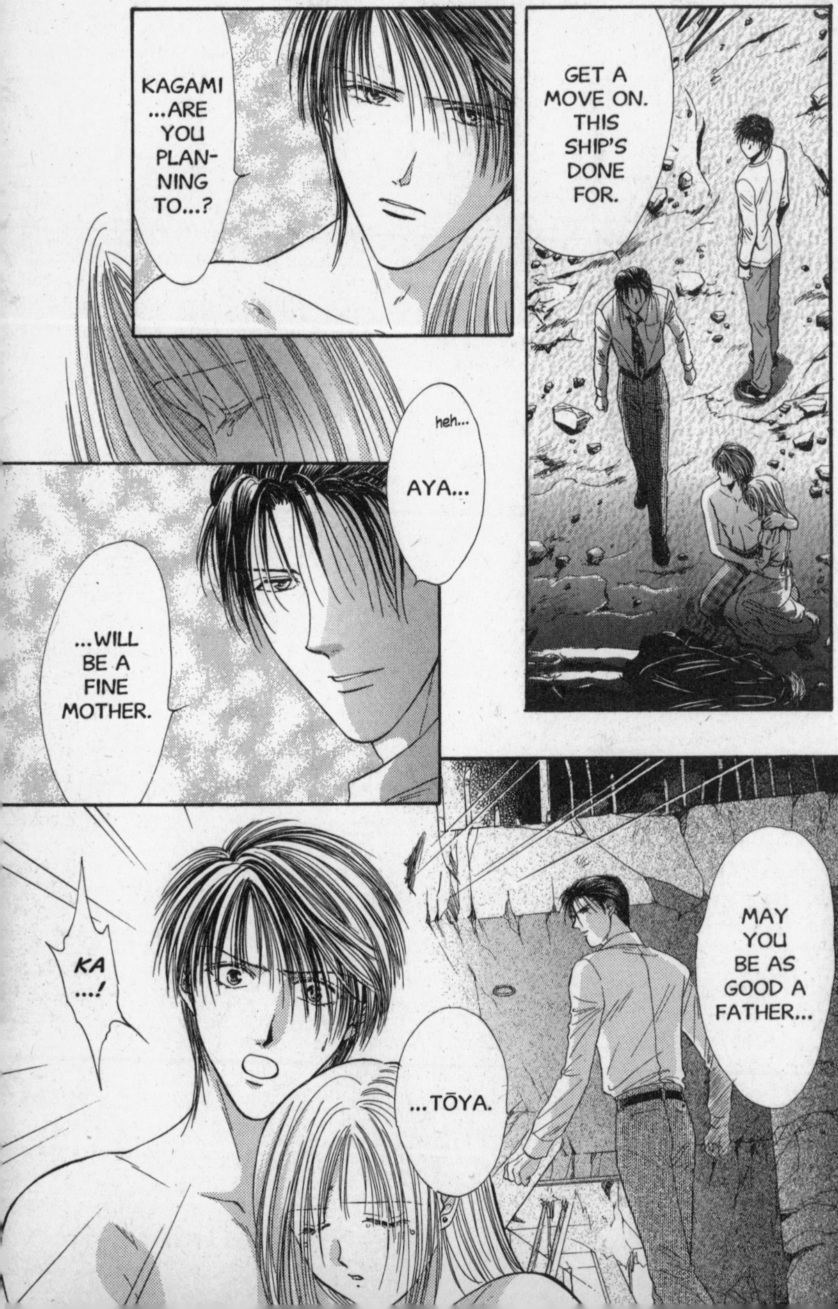
GET A MOVE ON. THIS SHIP'S DONE FOR.
KAGAMI ...ARE YOU PLAN-NING TO...?
heh...
AYA...
...WILL BE A FINE MOTHER.
MAY YOU BE AS GOOD A FATHER...
...TŌYA.
KA ...!

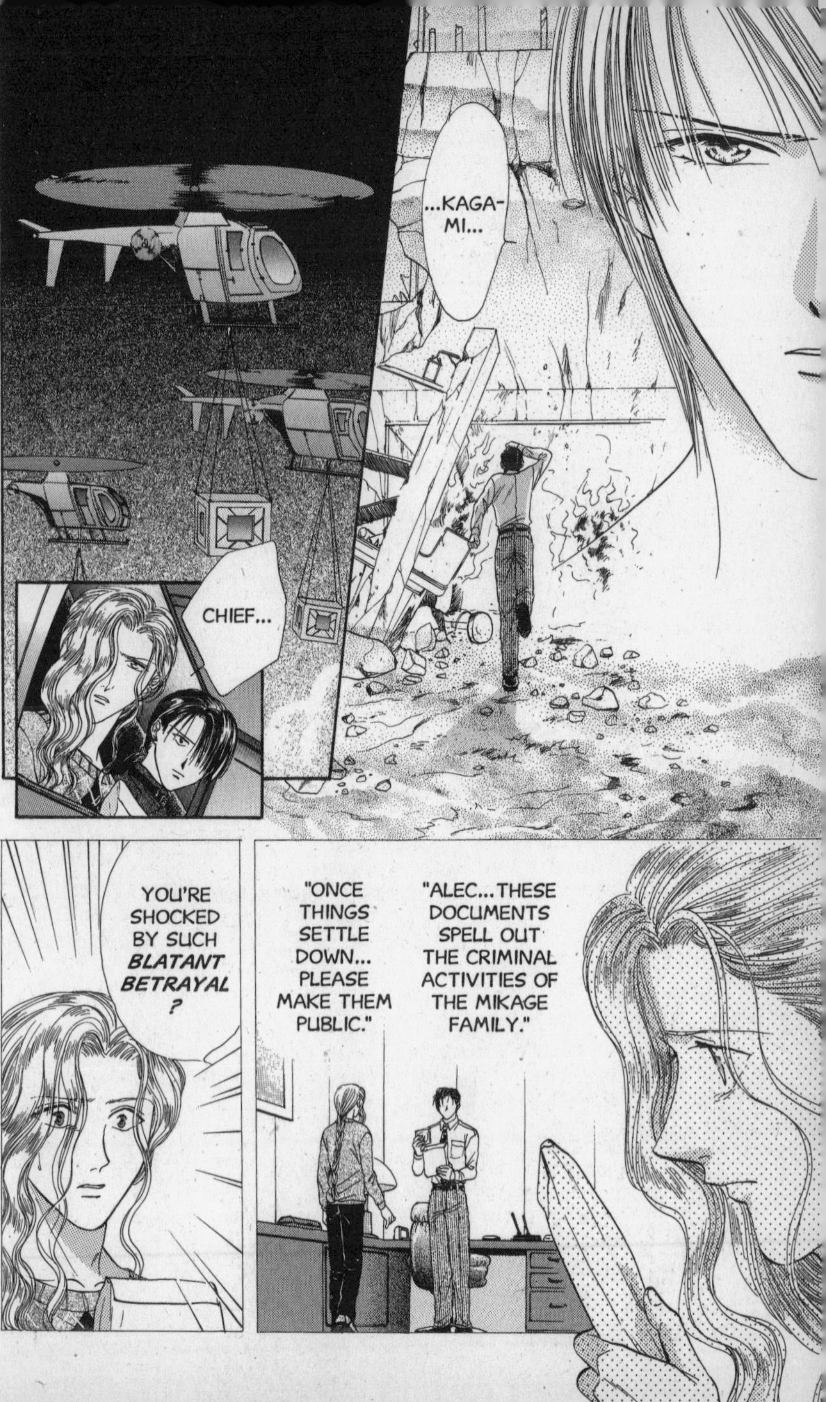
...KAGA-MI...
CHIEF...
"ALEC... THESE DOCUMENTS SPELL OUT THE CRIMINAL ACTIVITIES OF THE MIKAGE FAMILY."
"ONCE THINGS SETTLE DOWN... PLEASE MAKE THEM PUBLIC."
YOU'RE SHOCKED BY SUCH BLATANT BETRAYAL?

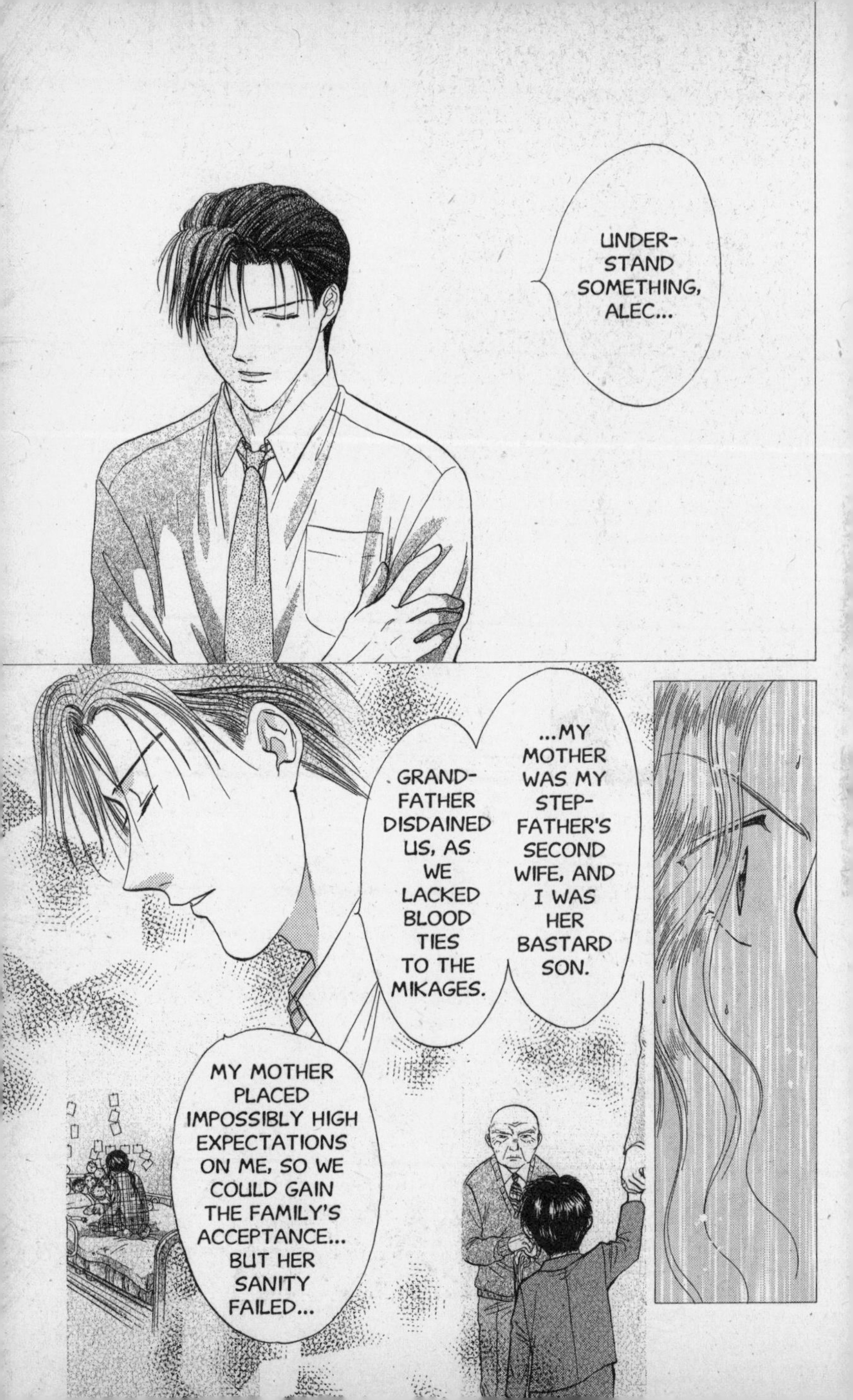
UNDER-STAND SOMETHING, ALEC...
...MY MOTHER WAS MY STEP-FATHER'S SECOND WIFE, AND I WAS HER BASTARD SON.
GRAND-FATHER DISDAINED US, AS WE LACKED BLOOD TIES TO THE MIKAGES.
MY MOTHER PLACED IMPOSSIBLY HIGH EXPECTATIONS ON ME, SO WE COULD GAIN THE FAMILY'S ACCEPTANCE... BUT HER SANITY FAILED...

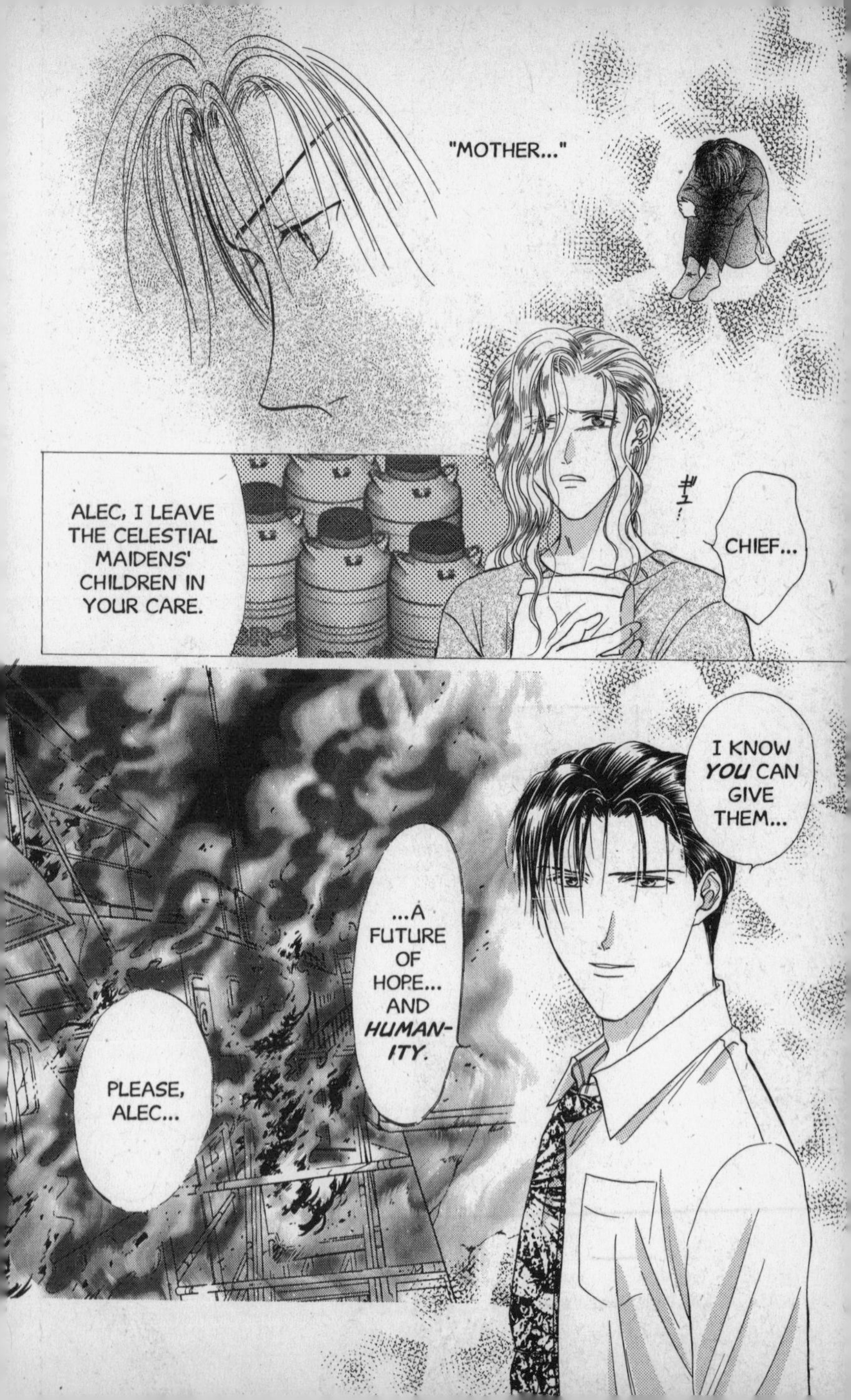
"MOTHER..."
CHIEF...
ALEC, I LEAVE THE CELESTIAL MAIDENS' CHILDREN IN YOUR CARE.
I KNOW *YOU* CAN GIVE THEM...
...A FUTURE OF HOPE... AND *HUMANITY.*
PLEASE, ALEC...

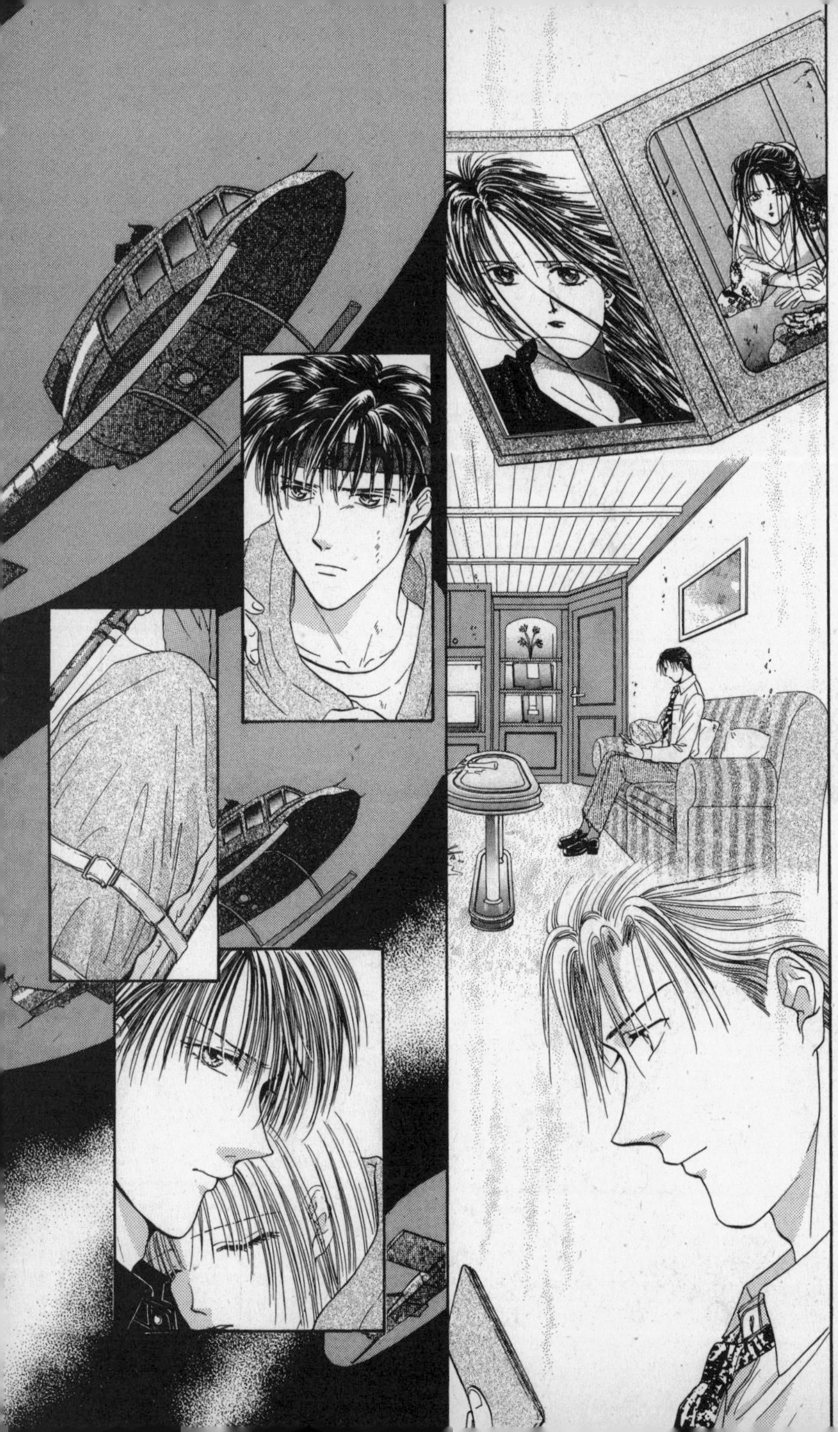

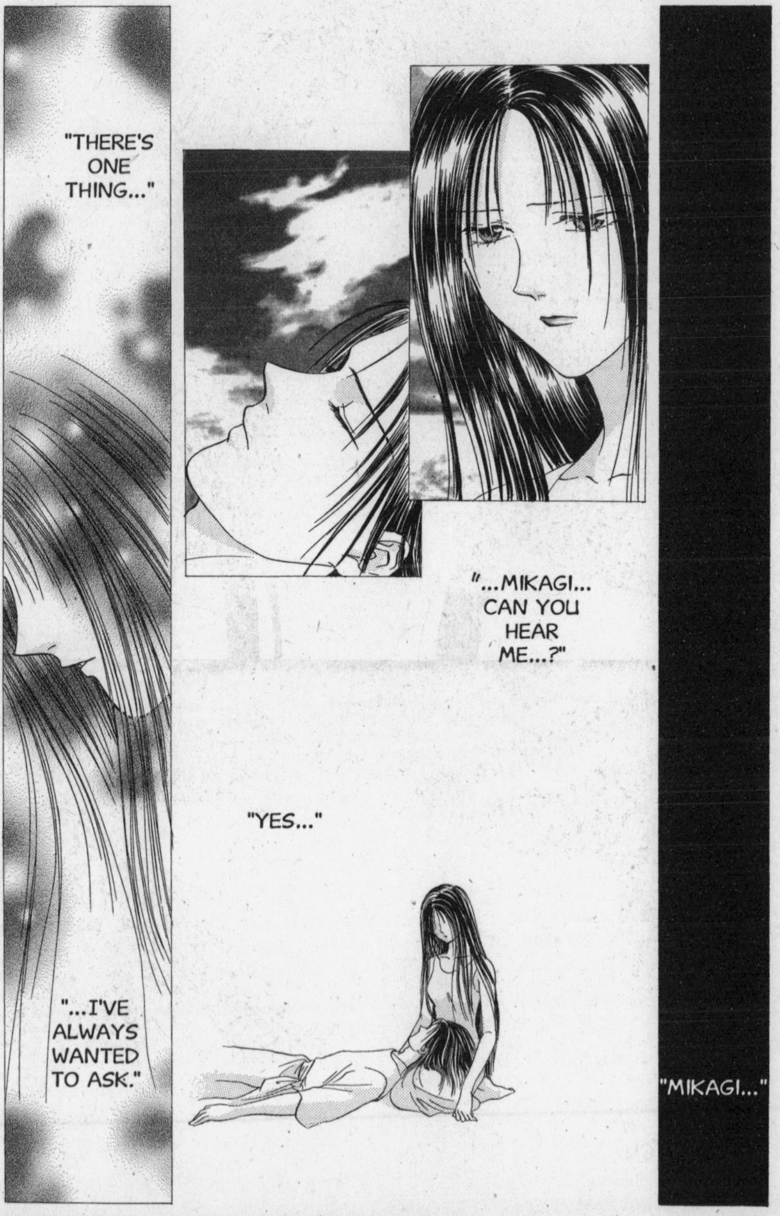
"MIKAGI..."
"...MIKAGI... CAN YOU HEAR ME...?"
"YES..."
"THERE'S ONE THING..."
"...I'VE ALWAYS WANTED TO ASK."

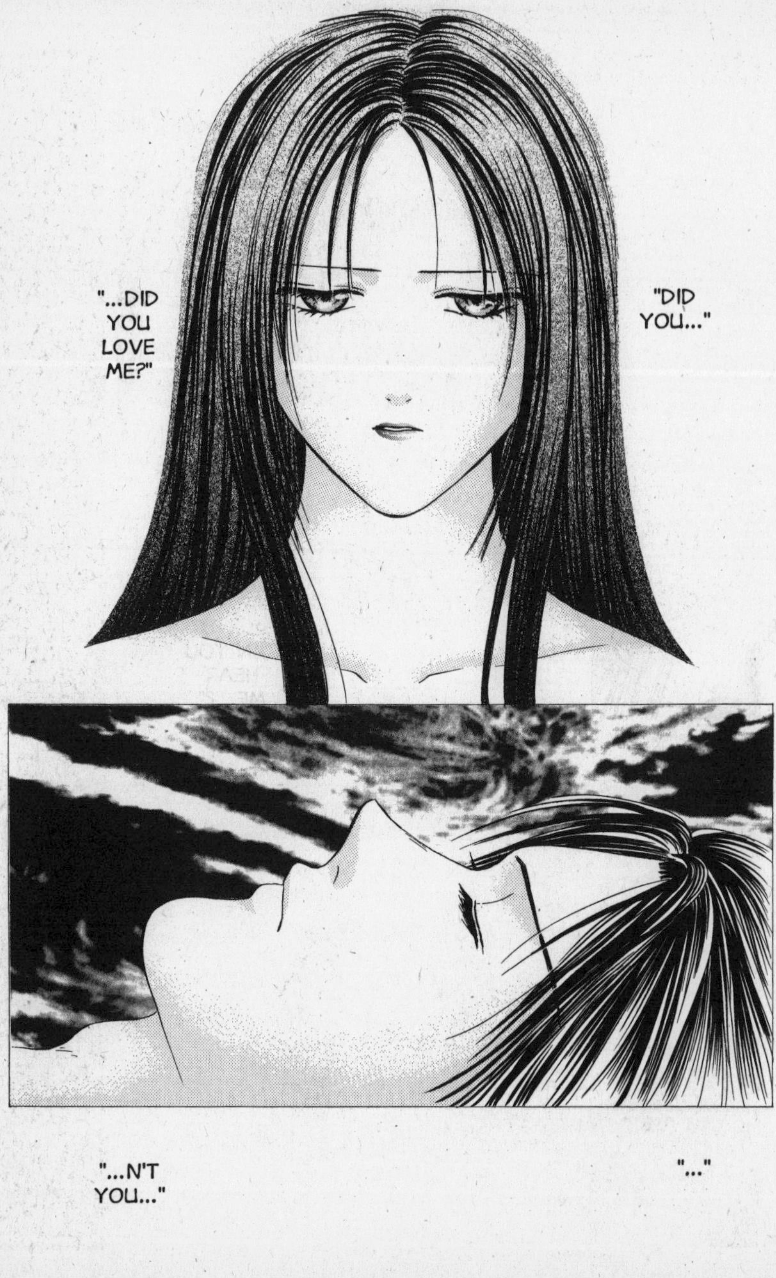
"DID YOU..."
"...DID YOU LOVE ME?"
"..."
"...N'T YOU..."

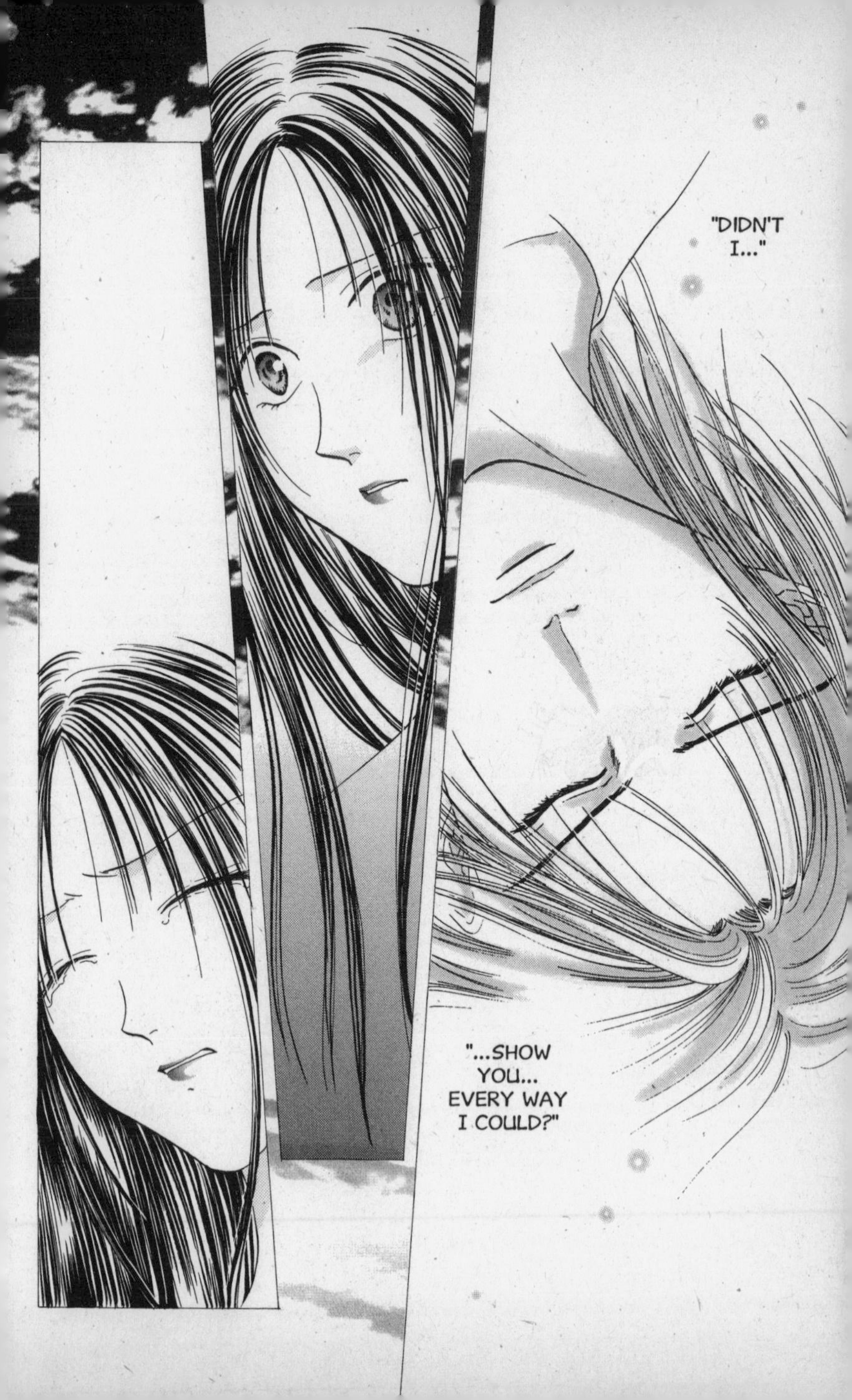
"DIDN'T I..."
"...SHOW YOU... EVERY WAY I COULD?"

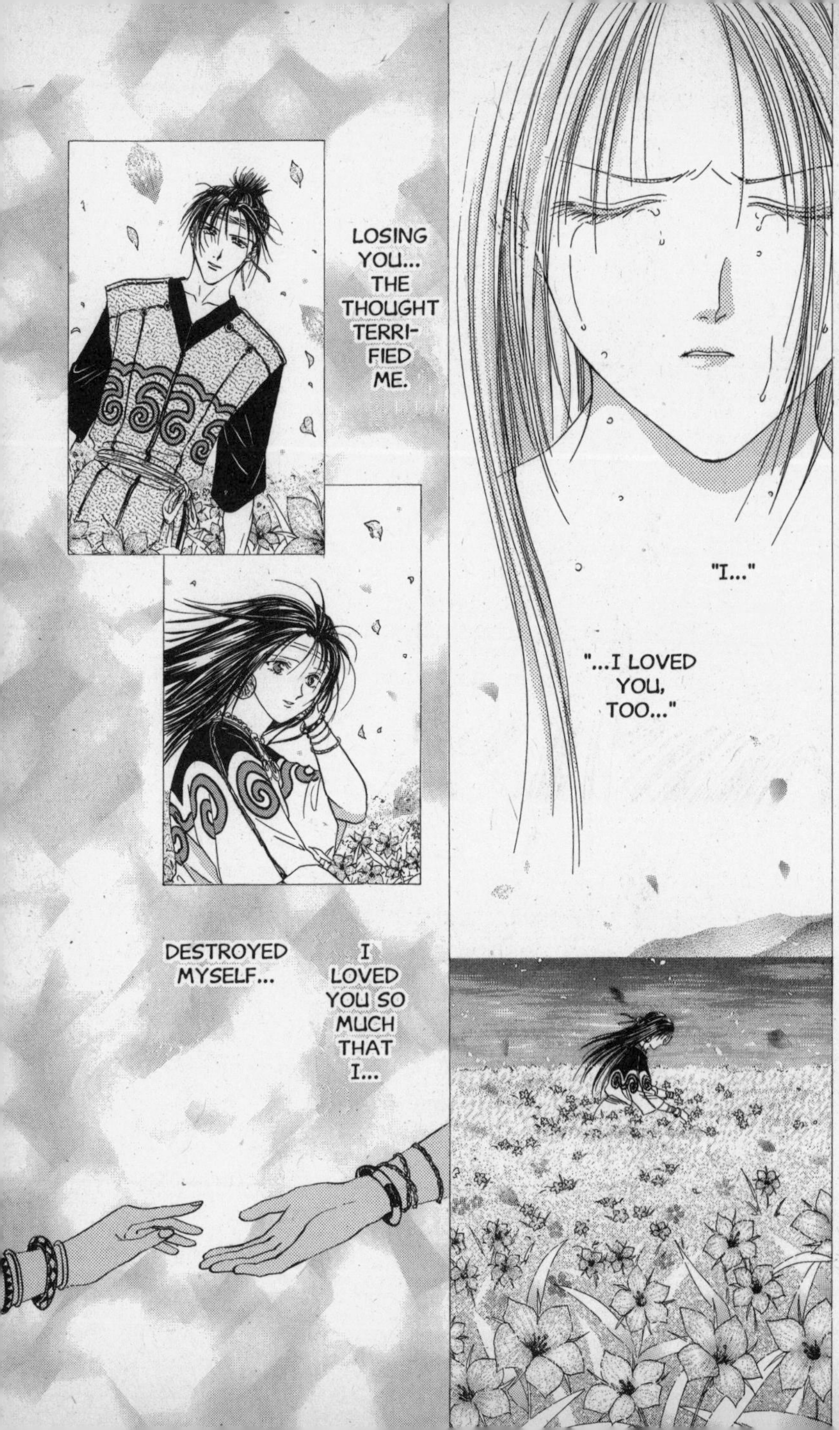
"I..."
"...I LOVED YOU, TOO..."
LOSING YOU... THE THOUGHT TERRI-FIED ME.
I LOVED YOU SO MUCH THAT I...
DESTROYED MYSELF...

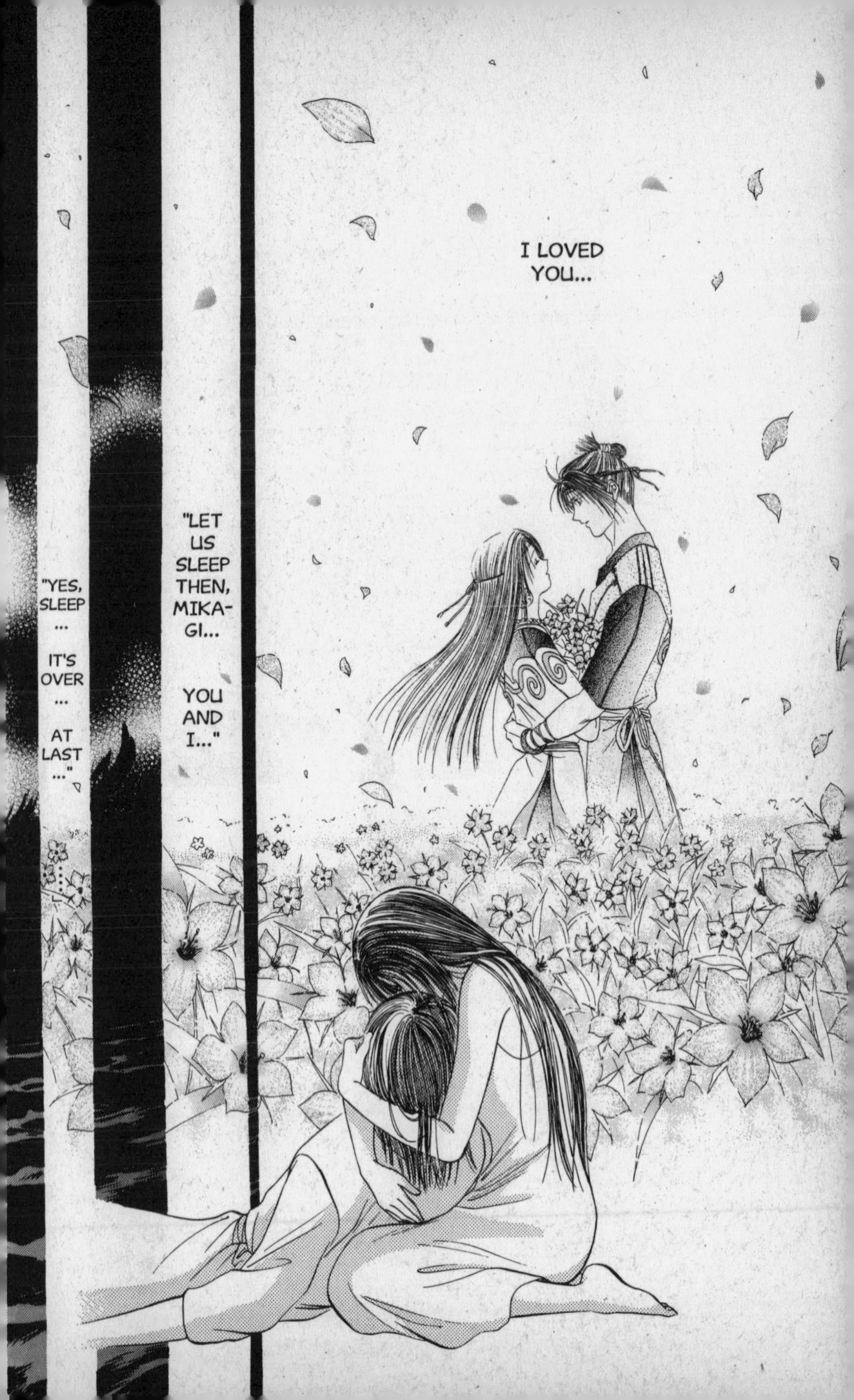
I LOVED YOU...
"LET US SLEEP THEN, MIKA-GI...
YOU AND I..."
"YES, SLEEP ...
IT'S OVER ...
AT LAST ..."

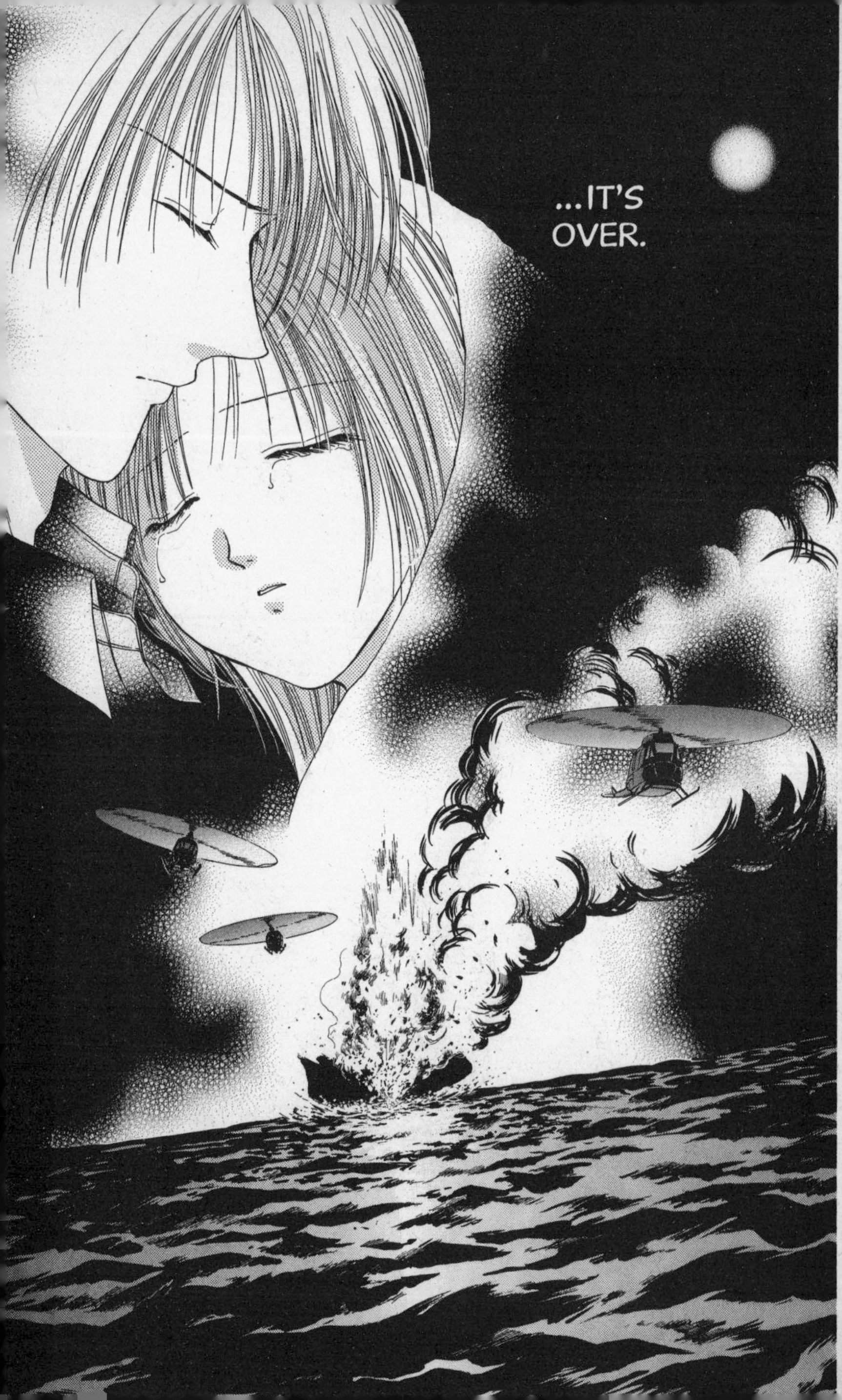
...IT'S
OVER.

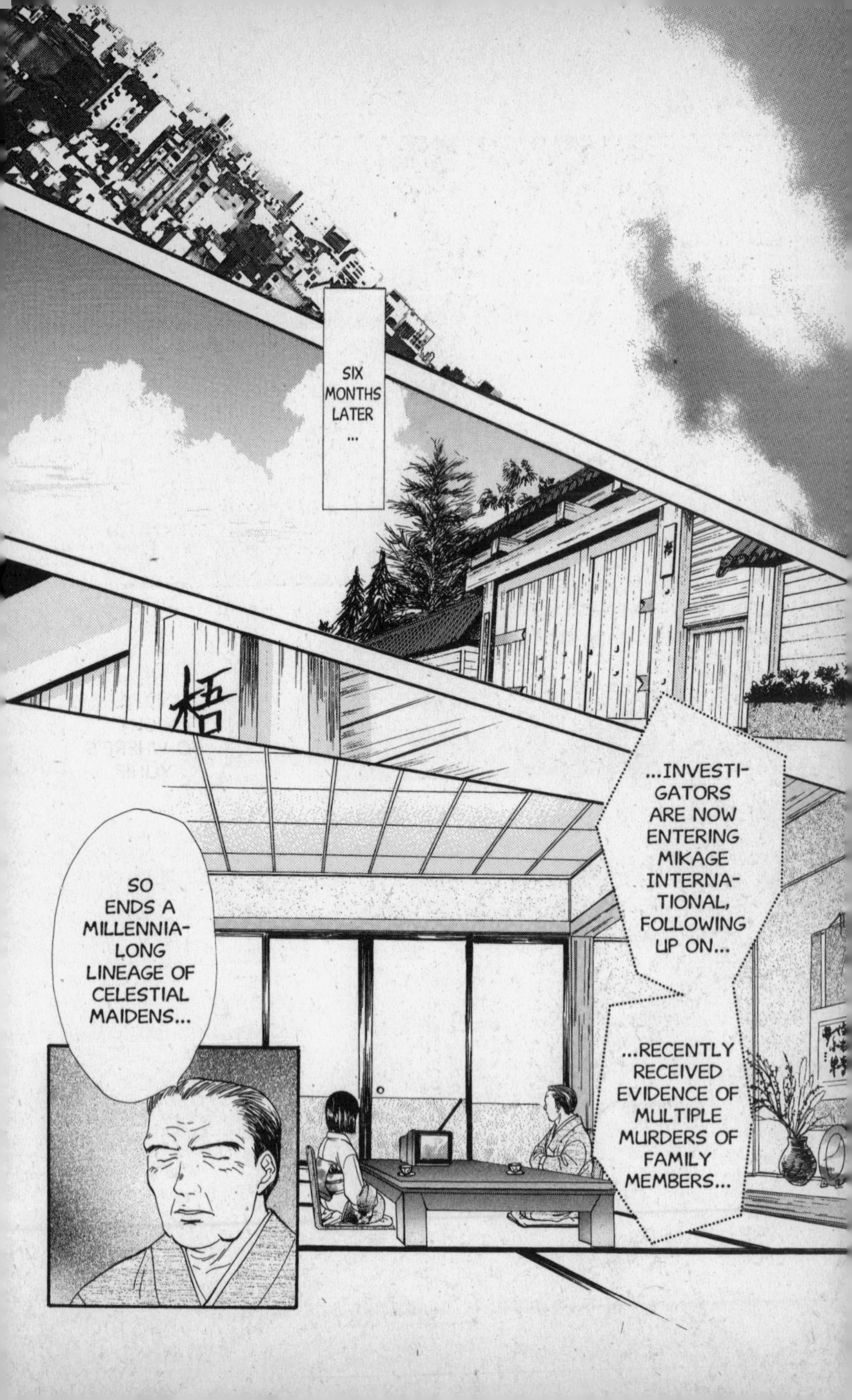
SIX MONTHS LATER ...
...INVESTI-GATORS ARE NOW ENTERING MIKAGE INTERNA-TIONAL, FOLLOWING UP ON...
...RECENTLY RECEIVED EVIDENCE OF MULTIPLE MURDERS OF FAMILY MEMBERS...
SO ENDS A MILLENNIA-LONG LINEAGE OF CELESTIAL MAIDENS...

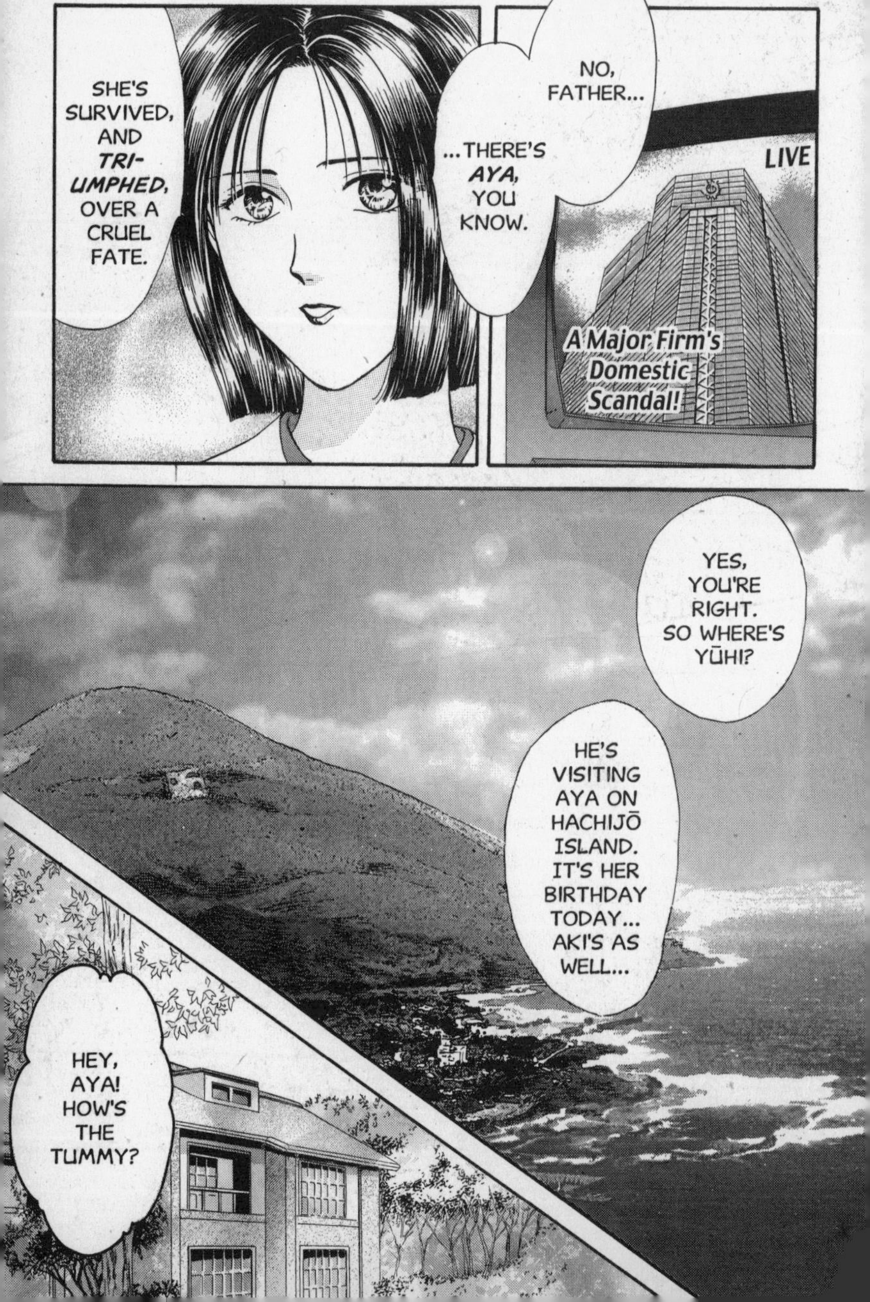
NO, FATHER...
...THERE'S *AYA*, YOU KNOW.
LIVE
A Major Firm's Domestic Scandal!
SHE'S SURVIVED, AND *TRIUMPHED*, OVER A CRUEL FATE.
YES, YOU'RE RIGHT. SO WHERE'S YŪHI?
HE'S VISITING AYA ON HACHIJŌ ISLAND. IT'S HER BIRTHDAY TODAY... AKI'S AS WELL...
HEY, AYA! HOW'S THE TUMMY?

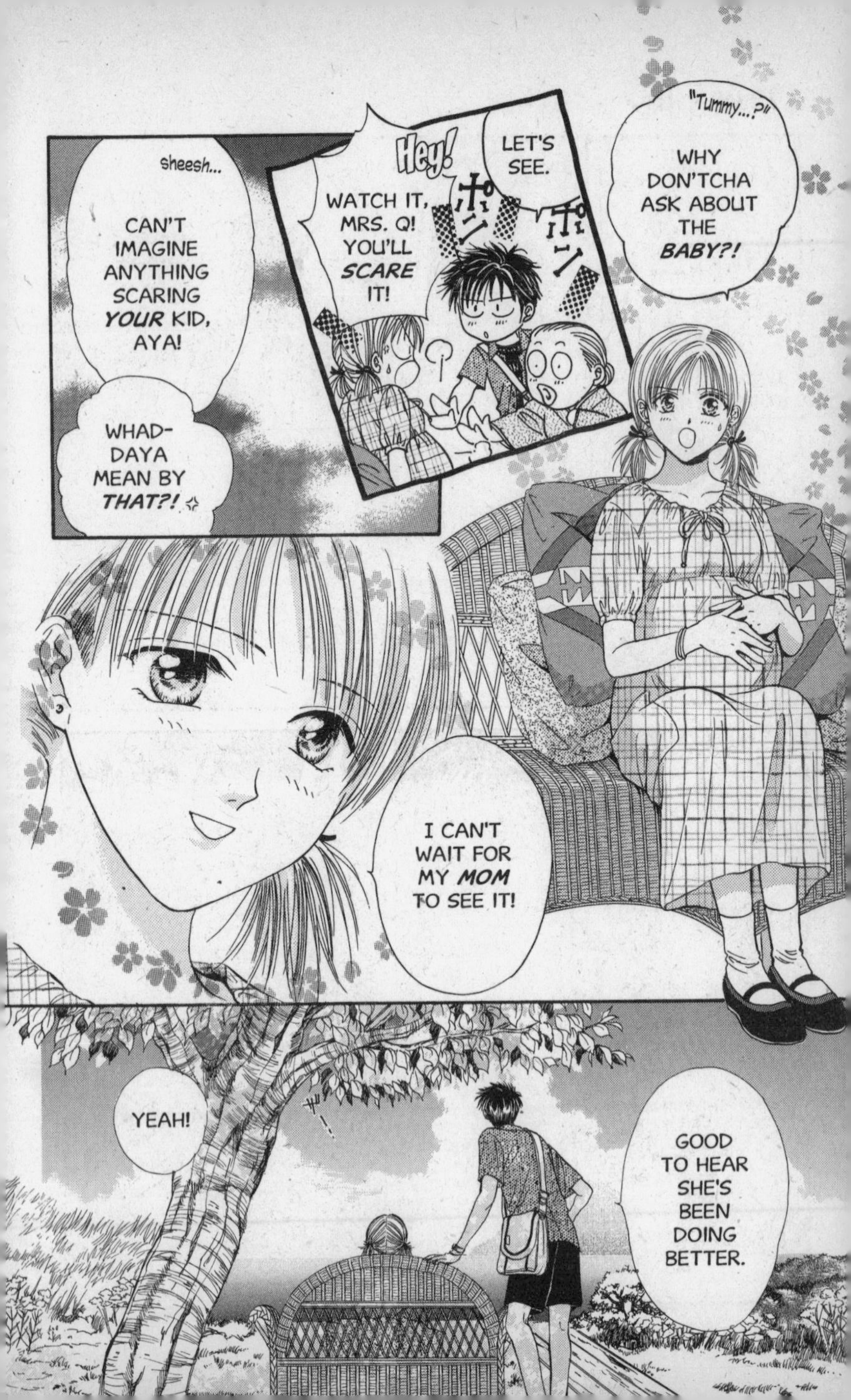
"Tummy...?"
WHY DON'TCHA ASK ABOUT THE BABY?!
LET'S SEE.
Hey!
WATCH IT, MRS. Q! YOU'LL SCARE IT!
sheesh...
CAN'T IMAGINE ANYTHING SCARING YOUR KID, AYA!
WHAD-DAYA MEAN BY THAT?!
I CAN'T WAIT FOR MY MOM TO SEE IT!
GOOD TO HEAR SHE'S BEEN DOING BETTER.
YEAH!

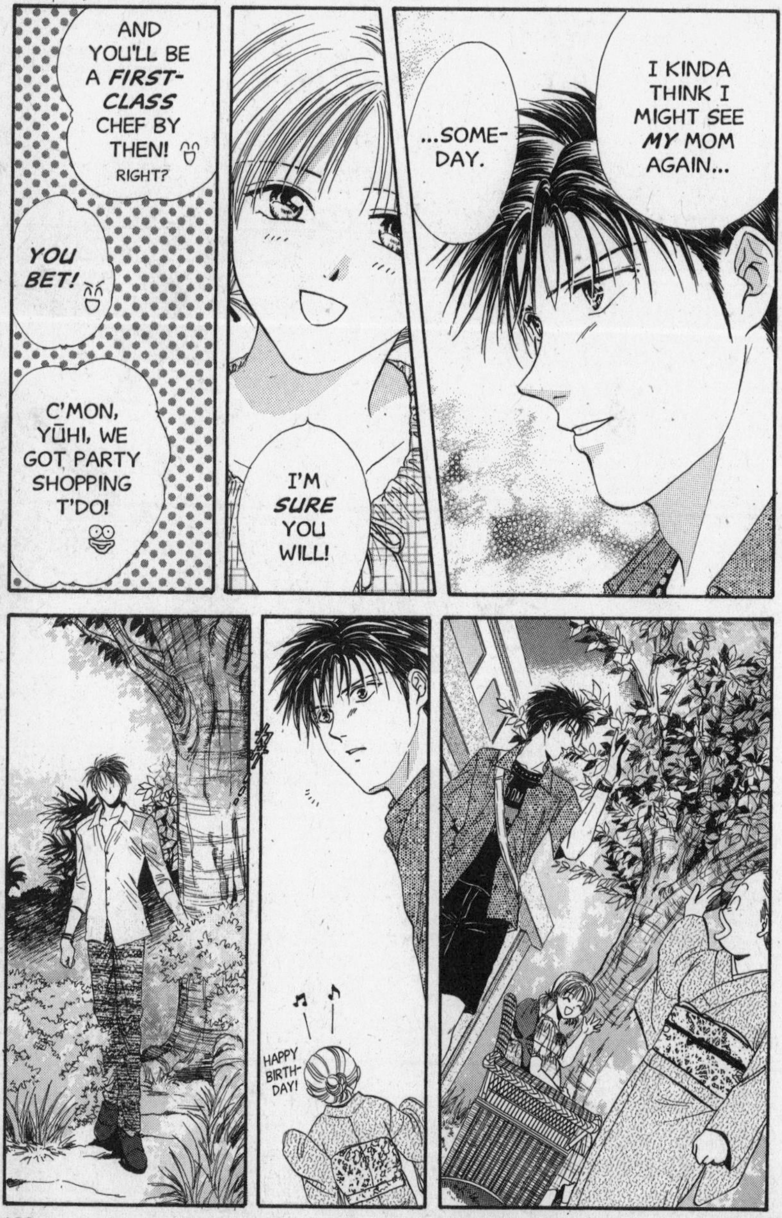
I KINDA THINK I MIGHT SEE *MY* MOM AGAIN...
...SOMEDAY.
I'M *SURE* YOU WILL!
AND YOU'LL BE A *FIRST-CLASS* CHEF BY THEN!
RIGHT?
YOU BET!
C'MON, YŪHI, WE GOT PARTY SHOPPING T'DO!
HAPPY BIRTHDAY!

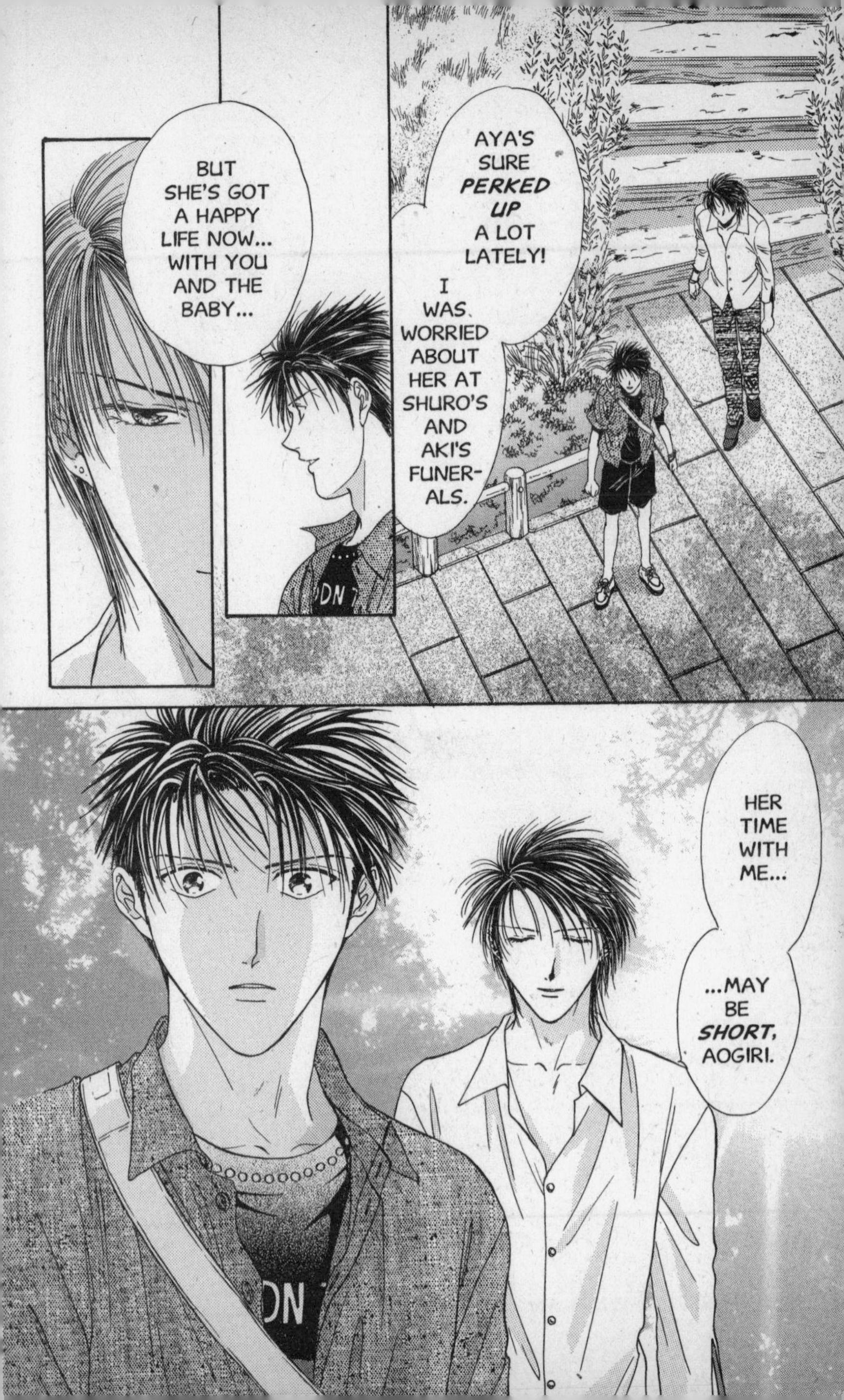
AYA'S SURE PERKED UP A LOT LATELY!
I WAS WORRIED ABOUT HER AT SHURO'S AND AKI'S FUNERALS.
BUT SHE'S GOT A HAPPY LIFE NOW... WITH YOU AND THE BABY...
HER TIME WITH ME...
...MAY BE SHORT, AOGIRI.

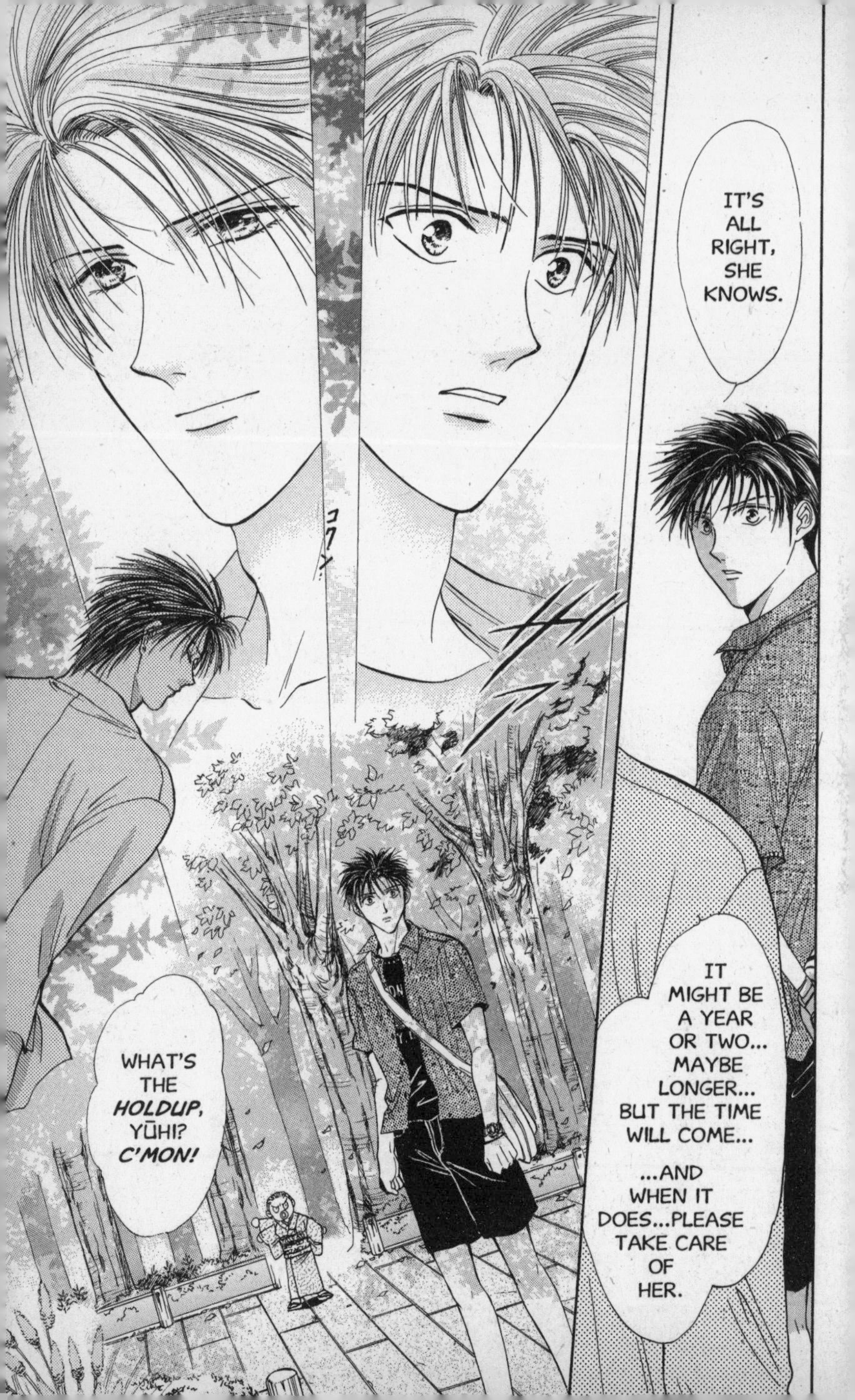
IT'S ALL RIGHT, SHE KNOWS.
IT MIGHT BE A YEAR OR TWO... MAYBE LONGER... BUT THE TIME WILL COME...
...AND WHEN IT DOES...PLEASE TAKE CARE OF HER.
WHAT'S THE *HOLDUP,* YŪHI? *C'MON!*

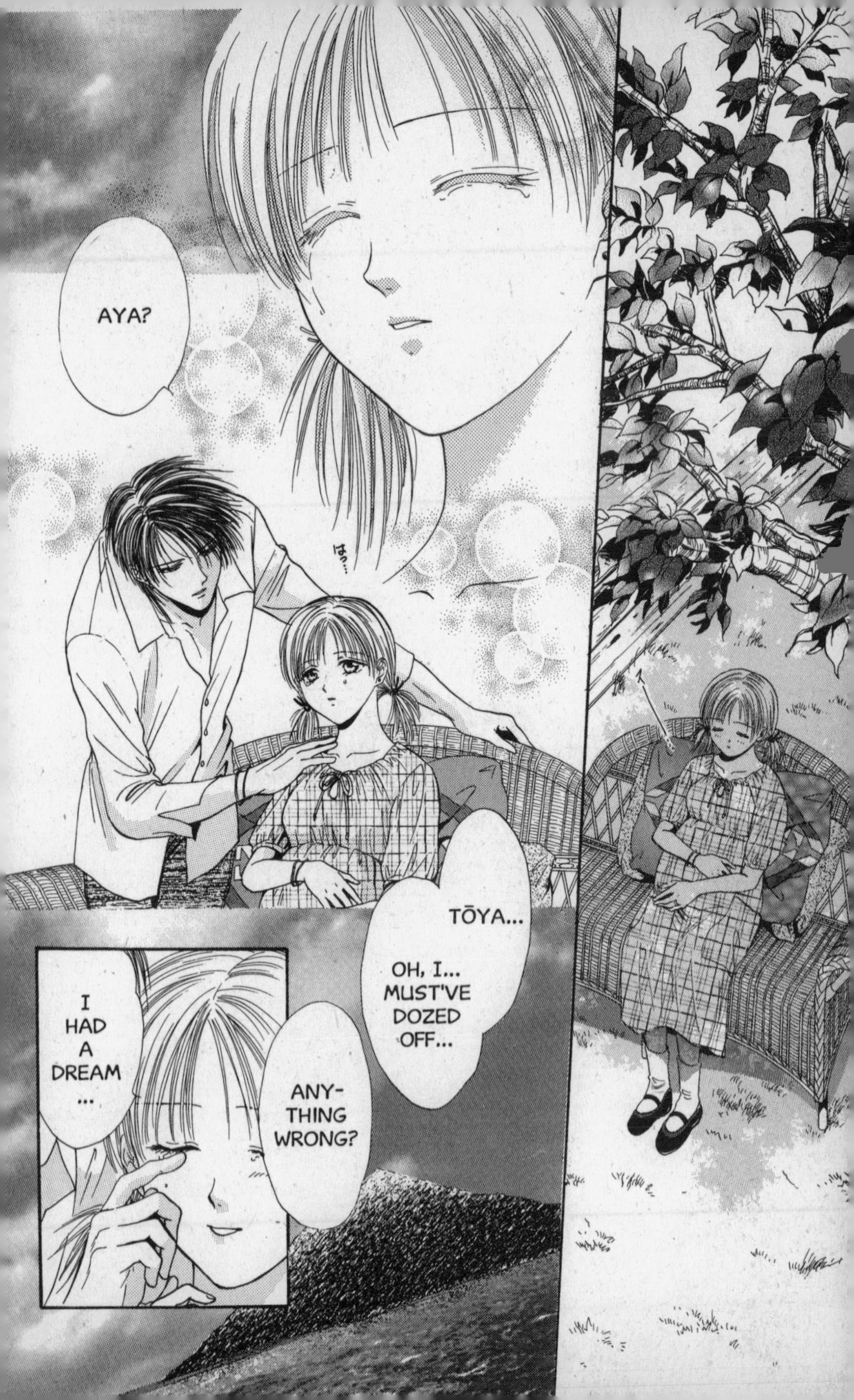
AYA?
はっ…
TŌYA...
OH, I... MUST'VE DOZED OFF...
ANY-THING WRONG?
I HAD A DREAM ...

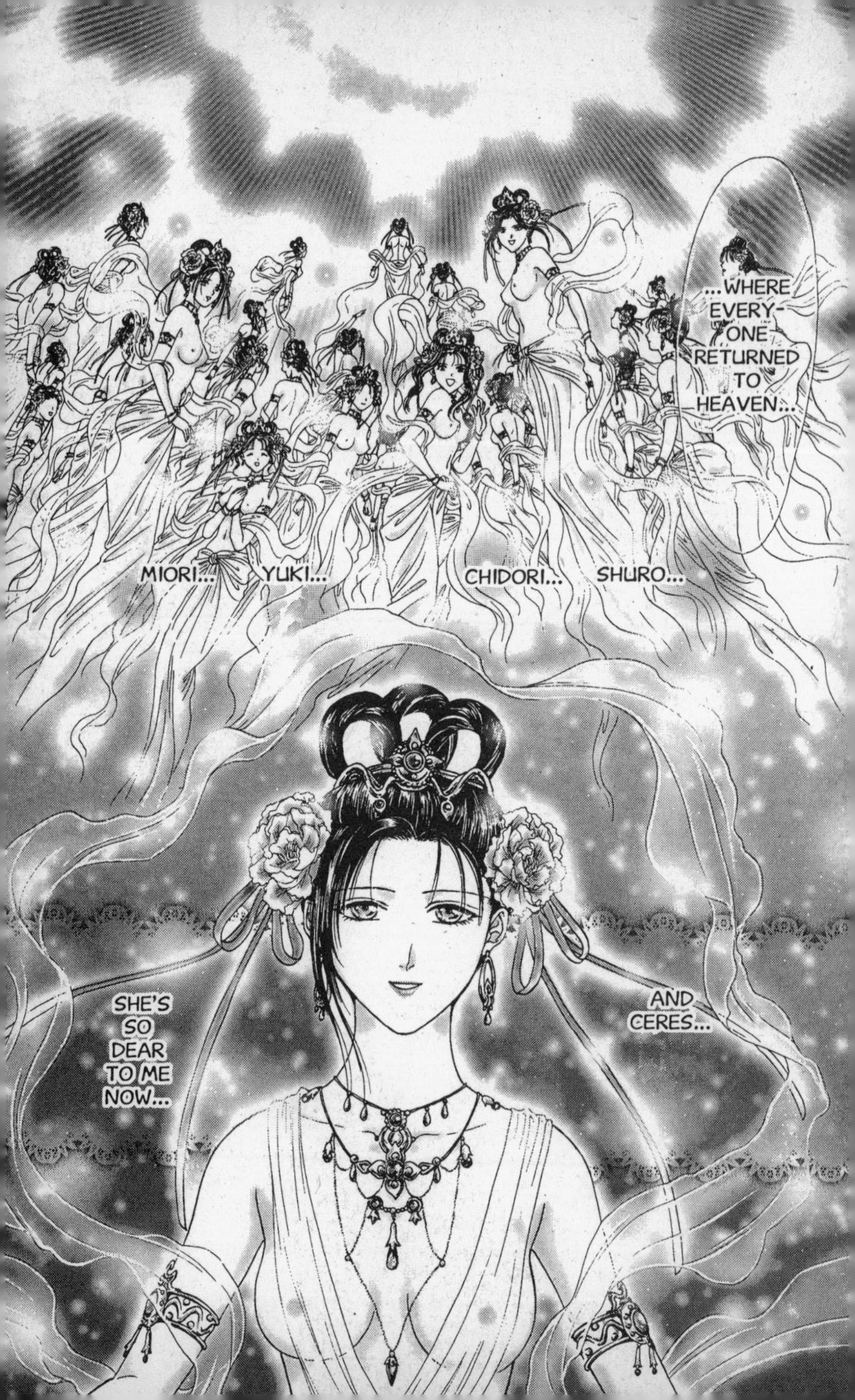
...WHERE EVERY-ONE RETURNED TO HEAVEN...
SHURO...
CHIDORI...
YUKI...
MIORI...
AND CERES...
SHE'S SO DEAR TO ME NOW...

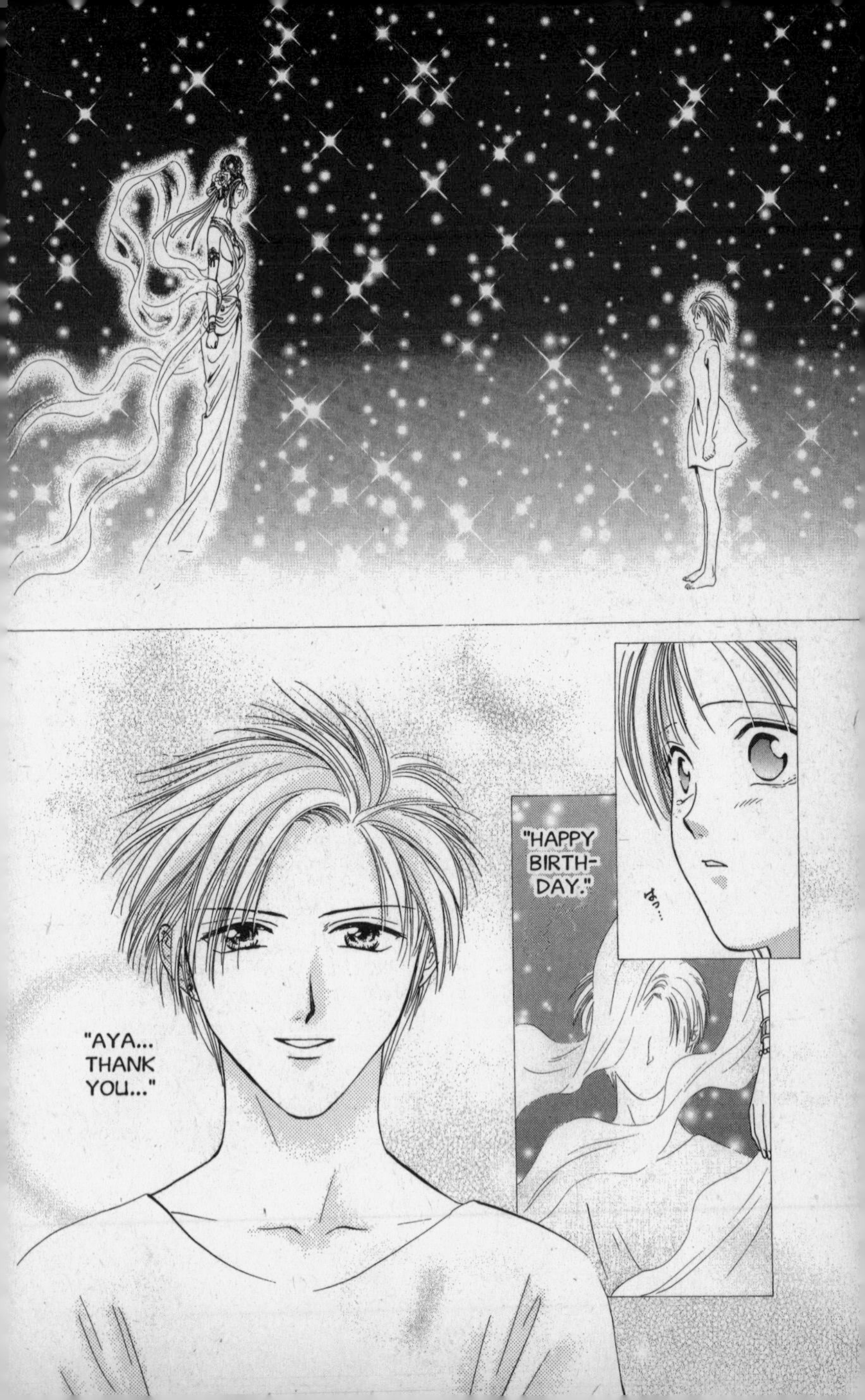
"HAPPY BIRTH-DAY."
"AYA... THANK YOU..."

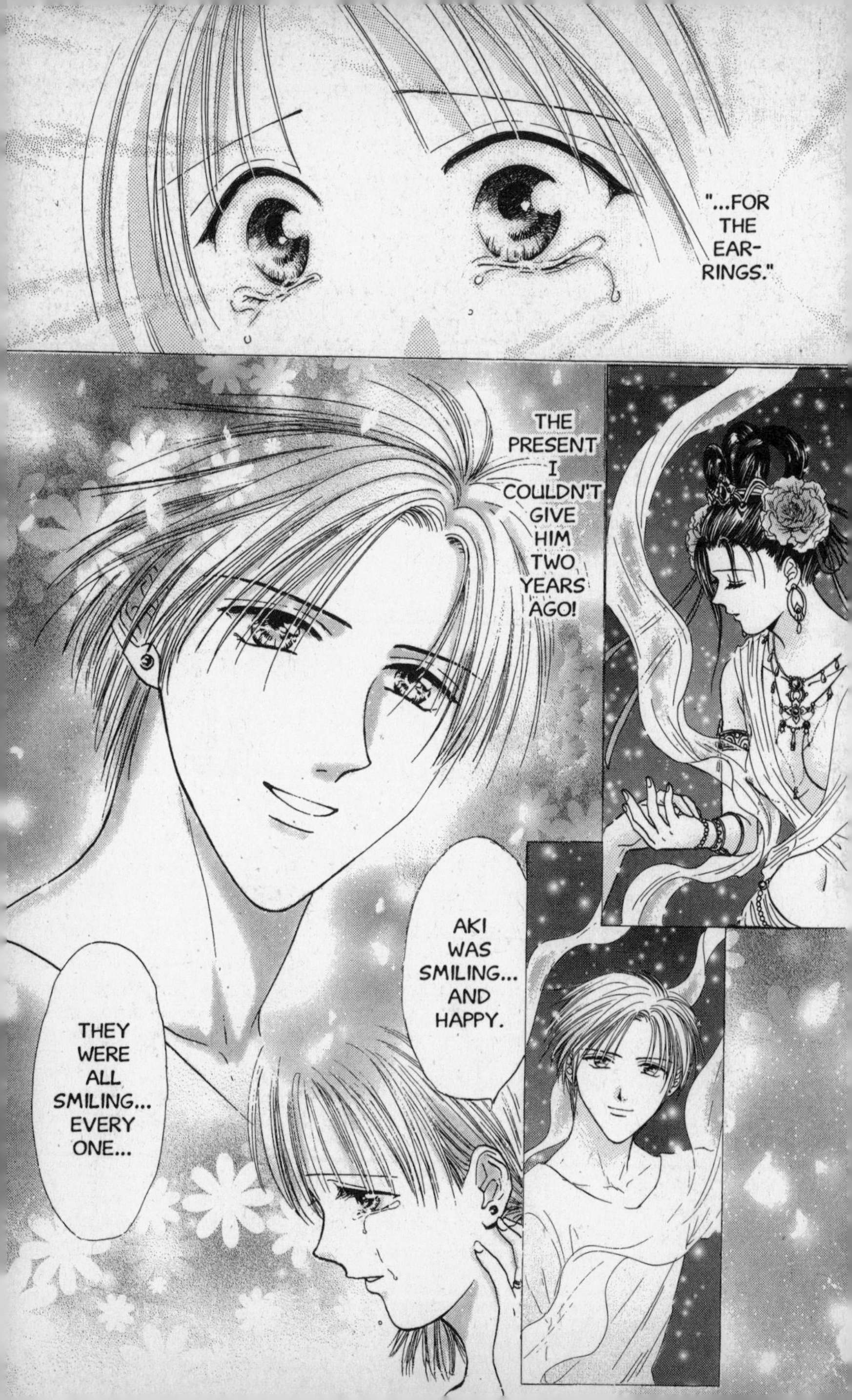
"...FOR THE EAR-RINGS."
THE PRESENT I COULDN'T GIVE HIM TWO YEARS AGO!
AKI WAS SMILING... AND HAPPY.
THEY WERE ALL SMILING... EVERY ONE...

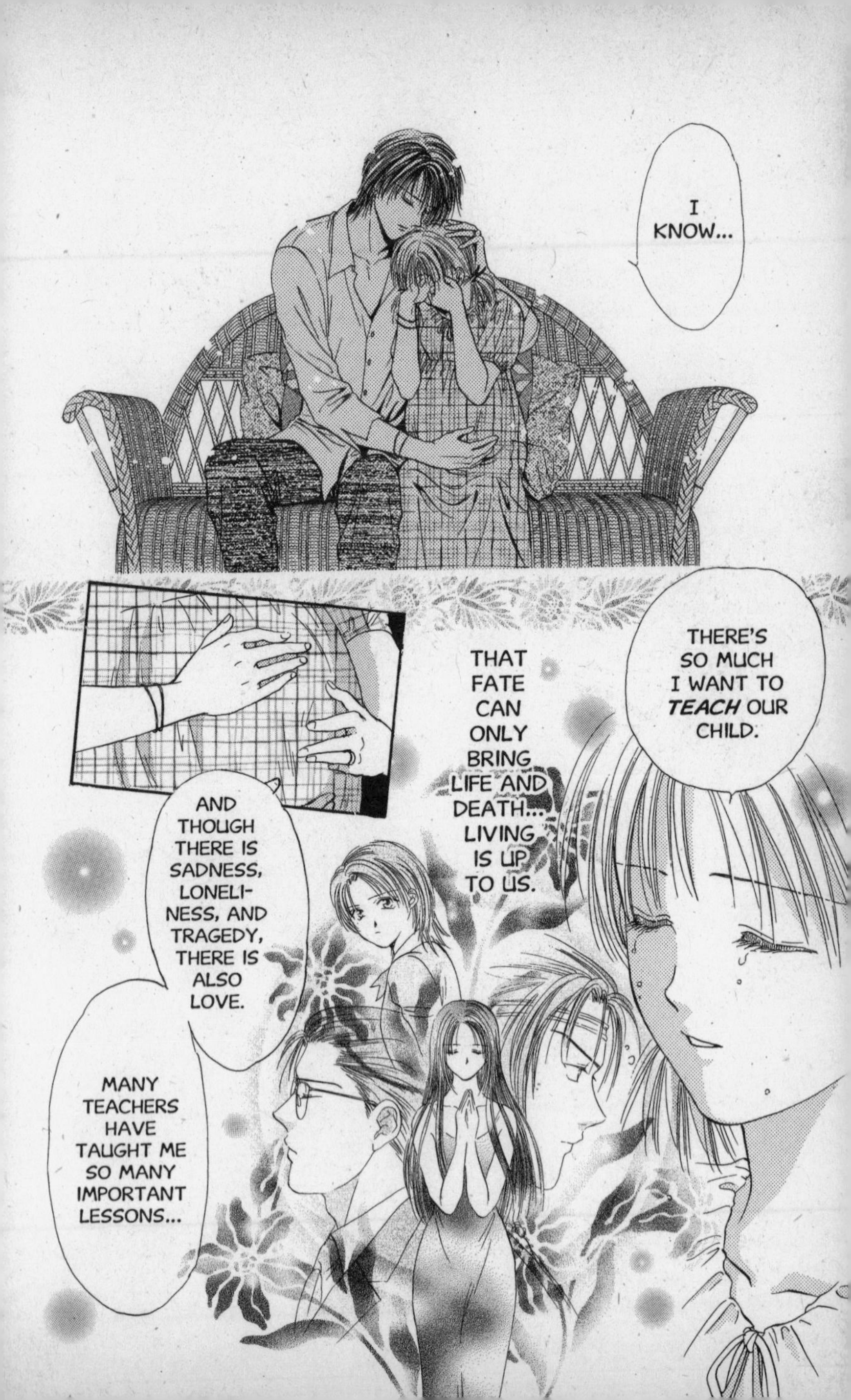
I KNOW...
THERE'S SO MUCH I WANT TO *TEACH* OUR CHILD.
THAT FATE CAN ONLY BRING LIFE AND DEATH... LIVING IS UP TO US.
AND THOUGH THERE IS SADNESS, LONELINESS, AND TRAGEDY, THERE IS ALSO LOVE.
MANY TEACHERS HAVE TAUGHT ME SO MANY IMPORTANT LESSONS...

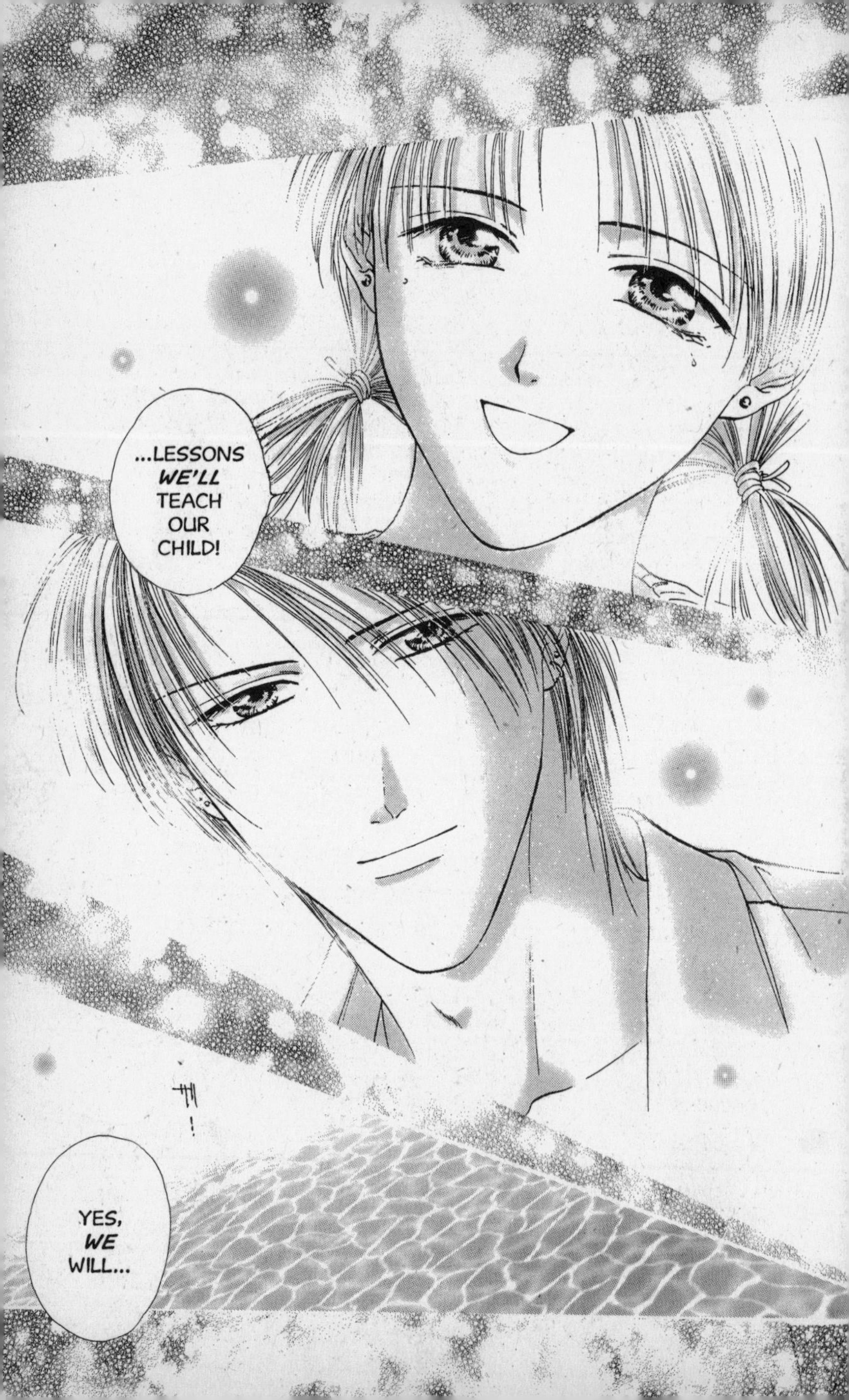
...LESSONS WE'LL TEACH OUR CHILD!
YES, WE WILL...

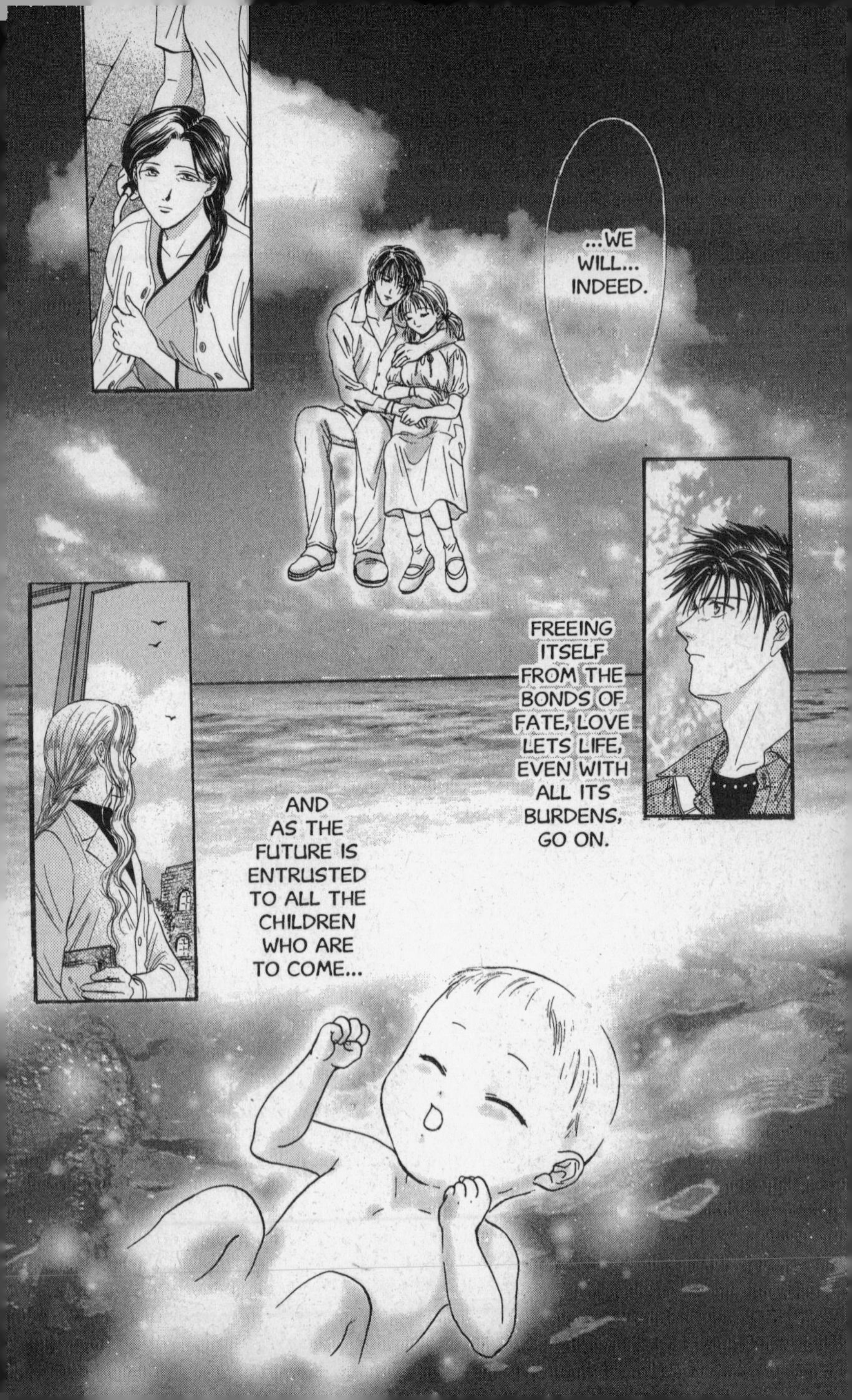
...WE WILL... INDEED.
FREEING ITSELF FROM THE BONDS OF FATE, LOVE LETS LIFE, EVEN WITH ALL ITS BURDENS, GO ON.
AND AS THE FUTURE IS ENTRUSTED TO ALL THE CHILDREN WHO ARE TO COME...

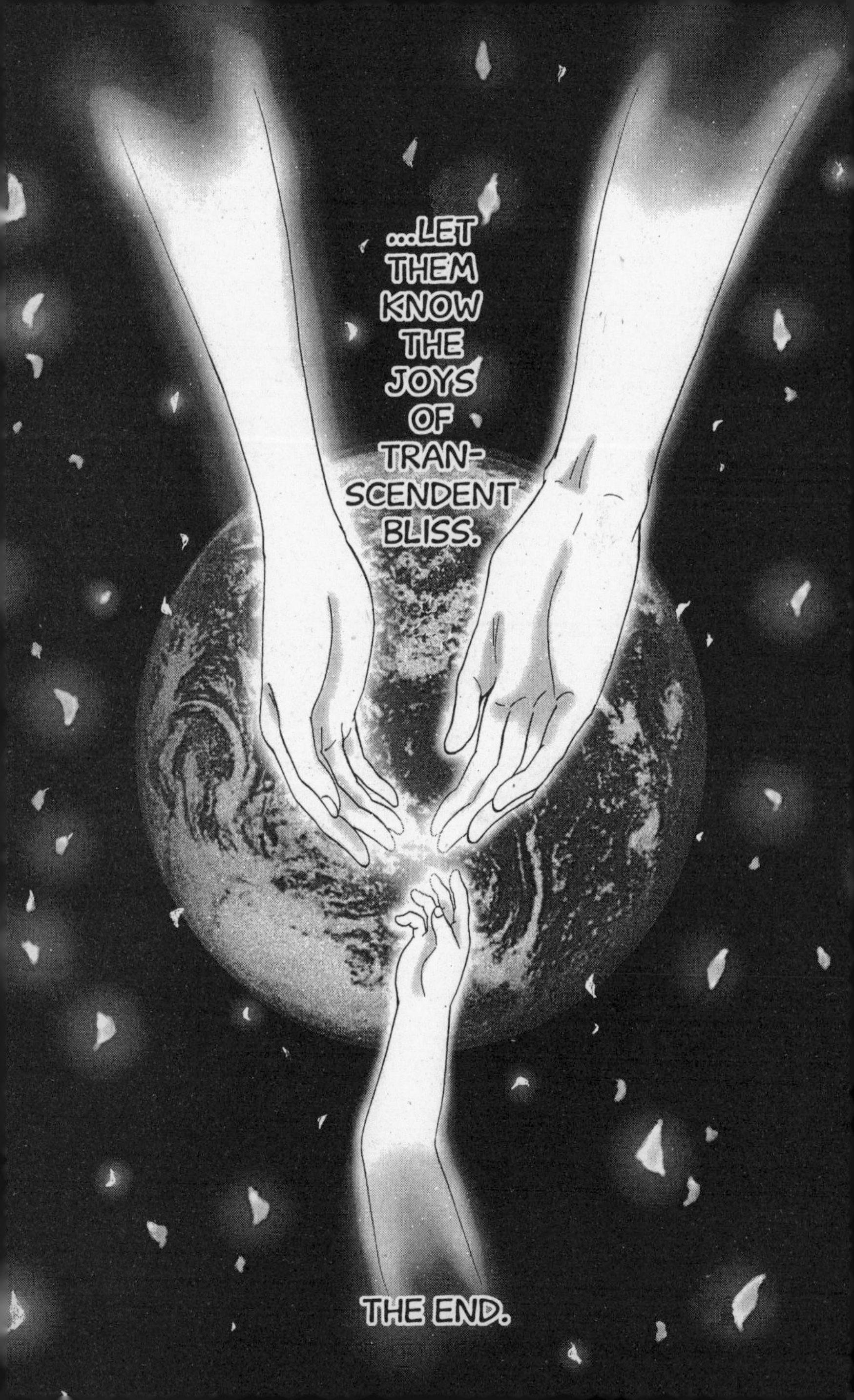
...LET THEM KNOW THE JOYS OF TRAN-SCENDENT BLISS.
THE END.

The CERES Guide to Sound Effects

We've left most of the sound effects in CERES as Yuu Watase originally created them—in Japanese. VIZ has created this glossary to help you decipher, page-by-page and panel-by-panel, what all those foreign words and background noises mean. Use this guide to impress your friends with your new Japanese vocabulary. The glossary lists the page number then panel. For example, 003.1 indicates page 3, panel 1.

006.3 FX:Dokun Dokun Dokun (heavy heartbeat)
007.4 FX:Fuwa (a "disappearance" sound)
010.2 FX:Suto (feet touch down)
010.3 FX:Gu (tug)
013.1 FX:Hyu (fft)
013.2 FX:Pishi (snap)
013.4 FX:Za (shk)
013.4 FX:Pakin (crack)
015.2 FX:Za (shk)
015.3 FX:Ba (fwap)
016.2 FX:Buwa (fwoosh)
017.1 FX:Zaza (slosh-waves)
017.3 FX:Guooon (vwoom-panel)
018.1 FX:Kira (glint)
019.2 FX:Guooon (vwoom)
020.1 FX:To (tump)
020.4 FX:Don (thump)
021.1 FX:Guoon (vwoom)
021.4 FX:Dogagaga (crash)
022.2 FX:Don Don (blam blam]
022.4 FX:Zuzu (zhoop)
022.4 FX:Poro (plop)
022.5 FX:Su (fft- fading)
023.1 FX:Zoku (brr)
023.2 FX:Tan (leap)
023.4 FX:Dan (slam)
024.1 FX:Biku (!)
024.3 FX:Zuzu (zhoop)
025.2 FX:Ha (!)
025.3 FX:Chaki (ch-chk)
026.3 FX:Pata (fwump)
027.1 FX:Zuru (slump)
030.1 FX:Go (rush)
030.3 FX:Ha (!)
031.2 FX:Gura (lurch)
032.1 FX:Fuwa (gentle touch)
033.2 FX:Tokun Tokun Tokun (heartbeats)
033.3 FX:Tokun Tokun Tokun Tokun (heartbeats)
036.1 FX:Za (sloosh)
037.1 FX:Patan (slam)

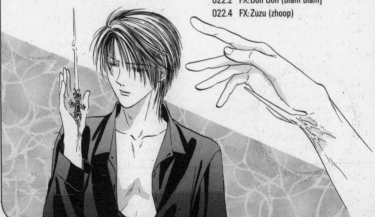

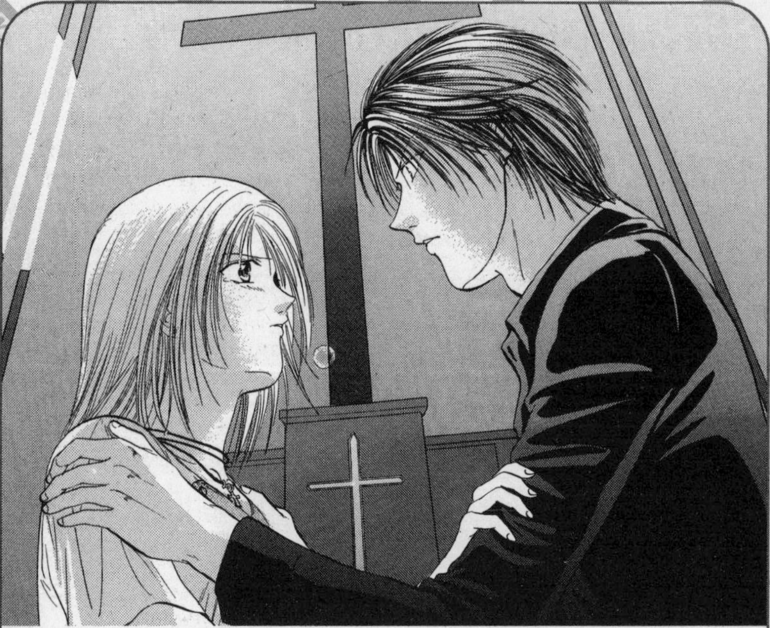

037.2 FX:Don (thump)
037.3 FX:Don Don (thump thump)
037.4 FX:Don (thump)
037.5 FX:Don Don (thump thump)
039.1 FX:Doka (boot)
039.2 FX:Doka Doka Doka Doka (pow pow pow pow)
040.3 FX:Gu (squeeze)
044.1 FX:Pi (clik)
045.1 FX:Za (sloosh)
045.2 FX:Bata Bata (tromp tromp)
046.3 FX:Ha (!)
047.3 FX:Za (shk)
049.2 FX:Zan (splash)
054.3 FX:Gaba (whump- getting up)
054.4 FX:Patan (slam)
055.3 FX:Gyu (squeeze)
057.3 FX:Dokun Dokun Dokun (heartbeats)
059.3 FX:Kura (swoon)
061.2 FX:Gyu (squeeze)
063.4 FX:Giii (creak)
064.2 FX:Fura (stagger)
064.3 FX:Ha (!)
064.4 FX:Pishi (crack)
065.1 FX:Pishi Pishi (crackle crack)
065.2 FX:Pishi Pishi (crackle crack)
065.3 FX:Ban (smash)
066.1 FX:Ha (!)
066.2 FX:Doon (boom)
067.1 FX:Buwa (whoosh)
071.1 FX:Ha (!)
072.1 FX:Gyu (squeeze)
073.1 FX:Gyu (squeeze)
074.4 FX:Parin (crack)
075.2 FX:Yura (billow)
075.4 FX:Gu (clench)
075.6 FX:Gusha (crunch)
077.4 FX:Do (wham)
078.1 FX:Ha (!)
079.5 FX:Ban (slam)
080.4 FX:Zaza (shkshh)
082.2 FX:Oooo (roarr)
082.3 FX:Ha (!)
084.1 FX:Don (slam)
084.3 FX:Hyu (fft)
084.5 FX:Ga (thok)

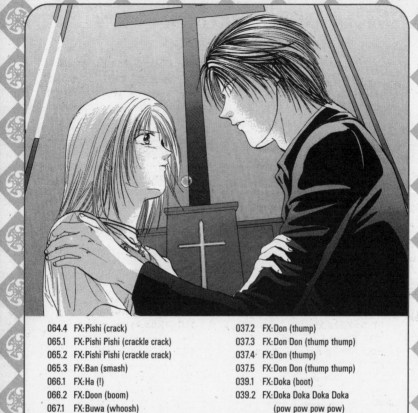

085.1 FX:Do (thunk)
085.2 FX:Za (shk)
085.3 FX:Su (fft- fading wound)
085.4 FX:Suu (melting)
086.1 FX:Ba (fwash)
086.3 FX:Dododo (bash)
086.4 FX:Dodo (crash)
087.1 FX:Don (boom)
087.2 FX:Zuzun (thoom)
087.4 FX:Ba (leap)
088.2 FX:Zun (boom)
088.4 FX:Do (slam)
090.2 FX:Zuzuun (thoom)
091.4 FX:Ha (!)
092.1 FX:Do (slam)
092.2 FX:Zaza (shkshh)
092.4 FX:Do (thunk)
094.1 FX:Zan (splash)
094.2 FX:Ba (leap)
095.1 FX:Za (splash)
096.2 FX:Paan (smash)
100.1 FX:Daran (slump)
103.1 FX:Bishi (pow)
103.2 FX:Gyu (clench)
104.1 FX:Ka (flash)
104.3 FX:Dosu (thunk)
105.2 FX:Zububu (rrg- digging in)
105.4 FX:Zuza (shk)
106.4 FX:Bababa (zzak)
106.5 FX:Ha (!)
107.1 FX:Ba (leap)
108.1 FX:Ha (!)
110.1 FX:Zazaan (slosh-waves)
113.2 FX:Gu (clutch)
113.3 FX:Dokun Dokun Dokun Dokun (heartbeats)
114.1 FX:Ha (!)
114.5 FX:Gu (squeeze)
115.2 FX:Ba (foosh)
117.3 FX:Zuru (stagger)
122.4 FX:Do (blam)
123.1 FX:Dododo (bash)
124.1 FX:Ban (slam)

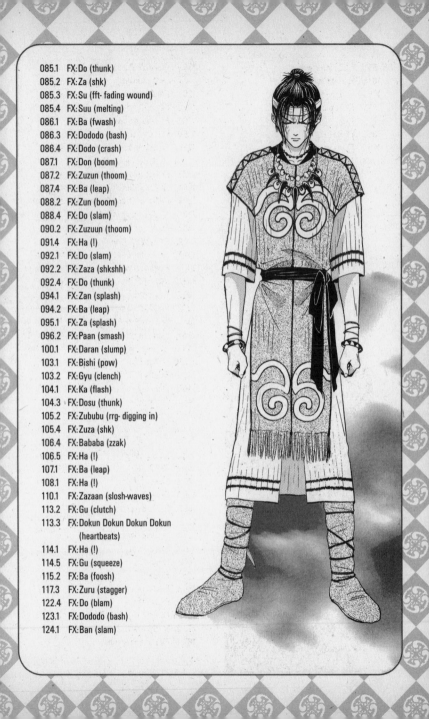

125.2 FX:Dokun Dokun Dokun Dokun (heartbeats)
126.1 FX:Dooon (boom)
126.3 FX:Ha (!)
126.3 FX:Zuzuzu (rumble)
126.4 FX:Ga (tug)
127.1 FX:Dokun Dokun Dokun Dokun Dokun Dokun (heartbeats)
127.3 FX:Haa Haa (huff huff)
128.1 FX:Dokun Dokun Dokun (heartbeats)
129.1 FX:Dokun Dokun Dokun (heartbeats)
129.4 FX:Dokun Dokun (heartbeats)
130.1 FX:Don (thump)
131.2 FX:Gashaan (crash)
131.3 FX:Do (thud)
132.1 FX:Zudo (thunk)
132.3 FX:Su (fft)
137.1 FX:Fu (fft)
137.2 FX:BAAN (crash)
139.1 FX:Fu (heh)
140.1 FX:Ba (fash)
140.2 FX:Doro (gloop)
142.1 FX:Suu (fft)
142.2 FX:Suu (fft)
144.3 FX:Bata Bata (running)
145.1 FX:Ka (tk)
146.3 FX:Doro (glorp)
146.4 FX:Zuru (drip)
147.4 FX:Ba (fash)
148.1 FX:Don (boom)
149.2 FX:Piku (!)
149.3 FX:Ha (!)
150.3 FX:Ha (!)
151.5 FX:Ga (wham)
157.1 FX:Su (shp)
157.4 FX:Doro Doro (gloop glorp)
165.3 FX:Fu (faint)
166.1 FX:Ka (tk)
166.1 FX:Ha (!)
166.4 FX:Baki (bash)
168.1 FX:Pa (flash)
168.2 FX:Bara Bara Bara (choppers)
172.2 FX:Gyu (clutch)
182.2 FX:Pon Pon (pat pat)
182.5 FX:Za (slosh-waves)
183.6 FX:Kasa (rustle)
185.2 FX:Zaa (rustle)
185.3 FX:Kokun (nod)
186.1 FX:Suu (z)
186.2 FX:Ha (!)
188.2 FX:Ha (!)
191.3 FX:Za (slosh-waves)

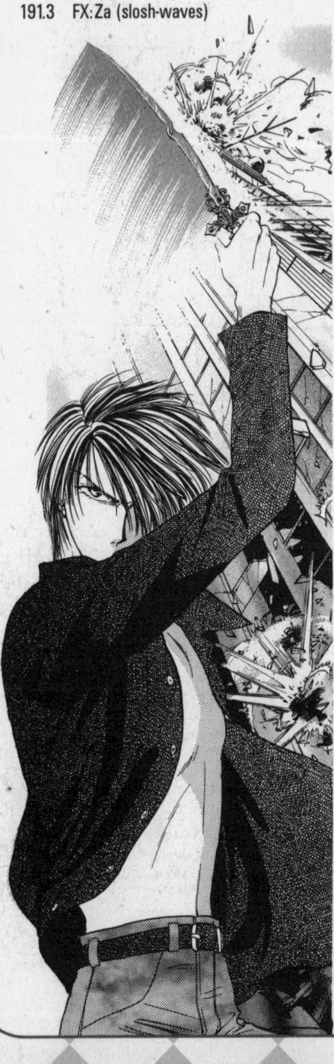

Yuu Watase was born on March 5 in a town near Osaka, Japan, and she was raised there before moving to Tokyo to follow her dream of creating manga. In the decade since her debut short story, "Pajama De Ojama" (An Intrusion in Pajamas), she has produced more than 50 compiled volumes of short stories and continuing series. Watase's beloved works CERES: CELESTIAL LEGEND, IMADOKI! (Nowadays), ALICE 19TH, ABSOLUTE BOYFRIEND, and FUSHIGI YŪGI: GENBU KAIDEN are now available in North America in English editions published by VIZ Media.

LOVE SHOJO? LET US KNOW!

☐ Please do NOT send me information about VIZ Media products, news and events, special offers, or other information.

☐ Please do NOT send me information from VIZ' trusted business partners.

Name: _____

Address: _____

City: _____ **State:** _____ **Zip:** _____

E-mail: _____

☐ Male ☐ Female **Date of Birth** (mm/dd/yyyy): ____ / ____ / _____ (Under 13? Parental consent required)

What race/ethnicity do you consider yourself? (check all that apply)

☐ White/Caucasian ☐ Black/African American ☐ Hispanic/Latino

☐ Asian/Pacific Islander ☐ Native American/Alaskan Native ☐ Other: _____

What VIZ shojo title(s) did you purchase? (indicate title(s) purchased)

_____

What other shojo titles from other publishers do you own? _____

_____

Reason for purchase: (check all that apply)

☐ Special offer ☐ Favorite title / author / artist / genre

☐ Gift ☐ Recommendation ☐ Collection

☐ Read excerpt in VIZ manga sampler ☐ Other _____

Where did you make your purchase? (please check one)

☐ Comic store ☐ Bookstore ☐ Mass/Grocery Store

☐ Newsstand ☐ Video/Video Game Store

☐ Online (site: _____) ☐ Other _____

How many shojo titles have you purchased in the last year? How many were VIZ shojo titles?
(please check one from each column)

SHOJO MANGA
- ☐ None
- ☐ 1 – 4
- ☐ 5 – 10
- ☐ 11+

VIZ SHOJO MANGA
- ☐ None
- ☐ 1 – 4
- ☐ 5 – 10
- ☐ 11+

What do you like most about shojo graphic novels? (check all that apply)

- ☐ Romance
- ☐ Drama / conflict
- ☐ Fantasy
- ☐ Comedy
- ☐ Real-life storylines
- ☐ Relatable characters
- ☐ Other ______________________________

Do you purchase every volume of your favorite shojo series?

- ☐ Yes! Gotta have 'em as my own
- ☐ No. Please explain: ______________________________

Who are your favorite shojo authors / artists? ______________________________

____

What shojo titles would like you translated and sold in English? ______________________________

____

THANK YOU! Please send the completed form to:

NJW Research
ATTN: VIZ Media Shojo Survey
42 Catharine Street
Poughkeepsie, NY 12601

Your privacy is very important to us. All information provided will be used for internal purposes only and will not be sold or otherwise divulged.